STUDIES ON CHINA

A series of conference volumes sponsored by the American Council of Learned Societies.

Perspectives on the Yi of Southwest China

EDITED BY

STEVAN HARRELL

UNIVERSITY OF CALIFORNIA PRESS

Berkeley   Los Angeles   London

University of California Press
Berkeley and Los Angeles, California
University of California Press, Ltd.
London, England

Library of Congress Cataloging-in-Publication Data

Perspectives on the Yi of Southwest China / edited by Stevan Harrell.
   p. cm.—(Studies on China ; 26)
Includes bibliographical references and index.
ISBN 0-520-21988-0 (alk. paper)—ISBN 0-520-21989-9 (pbk. : alk paper)
1. Yi (Chinese people)   I. Harrell, Stevan.   II. Series.
DS731.Y5 P47   2001
951'.3004951—dc21   00-055970

Manufactured in the United States of America
10   09   08   07   06   05   04   03   02   01
10   9   8   7   6   5   4   3   2   1

The paper used in this publication meets the minimum requirements of ANSI/
NISO Z39.48-1992 (R 1997) (*Permanence of Paper*). ♾

*To the memory of
Tong Enzheng (1935–1997),
the most broad-minded of men*

CONTENTS

TABLES, MAPS, AND FIGURES

TABLES

MAPS

FIGURES

ACKNOWLEDGMENTS

The First International Yi Studies Conference was supported by grants from the Joint Committee on Chinese Studies, the Wenner-Gren Foundation for Anthropological Research, the National Science Foundation, and the China Studies Program at the University of Washington. Yu Hongmo, Hsieh Jiann, Charles McKhann, and the late Tong Enzheng provided valuable expertise and commentary at the conference. Ren Hai, Almaz Han, and David Branner ably helped me translate original papers from Chinese to English and English to Chinese.

Norma Diamond, Louisa Schein, Kent Guy, and an anonymous reader provided valuable comments on various drafts of the manuscript. Bamo Ayi helped maintain contact with far-flung authors after the conference dispersed. Laura Driussi of the University of California Press shepherded the book through its first few drafts, Bonita Hurd ably copyedited it and Jan Spauschus Johnson finished it. And the guiding hand of Sheila Levine hovered benevolently over the whole project of transforming a pile of papers into a book.

Introduction

Stevan Harrell

SCHOLARLY DISCOURSES AND THE YI

There are nearly seven million Yi people, almost all of them in Yunnan, Sichuan, and Guizhou Provinces, with a few in Guangxi Province and Vietnam and a very small number of emigrants overseas. There are, in all, more Yi than there are Danes or Israelis or Cambodians. Yet it is quite probable that most educated people outside China have never even heard the name, let alone learned anything about the Yi. One goal of this book is thus to begin the establishment of a field of scholarship within today's cosmopolitan social-studies discourses: to inform scholars and students of China, of Southeast Asia, and of ethnic relations generally about a large part of the world that has remained largely inaccessible in European languages.

At the same time, there is no dearth of written materials dealing with Yi history, society, culture, and literature. These materials, however, belong to two widely divergent discourses,[1] both of them quite far removed in their assumptions, concepts, and methods of argument from the cosmopolitan discourses to which scholarship in European languages is usually addressed. One of these is Chinese language scholarship, encompassing the fields of ethnology *(minzu xue)* and ethnohistory *(minzu shi)*, which seek to locate Yi society and culture in a temporal and spatial framework of relation and interaction with other peoples in the region and with peoples in China generally. The other is traditional Yi-language scholarship, concerned with

---

1. In this introduction, "discourse" bears both its linguistic sense of a conversation among a group of people using an agreed-upon, somewhat specialized vocabulary, and something of its Foucauldian sense of a set of linguistic categories that define a regime of power (see Foucault 1984).

the recording of myths, legends, and poetry and, above all, with medicinal and ritual texts and formulas used by priests and other practitioners. Another goal of this book is to make researches in and about these two traditions accessible to English-reading scholarly circles.

In the eyes of the contributors to this book, however, these two goals remain little more than means toward a third and more important goal: establishment of a dialogue between the three scholarly traditions. Not only do the works of cosmopolitan ethnologists need to be circulated and discussed in Chinese scholarly circles, both national and Yi, but the concepts and results of scholarship from within China need to be taken into account by participants in the cosmopolitan conversations about China and about ethnicity and ethnic relations. We are missing a lot if we continue to have two different conversations about the same thing, one Chinese and one cosmopolitan, and we miss even more if we do not take the Yi-language materials into account either.

For this reason, I gathered twenty scholars with interests in Yi studies for what I rather grandiosely called the "First International Conference on Yi Studies," held in Seattle in March 1995. Eleven of the participants were themselves Yi: eight came from China, two from the United States, where they were already discourse-mixing as graduate students, and one from France, where she had recently mixed discourses in a Paris Ph.D. Others were American, German, Australian, and Chinese scholars who had conducted research on the Yi or neighboring peoples. We met for four days, using Chinese (the only language we all had in common) to discuss the papers that were the predecessors of most of the chapters in this book. Our conversations were, I think, inspiring to all participants as they realized that by recognizing the parameters of contrasting discourses, and by speaking about and against those parameters, we open up a wider field of view that cannot help but enrich and broaden our individual scholarly inquiries.

Our reasons for emphasizing the importance of, and committing ourselves to, a cross-discourse conversation all stem from the initial confrontations between our respective scholarly discourses. Anyone who doubts the utility of such a concept as a scholarly discourse need only observe the vast gulf across which Western and Chinese ethnologists and ethnohistorians confronted each other when they first started to interact again in the late 1970s and early 1980s, after thirty years of enforced separation. Westerners were debating the primordial versus instrumental basis of ethnicity and ethnic conflict (Keyes 1976; Bentley 1987; and others), speculating on the nature of state power in Chinese socialism and its immediate successors (Oi 1989; Shue 1988; and others), and writing from the assumption that state-society relations in China's "minority regions" consisted of state oppression and assimilation of local indigenous peoples (Dreyer 1976; Heberer 1989; and others). Chinese, by contrast, were writing about the success of ethnic identification (Fei 1981) and about the long and glorious histories of, and contributions to the nation by, various minority groups (Ma Yin 1984; Litzinger 1995; Harrell 1995b), using historiographic methods to trace the details of the history of each individual and scientifically organized group, and speaking of the steps of history along which various groups were advancing under Party tutelage.

In this atmosphere, attitudes of mutual contempt, condescension, and sometimes just plain wonderment quickly evolved. Western researchers, eager for "access" to remote and previously forbidden regions and peoples, dampened their public criticisms of an ethnological paradigm dating from Lewis Henry Morgan, which they considered to have been blown to insignificance before 1930 by the works of such as Franz Boas and Bronislaw Malinowski; they certainly took the Chinese ethnological and ethnohistorical paradigms seriously, but as objects of analysis, not as contributions to knowledge. An ethnological work about the formation of slave society in Liangshan, for example (Hu 1981), was a datum, just like an interview with a *bimo* (priest) or a photograph of a historical stela. On the other side, Chinese ethnologists and ethnohistorians were flabbergasted at the ignorance, narrowness, and arrogance of their Western counterparts. Often unfamiliar with classical Chinese, certainly unfamiliar with the local histories of the areas where they worked, the Westerners nevertheless brought the possibility of material support, access to sources that had been forbidden during the reign of radical totalitarianism, and even chances for these people to study and research abroad. Within a few years of the opening of China to Western ethnologists and historians, we had settled into a comfortable system of mutual back-scratching. Chinese provided the Westerners with access to the field and the archive; Westerners provided the Chinese with money and the opportunity to go abroad. We could remain mutually contemptuous of each other's concepts; the two discourses interacted hardly at all.

Almost as wide was the gulf between the Chinese national discourses of ethnology and ethnohistory, on the one hand, and the local discourse embodied in Yi-language materials, on the other. They had, of course, no enforced period of isolation from each other, but most scholars participating in the national discourse considered the Yi-language materials in the same way that Westerners considered ethnohistory in the Morganian paradigm—as data rather than analysis, and as data that could only be made sensible by insertion into that Morganian paradigm of the stages of history. At the same time, authors and transmitters of Yi-language materials were mostly unable to read the Chinese materials, and if they had been able to read them they would have shown little interest, because the goal of these materials was to synthesize, which was irrelevant to the local purposes of the Yi indigenous scholars.

This book is an indication that we have begun to grow out of that unfortunate situation. There are several reasons for the change. Probably first and foremost is the gradual but real liberalization of control over scholarship in

China in the 1990s. Ethnic relations and minority studies are among the more sensitive areas, and have certainly not experienced the degree of opening that has happened in, for example, literary criticism or women's studies. Nationalistic resistance in Tibet and Xinjiang is suppressed as ruthlessly as ever. But the particular view of history and society known in China as Marxism-Leninism, despite its current enshrinement as one of the "four cardinal principles," is no longer the only possible guideline for scholarship, leaving the way clear for questioning and, in some scholars' ambitions, dismantling that particular totalizing discourse.

In our own particular field, this has left the way open for attacks on the Morgan-Engels paradigm from two sides: a local-particularistic one led almost entirely by Yi scholars, and a cosmopolitan one in which Yi, other Chinese, and Western scholars have all had a hand. From the Yi side, what has been at issue is the "standard interpretation" of Nuosu (Yi) society in Liangshan and, by analogy or implication, of other Yi societies in other areas in earlier times. This interpretation took Liangshan before 1956 as the paradigm case of the "slave society," the second of the five universal stages of history, coming after the end of primitive society (sometimes referred to as "primitive communism" in the West) and before the development of feudalism. Field research on the Nuosu in the 1950s, a time when social class was held to be the most important factor in human society, had led to a paradigm in which the most important relations of Nuosu society were the relations of production between slaves and slave owners (Hu 1981; Sichuan Sheng bianji zu 1985, 1987). In the more political sections of these works, the cruelty of the system was also emphasized.

There was no other way to write about Yi society in the 1970s and early 1980s, but in the more open and tolerant atmosphere of the last few years, it has been possible to come forth with different models, and Nuosu scholars in particular have responded with a series of very different interpretations of social stratification and the caste system in Liangshan (Ma Erzi 1993; Pan Wenchao 1994). In another example, that aspect of the Morgan-Engels historical paradigm that enshrined the Han as the leading nationality and big brother to the backward minorities has also been challenged. Yi scholars, led by Liu Yaohan, have set forth a series of books and articles that places the ancestors of the Yi at the center and forefront of the development of early Chinese civilization and portrays them as having been pushed to the periphery only in the last thousand years (Liu Yaohan 1985).

But the weakening of the Morgan-Engels paradigm has stemmed not only from local pride and the resentment of outsiders less knowledgeable about local history but also from the increasing interpenetration of Chinese and cosmopolitan ethnological and ethnohistorical discourses. Within China, this perhaps had its strongest beginnings in mid-1980s self-critiques by those who had participated in the "ethnic identification" *(minzu shibie)* project of the

1950s, who conceded that Stalin's notions of "nationality" had not actually fit the Chinese realities of the 1950s, so that the identification project had proceeded on quite different grounds (Jiang 1985; Lin 1987). There was also recognition among experts, albeit expressed mostly privately, that it had been difficult in many instances to draw sharp boundaries between *minzu* (ethnic group or nationality) at all, and that situations had been much more fluid than the old hegemonic paradigm would admit (Li Shaoming 1986; Li Xingxing 1994).

The cosmopolitan attacks were, of course, more straightforward and less constrained. Western scholars earned many cheap points by pointing out the discrepancies between the paradigm and more interesting ways to view local realities (see the articles in the edited volume Harrell 1995 for examples). More significant was the effect these analyses had on Chinese scholars, both Yi and non-Yi, in their own analyses of ethnic relations. It is now common enough to hear arguments between an older generation of ethnologists, who insist that *minzu* categories are not, as overseas and Taiwan colleagues maintain, "invented," and younger scholars who are respectfully contrary in public and broadly dismissive in private of this "old thinking."

At the same time, the beginning of paradigm chaos in China has caused Western scholars, formerly contemptuous of Chinese counterparts as hopelessly brainwashed if admirably knowledgeable, to reconsider their Chinese colleagues as partners in dialogue with a depth of experience and local knowledge that almost no outsider can hope to match. And, in concert with the "indigenization" of anthropology and history in the "non-Western" world generally, the study of ethnicity and ethnic relations in China now seems destined to become a true transnational conversation that locals and outsiders can share in, and in which they can argue about the implications of local knowledge.

We are, however, still at the beginning stages of this process. Most Chinese scholars, Yi included, who are working out the possibilities of new paradigms for understanding their own history and current situation are doing so with only fragmentary knowledge of and exposure to the theoretical formulations that have so long been argued about in *waiguo* (foreign countries). There is the real danger that they will reinvent the wheel. Also, there are too many anthropologists and not enough historians studying ethnic relations in China (but see Lipman 1998); anthropologists tend not to be respectful of written sources in the Chinese and Yi languages because they do not have time to read enough of them. Further exposure to each other's work, and further collaborative work, is absolutely necessary before we can build a truly open transnational dialogue about these questions.[2]

2. Why we need a transnational dialogue about, for example, Yi social stratification and not about American inner-city social disintegration is not immediately clear, but is at any rate outside the scope of this book, which for better or for worse is about Yi society and culture.

Not only must there be more mutual exposure of Chinese and foreign scholars to each other's work and each other's thinking, there must also be conscious efforts made toward developing a viable translinguistic vocabulary for speaking about matters such as ethnic relations and Yi history. In order for us to keep the dialogue viable, we must write in Chinese and in English and, hopefully, in at least some kinds of Yi. More than that, we need to be aware of what changes when we move from one language to another, to develop what Lydia Liu (1993) has referred to as "translingual practice." Some of the papers from the 1995 conference have already been published in Chinese (Liangshan minzu yanjiu, 1995 issue), and versions of two of them in Japanese (Bamo 1996; Ma and Qubi 1996); they appear here in English. Are they saying the same thing to audiences who customarily read these three very different languages? What would they say if they were translated into Nuosu, Nisu, or Sani? Could they be? If not, why not; why have those languages not developed an ethnological and ethnohistoric vocabulary?

The 1995 conference and this volume derived from it represent the results of some of the first-stage efforts to wrestle with these problems, to resolve these contradictions. There are chapters written in the present-day versions of both the cosmopolitan and the Chinese scholarly paradigms (divided not by the ethnicity of the authors but by their place of scholarly training), and it is still easy, despite the beginnings of dialogue described above, to tell the difference. All those written in the Chinese paradigm (all by Yi scholars) are influenced by, and to some degree located in, the national discourse, but they take varied account of and put to varied uses the documents of the local, Yi-language discourse.

This book is thus an inevitable hybrid. But readers can approach the hybrid in more than one way. We can simply mine it for knowledge, for there is a lot here that is brand-new to the English-reading fields of ethnic relations, social structure, and particularly China studies. Or we can examine it as a concrete demonstration of the different ways in which participants in different scholarly discourses approach the same field of facts and data. Or, most interestingly, we can look at the interaction of discourses itself and hope to gain two kinds of insights from this interaction. First, we can gain a richer understanding of the material itself. We get a much better idea of Yi society, culture, and especially history if we synthesize the findings from different scholarly traditions. Second, we can learn about an example of the processes of transnationalization that must perforce reshape much social and cultural scholarship in the increasingly connected world of the twenty-first century. The remainder of this introduction will attempt to guide readers toward an approach to this material that may enable them to look for these kinds of insights.

WHO ARE THE YI?

The nearly seven million Yi constitute one of the fifty-six *minzu* (variously translated as "nationalities" or "ethnic groups," but best left untranslated here) into which the People's Republic of China divides its population. Like all the *minzu* but the Han, who constitute about 91 percent of the whole country's population, the Yi are one of the *shaoshu minzu*, or "minorities." About four and a half million Yi live in Yunnan, two million in Sichuan, half a million in Guizhou, and a few thousand in Guangxi (see map 12.1). The Yi are quite diverse linguistically: Chinese linguists have officially classified their languages into six *fangyan*, or "dialects," which are closely related but not mutually intelligible (see David Bradley, chapter 12 in this volume). Similarly, they are quite diverse culturally. None but the Nuosu of Liangshan have a caste system (though others, specifically the Nasu, most closely related to the Nuosu, may have traces of something like it). Other Yi groups, especially in Yunnan, have had much closer contact with surrounding Han society and culture than the Nuosu have had, particularly since the reunification of the Southwest with China by the Yuan rulers in the 1250s, and the massive immigration of Han military and civil colonies to the area that has gone on ever since—and that accelerated when the *gaitu guiliu* (replacement of local rulers by appointed bureaucrats) of the Yongzheng era (1722–36) incorporated most of their communities into the regular civil administration. And in fact, many sources attribute the divergence of language, custom, and social practices specifically to the differential influences of the larger Han environment. For example, Chen Tianjun writes that the slave-feudal transition occurred at three different times in the three different areas of Yi settlement. In Yunnan, it came earliest, at the time Nanzhao was taken over by Dali in the tenth century, whereas it persisted in Guizhou and northeast Yunnan until the Ming, and in Liangshan, in modified form at least, into the 1950s (Chen Tianjun 1987, 114–17).

This great linguistic and cultural diversity raises the question of what makes the Yi a people a *minzu*. The shortest answer to this is that they were so classified in the *minzu shibie* of the 1950s, which was undertaken according to "scientific" principles of classification first outlined by Stalin (Fei 1981). And the classification certainly could have been done otherwise. The Central and Western dialects of Yi, for example, are more closely related to Lisu and Lahu (languages of separate *minzu*) than they are to the Northern, Eastern, Southeastern, and Southern branches of Yi (Bradley 1990a). Earlier Western sources have often drawn the boundaries differently as well, incorporating Lisu, for example, or Woni (now officially classified as a branch of Hani) into the old category "Lolo," a pejorative term referring to the people we now refer to as Yi. And there is no commonly used term in all the Yi languages to refer to the Yi as a whole, though the term *Ni* is used in classical books. In addition, there are small groups of people in both Yunnan and Sichuan who are classified as Yi but who take exception to their inclusion in this category and would rather be separate *minzu* (see Harrell 1990, 2001).

Today, however, the question of whether the categories correspond to the previous reality of ethnic consciousness is unimportant in most areas, because for at least forty years the Yi have been the Yi, and ethnic consciousness, which distinguishes the local group from its neighbors, is intermixed with *minzu* consciousness, which distinguishes the Yi from the Han, the Tibetans, the Hani, the Miao, and so on. Diverse cultures exist, and the chapters in parts 1 and 2 of this book treat local customs and local differences in great detail. But it is clear that the Yi peoples are all related to each other historically, and that they retain greater or lesser amounts of cultural similarities in the present day. In other words, the slightly longer answer to the question of "Who are the Yi" is that they are the people who partake in Yi history, or the people whose history has culminated in those groups, culturally diverse as they may be, who are today classified as part of the Yi *minzu*.

Part 1 of this book explores aspects of this history and this historical relatedness. As might be expected, there is a lot of controversy about Yi history. For example, there are at least two major (and two or three minor) hypotheses about the earliest origins of the Yi ancestors. It is generally agreed that the ancestors of the present-day Yi fanned out from an original location somewhere in central Yunnan. But where they came from before that is a matter of dispute. Some maintain that they, like other Tibeto-Burman peoples, are the descendants of the Qiang peoples mentioned in classical historical sources as living to the northwest of China, who migrated to the Sichuan-Yunnan-Tibet-Burma-Himalaya region in the second and first millennia B.C.E. (Chen Tianjun 1987). Others maintain that they originated in Yunnan, perhaps as descendants of early humans whose remains from the Paleolithic have been found in Yunnan in abundance (see Wu Gu, chapter 1 in this volume).

Two chapters in part 1—by Wu Gu on traditional Yi historical records and Wu Jingzhong on the place of *nzymo*, or "royalty," in Liangshan history—draw primarily from Yi-language documentation to understand history, particularly social and cultural history, but in doing so they focus at quite different levels. Wu Gu offers a comprehensive survey of the kinds of materials other than traditional Han-language historiographical works that can be used as sources for writing Yi history, and in doing so, he stakes out the parameters of a unified history of the Yi as a whole. He makes a strong claim that the use of such sources (in his original draft, *guji*, which I have translated as "historical records") not only enriches our view of Yi history, extending it backward in time and adding cultural and social elements invisible in Han-language records, but also forces us to think differently about what is important in writing history. For example, notions of rulership found in the Yi-language *Classic of Ruling a Country and Pacifying a Territory* amend and alter the view of Yi rulership in Han-language sources. Similarly, there is much about ritual and etiquette, attitudes toward guests, military ideology, and so on that is recoverable from Yi-language books, even if they do not contain the precise historical dating that is so characteristic of national Chinese histories written in the Han language.

Wu Jingzhong, in his explorations of the role of *nzymo*, also draws entirely on Yi sources, in this case, Nuosu-language versions of several Yi classics that have recently been edited and published by *minzu* publishing houses, to reconstruct the possible origins and much of the cultural history of Liangshan before the Yuan dynasty. His account, unlike Wu Gu's, focuses on Liangshan Nuosu society exclusively and does not address the question of connections between Nuosu and other Yi. He finds his Nuosu-language sources to be particularly rich in descriptions of the kinship system, including strategies and behaviors people employ when arranging marriages among clans; descriptions of the relations between the *nzymo* and their servants, subjects, and retainers; of the role of certain rituals that we can easily recognize as ancestral to ceremonies being performed by *bimo* in Liangshan today; of the importance of certain subsistence pursuits, such as hunting, and of certain crops, such as tea, which lost their importance in Nuosu society in recent centuries; and particularly of warfare and military culture, something also taken up in chapter 7, Liu Yu's essay on the Heroic Age.

LIANGSHAN SOCIETY AND CULTURE

About two million of the Yi live in the regions known collectively as Liangshan, including what are now the administrative areas of Liangshan Yi Autonomous Prefecture, Panzhihua Municipality, and adjacent parts of Leshan and Ya'an Prefectures, as well as Ganze Tibetan Autonomous Prefecture, all in Sichuan; and in adjacent parts of Yunnan, most particularly Ninglang Yi Autonomous County in Lijiang Prefecture. Almost all of the Yi in Liangshan belong to what has been designated the Northern Dialect Group, and they call themselves Nuosu in their own language, a usage I will adopt here.

The ancestors of the Nuosu probably entered the Liangshan area early in the first millennium of the common era and occupied the eastern part of Liangshan, between the Anning River and the north-flowing leg of the Jinsha River, very early. They also spread northward fairly early in history, but their occupation of western Liangshan, from the Yalong west to the foothills of Tibet, came much later, and Nuosu were still expanding westward into northwestern Yunnan during the mid-twentieth century.

For most of their time occupying Liangshan, the Nuosu have been relatively independent of political control or even suzerainty from Chinese imperial dynasties or other local rulers. From the Yuan dynasty on, members of the *nzymo* stratum (see Wu Jingzhong, chapter 2 in this volume) were enfeoffed at various times in various places as *tusi*, or local rulers, and they owed allegiance and tribute to the imperial dynasties. But the rule of *tusi* was never very rigorous, and from the late Ming on, even those areas under *tusi* authority experienced rebellions from local aristocratic clans, who drove the *tusi* from most of eastern Liangshan and established the independent, tribal society known in nineteenth- and early-twentieth-century Western literature as "Independent Lololand" and known to Chinese scholarship as "the Liangshan Core Area."[3] Control by Nuosu *tusi* in northern Liangshan and by *tusi* of various other ethnicities in western Liangshan lasted longer than it did in the Core Area, but even in these peripheral districts the web of clan and caste relations was still the most important nexus of social structure. It is with this structure that all the essays in part 2 of this book are concerned.

Nuosu traditional society, like that of so many tribal polities formed in reaction to pressure from bordering states, is centered on the organization of patrilineal clans, called *cyvi* in the Nuosu language. Whenever two people meet, one of the first things they ask each other is the other person's clan membership, and people believe generally that clan loyalty is the basis of social peace and order, as well as the cause of strife and warfare. Clans extend all over Liangshan, and marriage alliances between clans tie together society both within local areas and over vast distances.

Chapters 3 through 6 of this book illustrate the various aspects of the clan system, and do so from the perspective of both cosmopolitan and local scholarly discourses. Ann Maxwell Hill and Eric Diehl, in chapter 3, put the Nuosu *cyvi* firmly in the orbit of comparative studies of social structure, showing the differences between patrilineal organization at the local level (for which they use the term *lineage*) in Nuosu and in Han society. Nuosu lineage organization, they show, is linked more to territorial organization, less to specific landownership. The Nuosu lineage does not cut across caste, of course, whereas in Han society, which has no castes, lineage organization cuts across class. And Nuosu lineages are more concerned at the collective level with marriage alliances than are the Han, for whom marriage is a matter of concern to the immediate and extended family, but not to wider kin groups: exactly the kind of difference we would expect to find between a tribal and a state society.

Lu Hui, in chapter 4, discusses considerations of marital alliance in more detail. Beginning with the paradoxical observation that bilateral cross-cousin marriage is the Nuosu ideal, but that one-sided matrilateral unions are more common than patrilateral unions and that true bilateral unions

---

3. I use the term *tribal* in the rather narrow sense advocated by Fried (1967): as a nonstate polity formed in response to military and/or ecological pressure from a neighboring state.

are quite rare, she discusses the strategies of alliance that motivate parents and local clan (or lineage) elders to marry their children into one clan or another. Again, this places the Nuosu social structure into the comparative framework of kinship alliance that has driven so much Western anthropological writing about mainland southeast Asia since Edmund Leach (1954). Also, it forms an implicit critique of the Morganian paradigm, which would have seen cross-cousin marriage as characteristic of a particular "stage" of social evolution.

The next two chapters, by Ma Erzi and Qubi Shimei, address Nuosu social structure from the standpoint of purely local scholarly discourse, but they elucidate still other aspects of the clan system. In chapter 5, Ma gives a thorough review of the Nuosu naming system, showing how clan names, birth-order names, and personal names serve to place individuals into the matrix of social organization in which they will live their lives. In chapter 6, Ma and Qubi together address another of the most important functions of the *cyvi*— the regulation of social order by means of unwritten customary civil and criminal law. The particular instance they write about concerns homicide within the clan, a situation that puts the clan organization into stark relief, because disputes within the clan must be regulated by law rather than warfare. The striking thing about the juxtaposition of the chapters by Ma and Qubi with those by Hill, Diehl, and Lu is that, even though Ma and Qubi write from purely local viewpoints, they make potential contributions to the cosmopolitan discourses of social anthropology and comparative sociology, and do it with material that is richer, because of their personal background in Nuosu village society, than any that could ever be compiled by an outside anthropologist.

If clans are the warp of Nuosu society, caste is its woof, and for the first forty years of the People's Republic caste was about the only feature that received serious scholarly attention in the national discourse of ethnology and ethnohistory. This attention was undoubtedly due to the conjunction of the Maoist emphasis on class struggle and the Morgan-Engels sequence that put slave society in second place, between primitive communism and feudalism. Long and detailed attempts were made to tie the caste structure of the Nuosu, including *nzymo*, or royalty; *nuoho*, or aristocrats; *quho*, or commoners; and various unfree or semifree castes, into a model of class oppression and exploitation based on slave labor—which would make the Nuosu the prime living example of the slave society that supposedly characterized Mediterranean antiquity but was already superseded by feudalism over two thousand years ago in most of China. In recent years, such scholars as Ma Erzi and Pan Wenchao have questioned the utility of the slave society model for understanding Nuosu stratification (Ma 1993; Pan 1994), and in chapter 7 of this volume Liu Yu tries out a different model—the "Heroic Age" of Homeric Greece, when patriclan loyalty, marital alliance, and martial values combined to produce a society and an ethos not unlike that described for the Nuosu in recent centuries. Whether the Heroic Age is the right model or not, this demonstrates the loosening of the hegemony of the Morgan-Engels model in China, as well as the increasing ability of people writing in the Chinese national discourse to draw on models and ideas from cosmopolitan scholarship.

The final aspect of Nuosu social structure touched on in this book concerns the specialist occupations. In a society with no formal political statuses (except the *tusi*, which was imposed upon it from the outside), there were still a large number of specialist roles that brought respect, social position, and income to their occupants. These included *ndeggu*, or mediator; *ssakuo*, or warrior; *surgat*, or person of wealth; *gemo*, or craft specialist (including carver, blacksmith, silversmith, carpenter, and so on); and two kinds of religious specialists: *bimo*, or priests, who worked with texts and perform textually based rituals; and *sunyi*, or shamans, who became possessed by spirits and used their acquired powers in healing. In chapter 8, Bamo Ayi writes about the education of the *bimo*, the importance of patrilineal transmission of knowledge, and the ideas of education embodied in the long training and apprenticeship before a *bimo* can perform rituals on his own.

For the national Chinese discourse, and to some extent for the local discourse of Yi identity, Nuosu society in Liangshan represents a kind of paradigm for the Yi in general—a society where outside influences were minimal (though of course by no means absent) and where one could see in the present what other Yi must have been like in the past, before their cultures were heavily intermixed with acculturative elements from the Han. The cosmopolitan discourse, in recent decades at least, has rejected such rigidly typological and general evolutionary schemes, and tends to view Nuosu society as something *sui generis*—historically related to the other Yi (and to other *minzu* as well) to be sure, but not indicative of anything except its own unique development (Pan Jiao n.d.). But Nuosu society, regardless of its typological position, does give us a picture of a Tibeto-Burman society in China in the absence of large-scale outside influences and in the absence of state organization. It also helps us to understand the relationship between scholarship and politics in both local and national Chinese discourses.

YI SOCIETIES IN YUNNAN AND GUIZHOU

Even though Nuosu have come to represent, rightly or wrongly, a kind of paradigm of unadulterated Yi-ness, they still comprise less than a third of the total population of the Yi *minzu*. The rest of the Yi, those belonging to the Eastern, Southeastern, Southern, Central, and Western "dialect groups," who are concentrated in Yunnan (over four million) and Guizhou (half a million or more), have a very different relationship with the surrounding Han society and culture. What they were like a thousand years ago is hard to tell (if we reject the notion that they must have been just like the Nuosu were in the 1950s), but we know that even as early as the sixth and seventh centuries they had established two-way cultural exchange with their neighbors, and that ever since the establishment of military and *tusi* rule under the Yuan and Ming, they have absorbed many elements of culture and social organization from the surrounding societies, particularly the dominant Han (see Wu Gu's chapter 1 for an overview of this cultural mixing). Part 3 of this volume contains chapters written about local communities belonging to three of the five "non-Northern" Yi groups, all of them located in Yunnan. All three chapters illustrate the complex position of these people culturally, socially, and politically. On the one hand, all of them are identified as belonging to the Yi *minzu*, and all have a strong local ethnic identity as well as an attachment to the Yi as a whole. And they preserve varying amounts of local language, culture, customs, and historical consciousness. At the same time, from the viewpoint of an outside observer, all of them seem culturally more like Chinese peasants than like the Nuosu tribal cultivators of Liangshan. They thus stand somewhere between being full and undifferentiated member communities of Chinese society, like their Han neighbors, and being connected to, but in many ways radically different from, Chinese society, like their Nuosu relatives. Each chapter shows this dual nature of Yi society among a different group and in the context of a different aspect of society or culture.

Li Yongxiang's chapter 9 emphasizes more than any of the others the continuity with the Tibeto-Burman tradition. In his study of the "cold funeral" rituals performed in his native Xinping County, Li paints a portrayal of a priestly tradition, its beliefs about the world to come, and the rituals its members carry out in support of these beliefs. The Nisu of Xinping (who belong to the Southern dialect group) are clearly still able to make connections to a tradition that is quite separate from that of the surrounding Han (Watson 1988). At the same time, Nisu bury their dead, and some of the deities ruling over that next world in fact have names borrowed from the Han language.

In chapter 10, Erik Mueggler begins to problematize the historical Yi connection, showing it as contested and threatened and describing the culture and power connection to the Han as a place of conscious boundary maintenance and cautious boundary crossing. The Lipo-Lolopo of Yongren County in north-central Yunnan live interspersed with Han and have absorbed many aspects of Han culture, particularly in their everyday life. But until the Democratic Reforms of the 1950s, they kept the surrounding culture at bay, absorbing only selectively. One way they did this was to appoint a local official whose entire purpose was to keep visitors and government officials—Han in general—at arm's length, so that other officials could carry out the "purely Yi" rituals necessary to the community's well-being.

In chapter 11, we move to the Sani of Lunan, familiar since the 1980s as handicraft sellers and money changers both at the Stone Forest, a tourist landmark in Sani territory, and near hotels in downtown Kunming. In this chapter, Margaret Byrne Swain describes how the Sani in Lunan have formulated and used their ethnic identity from the time they were first described (and, importantly, many of them converted to Catholicism) by French missionaries in the early 1900s until they became the tourism entrepreneurs of today. Though the ethnic bases of identity have changed, and though the outsiders trying to assimilate them have included Europeans as well as Han, what has remained constant is a sense of belonging to a place, much as it has been for the Lolopo in Yongren.

Taken together, these three accounts of Yunnan Yi communities outline a situation in which group identity works very differently from the way it does among the Nuosu in Liangshan. In a word, Yunnan Yi identity in all these places is more consciously constructed, more classically "ethnic" in the terms of Charles Keyes (1976), who sees ethnicity as the conscious use of common culture and common kinship to reinforce group solidarity and draw boundaries with outsiders. For Nuosu in most situations, the cultural differences are real and obvious and need no particular emphasis or valorization. Similarly, their common kinship is real as well, given the genealogies that can ultimately trace all Nuosu to two common ancestors, Gguhxo and Qoni, and given the strict prohibition on intermarriage with other groups. For Yunnan Yi, however, the cultural barriers have long been breached, and the degree of actual cultural difference from the Han varies but is nowhere near the distance between Han and Nuosu. Similarly, in many places intermarriage, dating from the time of the Yuan and Ming armies, is an established fact of life. In order to maintain ethnic boundaries, then, Sani, Nisu, and Lipo must ritualize, formalize, valorize their separate provenance, their group unity, their cultural distinctness. And yet, those cultural features that these Yi groups use as markers are precisely those that establish their historical connection to the Nuosu; and at one level these cultural elements, relatively complete and unself-conscious among Nuosu but relatively mixed and very self-conscious among Yunnan groups, are what makes everybody Yi.

THE YI TODAY

Parts 1 through 3 of this book are written as if there were such a thing as Yi culture, if not completely ahistorical (many of the essays here do, after all, tell historical narratives), then still separate from the social and political changes that have marked the nearly half-century rule of the People's Republic of China. But Yi in all three provinces are no less caught up in Chinese history than any other Chinese citizens, and in the final section of the book we turn to consider the condition of the Yi in modern Chinese society.

One of the first things the Chinese Communists did with the Yi, as they did with all ethnic groups, was to define them. This meant not only drawing the aforementioned boundaries between them and other *minzu* but also fitting them with a standard set of descriptors that nailed their stage of social development (slave in Liangshan, feudal serfdom in Guizhou, landlord feudalism in most of Yunnan) and their ethnolinguistic affinity (Sino-Tibetan phylum, Tibeto-Burman family, Yi branch). In the linguistic realm, this also meant classifying them into dialects, subdialects, and local vernaculars (see Harrell 1993). This was done not purely for scholarly reasons but also in order to facilitate the standardization and teaching of Yi languages. David Bradley, in chapter 12 of this book, provides a comprehensive view of this classifying process and of the three different projects of standardization that have resulted in very different modern scripts in Sichuan, Guizhou, and Yunnan. Although there are probably about a million members of the Yi *minzu* who do not speak Yi languages, this leaves nearly six million who do, and to varying degrees Yi languages have entered the modern world, especially in Liangshan (where the problems with dialect diversity are less) by means of school textbooks, daily newspapers, radio stations, and other modern media.

The problem with modernizing a minority language in any multiethnic polity is, of course, that the modernization is at least partially designed to fit the needs of the modernizers, who, especially in the areas of education and propaganda, are in this case overwhelmingly Han. Whether various standardized Yi languages can become "full service languages" that are useful in all social contexts, or whether they will retain the status of "local vernaculars" whose use will be restricted to home, village, and festival, is still a question. Much depends, one suspects, on the degree to which the "minority autonomous areas" *(minzu zizhi diqu)* of China are able to achieve a meaningful sort of autonomy, which is the subject of chapter 13 by Thomas Heberer. In that chapter, Heberer discusses the contradictions between the idea of local autonomy for China's minority peoples and the economic and policy imperatives of a centralizing government and Party. Dealing specifically with the case of Liangshan Prefecture, he shows how the current Autonomy Law is a law without teeth, a statement of principles without any measures for enforcement, and how in the absence of enforcement the problems of a colony-like extractive economy and massive Han migration shed doubt on the future possibility of real local control of local resources.

The problems of language, autonomy, and the future course of modernization come together, as does so much of nation building, in the schools and colleges, and it is from his experience in the Liangshan Nationalities

Middle School *(Liangshan Minzu Zhongxue)* in Xichang that Martin Schoen-hals draws material on ethnicity and education for chapter 14. In this chap-ter, he explores both the process by which Nuosu students from remote vil-lages become committed to education and careers, and the reasons why more of them do not. In the course of doing this, however, he confirms earlier ob-servations about the nature of Nuosu ethnicity: it is constructed not in op-position to some ethnic other, but rather as an essential characteristic of a group of related people. Nuosu do not see themselves as in any way inferior to Han; in fact, Schoenhals maintains, they see themselves as superior, both essentially and morally. For this reason, they are not the least bit conflicted about school success; while acculturation is possible, even pragmatically de-sirable in some situations, assimilation is unthinkable: once a Nuosu, always a Nuosu, no matter what one does or thinks or speaks. Thus ethnicity is no barrier to education, if people think education can help them get ahead.

In addition to problems of ideology and ethnic identity, Yi are also pre-sented today with the more objective problems of modernization—the econ-omy and health care, and these two issues are taken up in the final two chap-ters of this book: Wu Ga on women entrepreneurs in the reform era, and Liu Xiaoxing on changes and problems in the health care system. In chap-ter 15, Wu Ga details, on the basis of long-term, extensive field research among Nuosu in Ninglang County, Yunnan, the aspirations, obstacles, and contradictions that face women who attempt to manage their households to achieve prosperity in a commercializing economy. Not surprisingly, their suc-cess varies, often according to the degree of access they enjoy to markets for cash crops and livestock. In addition, gender roles in a reforming economy are also undergoing uneven change, with access to markets and male labor migration giving women more economic power in some areas, while in other communities women either see the demands on their labor increase with the introduction of new crops or, in the remotest areas, return to something resembling their role in the subsistence economy that existed before the great Communist experiments with collective agriculture.

In the final chapter, Liu Xiaoxing treats the changes in the health care system, and more significantly the lack of change in and the persistence of traditional healers, as another instance of the contradiction between ethnic autonomy and a centralized, state project of modernization. As with mod-ern schooling, Liu finds that both Nuosu in Liangshan and Lipo in Chu-xiong freely resort to cosmopolitan medicine when they see it as efficacious. But officials cannot understand why the Yi, when faced with what the officials see as the overwhelming superiority of scientific medicine, do not just reject their traditional healers and remedies outright and modernize their lives. The answer, of course, lies partly in the strong and persistent eth-nic consciousness of all Yi groups, regardless of their degree of accultura-tion. They cling to their traditions, however mixed their traditions may be.

At the same time, Liu emphasizes that Yi people do not choose one mode of therapy or another simply for reasons of tradition or ethnic loyalty. They perceive both kinds of therapies to be efficacious in different ways and choose one or both according to their particular circumstances. In such a situation, for the foreseeable future modern medicine and folk therapies will continue to exist side by side in Yi areas.

The essays in this volume thus present the Yi to the world through the voices of their own, increasingly widely broadcast and articulate local discourse and through the voices of others who have tried to link their concern with matters Yi to the cosmopolitan discourses of social science. In doing so, all of us, Yi and non-Yi alike, have also backed off a bit and examined what we are doing, how we can forge stronger links between local concerns of promotion and cosmopolitan ones of connection and comparison. There is, as yet, no comprehensive picture of Yi society and culture in any language. We hope that the essays presented here can serve as building blocks for such a comprehensive work in the near future.

PART I

The Yi in History

CHAPTER 1

Reconstructing Yi History
from Yi Records

Wu Gu

As a scholar who was born into a Yi family and who has devoted himself heart
and soul to the study of Yi history and culture for several decades, I have developed some knowledge of the comprehensive embodiments of Yi traditional culture, which we can call Yi historical records, and which include not
only written documents but many other kinds of materials that can be used
to document the history of this society. This essay represents some of what
I have learned.

YI HISTORICAL RECORDS ARE THE COMPREHENSIVE
EMBODIMENT OF YI TRADITIONAL CULTURE

Because the Yi have a long history and remote origins, they have amassed a
considerable cultural store. Already in the pre-Imperial period this attracted
attention from outside scholars: the earliest relatively systematic account occurs in the "Record of the Southwestern Aborigines" *(Xinan Yi liezhuan)* chapter of Sima Qian's *Shiji.* Ever since that time, accounts of Yi history and culture, perhaps owing to the influence of Confucian thinking, have taken this
as a model.

In the last hundred years, owing to the rise of ethnology a new group of
scholars have undertaken field research in Yi areas in order to gather new
material for the study of Yi history and culture. In their field researches they
found that many records still existed in Yi areas, which prompted an effort
among learned scholars in China and abroad to collect, collate, translate,
and research these sources. Gradually there emerged a systematic, planned
effort to open the world of Yi historical records. Later, because of the
influences of the anti-Japanese war, this particular effort was halted, but during that war, because Yi areas were turned into the great rear area of the

anti-Japanese effort, a large number of cultural workers was concentrated in those areas; and in their work to carry on the war effort in remote Yi areas, they recovered an even richer and more varied trove of oral records, as well as music and dances of obvious value as cultural records.

After victory in the anti-Japanese war, many of these cultural workers remained in the Yi areas and threw themselves into the revolutionary struggle. In promoting cultural activities in the base areas, they collected materials at the sources; and in the process of deepening their research and collation of materials, they also published several translations and arranged for musical and dance performances, thereby deepening their own knowledge of Yi culture. In the first years after Liberation, many of these cultural workers took up leading positions, and under their leadership and encouragement many Yi works were translated and published, such as *Meige, Axi Xianji, Ashima,* and *Mother's Girl.* Yi songs and dances from the "song and dance records," such as "Hearth Dance," "Axi Jumps over the Moon," "Sani Serenade," "The Big Song and Dance Show," and others took the stage and were presented to the world. But in the process of publication of these works and the move to present them on outside stages, certain portions that embodied characteristics of "primitive culture" were—because of limited knowledge about them—looked upon as feudal superstitions and unhealthy factors and discarded, weakening the historical and cultural content of oral records and song and dance records. At the same time, through the encouragement of several well-known scholars, Yi historical texts such as *Records of the Southwestern Barbarians, Collected Cuan Carved Texts,* and *The Origins of the Universe* were published in translation.

However, due to the fact that the Yi are relatively spread out, and that there are many branches and diverse dialects, combined with the fact that the Yi have always been rather xenophobic, there developed an attitude that there was a difference between insiders and outsiders. As a result, despite a hundred years of effort, the actual process of opening up access to Yi historical records was very slow and the results meager. The accumulated cultural embodiments of thousands of years could not be developed systematically and transformed into historical documents; the massive amounts of Yi historical records remained as they had been, transmitted from generation to generation in scattered and remote villages.

During the January 1980 "National Conference on Yi Language Work" in Beijing, a group of Yi scholars put forth the opinion that "in order to promote the contribution of Yi culture to human civilization, it is necessary to organize a group of research teams to carry out a systematic, relatively comprehensive effort at saving, collating, translating, and publishing Yi historical records." This opinion was enthusiastically received from the start by Chinese and foreign scholars and Yi people generally, and it received the support of governments. As a result, organizations for the collation and research of

Yi historical records were established at province, prefecture, and county levels in areas of Yunnan, Sichuan, Guizhou, and Guangxi, wherever there were concentrations of Yi people. In order to train the next generation of scholars, majors and classes in Yi historical records were established at the Central Nationalities Institute, the Southwest Nationalities Institute, the Yunnan Nationalities Institute, and the Guizhou Nationalities Institute. In the past ten years, there has developed a force of almost a hundred scholars, most of them Yi, working in organizations at all administrative levels. In order to strengthen cooperation, the Yunnan-Sichuan-Guizhou-Guangxi Work Group for the Collation, Publication, and Standardization of Yi Historical Records was established, with a mission to coordinate the systematic process of working with Yi records. After over a decade of effort, we now have a relatively comprehensive knowledge of Yi historical records: almost a hundred volumes of Yi texts have been published in translation, and books and articles resulting from research on these records have also appeared. This has provided a strong foundation for the development of work with Yi documents and the revival of Yi culture. If in the new century we continue in the same vein in all aspects of this work, Yi historical records will enable Yi culture to be known around the world and make a contribution toward enriching the cultures of humanity.

CLASSIFICATION OF YI HISTORICAL RECORDS

Yi historical records can be divided into the following types:

1. Primary material records. Because Yi are scattered about, with many branches and diverse dialects, and because Yi writing has for the most part remained in the hands of *bimo* (priests) and a few other specialists, among the common people, signs using primary materials have been the principal means of communication and recording of events. I term these primary material records, and of these the following sorts can still be found:
   a. Carved wooden symbols. In traditional Yi households, carved ancestral tablets are the object of worship. They can be made either of wood or green bamboo, and woven goods or hair can be added to the basic human figure to indicate a male or female spirit. In the homes of *bimo* or shamans, there are also human figurines carved out of ritual implements that represent their spiritual masters.
   b. Carved board symbols. Few of these symbols, called *sipei*, remain. They are made out of a rectangular wooden board, and on the exposed face are carved male and female human figures, domestic animals, slaves, tools, and other things; they are hung over the beds of older people to symbolize the continuity of the household.
   c. Symbols in clothing and jewelry. In traditional Yi clothing and jewelry, one's own status in the system of stratification, as well as one's lo-

cal group, are expressed in the differences in tailoring and embroidery. In women's clothing, differences in color, pattern, and manner of wear express differences in marital, kinship, and parity status. Even more strikingly, in some groups the designs on clothing express "maps of a thousand migrations," and from these we can read the history of the development of that group.

d. Musical and dance symbols. Music and dances that accompany ritual activity have their ritual and historiographic purposes. This means that instrumentation, melody, dance steps, and hand gestures feature patterns expressing metaphorically the stories of the creation myths. Still found in areas where Yi people are relatively concentrated are the "Hearth Dance," "Coordinated Songs," "Axi Jumps over the Moon," and "Sani Serenade"; these songs, along with their rather strict rules for performing them, have been transmitted over the generations to today, and they illustrate the hunting, agricultural, reproductive, and migration activity of the ancestors of the Yi through their history. This means that those who participate learn the history of cultural development. But since these performances have moved to the stage there has been a lot of alteration, and it is difficult to differentiate the genuine from the spurious.

2. Records in metal and stone. In areas inhabited by the Yi and their ancestors, archaeologists have discovered a large number of metal, stone, and pottery artifacts that function symbolically like writing. This legacy is particularly rich.

a. Pottery containing symbols. In the Sichuan-Yunnan border area, a large number of Neolithic pottery vessels have been unearthed. In the early 1980s, during the process of excavating the remains of Kunming Man, archaeologists uncovered three pottery shards with symbols that had characteristics of writing. According to dating procedures, these come from about 10,000 B.P., and they certainly have a connection with traditional Yi writing. Later on, in the process of excavating remains from the Chunqiu (771–481 B.C.E.) and Zhanguo (480–221 B.C.E.) periods at Caohai in Weining (Guizhou), another group of pottery pieces with incised symbols was found (now stored in the Guizhou Provincial Museum), and people have also matched these up with traditional Yi writing. In the classical Yi text *Hnewo* (Creation) *teyy* (Book) (see Wu Jingzhong, chapter 2 in this volume), it is recorded that the ancestors of the Yi, after the division of the six clans, lived at a place called Zzyzzypuvu (in Nuosu). Following the description in the book, this is probably around Caohai in Weining.[1] According to this text, the

---

1. Editor's note: Various scholars locate this place in Weining in Guizhou, or in Zhaotong or Huize in Yunnan. The precise location is still a matter of contention. Thanks go to Bamo Qubumo, Bamo Ayi, Qumo Tiexi, and Ma Erzi for their clarification of this matter.

ancestors of the Yi had been involved at that time in wars against people called So or Sa.[2] According to the site report, in the same layer were also found the remains of a large number of warriors killed in battle, along with accompanying artifacts. Therefore, we should be able to extrapolate that those symbols and Yi writing have a common origin; there is already considerable scholarship on the comparison of Banpo pottery symbols with Yi writing. In sum, symbols on pottery are historical remnants that can be studied in comparison to many kinds of writing, a field that has far-reaching significance for the study of the development of ancient civilizations.

b. Cliff records. Many paintings using pigments of iron or animal blood have been found in many places in steep mountains and deep valleys where the ancient Aimao used to live. Investigation reveals that these tell the stories of certain historical occurrences, which can thus be translated and "read." In 1984, researchers found at Xunjiansi in Mile County a Yi language couplet painted with the same pigments on two ends of a cliff. By the Nanzhao period, this kind of cliff document had developed into large-scale stone carving, such as the cliff sculptures at Shibao Shan in Jianquan and at Posiwahe in Zhaojue. Such cliff documents have long been treasures for research into early human civilization.

c. Tile and brick documents. During the excavations in the core area of the Nanzhao kingdom—Weibao Shan—a large number of brick and tile carvings were found. In addition to totemic images, there were a lot of talismans carved with Yi script. Talismans like these have also been found in stone grottoes at Jianquan, and they survive in great numbers in the foundation of a tower in Dayao County known as the Stone Chime Tower.

d. Metal and stone documents in Yi script. Yi ancestors, organized into tribes and moving from camp to camp, recorded their history by carving many stone stelae and casting many vessels, leaving behind a large quantity of Yi-language metal and stone inscriptions, along with a few bronze mirrors. Metal and stone documents such as these have lasted a long time because of their durable materials and are now valuable sources for research into Yi history.

3. Oral records. Because the Yi are dispersed in different groups and speak different dialects, if we compare their oral records with those of other peoples, we can say that they are voluminous and detailed, distinctive and praiseworthy, and have long been an important source of culture history. Because study of oral records was developed rather early, oral history has

2. These terms are probably cognate to the modern Nuosu *shuo,* which is a general term for outsiders, slaves, or Han.

already become a specialized field, and it will not be treated in more detail here.

4. Books. Because we can trace the origin of Yi writing back ten thousand years, and because it has been used in documents for two or three thousand years, it is no exaggeration to claim, as the old saying goes, that these sources are "plentiful as a sea of smoke, sweating the ox and bending the beams." According to historical sources, *tusi*, or local rulers, in various Yi areas carried out large-scale editing projects and established rather large collections of Yi-language books at today's Bijie, Jianshui, Wuding, and Xichang. Later on, because of the *gaitu guiliu* (replacement of *tusi* by appointed bureaucrats), Yi-language books were scattered in private collections. Yi books now preserved in Yi areas and around the world probably number over ten thousand titles.

Through analysis and comparison of Yi-language books, we can see that—even though currently preserved Yi books have a common origin—because they have not yet undergone comprehensive standardization, they display significant differences in different areas, with the three most important styles surviving in Wumeng, Liangshan, and Ailao. According to their content and use, they can be divided into two major categories: religious and ritual books and books for popular use.

Research into Yi books in recent years has produced a large number of monographs, and "those who know wisdom will find wisdom; those who know humaneness will find humaneness," as they say. But the most important reality is that because Yi books are so widespread, the work of collation and cataloguing is a long way from being completed. In addition, because the great majority of Yi texts are inseparable from ritual activities of *bimo*, if we try to separate the collation of the texts from their significance for ritual activity, we will never be able to understand their content in depth. For this reason, it is critically important in our work with Yi books to salvage their ritual meaning. Only when we have collected both a large number of books and various kinds of data on ritual can we undertake relatively scientific analysis of traditional Yi books.

5. Records embodied in material culture. The phenomena of material culture—developed and transmitted across the generations by each people in the process of carrying out cultural activities such as devising dress, food, housing, and transport—carry with them embodied documentary value. This kind of record is better developed than other kinds, because these activities are a response to the needs of the market. But because records of such activities have not heretofore been included in the sphere of scientific research, and because development of the activities themselves has recently been hurried by commercial considerations, there have developed both false and poor quality goods. If the tradition is lost, the results will be unthinkable. For this reason, some preliminary research into his-

torical records embodied in Yi material culture has been carried out in recent years. The analysis below reveals the pearls hiding in this mud.

a. Residential architecture. Yi peoples developed permanent, fixed housing very early in their history. In the early periods, the majority of people lived up against mountains beside waterways, and so developed the log-cabin style. Later, because of military considerations, the watchtower house built out of cut stone appeared. In their migrations, some branches moved to hot, humid climates, and in order to protect themselves against rain and mitigate the effects of heat, they invented the earthen insulated house, which is characteristic of a few counties, using mud mixed with straw in the walls and roofs of wood-frame houses. During the Nanzhao period, many styles were adopted from neighboring peoples. But the watchtower house remained the primary building style; sites for offerings to ancestral spirits are still built in this style. Watchtower houses were built during the height of the *tusi* system, right up to the imposing official residence built for Long Yun, governor of Yunnan in the 1930s.

b. Clothing styles. Because the Yi throughout history comprised a tribal confederation, the culture of each tribe has come down to us as the culture of a "branch" of the Yi. In addition, vestiges of "caste thinking," resulting from the long-lived slave society, caused Yi clothing culture to differentiate through color, cut, and pattern not only the branch but also the social stratum, marital status, and profession of the wearer.

c. Foodways. Because the ancestors of the Yi practiced agriculture very long ago, combining rice cultivation with domestic animal husbandry, they developed a culinary culture suited to this lifestyle.

They made alcoholic beverages primarily from grains, using the surplus grain from careful cultivation. Because different grains were grown in different areas, each area developed its own liquors, such as buckwheat liquor, wheat liquor, corn liquor, and rice wine, as well as alcoholic beverages fermented or distilled from a mixture of different grains. From the integration of alcoholic beverages into rites of propitiation for ancestral spirits came the development of drinking vessels as sacred objects, and the hereditary profession of manufacture of these objects. Liquor, drinking vessels, and the drinking songs that developed out of the ancestral ritual libations of different areas coalesced into the so-called alcohol culture typical of the Yi.

One group of Yi ancestors, who migrated to the southern part of Yunnan, began cultivating tea rather early, and a series of distinctive ritual practices of tea drinking developed to please the spirits and to please the practitioners themselves. Examples include the "Weishan eight steps tea," which has survived to the present as a typical example of the tea culture of the Yi.

Out of the custom of serving the meat of domestic chickens, pigs, cattle, and sheep to entertain guests and worship ancestors, there gradually developed a set of culinary practices. According to tradition, the ancestors of the Yi in their days of glory developed the "eight steps liquor" to welcome guests. They developed too the "jumping of dishes," a way of serving dishes with dance steps; *qiancai,* singing about the origin of the food while dividing it among the guests; the "liquor libation," in which up to 124 dishes were served in a "feast of whole sheep"; and an ordinary feast in which "eight bowls" of pork, mutton, and beef were served to guests. After the banquet, guests were entertained by the "eight steps tea," a display of dancing and singing. This whole tradition of feasting styles was known as the "three-eight" style of banqueting guests, and formed a distinctive culinary culture.

The Yi thus constituted, developed, and transmitted from generation to generation a rich and varied culture consisting of the categories described above.

RECONSTITUTING THE HISTORICAL DEVELOPMENT OF YI CULTURE THROUGH YI HISTORICAL RECORDS

In the last few decades, it has been the constant hope of historians to prepare a history that would straighten out the origin of the Yi. But because all of the historical records and interview materials used have their own particular characteristics, all the results announced so far have become the focus of disputatious debates. In extreme cases, published statements have led to ethnic hostility and the phenomenon of "discuss Yi history and blanch with fear."

I hope that several decades of editing and researching Yi historical records will eventually enable us to reconstitute the historical development of Yi culture and add a new voice to the disputations over Yi history. Here I will use a general summary of the newly edited *History of Ancient Yi Culture* (Zhang Fu 1999) as a source for some basic information.

The Origins of the Yi

Research on a large number of Yi poems about the creation of the world shows that the majority of the original Yi were probably descendants of ancient humans of the Sichuan-Yunnan border area who gradually developed and expanded their numbers over the course of about a million years; about ten thousand years ago they entered the period of formation of the Yi as a group. During this period, there arose the simplest of primitive human cultures. The early ancestors of the Yi had an animistic outlook, and thought that all life originated in water. Water was created by snowmelt; as it flowed

downward, there gradually emerged a creature called Ni, who in the movement of water gradually evolved into all forms of life (very much resembling
the view of Lao Zi's *Daode Jing,* which says, "One gave birth to two; two gave
birth to three; three gave birth to all creatures," especially since the Chinese
word *Yi* (one) resembles the Yi word *Ni* in its form, meaning, and sound,
and probably comes from the same origin). So all creatures have the spiritual energy of Ni, and Ni became the highest object of worship of the ancestors of the Yi and is still today one name for the ethnic group. (Also, because Yi people respect black and think of black as a precious thing,
contemporary people continue to translate *Ni* as *black.*)

About ten thousand years ago, Yi people began to invent a form of writing (the signs, which can be read in Yi, found on pottery from about ten
thousand years ago during the process of excavating the remains of "Kunming People" at Jinbao Shan in 1980, are an example).

The ancestors of the Yi at about this time mostly lived in riverine or la-
custrine lowlands, called *bazi* in Chinese, and subsisted primarily by rice cultivation supplemented by fishing and hunting, making theirs the earliest agricultural civilization.

The highly involuted topography of the Sichuan-Yunnan area was created
by pressure from the collision of the Indian subcontinent, which also exposed
many deposits of precious minerals. Their presence resulted in the world's
earliest bronze metallurgical activity (in ancient Yi written documents there
are records of bronze-smithing; in the Yi classical text *Yypuquopu,* it is
recorded that when the six ancestral branches of the Yi divided, their ceremony of division was conducted at a sacred place known as Bronze Cave).
The development of bronze-age culture was one aspect of the primitive culture of this period.

Spurred on by the material and mental cultural advances related above,
the ancestors of the Yi gradually evolved into a tribal society. They evolved
productive activities that fit ecologically with the particular environment of
the *bazi,* and evolved into separate tribal cultures with particular characteristics (the multiplicity of the current branches of the Yi probably has something to do with this).

Division and Migration

The ancestors of the Yi, in the process of continually improving their means
of livelihood, also developed the idea that relatives could marry each other
after a certain number of generations (i.e., some groups permitted marriage
only after three generations, some only after six, and some only after nine)
and thus improved their reproductive capacity. When the population growth
outstripped the capacity of the *bazi,* they began the pattern of dividing into
branches and migrating.

A rather complete set of records of the process of division into branches has come down to us, and it contains characteristics of the lineage system typical of the early stages of slave society. For example, it states, "The elder is the lord; the younger is the slave," and "The issue of stratum endogamy is a lord; the issue of exogamy is a slave." Younger brothers who did not wish to be slaves could carry out certain rituals, establish themselves as a *xing* (surname group), move elsewhere, pioneer the area, and establish, according to the traditions of the lineage system, a new hereditary domain. Gradually, over generations, there emerged a "culture of migration," which included the creation of "migration epics," a rich and valuable source of historical documentation.

According to numerous Yi historical records, about five or six thousand years ago among the ancestors of the Yi there was a hero, called Zhygge Alur in the Nuosu language, who completed the military conquest of a large number of tribes and established a tribal confederation, giving himself the royal title (in Yi) of *emu,* which can be translated as *emperor.* (According to the account in the historical book *Yypuquopu,* the symbol of the *emu* later evolved into the hairstyle of the nobility. It is probably connected with the hairstyles of certain peoples of the Dian culture.) About four thousand years ago, because of destruction caused by floods, the ancestors of the Yi carried out the largest-ever ceremony of tribal division at a place in northeastern Yunnan called either Lenyibo or Lonibo in Yunnan and Guizhou Yi-language books, and Nzyhxolynyiebo in Nuosu.[3] This began the "division of the six branches"—which so greatly influenced the later history of the Yi—and brought about the further enrichment and development of the migratory practices of the Yi.

Their migratory activities certainly influenced the cultural relations of the ancestors of the Yi. The particular topography of the Sichuan-Yunnan region and the Yunnan-Guizhou plateau determined the direction of migration along the watersheds of the "six rivers." This gave these people the possibility of moving eastward along the Upper Yangtze into the area of Ba and Chu (eastern Sichuan and Hubei), moving southward along the Mekong River into Southeast Asia, moving westward across the peaks of the six-river region into the Indian subcontinent and even into Europe, and moving northward upstream into the northwest of China and the north China area. This gave rise to a large-scale cultural interchange of the ancestors of the Yi and, unavoidably, to much mixing of ancestral strains.

Thus, the Yi are a mixed group of diverse origins, one that began with the ancient humans of the Sichuan-Yunnan area; incorporated descendants from Chinese, Mon-Khmer, Aryan, and Mongolian groups; and culminated

---

3. Editor's note: Again, there is much scholarly speculation about the exact location of this place, but it is generally agreed that it must have been in the area surrounding the current city of Zhaotong, now divided among the provinces of Yunnan, Guizhou, and Sichuan.

in the Dian culture. This is another characteristic of the Yi that has survived from the "time of migrations" and the "division of the six ancestors" that is recorded in Yi documents.

The Flourishing of Yi Culture during Nanzhao

Nanzhao (c. 734–902) was the most brilliant period in the development of the ancestors of the Yi, when they developed a polity based on a combination of historical developments—which they recorded in the *Classic of Ruling a Country and Pacifying a Territory*—and experiences learned from Han areas. The *Classic,* a very important text, is lost to posterity, but from a large number of other surviving texts we can reconstitute its essence: the *emu* was said not only to manage the affairs of the world in concert with the heavenly gods but also to manage the affairs of all the Yi tribes of the time. At that time, Yi tribes were organized as associations of five social statuses—rulers, ministers, priests, artisans, and common people. As recorded in the *Classic,* "The ruler makes the overall plans; the minister makes concrete decisions; the priest supervises the rituals; the artisan manages indoor labor; and the people cultivate the fields." Each tribe's administrative territory was demarcated by anywhere from a few to a few tens of boundary rivers. A central administrative area was directly governed by the ruler, minister, and priest, and this area, along with its boundary rivers, was assigned to a *mase,* or marshal, who held overall military command. Under the *mase* were several *mayi,* and the *mayi* in turn commanded *yidu,* or battle commanders. The *yidu* were the lowest level of officialdom, leading military expeditions against other polities under the command of the *mayi,* capturing prisoners to be used as slaves, and taking direct charge of the labor activities of commoners and slaves in their own areas. From the *Classic,* it is not difficult to see that this was a set of institutions that served the stratified slave society of the time and had allowed the Yi slave society to continue for several thousand years.

The Yi of the Nanzhao period, because of interactions with neighboring countries, left behind a rich cultural legacy: they gradually developed the architectural, culinary, and sartorial practices described in detail above, as well as music, choreography, and other aspects of high culture.

Music and dance had already reached high levels, owing to the early development of ritual activities and their consequent ritual dances, as well as continuous dance activities for the pleasure of the gods and the participants. Add to this the interaction with neighboring countries, which brought in outside music and dance, and the music and dance of the Yi stood out among neighboring ethnic groups and formed an example for others to emulate.

We can thus see that during the development of the Nanzhao, Yi culture not only maintained the traditions of its past but also absorbed much from abroad, becoming a comprehensive culture. Had it been able to continue developing, it could well have become an independent national culture in its own right. But because of the changes in regime, the Nanzhao period left only a regional culture; putting an actual national label on it would be nothing but ethnic chauvinism.

Cultural Divergence after the Fall of Dali

The replacement of the Nanzhao and Dali (902–1253) regimes, the collapse of the thirty-seven districts, the scattering of a unified ethnic group, the rise of the different ethnic groups of the Yi language family together comprised the most important change in the southwestern area during this time, and it has an intrinsic connection with Yi historical culture.

Extending throughout the history of the development of the Yi was the continuous thread of descent relations, which gave rise to the primitive practice of ancestral worship and was expressed in ancestral genealogies. People could not escape the limitations of the mountainous topography of the Sichuan-Yunnan region or the Yunnan-Guizhou plateau during their long-term migrations, and so they continued to migrate back and forth along rivers and beside lakes and thus developed cultural commonalities based on the concentration in the *bazi,* or plains areas. The vertical environmental variety of the high mountains and deep valleys meant that these people had to adapt to different ecological circumstances in the different areas in which they settled, and this gave rise to the changeable nature of their cultures. As a result of historical developments and the accumulation of cultural features, groups gradually developed an independent existence based on tribal culture, which led to collapse of the historical tribal confederation. As soon as the Nanzhao and Dali confederations felt the power of the great armies of Qubilai, they collapsed and the union of the thirty-seven tribes wilted like an ephemeral flower. The divergence of the different ethnic groups of the Yi family was historically inevitable.

As a result, Yi culture developed as multiple streams from the same source, and the division of one ethnic group into a large number of ethnic groups (or branches) spawned multifarious ethnic cultures.

According to evidence found in Yi documents, certain practices evolved: Participation in sacrifices is a fundamental duty of all group members. (Yi-language books detailing sacrifices to the ancestral spirits are among the most important ritual articles transmitted in *bimo* households.) Ancestral genealogy must be studied by all adults, and nearness or distance of kinship relationships based on descent is a means for determining relationships between people. The recitation of Scriptures for Showing the Way during sacrifices to the ancestors leads members of the group to know the routes taken by previous generations during their migrations.

Like the archival materials and historical records mentioned above, most other documents that are related through a common cultural origin demonstrate—as a result of their divergent origin from a common source— a set of common cultural characteristics with regional cultural variations:

1. There are several particular characteristics in stories about the origin of the race. For example, the descriptions of the origin story, in which "water gave birth to the myriad creatures, and the dragon nourished the first ancestors," that appear in the original stories of all of the regional cultures attest to the specific characteristics of "totems" as symbols of clans.

2. All sorts of characteristics of architecture, food, and dress have been divergent from area to area.

3. Methods of public praise, along with music and dance, which originally carried specific cultural characteristics, have also had considerable interchange, intermixing, and mutual absorption with other groups, and have developed large-scale differences.

4. Medicine and pharmacology depend even more on materials occurring naturally in different environments, and undergo selection, so the local nature of Yi medications is particularly apparent. Nevertheless, the intertwining of spirits and medicaments as two kinds of solutions to health problems is a common characteristic of medical documents. So the document Scripture for Exorcising Spirits and Expelling Ghosts is still in use in many Yi villages.[4]

5. Agriculture, rice growing, and animal husbandry are traditional subsistence practices of the Yi, and success in these governs the ability of Yi populations to flourish or even survive. The need to "divine the day and fix the time for cultivation" is universal among rice-growing and other agricultural cultures all over the world, and the Yi are no exception. For this reason, astronomical texts and the calendar are important Yi historical documents, but because of differences in latitude and elevation encountered in the course of migrations, many different versions of these documents have been developed to suit particular circumstances. The Scripture for Exorcising Spirits and Expelling Ghosts, as well as the Almanacs for Divining the Auspicious and Inauspicious, which guide those who seek divine assistance in countering the inevitable natural disasters and human depredations, testify to the continued relevance of inherited astronomical and calendrical knowledge.

We thus can see that the Yuan and early Ming comprise the period of the maturity of Yi culture, as well as the time when existing Yi historical records received their lasting form.

4. A translation and commentary on a Nuosu version from Zhaojue has recently been published: see Taipei Ricci Institute 1998.

Pressure from the Outside and the Making of Modern Yi Cultures

Starting in the Ming and Qing periods, central dynasties, implementing their policies of securing the borders and stabilizing the frontiers, constantly sent troops and dispatched military expeditions into ethnic areas. In the vast Yi areas on the distant southwestern frontiers, people were driven from their original areas of occupation into the high mountains and ancient forests. In the wake of the frontier consolidation undertaken by civil and military colonies, and the shock of having native officials replaced with appointed officials, the Yi also experienced the double shocks of the assimilation policy of Han-centered central political authorities and the alienation policy that preserved ethnic cultures and local power. This was a baptism of blood and fire for Yi culture, and a trial of existence or annihilation for ethnic historical documents.

The history of the Yi, which began ten thousand years ago, has been a process of development, maturity, and flourishing; and the cultural documents that have come from it also have a history in which they have changed and then finally assumed a fixed form. As a result, Yi historical documents have taken on a living strength that transcends time and place.

In sum, Yi historical records, the comprehensive carriers of the Yi culture through the long period since its origin, are a rare treasure of human culture because they re-create a ten-thousand-year ethnic history. Studying them can lead us to a greater understanding of ourselves as humans.

CHAPTER 2

Nzymo as Seen in Some Yi Classical Books

Wu Jingzhong

Nzymop is a Nuosu-language name for a member of a ruling stratum, a name that has long been used in Yi history, and which means "one who wields power."[1] The Yi had a caste society for much of their history; during this time people were divided into several strata with different social positions, and the *nzymo* was the highest stratum in this society.

Because the *nzymo* held this illustrious position for a long period, they had great influence on every aspect of Yi history. As a result of their close relations with the feudal dynasties throughout history, the study of the *nzymo* is an important aspect of the study of Yi history.

China's feudal dynasties, beginning with the Yuan, practiced the *tusi* system among many minority peoples in the northwestern and southwestern areas of the country (see Herman 1997). They enfeoffed existing leaders of these minority peoples as local rulers, giving them titles such as *tusi* and *tumu*. The *nzymo* of the Nuosu in Liangshan were also deputed with the titles *tusi* and *tumu*. Consequently, *nzymo* were mostly referred to as Yi *tusi*. After the rulers of the Yuan dynasty began enfeoffing the *nzymo* as *tusi* and *tumu*, the Ming and Qing continued the Yuan system. Even though the policy of *gaitu*

---

1. In the romanized form of standard Nuosu orthography, tones are indicated by an iconic "musical scale" graph, with "t" indicating a high tone, "x" a midrising tone, no graph a midlevel tone, and "p" a low falling tone. The standard romanization here is thus *nzymop*. To prevent unaccustomed English-language readers from interpreting the "p" graph as a bilabial stop, we omit the tone marks in this book.

Nzy and *Nzymo* are equivalent terms. The suffix *-mo* occurs in many nominal forms, often indicating large size, high rank, or seniority, and sometimes opposed to *-sse*, meaning small or junior. Thus *bimo* is a priest, *bisse* a disciple; *gemo* a senior artisan; another *gemo* is a large wardrobe, while a *gesse* is a small chest of drawers.

guiliu (replacement of *tusi* by appointed bureaucrats) effected large changes, the *nzymo* among the Nuosu of Sichuan remained in power until the Democratic Reforms took place following establishment of the People's Republic. *Nzymo* were thus important in Yi history for two thousand years, and their influence on Yi society cannot be ignored. Investigating the *nzymo* can help us deepen our understanding of Yi history, as well as of the ethnic policies of Chinese imperial dynasties.

There are many in China's scholarly circles who have researched the *tusi* system, including quite a few who have studied the *tusi* system among the Yi. But the bulk of the data for this research has come from Han-language history books or from field investigations. Comparatively few scholars have directly consulted Yi-language classical books for such studies. For this essay, which begins my exploration of the history of the *nzymo*, I have used material on them recorded in several Nuosu-language books that have come down to us from Liangshan.

Han-language sources are reasonably clear in recording the position of the *nzymo* from the Yuan dynasty on, but their understanding of them before that time is superficial at best. Yi classical sources are different: they are not arranged according to the successive historical dynasties of China, but rather according to the history of their own people. Because of this, they have relatively rich records of the *nzymo* in the period before the Yuan, so we can use Yi-language classical books to supplement or strengthen our understanding in places where Han-language sources are incomplete.

We can date the events recorded in Yi historical books to particular Chinese dynasties by using the abundant data found in the father-son linked genealogies of Yi clans, counting thirty years per generation as a standard. By this method, we can not only determine in which historical dynasty a particular *nzymo* mentioned in Yi historical sources lived, but we can also assign a tentative historical progression to the events found in such sources.

TEXTS USED IN THIS ESSAY

In compiling this essay, I have used four Yi-language texts in particular: *Hnewo teyy, Vonre, Hxoyi Ddiggur,* and *Gamo Anyo.*

Hnewo teyy can be roughly translated as *The Book of Origins,* and it is the most famous Nuosu-language text to come out of Liangshan. It was probably first written down in the Ming period but is clearly based on much older, orally transmitted traditions. It recounts the origin of heaven and earth, as well as the origin and early migrations of the Yi people, along with descriptions of life and society during earlier periods.[2]

2. There are at least four modern editions available: Jjissy 1980 and Qubi Shimei n.d. are in standardized Nuosu, and SFAS 1960 and Feng 1986 are in Chinese translation.

Vonre can be translated as *The Snow Clan*. It too appears to be a collection of orally transmitted stories that was compiled in written form sometime during the Ming. It describes the origin of humanity, as well as life in earlier times and the genealogies and migration histories of many Yi clans (Leng 1983).

Hxoyi Ddiggur takes its name from its principal character, a retainer of the famous *nzymo* Miajy. In the course of recounting the exploits of its hero, the book gives detailed descriptions of life in his time, which was probably sometime during the Tang period. Several versions of the story were recorded at various times during the Ming and Qing periods at different places in Liangshan (Ggelu 1986).

Gamo Anyo also takes its name from its principal character, in this case a beautiful woman who probably lived in Ming times. The tragic story of the heroine has been sung by bards for several hundred years all over Liangshan; recently, modern scholars have collected and collated this material to form the present book.

THE ORIGINS OF THE *NZYMO*

With regard to the time and origin of the *nzymo*, there are many questions that remain to this day. We can explore them through Yi-language histories and Nuosu genealogies.

According to Nuosu genealogies, *nzy* originated twenty-five generations after the Yi became patrilineal, at the time of Vobbuddebbu. The period covering from the time of Vobbuddebbu to that of the original ancestors of the Liangshan Nuosu, Gguhxo and Qoni, encompasses about ten generations, or about three hundred years. And the period from Gguhxo and Qoni to the present encompasses about seventy generations. If one generation averages thirty years, we find that the *nzy* appeared about twenty-four hundred years ago. Naturally, this is not a precise date, but we can see that they originated quite long ago.

It is difficult today to discover the original circumstances under which the *nzy* first appeared, but we can gain a glimpse from the tradition of the origin of the Lynge *nzymo* of Liangshan. Many years before, according to this tradition, among the ancestors of the Lynge *nzymo* there were seven brothers. Among the seven, who would be *nzymo*? Their old mother thought of a way to decide.

At that time, all of Liangshan was dense forest, with many wild animals that often disrupted people's lives. Near where the Lynge lived there was a fierce beast who frequently caused trouble, even to the point of stealing corpses from the cremation ground. Because of this, the old mother suggested to her sons that they eliminate this beast in order to prevent it from stealing her corpse after she died. Whoever distinguished himself as a hero in this fight would become the *nzy*, and the others would all have to follow his orders. The eldest son shot the beast dead, and he became the Lynge *nzymo*.

The preceding tale demonstrates that the *nzy* originated in the struggle between humans and nature. The conditions for becoming *nzy* are, first, courage and a positive contribution; second, respect for the elderly. From this it is apparent that the elders, represented by the mother, played an important role in deciding who became *nzy*. This example is not necessarily the first example of the origin of a Yi *nzymo*, but it demonstrates that at that time *nzy* were chosen according to definite standards.

EARLY *NZYMO* AS RECORDED IN
THE *HNEWO TEYY* AND OTHER TEXTS

What was it like for the early *nzymo?* Yi classical books, as represented by this excerpt from the *Hnewo teyy*, offer some hints:

> Leading people and horses from his own command, they moved around for a long time on the two banks of the Jinsha River, looking for an ideal place to settle. Their route went from Miti to Galumobbo [now Leibo], then to Guzyjjiggur [now Xiongba], and then along the Lagu Mountains: Sakulur-jjo—Mohxoladda [Mabian]—Jiejyyydda [Ebian]—Jjieggurgalo [Ganluo]—Pohxoladda [Puxiong]—Xinziladda [Yuexi]—Xiddoladda [Xide]—Aqybilu [Hongmo in Mianning]—Nieyylyjjo [Anningchang in Xichang]—Labbuorro [Xichang]—Mutedoli [Daxing Chang]—Salandipo [Lanba, Zhaojue]—Syngaladda [Sikai, Zhaojue]—Hxuoggurjojjo [Zhaojue]—Limuzhuhxi [Zhuhe]—Yyyishuonuo [Huangmaokeng]—Rawalomo—Tejjoladda—Nyungelolo. Afterward he exhorted his descendants to continue the effort, and they finally settled at Zzyzzypuvu.

This description of migration is the history of several generations of people continually searching for an ideal dwelling place. The story reflects the difficulty of such a search in the face of natural adversity and social confusion in Liangshan. Migration under the leadership of the *nzy* was continuous because many places did not meet the *nzy's* ideal.

First there were the poor natural conditions. For example, in Miti "there were trees on the mountains, and no water in the valleys." In Guzyjjiggur the climate was cold: "The land was cold as a mud pillar, the wind blew through the branches like a flute; . . . the grass stalks were like swords." Ganluo was a place where the wild animals lurked: "A place where wild game sharpened their teeth." Yyyishuonuo was a place where "the long grass that grew was poison grass; when Yi people touched it they were poisoned; when Han people touched it they, too, were poisoned, and would die from poisoning in a day."

In some places, local customs were peculiar, and the *nzy* did not want to live there. For example, in Aqybilu "they plow with the black water buffalo, and they eat with the short-handled spoon." In Laggeorro (Xichang), "the sun sears your back, and you get boils on your chest; the water buffalo and the ox both plow; they are together when they work, but after plowing they go their separate ways. The Yi and the Han live mixed; when they go out they are together; when they scatter they go their separate ways.[3] The Han wrap their heads in cloth turbans; Han women wear narrow trousers."

In some places, the social environment was dangerous. In Galumobbo (Leibo), "sons of the *nzymo* were imprisoned." In Xinziladda (Yuexi), "the male eagle is eaten by the frog and pollutes nine ranges of mountains;[4] the crow drinks human blood and pollutes nine villages; the white dog gnaws human bones and pollutes nine households; the raven swallows the ashes of the cremation ground and pollutes nine patches of forest." In Jjotumuggu (today's Haogu), "evil spirits gather, and you have to watch your head all day long." In Hxoggurjjojo, "there are a painted saddle and bridle on the brown horse—if the lord is strong the lord rides; if the slaves are strong the slaves ride; there is no division between high and low." And in Nimuzhuhxe there are an intolerable number of guests: "The guests gather like clouds; if the hosts' wooden serving dishes are enough, still there are not enough spoons: if you can offer hot food and drink, you still can't offer hot soup."

At that time, the *nzymo* also paid great attention to the family's ability to select marriage partners. The *nzy* chose only from among the leading families of any clan or tribe. Yi classical books record the situation of intermarriage among the six *zu*.[5] When members of the Vonre clan were seeking affines, the Ggeqo clan came to marry; when Hxuohe were looking for affines, Ggenbo came to marry; when Bbuhmu were looking for affines, Shynra came to marry. This demonstrates that leaders of various clans came to arrange marriages. The *Vonre* also says, "When Legge had passed one generation, Vositi came to marry; when Legge had passed two generations, Voddibo came to marry; when Legge had passed three generations, Voddile came to marry; when the fourth generation was reached, Votinyi came to marry," and so forth.

3. Editor's note: Nuosu often use pairs of animals to distinguish themselves from Han. Water buffalo (who live in the lowlands only) are Han; oxen (who can thrive in the highlands) are Nuosu. Similarly, goats (who have beards) are Han, while sheep (who have no beards) are Nuosu.

4. The numbers 9, 90, 900, etc. are used in many Yi sources to indicate a large number. They should not be taken literally. For uses of 9 and its multiples in a different context, see Qubi and Ma, chapter 6 in this volume.

5. Editor's note: The six *zu*, or ancestors, occur in classical Yi texts from many parts of the southwest; many scholars believe that these six legendary ancestors, who are said to have founded the various Yi peoples of today, were actually six tribes that dispersed from a common point of origin, usually thought to be somewhere in Yunnan.

Another point that deserves our attention is that at this time *nzymo* were particularly concerned with trying to expand the population. This is not difficult to understand. And population increase was connected with the ritual activity called *nimu*,[6] which means ancestor worship (see Bamo 1994). In the *Vonre* there is a story of the flourishing of the human population because of *nimu*: "The two eldest sons, Vo and Nra, lived at Chochulaie, and Vo and Nra did *nimu* together, and between them they had nine sons, whose descendants flourished all over the world." It also says that "Siti did six *nimu*," and he too had nine sons. The Ashuo clan also had six sons as a result of ancestor worship, and also began to be prominent at this time. In sum, people at that time thought the flourishing of the human population was closely connected with the performance of religious rituals.

NZYMO AS SEEN IN THE *VONRE* AND OTHER CLASSICAL TEXTS

About thirty generations after Gguhxo, there was a period of great flourishing of Yi culture, and at this time many famous *nzymo*, such as Heatu, appeared.

According to genealogies, from Heatu (also called Ahe Atu) to the present there have been about forty-five generations; if we figure thirty years per generation, Heatu probably lived about thirteen hundred years ago, during the Tang period. He was born in a place called Yyyyhxeke, and Yi-language books refer to the period following his birth as the time of Heatu. In the texts we find many references to his mark on history.

According to Yi-language history books, Heatu belongs to the line of Gguhxo: "After leaving Yyyyhxeke, Gguhxo performed ancestral sacrifices, and his clan divided into branches: one was Helinge, who lived on Lepu Mountain; one was Hessely, who lived at Vovyddirro; one was Herromi, who lived at Mahnibbovu; one was Herrovy, who lived at Ddipuhxeke; one was Helenge, who lived at Lengeshoshy; one was Heavy, who lived at Avyjjurrro; one was Heatu. In the time of Heatu, they moved away from Cheyuyu to live at Yyyyhxeke." This shows that Heatu belonged to a branch of Gguhxo's line.

Heatu's mother was called Ddijysasse. The *Vonre* says, "In the time of Heahxo, at the place called Kilinreggo they established marriage relations with the Dijyshuote clan; the bride was called Ddijysasse; she was the mother of Heatu."

At the time of *nzymo* Ahe Atu, there were also *Mo* Ahe Avy and *Bi* Ahe Aggo. A *mo* was a mediator of disputes, and a *bi* was responsible for sacrifices to the dead. Because of this, the time of Heatu is also referred to as the time of the three worthies. The situation of the *nzymo* at this time is as follows: In subsistence pursuits, hunting had an important place. According to the *Vonre*,

---

6. Editor's note: The syllable rendered *mu* in the Romanized orthography is in fact pronounced as a syllabic *m*, with no accompanying vowel. *Nimu* is thus pronounced *nim*.

the *nzy* at that time went in person on horseback to take charge of the hunt. The results of one large-scale hunt were quite evident, as noted in the text: "When he was living at Mynyibati, *Nzy* Ahe Atu released seven hunting dogs, and they went to the mountain tops; when he brought his dogs back in, he gathered up the catch. The bodies of tigers and leopards made a heap; the heads of tigers and leopards were like a pile of stones. The deer that he bagged numbered in the thousands; the tiger and leopard skins he distributed in nine places. In one cedar forest, they hunted in three locations in three days. They bound up the animals and carried them on their backs." Accomplished all in one hunt: tigers and leopards in a heap, carcasses piled up like logs, skins in a huge stack, deer without number. This was quite an organized hunt.

The text *Hxoyi Ddiggur* records the story of the hunting hero Hxoyi Ddiggur. According to the book, he was a thirty-sixth generation descendant of Gguhxo. If Gguhxo lived twenty-one hundred years ago, then Hxoyi Ddiggur lived about twelve hundred years ago, and this makes him a contemporary of Ahe Atu. One of Hxoyi Ddiggur's claims to fame was that he became a close companion and an accomplished hunter as a follower of *Nzy* Miajy and Miajy's family. He also hunted with dogs. It is said that he took along three packs of dogs when he hunted. On the first day, he bagged only a few rabbits. Because Ddiggur did not eat rabbit meat or rabbit soup, he divided the meat among his dogs, so the dogs were particularly obedient; on a later day he bagged a beaver, and on another day a muntjac (small deer); both times he gave the meat to his dogs in order to train them. Later, in a cedar forest, he bagged three small river deer. Ddiggur tanned the three deer hides and gave them to three old people, who used them as bags to carry roasted flour and eggs. He also bagged three musk deer and gave the musk to nine boys. The boys, carrying the musk, went to nine different places. Thus they brought the smell of musk to nine places and also carried Ddiggur's fame to nine places. At the same time, Ddiggur had not forgotten the labor of his hunting dogs: he took out the innards of the river deer and gave them to the dogs, making the dogs even more obedient.

Later, Ddiggur bagged a doe. This day, Ddiggur was even happier, and he jumped for joy on the way home; the worth of the doe was even greater. For one thing, the antlers were long and had nine points. For another, the doe's meat was plentiful: there were nine layers on the legs. Because of this, *Nzy* Miajy's family was also happy. All this bounty was the result of Ddiggur's abilities. *Nzy* Miajy himself got up to welcome him, and he got out liquor for him to drink. The venison was cooked in nine large pots, and nine villages all received shares of the meat. People in the nine villages all ate the meat and felt very satisfied.

This book also discusses the fact that when Hxoyi Ddiggur went hunting, *Nzy* Miajy and his family all considered it very important: they were concerned about every detail, everything from arranging food for the hunting dogs to organizing the men for the hunting party. On the night before the hunt, the hunters did not sleep well. Early on the morning of the hunt, they called *Nzy* Miajy and Mokeddirry, his household manager, to get up and join the hunt. The ruler also brought three young men to assist with the hunt.

Another component of hunting, in addition to dogs, was bows and arrows. When animals were driven (by dogs) for Mokeddirry to shoot, "in his left hand, he held a copper bow, which was curved and more curved; in his right hand he held his iron arrows, which were sharp and more sharp." He ran into a man called Bylussechy. This man was probably rather poor, since he was carrying a wooden bow and bamboo arrows. Afterward, he ran into *Nzy* Miajy, who was carrying a bow and arrows of the finest kind: "In his left hand he held a silver bow, and in his right hand golden arrows." Hxoyi Ddiggur had an array of hunting weapons: in addition to the bow and arrows, he had a knife, nets, and other implements.

Hxoyi Ddiggur also records that when Ddiggur went hunting, he ran into animals that he offered to spirits. After killing a river deer, he took out the deer's gallbladder and put it in the fork of a tree. Afterward, he inserted it in three directions—east, west, and north. This is clearly an offering to a spirit. It seems quite natural that people would have held this sort of belief at that time.

There is another aspect of subsistence in the time of *Nzymo* Ahe Atu that we should pay close attention to: tea. Nowadays, in the Nuosu core areas of Sichuan, the custom of drinking tea has disappeared. But historically Yi people were very fond of it, as noted in the *Vonre*. When the descendants of Heatu lived at a place called Shygulur, they ran into a large snake with yellow and black stripes. People took this to be a spirit of a cedar tree, and perhaps also a spirit who would protect people. When they gave it room to retreat, it did not retreat. Even when they took off their silver jewelry to plead with it to retreat, it did not retreat. Finally, when *Bi* Ahe Ago made an offering of tea, it left:

> They went to a place above the village;
> above the village there were tea plants;
> they picked three trays of leaves.

> They went to a place below the village;
> below the village there was water for brewing tea;
> they brewed three cups of tea.

> One cup they placed before the fog;
> the fog retreated to the layers of clouds.

> One cup they placed before the rain;
> the rain retreated to the mountains.

> One cup they placed before the snake;
> the snake retreated to the woods.

Today the custom of drinking tea remains in only a few Nuosu areas.[7] But even in the places where people do not drink tea, traces still remain of customs that indicate respect for tea. For example, in some places, tea is offered to spirits during religious ceremonies. In some places, tea is given to affines during marriage ceremonies to show respect. In ordinary speech, Yi people still mention tea and rice together.

In terms of politics, at this time the *nzy* already held power over the masses and had many special privileges. In several classical books there are records of *nzy* who had great power and authority. Ango Ngole, as recorded in the book *Hxoyi Ddiggur,* was a *nzymo* with great power. He even caused *bimo* who had been invited to perform ceremonies to be put to death, something rarely encountered in society at that time. He also cruelly killed the father of the subject of this book, Ddiggur. This family of *nzymo* lived at Jyssy in Ganluo. They were extremely rich and had political influence over a wide area. They also had a precious sword that could not be unsheathed, because it was said that as soon as it was unsheathed it would wound people. They had wolf dogs who could kill people, and a book that could manifest all sorts of spirits; any person's secret could be found out by means of that book. When Ango Ngole went out he was an awe-inspiring figure: "Riding a fine horse, he had nine thousand preceding him and nine hundred following; and another ninety in the clouds and mist."

Also recorded is the story of *Nzy* Miajy, whose family resided at Zzyzzylajjie. He too was extremely rich: he had a magnificent dwelling; a glistening precious sword; a colt with a radiant voice; large herds of pigs, cattle, and sheep; a great pack of hunting dogs whose barking was thunderous; and so on.

The many Yi-language classical books that tell about *Nzy* Ahe Atu also mention *Mo* Ahe Avy and *Bi* Ahe Aggo as his helpers in governing. The records show that the three traveled everywhere in search of an ideal dwelling place, and that they sacrificed chickens and dogs in religious rituals in order to solidify the slaveholding system.

At that time, the *nzymo* of the Yi already kept slaves, or *lurjji;* this is recorded quite clearly in the texts. In *Hxoyi Ddiggur,* slaves and servants appear prominently among those who do the work to prepare for a hunt and among those

---

7. In the Anning River valley and areas to the west, where Nuosu live mixed with Han, Prmi, and other ethnic groups, they drink different kinds of tea, including bitter tea reminiscent of local Han practice, and yak-butter tea with salt, where Tibetan-influenced people such as the Prmi live. It is clear that they did not bring the custom there but learned tea drinking from their neighbors.

who welcome Hxoyi Ddiggur when he returns triumphantly. In the *Hnewo teyy*, however, slavery is even more apparent: in the time of *Nzy* Ahe Atu, the slaves had been disobedient to their masters, and so, at a place called Yimuzevo, the masters performed rites in which they sacrificed chickens and dogs and recited curses and oaths. And from this time forward the position of the *nzymo* was elevated and the position of the *lurjji* was further depressed: "From this time on, if the *nzy* spoke the slaves obeyed, and the line between masters and slaves was clearly delineated." This text offers valuable information on the slave system in Yi history.

Yi-language texts also record that when Heatu was leading the people in their migrations, he continuously experienced conflicts with other branches of the Yi and with other peoples. These were sometimes quite violent; the *Vonre* records several instances of particularly large-scale battles. One occurred at a place called Yyyhxeke, a conflict in which Heatu and his people conquered the Vo'ozzur people. In another they defeated the Legge Yi people. The text also mentions that they fought the Pu and the Ba peoples; they pursued and killed the Pu until they came to a place called Puqyyysi, where they chased the Pu to a place under a cliff. Important here is that every time there was a fight, Ahe Atu consulted his own followers at length before going into action. For example, in the battle with the Vo'ozzur, "these three worthies [*Nzy* Heatu, *Mo* Ahe Avy, and *Bi* Ahe Aggo], after consultation, sent out their fighters and rustled the cattle of the Vo'ozzur. They killed a thousand of the enemy, and they brought back hundreds of cattle." During the consultations, they ate "cattle of consultation," that is, an ox sacrificed for the consultations. When the *Vonre* mentions their fights with the Vo'ozzur, it also notes that only after earnest consultations do they attack. As a result of their battle, the Ahe clan achieve a complete victory, kill many of the enemy, and bring back much of the enemy's livestock as prizes.

The story of internal conflicts among the Yi told in the *Hxoyi Ddiggur* is even more detailed and interesting. The two clans of Ajy and Agge had been at odds for many years, and the situation had developed to the point where they were drawing arrows against each other. Finally, when Ddiggur, a member of the Ajy clan, returned to his original home to visit his sick mother, the Agge clan sent a scout to check out this affair. They proposed a scheme: the Ajy, led by *Nzy* Miajy, had a thousand soldiers and ten thousand horses, but what the Agge were really after was one person: Hxoyi Ddiggur. Now, since Ddiggur was not at home, this was a great opportunity to attack; one stroke would guarantee victory. So the Agge launched a large-scale attack on the Ajy.

In the first stage of the fight, because the Ajy had made relatively good preparations and particularly since they had an enchanted bugle that could rouse the military spirits, they won the battle. But later on, in another battle, their bugle was captured and they lost the battle. After this, the Ajy could not win a fight, and the Agge pushed them back one step at a time. Finally, the Ajy army was surrounded, and Miajy himself captured and killed.

As the Agge prepared to execute Miajy, they asked him if he had any final wishes. He said that as an *nzy* he was not afraid to die, but he had to die in a particular way. He wanted to leap to his death, and they consented. His motivation was, first, to demonstrate in front of the enemy that an *nzy* was not afraid to die; but second and more important, he hoped that while he was being chased, Ddiggur would come to rescue him. He delayed his final leap—he "leapt around below the slope three times, and leapt around above the slope three times, but still Ddiggur did not come."

Hxoyi Ddiggur was extremely brave and very loyal to *Nzy* Miajy. Also, he was very organized, which gave him the ability to be a military leader. When he got back to Miajy's home, he resolved to come to his aid against the enemy and immediately organized Miajy's fighters for a counterattack against the Agge clan. In the end he defeated them.

There are several things in this counterattack by Ddiggur that deserve our attention. First, he convened a council of warriors called a *momge*. At the council, he talked about the duty to defeat the enemy on behalf of *Nzy* Miajy. He used the reasoning that "if you don't protect a crop, the whole field will be stolen; if you don't protect a family, the whole bunch will be made captive; if you don't protect a person [the ruler], the whole territory will be occupied." And in preparation for this council he brewed liquor, which he invited all the participants to drink.

He also made military preparations, which included gathering armaments and provisions, and recruited fighters. With regard to recruiting, the text says: "He sent out ten young men to four places to recruit fighters. . . . Before they went to recruit there were already nine thousand fighters; recruiting doubled the number." This demonstrates that the men were enthusiastic about fighting.

The organization and armaments of the fighting force were also quite magnificent. In the ranks "there were officers and there were soldiers; they were divided into the main force and the scout squad, the spear-and-shield infantry and the archers. There was also a swordsmen's company following." The dress of each force was different: "The spear infantry wore yellow capes; the archers wore white capes; the swordsmen wore red capes. To the eye it was a full field of yellow."

When Ddiggur's army moved to attack the Agge troops, they presented a magnificent military spectacle. The text records that at every mountain, bridge, or pass, there were armies passing by; their "spear shafts were like cedar trees, their spear points were like stars; the wall of their shields was like a great cliff; their shin guards leapt like jumping fish; when they drew their swords, there was a great flash of light."

When Ddiggur's forces arrived at the territory of the Agge and began their attack, they deported themselves bravely. Hxoyi Ddiggur himself charged to the fore. As a result, the forces of the Ajy immediately routed the Agge troops: "They breached nine layers of defense; they routed nine detachments of soldiers; they captured nine officers." They routed hundreds or thousands of Agge fighters. Their corpses filled the fields; their blood flowed as a river. They also burnt the enemy's houses: "The thick smoke engulfed everything; even the crows fled from the smoke." Ddiggur's armies returned triumphant, having gained revenge on behalf of the Ajy clan.

The text also records that among the observers of the battle was a woman called Leggemo Ala, who reflected on the reasons why Ddiggur's army won, comparing his army with the troops led by Ajy. In the text, it says that the comportment of Ddiggur's troops was regulated and disciplined without violation, but that "Ajy's troops were not concerned with courtesy or discipline, and no matter where they went, they asked people to give way." They frightened people into saying, "If you don't make way for them, the spears will prod people and the swords will wound people; the fine horses will stampede people." Because of this, the ordinary people were all afraid of them and did not give them aid. But Ddiggur's forces were different: they understood manners and courtesy, so no matter where they went, they had friends. This kind of a fighting force "would definitely win whenever they fought."

In the time of *Nzy* Ahe Atu, there were many circumstances covered by religious ritual, as stated earlier. For example, when clans divided, the "crossing over" sacrifice had to be made to the ancestors; the *Vonre* says, "Crossing over must be done for the partition of the clan." If a large-scale death occurred while the clan was moving from one place to another, then they had to have a *bimo* do a ritual to chase it away. When *Nzy* Miajy fought a battle, he mustered the troops and horses with a bugle whose sound could reach Heaven. There is also the case of *Nzy* Ahe Atu killing a chicken or dog in order to solidify the boundary between master and slave. All of these demonstrate the utility of religious ritual for social control by the *nzymo*.

NZYMO AS SEEN IN *GAMO ANYO*

This book is about the unfortunate occurrences in the life of a beautiful woman called Gamo Anyo. Her clan belonged to the descendants of Gguhxo. The clan home was in a place called Jiejyyyda (which is in present-day Ebian County). According to Yi genealogies, there were fifty-three generations from Gguhxo to Anyo, and thirty-one more generations from Anyo to the present day, meaning that Anyo lived about six hundred years before the present, in the early Ming period. The material in the text, in addition to telling Anyo's story, reflects conditions of that time.

According to the text, the status of the *nzymo* had developed greatly by then. All had titles from the Chinese imperial dynasties. One of the central families in this text was the Ngafu of Lizhou, which we can take as an example. They were called "Lords of the Official Seal." They controlled a great territory; it took nine days to cross it on horseback. It extended eastward to Jiejyyyda and westward to the foothills of Gongga Mountain (Minyak Konkar). Their retainers and slaves were so many that the local crows suffocated in the smoke from their fires, and their territory was so great that a bird in flight would have to rest nine times before crossing it. And the beams and rafters of their houses were made of gold and silver. In short, they were rich beyond compare. The descriptions in this text may be somewhat exaggerated, but they do reflect the family's wealth and power.

The book also speaks of the Lili *nzymo,* the Shama *nzymo,* and the Zyndi *nzymo,* all of whom were powerful, each ruling his own territory. In addition there was also one evil ruler called *Nzy* Apopo, who was feared by everybody.

At that time, the economy of the Nuosu under the rulership of the *nzymo* compares favorably with that of the present day. Hunting and fishing are things that the Nuosu could not entirely forsake, but these had already fallen to a distinctly secondary place. Agriculture and animal husbandry had become the most important economic activities. The people still used swidden methods in farming, but they concentrated on growing oats and bitter buckwheat on large farms. The Yi had also developed sericulture in the Jiejyyyda area by this time, and they could themselves weave beautiful silks. Sheepherding was even more important—the book specifically describes the beauty of a fat sheep: "A white domestic sheep, a sheep of the place called Yyyihxoshy, it eats the grasses of the high mountain pastures, it drinks the water of the Dadu River. The horns of the sheep are curved and curved again, its bleat sounds to faraway places, its loins are thick and sturdy. Its tail is fat and beautiful; when it goes to pasture it walks in front; when it comes back in, it walks in back. We shear the wool of the ram to make a white cape; Anyo is beautiful when she wears it."

One particularly noteworthy point is that at this time the Yi were already trading with people in Han and Tibetan areas. The story tells of fine liquors bought from Chengdu, of large-grained, snow-white rice bought from Jiading, and of jewelry bought from Kangding.

In wartime the beautiful lady Anyo of the house of *Nzymo* Ngafu was captured, and there was a war with her captors. In addition to recording the use of daggers, arrows, and long spears by the brave and strong fighters of the Ngafu, the book mentions *Nzymo* Ngafu Muga using mounted cavalry. This is rare in Yi warfare. Even more extraordinary is the mention of both men's and women's fighting units. This is otherwise unknown.

There are also considerable records of religious activity. Among them are records of the *Bimo* Ashy Lazzi, famous in Liangshan Yi history. The clan of the *Nzymo* Apopo employed Ashy Lazzi to conduct rituals. But then Lazzi received news that *Nzymo* Apopo was plotting to kill him and capture his daughter. So the father and daughter fled together. He used magical methods to aid in his flight. He caused *Nzymo* Apopo to go off in the wrong direction, and later was able to escape from his own body.

CONCLUSION

The Nuosu-language historical sources described in this essay show that Nuosu historical writing is concerned primarily with politics, economy, marriage, religion, and warfare. If we compare the content of these sources with what has been published in other sources, the following points deserve to be emphasized:

1. Marriage. Nuosu have a long history of practicing stratum endogamy. In this way, Nuosu rulers have preserved their so-called purity of blood and noble status. This long-lasting system of status endogamy was already in place at the time of the two ancestors of two thousand years ago, Gguhxo and Qoni.

2. Hunting. The hunting economy had an important place in Yi society for a long time. Descriptions of hunting are recorded in several Nuosu historical books, and in some of them hunting is recorded in great detail. This is quite a different picture from that given in other contemporary accounts, which emphasize the early importance of pastoralism.

3. Warfare. That Yi have historically been a martial people is well known. This is richly expressed in several of the Nuosu historical books; many of the accounts are detailed and lively. This has great value for research into historical Nuosu warfare.

4. Religion. Religion has had an important place in Yi society from ancient times to the present. From Nuosu-language sources, we can see the development of Yi religion, as well as the changing attitudes of the *nzymo* stratum toward religion.

In conclusion, only by investigating *nzymo* through the use of Yi-language historical sources can we gain a comparatively complete, objective, and scientific view of the role of the *nzymo* throughout Yi history.

PART II

Nuosu Society in Liangshan

CHAPTER 3

A Comparative Approach to Lineages among the Xiao Liangshan Nuosu and Han

Ann Maxwell Hill and Eric Diehl

A recent period of fieldwork among the Nuosu of the Xiao Liangshan area of northwestern Yunnan Province in the People's Republic of China provided convincing evidence that lineage organization was at the heart of Nuosu society and culture in the days before the Chinese Communist pacification of the area in the mid-1950s.[1] While much has been written about Nuosu kinship by Han Chinese scholars and, more recently, by a new generation of Nuosu ethnologists, generally there have been no systematic discussions of the Nuosu lineage in the context of Western anthropological conventions about lineages. Taking the first step in the direction of a fuller, comprehensive treatment, we present here some insights into the Nuosu lineage, or *cyvi*, derived from a limited comparison with Han (Chinese) lineages. Because the "lineage paradigm" in the anthropology of China has informed so much of our thinking about lineages—certainly for those of us studying China's minorities—and because historically the Nuosu have lived "lips by teeth" with the Han, a comparative perspective on this dimension of Nuosu and Han cultures may provide a better understanding of the internal structure of Nuosu society, as well as some facets of Nuosu relations with local Han groups.

1. This fieldwork was funded by Dickinson College's Mellon Student Faculty Research Fund. We wish to thank our colleague Mr. Lasha Lunuo (Zheng Chengjun) from the Yunnan Academy of Social Sciences for sharing with us his expert knowledge of the Ninglang Nuosu and for his translations from Nuosu into Han. We also are indebted to the head of the Foreign Affairs Office in Ninglang Yi Autonomous County, Mr. Su Xuewen, who accompanied us on many of our interviews and extended to us all the courtesies of his office. A special thanks to Ms. Yang Wenying, also of the Ninglang County Foreign Office, for her help with arrangements and for her enthusiastic support of our research project.

XIAO LIANGSHAN AND THE NUOSU

The area colloquially called Xiao Liangshan, or the Lesser Cold Mountains, takes its name from the place of origin of most of the area's Nuosu people, Da Liangshan, or the Great Cold Mountains. This homeland territory lies just to the east of Xiao Liangshan in the province of Sichuan. Whether the diminutive *xiao* refers to the lower altitude of Xiao Liangshan, roughly between twenty-five hundred and thirty-five hundred meters above sea level, or merely to the historical fact of later settlement, is not clear. The heart of Xiao Liangshan Nuosu land is Ninglang Yi Autonomous County, where there are about a hundred thousand Nuosu, roughly half the county's population.[2] There are other ethnic groups in Ninglang: Pumi, Mosuo, Lisu, and Han, the most numerous, but also Zang (Tibetan), Naxi, Miao, Zhuang, Bai, and Hui (Muslim).

On the grounds of language, culture, and other criteria, the Nuosu in Ninglang are included in the official nationality category, Yi, a designation they share with more than six million other people living in Yunnan, Sichuan, Guizhou, and Guangxi Provinces (Long Xianjun 1993, 1; see Harrell 1989 for a discussion of problems with official nomenclature). Most of the Yi in Ninglang call themselves Nuosu, as do their brethren in Da Liangshan, and speak the northern dialect of Yi. Older men among the Nuosu all trace their genealogies back to Da Liangshan, and some of their families still have marriage relations with Da Liangshan Nuosu. While written sources cite warfare among Da Liangshan Nuosu elites and uprisings among their dependents as reasons for migrations out of Da Liangshan into Xiao Liangshan (and some earlier movement of people in the opposite direction), only one of our informants, a Nuosu scholar, volunteered this interpretation (Du Yuting 1984, 1–2; NYZXGBZ 1985, 9–10). Other people said their lineal ancestors left because they followed their masters to Xiao Liangshan or were called to this area by groups that were their traditional marriage partners. More recent immigrants to Ninglang, those who arrived four generations ago or even later, said they came for the land, which they described as relatively empty.

Because the Nuosu, inveterate genealogists, reckon historical time in terms of generations of patrilineal forebears, pinpointing precise dates for settlement of Ninglang is difficult. The earliest generation count we heard in the field was ten generations ago for the Jjiggu *cyvi*, but this claim was hotly disputed by everyone else present. With this exception, there was some gen-

2. Thanks to Mr. Su Xuewen for this up-to-date estimate. An earlier figure from the mid-1980s indicated that the Nuosu in Ninglang comprised about 56 percent of the county's population, or about 90,000 people (NYZXGBZ 1985, 9). According to figures based on research in 1963, there were 70,000 Nuosu in Ninglang County (Du Yuting 1984, 8).

eral agreement among informants that the earliest Nuosu to arrive in the areas where we interviewed came seven generations ago. In translating generational reckoning among the Nuosu into Western historical chronology, we also had to keep in mind the practice of early marriage and the spread of groups of brothers over the reproductive span of their mothers. Using the conventional twenty-five years per generation means that the first Nuosu came to Ninglang roughly 175 years ago, in 1820; that may be a bit early, but one source, estimating on the basis of elite family genealogies, says not quite 200 hundred years ago (Du Yuting 1984, 1). One man reported that his patrilineal ancestors, having arrived in Xiao Liangshan seven generations ago, later helped the Han drive out the Muslims. This would have been sometime during the Muslim Rebellion (1855–73), so it is likely that his forebears came before the 1850s.

Although the Ninglang Nuosu are now settled in permanent villages, before 1956 they were a much more mobile population. They were swiddeners, clearing land by burning the upland forests, then planting in the ashes. The need for more land, when the fertility of some fields was exhausted, as well as the search for pastures suitable for grazing sheep, horses, and cattle, compelled some families to move to high-altitude, empty land when the opportunity arose. On the other hand, in Ninglang the Nuosu's most productive fields, where they grew potatoes, buckwheat, and oats, were fertile year after year, owing to a fairly sophisticated agricultural technology including the oxen-drawn plow and the application of animal manure. So it is not surprising that two villages among the ten in which we interviewed had long histories coincident with the earliest arrival of the Nuosu in Ninglang.[3]

According to Han ethnologists writing since 1949, the Nuosu in Ninglang were a "slave society," with small numbers of servitors attached to households as field laborers and servants. Most of these people, of whom we shall say more below, originated as captives taken by the Nuosu in raids on adjacent ethnic groups, especially the Han. When looking at individual families, through the window of genealogy, we found that Nuosu "slaves" had complex, variable relations with the rest of Nuosu society that call into question the rubric "slave society." Nonetheless, the Nuosu in the old days maintained strict distinctions among various social strata, a system that functioned

3. But villages, as opposed to *cyvi*, were not a significant source of identification for Nuosu in the past, nor were they always neatly bounded, nucleated spaces, since married couples had considerable autonomy in moving to areas "outside" the village, where land was more plentiful. As far as we were able to determine in interviews, the Nuosu in Ninglang, unlike some other Tibeto-Burman groups, do not have special ceremonies for village renewal, nor are there village guardian spirits (cf. Alting von Geusau 1983, on the Akha; and Durrenberger 1983, on the Lisu, both groups in northern Thailand). It is also possible that the two villages with long histories in Ninglang maintained the same names, even as they moved around in one locality.

within living memory of many of our elderly informants. These strata comprised four exogamous groups: the *nuo,* or elites; the *qunuo,* or commoners, making up the majority of Nuosu people in Ninglang; the *mgajie,* a residual category of semi-independent farmers; and the *gaxy,* or recent captives and their immediate descendants. Families in all four groups, we were told, could have their own *mgajie* or *gaxy,* depending on the household's access to land and wealth. However, in thinking about the system, the Nuosu regard the *mgajie* and *gaxy* as not of the same order as *nuo* or *qunuo,* as somehow outside the system, perhaps because they were so closely identified with ethnic origins outside Nuosu society and attached as individuals to particular Nuosu households. The relations among the four groups were ritual, economic, sometimes personal, and bound up inextricably with descent lines and the *cyvi.*

The Nuosu *cyvi* was not the original focus of our research: we went to Ninglang intending to gather preliminary data on ethnic identity and the pre-1949 social stratification system of the Nuosu in Ninglang. During our first interview, it quickly became apparent that neither of these topics was accessible without some basic understanding of descent lines, genealogies, and the *cyvi.* Settlement patterns, local identity, social stratification, indeed, most of Ninglang's local history, were framed by our informants within the idiom and structure of *cyvi.* In our brief, four-week stay in Ninglang, we conducted twenty-two interviews, most of them in rural Nuosu households in Shaliping *xingzheng cun,* or administrative village, in Paomaoping Township, and in Shuicaoba *xingzheng cun* in Lanniqing Township. Conducted in the convivial spirit of Nuosu hospitality, interviews tended to last three or four hours, sometimes the entire day. Although we addressed our questions to our host, our visits usually attracted a crowd of people from neighboring households who came to eat, smoke, and chat. So our notes reflect the responses of onlookers, some of the issues of their historical and genealogical debates, and sometimes the consensus of the adults present. Interviews were conducted entirely in the Nuosu language and translated for our benefit into Chinese. Due to the brevity of our stay in the field, our work on the *cyvi* is far from complete, but we view this essay as an opportunity to summarize what we learned, raise questions deserving further research, and elicit critical comments from scholars whose fieldwork with the Nuosu has been of long duration.

In taking a comparative approach to the *cyvi,* we have implicitly anticipated the fact of its difference from the Han Chinese lineage. But what commits us, in the first place, to labeling the institution and its ideology a lineage? Drawing on British social anthropology, whose traditions most fully defined and elaborated the notion of the lineage, we find in the Nuosu *cyvi* the following attributes that resonate with conventional understandings of the concept among anthropologists: unilineal descent, corporateness, localization, segmentation, and group identity. By all these criteria—articulated by Fortes (1953) in his classic essay on unilineal descent groups in Africa and later refined by Keesing (1975) in his primer on kinship—the patrilineal, exogamous *cyvi* in its ideology and social reality exemplifies the lineage. How much so becomes clear below, as we juxtapose the Nuosu institution with the Han lineage, itself deeply embedded in Western analytical discourse on the organization of Chinese society (cf. Freedman's work [1958 and 1966] on lineages in southeastern China; Watson [1982 and 1986] on the history of studies of Chinese lineages; Cohen [1990] on lineages in north China).

PATRILINEAL DESCENT, GENEALOGIES, AND SEGMENTATION

In the old days, we were told, when two Nuosu men met as strangers on the path, they recited their genealogies. Such potentially prolonged greetings were shortened by the mnemonic convenience of patronymic linking where the last two syllables of the father's name become the first two syllables of the son's name. Although actual terms of address differ from this system and only the most formal, personal name is reflected in it, the system was indispensable for locating individuals in the complex, kin-based society of the Nuosu (see Ma Erzi, chapter 5 in this volume). Genealogical recitations, demonstrating descent from a male forebear at least seven generations in the past, established in the first place whether the two strangers were of the same *cyvi* or, if memories were long, shared a common ancestor in the distant past. Some of the men today know a few names in the descent lines of "brother" lineages *(vynyi)*, even if they cannot recall the shared ancestor responsible for the "brother" relationship. The same partial recollection holds for lineages with whom they have traditionally intermarried *(vusa)*. So it was possible to claim an affinal relation, or better yet a consanguineal one, with the stranger, thus ensuring a measure of hospitable treatment at the hands of the new acquaintance. To the extent that genealogies could locate strangers within a particular *cyvi*, one could not only determine whether they were allies or enemies, but also whether they were one's social inferiors or superiors. Lineages tended to be identified with one social stratum, although there were cases of the same lineage having segments, or branches, in different strata. It all depended on genealogy.

It is well known, of course, that most of the large, wealthy lineages of southeastern China studied by Freedman had written genealogies (1966, 15). Cohen reports similar documentation for lineages in north China, although the information was likely to have come from scrolls and ancestral tablets or been symbolized in the arrangement of graves in a lineage cemetery (1990, 515–19). Chinese genealogies were rather remote from the everyday social lives of peasant farmers in late traditional China, most of whom were illiterate. Somewhat like intellectual property, written genealogies were the concern of lineage elites, rather than the hoi polloi. Genealogies were such valued property, in fact, that teams of scholars were sometimes hired to "fix" them in their higher, more distant levels to establish connections between two large and powerful lineages of the same surname that lacked demonstrable kin links, to facilitate an expeditious union (Freedman 1958, 70–71). Mere possession of genealogical records, in whatever form, was in itself an assertion of the high status of one's lineage or segment, and such records tended to be associated with sites of lineage ancestor commemoration, whether in halls or side rooms in family compounds.

Although when you first think about it, written genealogies seem to have a concreteness and historical resiliency that oral genealogies lack, in fact Nuosu genealogies may be much less abstract and much more resistant to manipulation than Chinese ones. In our experience, genealogies are in the public domain, so to speak. Men in rural areas over the age of twenty-five, and even some younger, know their patrilines for at least seven generations back. If they falter or get confused at certain junctures in the recitation, others chime in to correct or dispute. To be sure, the *bimo,* literate ritual specialists among the Nuosu, know more genealogies than do nonspecialists and monopolize historical knowledge generally, but their high rank does not entitle them to the exclusive possession of genealogical data. In a society where patrilineal origins, rather than the ownership of property or commercial wealth as among the Han, played such a disproportionate role relative to other factors in determining an individual's social status, it is hardly surprising that the Nuosu do not take their genealogies lightly nor cede them to the memories of a small number of specialists.

Patrilines were the bulwark or "skeleton" of Nuosu *cyvi.* Just as in some areas of Han society, patrilineal descent provided individuals a "natural" affiliation with a localized group of men claiming descent from a common ancestor and sharing a common identity, so too for the Nuosu the *cyvi* was the basis for group membership and identity. Yet behind this general resemblance between Nuosu and Han lineages lurks many differences. We have already noted the personal and social salience of genealogies for the Nuosu, a significance far exceeding the role of genealogies in Han society. So in the Nuosu case, when we speak of *cyvi* as localized descent groups, we need to acknowledge that the genealogical ties within them are known and demonstrable to the people who claim membership in them, even though *cyvi* men and their households may be widely dispersed over an area covering a thousand or more square kilometers and living among households of different *cyvi.* Now, it was also the case that among localized lineages in China, at least for a "substantial minority" of them, written genealogical records spelled out the lineage's male agnates and forebears (Freedman 1966, 15). But in my own experience, Chinese patriarchs do not routinely commit to memory long lines of patrilineal ancestors, and a remark made by Cohen about lineage scrolls in a north China village suggests that without reference to written records, people could recall only the names of the most recently deceased family members and their immediate ancestors (Cohen 1990, 516).

This difference in the relative knowledge of genealogical connections within lineages perhaps makes more sense if we consider the literal extent of localization for lineages in the two cases. We have described Nuosu *cyvi* as localized not only because the Nuosu themselves talk about them this way. Historically, certain *cyvi* have predominated in particular areas of Nuosu settlement, in Xiao Liangshan often localized on the mountain slopes surrounding a high valley. And, as we shall see below, the existence of dominant lineages in any one area has a great deal to do with sequence of settlement and the related phenomenon of lineage branching or segmentation. But at the same time, people we interviewed were quick to point out that many Nuosu *cyvi* were spread out all over Ninglang, or throughout Xiao Liangshan and sometimes into Da Liangshan (and at this point we would hear stories about the two strangers on the path reciting genealogies). Although we need much more genealogical data on the distribution of *cyvi* to lend more precision to our understanding of lineage localization, if we accept that lineages were dispersed over wide areas where communication was problematic at best, then ready knowledge of *cyvi* patrilines, genealogical connections, marriage partners, and so forth was essential, practical information for initiating any sort of relationship. By contrast, Han lineages were more narrowly circumscribed territorially and, one could argue, more strongly localized, especially if there was an estate. Southeastern China is well known in the anthropological literature for its single-lineage villages or single-lineage territories encompassing several adjacent villages; dispersed lineages were the exception, but even those were centered on a core village likely to have a hall and property (Freedman 1966, 1–21). Under these circumstances, where communication was much easier and face-to-face interactions more frequent, villagers were likely to know others' surnames (and hence, lineage membership) and kin relations without having to mentally climb the genealogical tree. And when matters of lineage property were at issue, lineage elites had written records to wield in interpreting entitlements.

Segmentation of the *cyvi* was related to localization and to other factors as well. For example, one segment or branch *(nji)* of the Alu *cyvi* is traced to an ancestor who came from Da Liangshan to Shaliping in Xiao Liangshan seven generations ago. He was the younger of two brothers, each of whom is regarded as the ancestor of a separate branch (Yan and Liu 1984, 74–75). We heard the younger brother's story from two informants, one of whom was the oldest living descendant of the branch founder. According to these accounts, the first people in Shaliping were a Han family called Wang and a few Hui, or Muslims; most of the land in the narrow valley and its hillsides belonged to the Wangs. The Alu ancestor, Alu Jjiyzu, renowned as a hunter, one day killed a deer and took its leg to present to the Wangs. They lived in a compound guarded by two vicious dogs, one on either side of the gate. As a general rule, the dogs attacked and killed any stranger who approached the Wang compound, but when Alu Jjiyzu arrived at the Wang gate with the deer meat, the dogs were asleep so the hunter walked right into the Wangs' house. Old Wang, amazed by the dogs' strange behavior, felt that Alu Jjiyzu was somehow extraordinary. From that day on, they were friends. Wang hired the Alu man to work for him, and when Wang died, having no sons, he left his land to the Alu ancestor. Later, the Han government gave more land to the Alu *cyvi* to recompense them for their help against the Hui (Muslims) during the Muslim Rebellion (1855–73). When asked why the particular Alu ancestor came to Shaliping in the first place, his descendant said that the Alu left their original home, Lakagu in Da Liangshan, because there was not enough land and the land itself was poor. Others from Lakagu, including their traditional marriage-partner lineages and their master, the Bbuyo *nuo*, then followed the Alu to Shaliping.

We encountered several other cases where localization played a role in lineage segmentation; the depth of lineage segments, named after the first-generation ancestor, tended to coincide with the length of time the *cyvi* had been settled in Ninglang. Other evidence comes from people's general statements about *cyvi* branches. In Shaliping, we encountered many descendants of the area's three "brother" lineages: Jjiggu, Jjiezy, and Jjiho. These three *cyvi* do not intermarry, because of a common ancestor: the lineages trace their descent to three brothers who came from a union between a high-status Nuosu and his female *gaxy* in Da Liangshan (cf. Yan and Liu 1984 on this point). Because of strong prohibitions against marriage between different social strata, the brothers and their descendants could not claim the high-ranking *nuo* as their legitimate father (let alone lay claim to his status). Each brother then came to be regarded as the founder of a *cyvi*, each in its turn producing several branches or segments. Today, Shaliping people claiming membership in one of the three brother lineages talk about their *cyvi* branches as if they were localized: "No one in my segment of the Jjiggu belonged to the local Bbuyo *nuo*, because we all came from Zhan He," or "All of us Jjiezy here [in Shaliping] are of the Amge Pydi segment."

Marriage and population dynamics are other factors that may have led to segmentation. We were told that among Ninglang's *nuo* families, segments within one *cyvi* could intermarry after seven generations. This exception to the general proscription of marriage between any two people sharing a known common ancestor was necessitated because of the small size of the *nuo* stratum, in Ninglang probably only 4 percent of the total Nuosu population (Du Yuting 1984, 11). In other words, to produce legitimate heirs, *nuo* had to marry other *nuo*, and when marriage partners were in short supply, marriage between two people in the same *cyvi* was permitted, as long as the appropriate genealogical distance was maintained (seven generations). This practice among the *nuo* was marked by a ritual for splitting the lineage, called *nimu vijjie*. Nuosu scholars describe the ceremony as an artifact of the past and no longer necessary among contemporary Nuosu with access to a greater number of marriage partners (Jiemei Yi xue yanjiu xiao zu 1992, 68; Lasha Lunuo 1995, personal communication). The ceremony called for the services of the *bimo*, who chanted from a text for splitting the lineage and presided over animal sacrifices intended for ancestral spirits. The ritual was concluded when "tablets" for the spirits of each founding ancestor of a new lineage were hidden in separate caves.

Marriage down, or a union with someone of a social level below one's own, also may result in segmentation, as the story of the three brothers indicates. These kinds of cases, though, are difficult to document through interviews because people to this day are sensitive about downward mobility and adamant about their adherence to the proscription on marriage with people in other classes.[4] We were also told that cross-cousin marriages, if conducted over two or more successive generations between two *cyvi*, may have created alliances between two lineages or groups of lineages over time, resulting in segmentation. Finally, we have indirect evidence that segments may have been created in response to proliferation of descendants in collateral lines with a common forebear, or conversely, when some lines died out, leaving only the descendants of one of a pair of brothers. We have people's random remarks about this line flourishing and another dying out, and about "large" segments and "small" segments, to suggest this phenomenon.

When people talked about the process of segmentation within a *cyvi*, it was always with reference to groups of brothers, each of whom was cited as fathering a new segment. However, there was no indication that the Ninglang Nuosu regarded some segments—for example, those originating with eldest brothers—as superior in any way to the others, unlike the "fixed genealogical mode" that Cohen describes for lineages in north China (1990, 510).[5] *Cyvi* segments, each named after its founding ancestor, conventionally included seven, or at most nine, generations; depending on context, people could identify with segments at any genealogical level. In other words, the rhetoric of *cyvi* segmentation would indicate that the process was symmetrical and based strictly on genealogical reckoning, producing segments of similar genealogical depth nested in neat hierarchies. Experts on Nuosu culture, college-educated Nuosu and *bimo*, contributed to these conversations

4. See the discussion of social mobility, which sheds some light on the relationship of marriage to mobility.

5. For the exception to the rule that elder brothers did not found "superior" segments, see the Nuosu origin story in the discussion of social mobility. But this exception is different from the "ritual" superiority granted to senior branches in Cohen's Han Chinese village.

the observation that *cyvi* segments, unlike Han lineages, were never based on the accumulation of property or wealth, resources that in southeastern China led to asymmetrical segmentation (Freedman 1958, 48–50). But our interviews indicated that variables such as localization, marriage patterns, including particular unions cross-cutting "class" lines, and number of male descendants in any one generation—those we have discussed above—were historically random and over time could result in unequal, or asymmetrical, segmentation. And certainly at the higher levels of Nuosu genealogies, beyond the segment of living descendants, named branches appeared more frequently than every seven generations.

The phenomenon of telescoping, to describe the tendency to abbreviate upper-level genealogies to focus on only a few ancestors, may account for the appearance of more frequent segmentation among the more remote patrilineal ancestors of Nuosu *cyvi* (Fortes 1953, 32). Some authors reserve the term *clan* for these larger, descent-based configurations traced back to ancestors of near-mythical status (e.g., Keesing 1975, 31). Terminologically, however, our Ninglang informants made no such distinctions, other than to acknowledge branches within *cyvi* called *nji,* discussed above, named after the branch founders.

THE *CYVI:* CORPORATE OR NOT?

The "lineage paradigm" developed in the study of lineages in southeastern China highlighted the importance of corporate landholdings and joint economic activity in determining the strength and cohesion of lineage organization. Land owned by the village, a lineage, or segments of a lineage often played the most important role in local economies. Lineage property and any subsequent income was used to strengthen the lineage's political power and prestige (Freedman 1966, 68–96). While often these "classic" Chinese lineages relied on economic activity, in the north lineage solidarity and strength were not limited to the scope of material resources. North China lineages lacked the large corporate holdings found in Guangdong and Fujian but were nonetheless significant in structuring village social relations and as sources of group identity. African lineages, too, of the sort described by Fortes, tended not to have corporate holdings. As political and jural structures, however, they were strongly corporate. They related to one another as single entities for marriage, political alliances, feuds, and dispute settlement. And an individual had "no legal or political status except as a member of a lineage" (Fortes 1953, 26).

Lineage affiliation, as a condition of full jural personhood, was the sine qua non of membership in Xiao Liangshan Nuosu society and, as we discuss below, an important dimension of upward mobility strategies among Han and other folks attached to Nuosu households. The *cyvi* was an exogamous group related to others through ties of marriage and, in some times, united against others in disputes or outright warfare. The *cyvi*, rather than society's upper strata or the Chinese imperial government, was responsible for breeches of the social order and had mechanisms, based on precedent, for the restoration of good relations among its members and between affinally related lineages (see Qubi Shimei and Ma Erzi, chapter 6 in this volume).

Elderly informants told us that the most serious crimes were those that threatened *cyvi* solidarity. In these cases the only honorable thing to do was for the perpetrator to take his own life. If he could not be persuaded to suicide, he faced expulsion from the *cyvi*. Without the support of his *cyvi*, a man's only option was to leave society. And by choosing expulsion, a man also left the stain of the crime on his family, which would have to seek *cyvi* permission in order to remain a part of the community.[6]

Lineage elders were instrumental in settling cases involving members of their own *cyvi*, often with the help of a *bimo*, who was compensated for his services as part of the settlement. We were told that *cyvi* elders were also important in arranging marriages or deciding a move. In general, these men were from the lineage's oldest generation, although younger men who were particularly capable might also be leaders. The respect given these older men and their wives in one's *cyvi* was obvious through seating arrangements and how food and alcohol were served.

Cyvi leadership, though, was never authoritarian. For example, if there was a decision among *cyvi* leaders to move to a new territory, individual households were not compelled to comply. At marriage, sons tended to settle on land near their fathers' houses, but this was more a reflection of inheritance patterns than the existence of bounded lineage territory managed by the group's elders. To the contrary, lineage property was nonexistent. As we understand the land tenure system in Xiao Liangshan before the 1950s, land was held by particular households. They acquired usufruct rights to land in several ways, one of which was through patrilineal inheritance. Sons, ideally married in order from eldest to youngest, received a share of land identified with their fathers' household at marriage; the youngest son, the last married, took over his father's portion and his father's house. He also had the greatest day-to-day responsibility in caring for elderly parents, who usually lived in a newly built, small house in the original family compound. A daughter could also receive a portion of her father's land when she married, al-

---

6. The circumstances of our interviewing, conducted in public and surrounded by government cadres, seemed to preclude women's full participation in the interaction. Furthermore, men's normative statements about Nuosu society, as well as their examples, invariably assumed that men were the principal actors. Common sense tells us that women also were involved in disputes, but our notes on social disruptions among the Nuosu have only one allusion to a women: she committed suicide. Her suicide resulted in a break between the two *cyvi* (hers and her husband's) that were party to the marriage. We have no other information.

though she was unlikely to live on it. Rather, a daughter, after marriage and after becoming pregnant, moved into the husband's house.

We use the term *usufruct* for several reasons. In the first place, land in Xiao Liangshan was not owned by anyone: there were no landlords, no tenants, and no rents because there was no private property among the Nuosu (but see note 8). In the second place, with the exception of original settlers to a particular area, such as the Alu ancestor and his descendants in Shaliping, latecomers who settled on land claimed by earlier groups gave a portion of their harvest to the original inhabitants in return for rights to work the land; this practice was precisely an acknowledgment of a prior claim, nothing more or less. Grain was paid to individual families and not to a corporate lineage.

Having said that, we frequently heard land and localities named after *cyvi*. Since the Alu in Shaliping are such a striking example of this phenomenon, as well as of other facets of land tenure and its relation to *cyvi*, their *cyvi* history bears further examination. Recall that one major segment of the Alu lineage traces its roots back to the first Nuosu settler to arrive in Shaliping. This Alu ancestor received some land from the Han Wang family, although the exact terms of this arrangement are not clear; other land came to him and other Alu from the Chinese government in recognition of their help against the Muslims. My guess is that this came along with some kind of frontier-pacification title or office awarded an Alu ancestor. Whatever the case, we frequently heard that all land in Shaliping was originally "Alu land." According to the story, the Alu settlers then called their traditional marriage partners to the area and also their former *nuo* of the Bbuyo *cyvi*. These later settlers, though, were not given land outright by the Alu. They had to give a portion of their harvest to the Alu in return for usufruct rights. Even the Bbuyo *nuo,* of a higher social stratum than the Alu, was obligated in the same way as lower-ranked *qunuo* occupants of Alu land.

We heard another story of an Alu man who lost his land because of opium addiction; he then had to pay harvest rents to his Alu relatives for use of their land.[7] From this and other anecdotes, we concluded that economic cooperation among families descended from the same *cyvi* was limited to life crisis events, the borrowing of draft animals for plowing, and occasional contributions to destitute families.[8]

7. In fact, we were told that this fellow "sold" his land. The traditional land tenure system of the Nuosu in Ninglang probably was affected early on by Han encroachment and Han notions of property, especially in the several decades before 1956 when opium growing in Ninglang was at its peak.

8. Yet if we are to believe Winnington's account of Ninglang in the 1950s just prior to collectivization, poverty, resulting in debt and ultimately enslavement, was fairly common (Winnington 1959, 71–72). His observations bear on the limits to mutual assistance among *cyvi* members.

Group ritual activity among *cyvi* members, of the sort that characterized the annual cycle of commemoration of lineage ancestors among the Han, was not typical of Nuosu lineages (cf. Watson 1982, 596–97, on the ritual unity of Han lineages). But it may be that funeral rituals, where lineage mates and their families gathered to celebrate the death of one of their members, provided such occasions. Unfortunately, we were not able to observe any funeral ceremonies in the field. Ancestor commemoration, as far as we could determine, was and is a domestic affair. Most of our hosts offered libations to the spirits of patrilineal forebears at a place above their beds, called *hlipi,* before drinking. While every household, in theory, could have a *hlipi,* only the household of the eldest among a group of brothers had an *apukuo.* The *apukuo* is made after the death of a father and requires offerings different from those given at the *hlipi.* The *bimo* whom we interviewed told us that the *apukuo* was for the spirit of the founder of the *cyvi,* but others, lacking *apukuo,* were uncertain about this distinction.

SOCIAL MOBILITY AND THE *CYVI*

Although landholding Alu families were generally more prosperous than their neighbors, they did not belong to the highest social level in Nuosu society. The Bbuyo *cyvi* in Xiao Liangshan were all *nuo,* and in several localities, including Shaliping and Shuicaoba, they annually received tribute from their *qunuo,* such as the Alu. Tribute, presented to the *nuo* at the New Year and at their weddings and funerals, usually consisted of meat, food, and wine; it was not necessarily an acknowledgment of *nuo* claims to land, though the *nuo,* as first settlers, could also demand harvest shares. Nor was tribute, strictly speaking, a claim on people's labor, since families in any stratum could have slaves as servants and field hands. Prestations to elite families were, in the simplest terms, symbolic expressions of deference to one's superiors. In the field, we probed for insights into the basis for people's beliefs that the *nuo* were superior and essential to "normal" Nuosu life. We found the beliefs so thoroughly naturalized in the rhetoric about the "old" society, and the system so taken for granted by the older people who lived in it, that our earnest questions were laughable. Ethnologists speculate on the martial origins of the rise of powerful families in Da Liangshan, or in a more Marxist vein, their economic origins (e.g., Ma Erzi 1993, 41; Li Shaoming 1992, 68), but scholarly debates about how stratification evolved bear no necessary relation to people's constructs of a system that, by their own admission, was not based on *nuo* coercion or the prerogatives of wealth.

Some clues to *nuo* superiority emerged from our interview with a *bimo* in Dalaba, a Nuosu village not far from the Ninglang county seat. His history of Nuosu origins, like all Nuosu histories, was framed in the idiom of patrilineal descent. We present here an abbreviated version. According to the *bimo,* the *nzy*, a stratum not present in Ninglang but the highest-ranking group in Da Liangshan, and the *nuo* all originated in a group of brothers; the youngest, the *nuo*, because of birth order, ranked below the others. The brothers, founders of specific *cyvi*, were all "pure" Nuosu because of their close genealogical connections to even earlier ancestors and because they never married outside Nuosu society. The *qunuo* were considered only relatively pure because sometimes they were descendants of marriages with people in other ethnic groups. The *mgajie* and *gaxy* were the least pure, given their known historical origins among people who were not Nuosu. In this scenario, *nuo* superiority was rooted in bloodlines and strict adherence to group endogamy. This notion of purity through descent and marriage resonated strongly with our informants' narratives of the past, when genealogical recitations determined whether a stranger was friend or foe, when land and villages were named after dominant lineages, and when marriage proscriptions were strictly observed.

It was perhaps inevitable, then, that one of the most common strategies for upward mobility among the "slave" groups was a successful assertion of membership in a Nuosu *cyvi*, ensuring a descent link to all other Nuosu (cf. Ma Erzi 1993, 39). From our interviews, we glimpsed how this process might have worked historically. One informant in Jjiggu village told us that his father was a Jjiggu, but that he was a Qiesa. How to explain this anomaly? Reaching back into family history, he said that his Qiesa ancestors in Shaliping were originally *mayo* to one of the Alu families. *Mayo* is a term commonly used in Ninglang for *gaxy* of the *qunuo*. The implication is that his Qiesa ancestor was brought in from Da Liangshan with his Alu master. Some time afterward, his forebears were sold to a *nuo* family, then sold to a Jjiggu household. Hence, his father was a Jjiggu man, although it is not clear how widely accepted this affiliation was. After 1956, he (our host) recovered his Qiesa patriline and *cyvi*. Significantly, our host claimed as marriage partners *qunuo* lineages, including those that were the traditional marriage partners of the Jjiggu. Others present later challenged his claims, skeptical that a *gaxy* lineage could intermarry with *qunuo*. While interviewing in Axi village, members of the Axi *cyvi* told us that they were descendants of a marriage between a *nuo* and a *gaxy*. After a split in the *cyvi* seventeen generations in the past, our host's segment had become *qunuo*, while the other segment had retained their *gaxy* status. Investigation into the historical marriage partners of our host's segment confirmed that this was indeed the case.

Histories such as these led us to believe that over the long haul, upward mobility in Nuosu society was possible. Men could claim the *cyvi* of their masters and, in some cases, eventually assert a new "class" status. How long they would have to wait and what figured into successful claims is not clear, beyond the fact that one's marriage partners were important sources of validation of social status. Certainly first generation slaves would not have this option and would have a somewhat anomalous position in Nuosu society. Slavery was in most cases precisely the condition of not having a *cyvi*. We met one elderly woman, reputedly a Han from the adjacent county of Yongsheng, who had been the mistress of the local *nuo*. She claimed no *cyvi*, but said that the lineage of her husband was Bbuyo. Because she had a son and a daughter, both of whom were married and well into adulthood, we were eager to ask further questions about her and her children's histories. However, everyone's extreme discomfort with the interview led to a halt.

CYVI AND SOCIETY

One factor we have failed to discuss in our essay, but which has much to do with the differences noted between Nuosu and Han lineages, is political economy. Nuosu lineages in Xiao Liangshan structured a society that by and large lived off a subsistence economy and had little recourse to political authority beyond *cyvi* elders. While Da Liangshan had powerful *nzy*, some of them formally recognized by the Chinese imperial government as *tusi*, or local rulers, responsible for their territory's tranquillity, Xiao Liangshan Nuosu had only sporadic contact with the Mosuo *tusi* in their area. And their own *nuo* were not, in people's memories, involved in the maintenance of social order. Rather, the *cyvi* loomed large as the most significant political and reference group in everyday life.

By contrast, Han society in the late Qing was commercialized and bureaucratized. The Han state was a class society, where family status was based on access to commercial and property wealth and to the perquisites of imperial offices. While lineages were important in particular localities, their strength and influence reflected to what degree they afforded their members access to wealth and bureaucratic position, opportunities that in turn depended heavily on a lineage's corporate holdings. In Nuosu society, too, there were differences in wealth, deriving from control of land and people and cross-cutting the castelike groups that have attracted so much scholarly attention. But restricted contact with Han markets and the relative absence of private property, as well as Nuosu ethics concerning hospitality and generosity, in Xiao Liangshan worked against the concentration of wealth in particular families and the formation of socioeconomic groups per se. The only possible exception to this generalization was the production and marketing of opium in Xiao Liangshan in the last few decades before the fifties; left unchecked, opium production and its attendant politics might have drastically altered traditional relationships, as it entailed extensive contacts with Han markets and a sudden influx of money and guns.

As the brief discussion of markets implies, the Nuosu in Xiao Liangshan lived apart from other ethnic groups. Most of them arrived in Xiao Liangshan later than other peoples, such as the Mosuo, Pumi, Han, and Hui, and they tended to occupy land at the highest altitudes, which had not been set-tled. Nuosu settlement of the high mountain slopes, their subsistence econ-omy, and strong cultural prohibitions against marriage with other groups contributed to their relative isolation. But they were not by any means a closed society. Slaves, who were Han in every case we had any information on, were continually brought in, in small numbers, usually from areas outside Ning-lang, to work the land or to be sold to Nuosu neighbors for cash. Assimila-tion of outsiders, first through the *cyvi*, was inevitable over the long haul and ultimately swelled the ranks of the *qunuo*, always the largest social stratum in Xiao Liangshan Nuosu society (Ma Erzi 1993, 39).

Whether one looks at the historical process of becoming Nuosu or the logic of the system based on descent and marriage, the *cyvi* takes precedence over all else as the foundation of Nuosu society in Xiao Liangshan. People became accepted as Nuosu not because of their position in the ranked so-cial strata but through the agency of the *cyvi*. The *cyvi* themselves were, and in rural areas still are, charters for Nuosu identity. Because the *cyvi* offered the most immediate genealogical connections for men and their families, the identity bestowed by such descent links gave one a place in the stratifi-cation system. As individual families, having acquired a *cyvi* identity, made the first initiatives to move up through the stratification system, it is significant that they did so through marriage alliances with upper-level families, and that a move upward was the impetus for establishing a new *cyvi* segment. In effect, it was ultimately not families or individuals that were ranked in the stratification system, but *cyvi*.

RETROSPECTIVE QUESTIONS

As we anticipated, our limited comparison of Yi and Han lineages has left many lacunae and unanswered questions. One conspicuous shortcoming con-cerns rituals. While our interviews led us to the conclusion that lineages, rather than social strata, were more important in structuring Nuosu society and con-ferring Nuosu identity, our case would be strengthened if ritual activity among the Nuosu were better understood. As many anthropologists across a wide spectrum of theoretical orientations have noted, ritual, whether construed as mirroring social relations, reproducing them, or transforming them, speaks to people about their place in the social universe. Given the high sta-tus and high visibility of ritual specialists, the *bimo*, in "old" Nuosu society and their ubiquitous presence at funerals, dispute settlements, and some phases of marriage rituals—all occasions freighted with issues of lineage identity and status—we think that ritual life among the Nuosu was once very rich. Even in the absence of lineage-wide, ancestor commemoration rituals typical of the Han Chinese, we hardly expect that rituals for life crisis events and dis-pute settlements in Nuosu society were silent on the subject of the *cyvi*.

And we feel our data raise many questions about lineage branching or segmentation. This process is important because it is critical to people's identity, to their standing in the stratification system, and to social mobility. We know, for example, that the relationship between elder and younger brothers is much more central to the Nuosu than to the Han, yet the evidence that it affected ranking among lineage branches is equivocal. What we have dubbed the "seven-generation rule" is also culturally salient to the Nuosu, but data on lineage segmentation point to other factors such as localization, marriage patterns, and demographic variables that seem to work against the cultural norm. If the rule is so often honored in the breach, then does it motivate retrospective adjustments to genealogical connections that we have claimed are, in our comparison to the Han lineage, rather resistant to tampering? And can we hope to appreciate Nuosu society as anything but static, unresponsive to relations with other ethnic groups, to the Han state, to larger economic changes, if we do not understand a major frame of reference in the rhetoric of Nuosu ethnohistory, namely *cyvi* genealogies and the process of segmentation?

Finally, our comparison, because centered in Western anthropological discourse, has not directly confronted the implications of the legacy of Han ethnologists, who brought to the field their own culture's constructs of the lineage, for all of us as we approach the *cyvi*. This legacy and the medium of the Chinese language need closer scrutiny for how they have shaped our discussions of lineages and other social dimensions of Nuosu society.

CHAPTER 4

Preferential Bilateral-Cross-Cousin Marriage among the Nuosu in Liangshan

Lu Hui

Until 1956, the Nuosu (Yi) society that we know of in Liangshan was almost completely free from control by the central government (especially in the hinterland). Yet it did not form a separate state but was a slave society divided and ruled by various *nuoho* clans.

At the same time, it was also a castelike social system. The hierarchical order of castes and even of clans was demarcated by the degree of "hardness of bones." Such a social system had divided the Nuosu society into two sides: the aristocratic "hard bones," including *nzymo* and *nuoho* ("Black Yi" or "Black Bones") categories on one side, and on the other their subordinate castes, the three categories *quho* or *qunuo* ("White Yi" or "White Bones," commoners), according to the region; *mgajie* (serfs); and *gaxy galo* (slaves). Marriage between castes was, and still is, considered a grave violation of social rules and punished severely, by death before 1956 and by exclusion from the clan or even caste today. The whole society, then, followed the principle of strict endogamy of caste and exogamy of clan. On the basis of this principle, bilateral-cross-cousin marriage was, and is, practiced and parallel-cousin marriage was, and is, forbidden.

The principle of clan relationship applies not only among *nuoho* clans but also among *quho* clans, just as the concept of "bones" is generally acknowledged by every Nuosu caste. This fact further illustrates the hierarchical distinction in the caste system, especially the distinction between the *nzymo,* the *nuoho,* and the *quho.*

Nuosu society is a patrilineal society; consanguineal relatives are reckoned patrilineally. The clan consists of a group of people descended from the same male ancestors; females are excluded from oral genealogies. Sons have the privilege of inheritance in a family; men practice levirate and polygamy; married women do not move into their husbands' households before becoming pregnant.

In patrilineal societies such as that of the Nuosu, the most common rule is to forbid parallel-cousin marriage. In preferential bilateral-cross-cousin marriage, whether preference is shown for the mother's brother's daughter or the father's sister's daughter varies according to the social conditions. In this essay, I will discuss in detail the practice of the preferential bilateral-cross-cousin marriage among the Liangshan Nuosu and the factors that affect their decision making.

THE LOGIC OF CLAN COMPETITION IN MARRIAGE

From ethnographic literature recorded in Chinese, we know of two sayings in Liangshan: "The father's sister's daughter is naturally the daughter-in-law of the mother's brother" and "It takes no effort for the father's sister's family to obtain the mother's brother's daughter." Although these sayings are recorded in Chinese, using Chinese terms, they still illustrate the marriage principle of the Nuosu. The truth of the sayings has been verified by scholarly investigations. In other words, according to this marriage custom, both in theory and in logic, the MBD is very often in fact the FZD: MBD = FZD (see Figure 4.1).

According to the kinship terminology in Figure 4.2, however, we can see that for the Nuosu *assa* (MBD) is not always *ahmi* (FZD).[1] The reason is that, unless father's sister actually married mother's brother (a common but not universal occurrence), father's sister's daughter and mother's brother's daughter belong to different clans. Clans are the core of the Nuosu social structure. They function like pillars in the structure, and their interrelationship crucially influences other aspects of social lives, including the marriage system.

Let us examine the Nuosu clan organization by using *nuoho* clans as an example. I have mentioned that the hierarchical order of each caste in Nuosu society is differentiated by "softness" or "hardness" of their bones. Among them all, *nzymo,* or *tusi* (the Chinese term), have the hardest bones and have the purest aristocratic blood. *Nuoho* are second in the hierarchy and are in turn followed by *quho* or *qunuo.* The Han laborers, who are seized and kept as slaves, are usually considered to "have no bones." Although the ruling *nuoho* clans originated from two brothers, Gguhxo and Qoni, their descendants eventually divided into hundreds of clans. The populations of these clans range from less than one thousand to ten thousand or more. The name of each clan serves as the surname of its members. These clans form themselves

---

1. Ego = male or female; F = father; M = mother; Sp = spouse; H = husband; W = wife; S = son; D = daughter; B = brother; Z = sister; C = child.

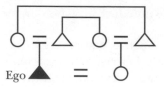

Figure 4.1. The equivalency of MBD and FZD in the ideal Nuosu marriage system.

into exogamous groups. Among *nuoho* clans, the hardness of bones of one clan is measured by the number of generations in their oral genealogy and the number of male members. The so-called Big Black Yi clans are those that have about thirty generations or more in their genealogy. Although all the clans descend from Gguhxo or Qoni, a long history of a lineage clearly ensures a clan's aristocratic position and signifies the hardness of its bones. Very often, daughters of these Big Black Yi are married into the *nzymo* families. A clan can be subdivided into several segmented lineages. Each segmented lineage inhabits one or several neighboring villages, according to its population and power (see Ann Maxwell Hill and Eric Diehl, chapter 3 in this volume).

There are eight *nuoho* clans in Butuo County, where people speak "narrow trouser legs" dialect (Suondi). Every clan also contains segmented lineages of varying sizes extended into neighboring counties, such as Puge, Jinyang, and Zhaojue. Two clans are relatively concentrated and have resided for a relatively long time (at least fifteen generations) in Butuo: the Jjidi and the Bibbu clans. Each of the clans consists of about two thousand members. Until 1956, the two clans almost divided Butuo into two parts, using the Temuli River as the boundary. Because the two clans were evenly matched in power, they became conventional allies, although there was no prescribed rule of alliance between their lineage segments. If we further observe the alliance between their lineage segments, we will find that not every Jjidi lineage segment has a Bibbu lineage segment as its main ally; the main ally could be Mgevu, Jire, Mokui, or Moshe, or even Hma or Awo residing in other counties. On the other hand, almost every lineage segment (five were investigated) has some families that marry with the Bibbu clan. Actually, the eight *nuoho* clans describe the relationship among themselves this way: "All are allies and all are enemies." When they collaborated in attacking the Adu *tusi* who ruled Butuo, their military alliance was formed on the basis of affinal kinship relations. When the Jjidi Acho clan in Siqie Village fought with one segment of the Mokui clan over cattle in the 1940s, the scale of the conflict and the interests involved were small enough that none of the lineage segments or allied clans on either side took part in the fight.

As to the power distribution among the *nuoho* clans, clan members often say, "*Nuoho* clans are of the same size, as chicken eggs are." This saying

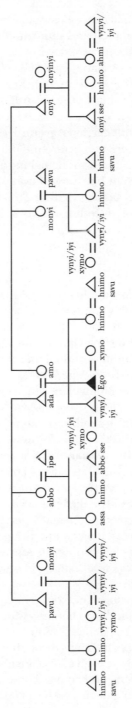

Figure 4.2. Nuosu (Suondi dialect) kin terms.

projects an egalitarian ideal of a tribal society, in which every clan enjoys equal status and there is no domination and subordination of one another. In reality, however, clans are most concerned about how to maintain and increase the hardness of their bones. A clan's hardness of bones is exhibited in the betrothal gifts that its daughters receive. In other words, the more powerful the bride's clan is, the more valuable the betrothal gifts. Thus, clans have no absolute equality in power or status. The variation and change in the preferred bilateral-cross-cousin marriage around the notion of bones best manifest the political, military, and economic interrelationship among the clans. One of the major considerations in making a choice between the MBD or the FZD for marriage is their hardness of bones. We have mentioned that often the MBD and the FZD belong to different clans, that is, the hardness of their bones might be of different degrees. Thus, the betrothal gifts needed would be different.

CLAN INTERMARRIAGE AND KINSHIP TERMINOLOGY

In Village A there are six households that belong to lineage segment A of Butuo Jiddi. Three households among them have been allied with the Awo clan for four generations; two among them marry daughters of the Bibbu clan; the last one marries the Hma clan. In lineage segment B in Village B, most of the males marry daughters of the Hma clan; most of the females are married into the Bibbu clan. In lineage segment C in Village C, most of the males marry daughters of the Bibbu clan. Thus, we have Lévi-Strauss's "generalized exchange" among at least three lineage segments.

The exchange pattern is also similar to that practiced by Kachin. That is, one clan or one caste provides women for another higher social stratum, which is the clan with harder bones in the Nuosu case, and obtains women from a third clan, and so on. And matrilateral-cross-cousin preferential marriage is the best way to guarantee the smoothness of this exchange cycle. Because of the vast territory and the dispersion of the Nuosu clans, however, matrilateral-cross-cousin marriage is usually performed on the basis of lineage segments or even villages, instead of among clans. For example, each lineage segment of the Jjidi clan chooses its affines according to its own interests. For the whole clan, the total range of its alliance is thus enlarged, as shown in Figure 4.3.

It should be noted that before 1956, the rugged topography and dialect differences rendered communication between widely dispersed clan branches in Liangshan very difficult. For military and political reasons, alliances were easier to form among neighboring clans through marriage exchange. Therefore, there exist complex terms in each dialect area, such as Vazha-Baqie, Sugga-Aho, Luoho-Lomu, Jjidi-Bibbu, and so on. These clans, which have formed fixed alliances with each other, practice preferential bilateral-cross-cousin mar-

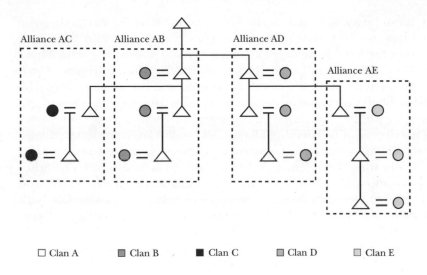

Figure 4.3. A hypothetical alliance network.

riage; that is, restricted exchange, like the above-mentioned marriage between lineage segment A in Village A of the Jjidi clan and the Awo clan.

The two clans involved in this kind of exchange usually have the same degree of hardness of bones and share common political, economic, and military interests. This kind of exchange, however, does not hinder a clan's lineage segments from forming a short-range alliance with lineage segments of other clans with which the clan is not customarily allied.

The notion of bones applies not only to the *nuoho* and the *nzymo* but also to the *quho*. Since all are "White Bones," however, *qunuo* cannot marry other white-boned castes, such as *mgajie,* not to mention the *gaxy,* who are slaves. Furthermore, the hardness of bones is also differentiated even within the same *qunuo* clan. At the level of the *gaxy* caste, those with Nuosu roots do not marry those with Han roots.

In the social hierarchy, it seems that wealth is not as important as the hardness of bones, just as an individual is less important than his or her clan. The choices that individuals make in marriage must accord with the interests of the entire clan. In choosing a partner for marriage, the hardness of a candidate's bones is first determined, and then political and economic interests involved are considered.

Now let us look back at kinship terminology of the Suondi dialect, using Ego, a male, as an example. From the terms, we know that the mother's brother's daughter is called *assa* and the father's sister's daughter is called *ahmi.* It can be seen, then, that the MBD is not always the FZD, otherwise there would not be two different terms. However, *ahmi-assa* (MBD-FZD) is a complex term referring only to (female) cross-cousins. The term *hmazy-hnimo* (FBC-MZC) is another complex term, which includes all bilateral-parallel cousins of opposite sex, as well as brothers and sisters. Accordingly, bilateral-parallel cousins and bilateral cross-cousins form two opposite groups: consanguineal kin and affinal kin. Among consanguineal kin, no matter what the degree of collaterality, all parallel cousins are considered consanguineal and are equated with sisters or brothers. Sexual relations among people with these kin relations would be labeled as incestuous. The other group is composed of affinal relatives, including all the preferred bilateral cross-cousins. Although these two complex terms may in fact include both bilateral-parallel and cross-cousins, most of the time they designate separate groups.

There are two major kin groups in Nuosu society: *cyvi,* or consanguineal kin, and *vusa,* affinal kin. There are also two terms in Suondi for the wife's parents: *onyi* = MB, *onyinyi* = MBW, *ipo* = FZH, *abbo* = FZ. Obviously, the aunt and the uncle might belong to different affinal kin, so they are assigned different terms. The fact that there are different terms also suggests that their children are not necessarily regarded as equally suitable marriage partners.

Let us now compare the status of the mother's brother with that of the father's sister. The mother's brother is not only paired with the father in terminology but also lives in the territory of the affinal kin. Until Ego gets married, the mother's brother is the closest affinal relative. In contrast, the father's sister is from the consanguineal kin of Ego. She does not become a member of the affinal kin until she is married. She is in a situation similar to that of Ego's mother. The latter comes from the affinal kin, but after she is married she becomes consanguineal kin to Ego, as his mother. The kinship term *abbo* (FZ) does not change after she gets married. Even though she becomes the cross-cousin's mother, she still remains Ego's consanguineal relative to some extent. As an affinal relative, however, her status is not as clear as that of the mother's brother.

In Nuosu society, the status of the mother's brother is very important. This is reflected in many Nuosu legends, folk tales, and sayings. When he comes to visit, his seat by the hearth is the place of honor. In the marriage, the person who accompanies the bride to the groom's home is her brother, the future maternal uncle of her children. Since Nuosu society is established on the basis of an egalitarian ideal with the clan as the basic unit, far more significant than the nuclear family, the mother's brother is most important as the representative of the mother's clan, Ego's affines. At the same time, he and his clan are important political and military allies. Especially when we understand the significance of warfare in traditional Nuosu society, we can see the importance of the affinal clan, symbolized by the mother's brother, and the importance of the relationship between Ego's clan and his mother's clan.

My and others' investigations have shown that it is more common for Ego to marry his mother's brother's daughter than his father's sister's daughter, when they are not the same person. Although Nuosu people usually think that the FZH (*ipo*) is equal to the MB (*ipo*=MB=FZH) and emphasize that there is no difference between the two, in real life, however, the mother's brother has another name, *onyi*. That is to say, the FZH belongs to the category of mother's brother but is not absolutely the same. Some examples below may help us understand the way this expresses the flexibility in marriage alliance among the Nuosu.

SOME CASES OF CROSS-COUSIN MARRIAGE

Case 1

According to Ego, his parents started to think about arranging his marriage when he was twelve years old, in 1954. At that time, an elder in his clan advised his parents to form an engagement with the Jienuo clan of Jiao Jihe Village, which is twenty kilometers away. The elder said, "The Jjidi clan shouldn't always intermarry with the Bibbu clan. Bibbu also marry with the Jienuo clan in addition to Jjidi; so we should have marriage relations with other clans as well. Otherwise, if we have war with Bibbu someday, and they get help from the Jienuo clan, then who can help us? In addition, one family of our Jjidi clan in the village gave one daughter to Jienuo many years ago. Thus, we ought to get a wife from the Jienuo clan." See Figure 4.4.

In 1963, after the Democratic Reforms were instituted, Ego married a daughter of the Jienuo clan. In 1980 Ego's son married uxorilocally into his mother's brother's house. In 1989 he got divorced and returned to his natal village. In the following year, he married another daughter of the Jienuo clan, and then died of an overdose of heroin in 1994. On the day of his funeral, his clan members decided that his widow would marry his younger brother, who was fifteen at the time, after the latter graduated from high school. The young man's widow, however, was not willing to marry her husband's brother, and she ran back to her natal home. A local member of the Jjidi said, "Well, that's OK if she is not willing to marry him, but the Jienuo family should repay us our money."

One informant told me, "Marrying fathers' sisters' daughters is certainly good, but it would cost 1,000 to 2,000 yuan more to marry daughters of fathers' sisters' families than daughters of mothers' brothers' families. Furthermore, when a clan is in need, the mother's brother's clan is more inclined to help. The mother's brother may give us money or liquor. But fathers' sisters' families are outsiders; it's not easy to ask for their help."

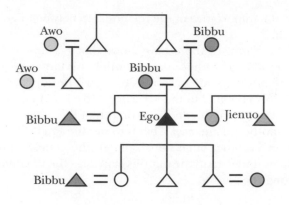

□ Clan Jjidi   ■ Clan Bibbu   ■ Clan Jienuo   □ Clan Awo

Figure 4.4. Alliances between the Bibbu and other *nuo* clans.

The fact that the betrothal gifts to the MBD and to the FZD are different in value also proves that the FZH is not necessarily the same as the MB. This is to say that if the bride does not come from the mother's clan, more betrothal gifts are needed. The bride is worth more in this case because she has harder bones, although she comes from a clan that is more distant in relationship than that of the MB's. When she for some reason does not marry the son of the MB, she has to symbolically give part of her betrothal gifts to her MB.

In a society with such a strict caste system as that of the Nuosu, an ideal marriage would be one that would increase the hardness of the bones of the family and consolidate its social position: in consequence, the FZD is the best choice. However, in reality, a family often marries a son to the MBD for political or strategic reasons, sometimes even to the daughter of other non-usual affinal clans. In the latter case, the wife's father is called *onyi* = MB, and the wife's mother *onyinyi* = MBW. That shows that the wife's father is considered or classified as the mother's brother, not as the father's sister's husband.

There is a clear boundary between the territory of one's own clan and the territory of one's mother's brother's clan, also the clan of alliance. In times of peace, both areas would be open for the best use, whether agriculture, herding, water sources, or hunting; a dispute over a stream, piece of land, or slave could turn the two sides into enemies and be cause for war.

Case 2

Figure 4.5 demonstrates the marriage alliance between the Long and Lu clans, which is traced as far back as possible based on the oral genealogy. The Jjidi clan (which adopted the Han family name Lu) moved from Butuo

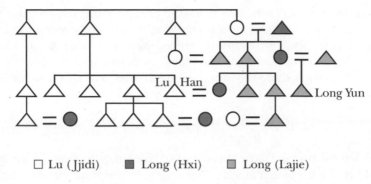

□ Lu (Jjidi)   ■ Long (Hxi)   ▪ Long (Lajie)

Figure 4.5. Alliances between Lu (Jjidi) and Long (Hxi and Lajie).

to Yanshan in Yunnan, and the Hxi clan (which adopted the Han family name Long) moved from Jinyang to Songle Village in Longshan. They have been allied for at least three generations. Although the Lajie clan was also once allied with the Hxi clan because of war, we can see from Figure 4.5 that marriage exchange has taken place mainly between the Lu and Long clans. The Lu and Long clans in Yanshan have adopted many Han customs in their lifestyle. For instance, they use Han family names instead of Nuosu clan names, they hire tenant-peasants to farm their land, they are educated in Han schools, and they use wood coffins and stone tablets for the burial of the dead. But they still subscribe to the Nuosu marriage system and marry only within the *nuoho* caste. And they still invite *bimo* from Zhaotong or Liangshan to take charge of important sacrificial rituals.

Until 1949, the Lu and the Long clans were the biggest landowners and the only *nuoho* clans in Yanshan. Their alliance kept their land from falling into the hands of Han people. In addition, transportation in Yanshan was very inconvenient due to the high mountains and deep valleys. It would take several days for one to get to the nearest town, Zhaotong, on foot or by horse, and it was no easy thing to come down the mountains to cross the Jinsha River, either. Geographic isolation helped promote the alliance between the Lu and Long clans as they sought to consolidate their status and counter local Han families. However, because the number of members in the two clans was very limited and the sex ratio was unbalanced, they still had to find spouses from outside. They married the An clan of *nuoho*, who originated from Guizhou, and the Hma clan from Liangshan.

Early in this century, members of the Lu and Long clans started to leave Yanshan to join the army and government in Zhaotong and Kunming. Eventually, they ruled all of Yunnan province. After they left Yanshan, they were influenced by the outside world. They were disturbed to hear such comments as "A is not as smart and healthy as B, because A's parents are cousins." There was a difference between their marriage practices and those of the Nuosu in Liangshan: the cross-cousin preferential marriage between the Lu and Long clans involved first cousins rather than more distant classificatory cousins as in Liangshan. After they took up permanent residence in Kunming in the 1930s, there was only one case of intermarriage between Lu and Long.

Case 3

Ego A left his home village at the end of the 1950s to study in the county seat. Later he became a teacher. According to the tradition, he married a daughter of the Bibbu clan in the village; he had three daughters and two sons. After several years, his wife brought their children to the city to live with him. The children received a Han-language education in school. Later, his two sons both worked in government institutions. The oldest daughter was engaged to a son of the Bibbu clan in her childhood. A had accepted one-third of the betrothal gifts—one thousand yuan. Later, liberal-minded A decided to break off the engagement so that his daughter would not marry back to the countryside to become a farmer, but could have her own career in the city, instead. His decision enraged the Bibbu clan. They found it hard to accept A's family's withdrawal of the commitment as a *nuoho* family. In addition, it was even more unacceptable that A looked down on villagers once he had moved to the city. However, A had made up his mind, and his daughter did not want to get married and live in the countryside either. Therefore, A initiated a difficult negotiation with the Bibbu clan. Finally, the conflict was resolved by A paying back double the betrothal gifts and thus incurring great debt. He sighed at the peaceful resolution of the conflict: "If this had happened in former times, the Bibbu family and I would probably have become enemies."

After this problem was over, A began to worry about the marriage of his oldest son, B. B had a secondary school education and a nice job. Certainly there were a lot of marriage proposals. Although all the girls proposed were from *nuoho* families, they all lived in the countryside and were considered "uncultured." A did not think that they were fit for his son. B agreed that the gap between his lifestyle and that of those women was too big, and said he would like to find a *nuoho* woman who had job in the city. B did not want to marry a Han woman, let alone a *quho* woman. However, there were really very few *nuoho* women who were both educated and had jobs in the city. After many inquiries made by clan members, a year later they finally found a daughter of the Elu clan in another county, which was hundreds of *li* away. B was successfully married. A did not incur great expense on the betrothal gifts because the bones of the bride's family were not hard enough to merit that. Many Jjidi clan members brooded on this marriage, and they said in regret, "It's certainly nice to marry a *nuoho* daughter, but her bones are not hard enough. It wouldn't have worked in former times."

The political and social life in Liangshan has radically changed in the last few decades. The Nuosu castes consciously or unconsciously followed along with the process of social transformation. But this does not mean that they have gradually given up their traditions completely. On the contrary, not only do the Nuosu not depart from their own history in the face of these new changes and the pressure of Sinicization but they also reinforce their relationship with the Nuosu tradition through various means. This is manifested in their marriage practices. The *nzymo* and the *nuoho,* who are of the aristocratic stock and who have lost their privileges, still preserve the custom of complete caste endogamy so as to maintain their aristocratic characteristic in today's world. The *quho* also stick to their own marriage rules. The *qunuo* clans, which have harder bones, are still reluctant to marry with other clans, let alone with other castes, such as *mgajie* or *gaxy.* In Liangshan, we still hear government officials, intellectuals, and farmers from *qunuo* clans say, when they comment on their marriage rules, "We don't marry with other *quho* at random."

The story in Case 3 illustrates the difficulty and dilemma in spouse selection that many *nuoho* and *quho* officials as well as urban residents commonly encounter and the compromises that they often have to make. On the one hand, the concept of bones is still the same as it was in the past and is still the decisive factor in spouse selection; on the other hand, the concepts of power, prestige, and status have changed. The degree of Sinicization and the level of education and professional success have replaced the old signs of wealth and power—land, livestock, and slaves. In addition, these factors act to contend with the notion of bones. Nonetheless, the notion of bones, as the basis of the Nuosu caste society, always reminds every Nuosu that one of the markers of his identity is his obedience to the rule of the Nuosu ancestor—one can marry only within the caste and with a family with equivalent bones.

CONCLUSION

The Nuosu society, which was a forest of clans, was never organized into a state. The egalitarian relationship among the clans, where there was no domination and subordination, was a means to coordinate the clans in order to attain political balance. Nuosu history showed that, as an aspect of ethnicity in the social system, this coordinating relationship was manifested in frequent military confrontations and conflicts among clans, on the one hand, and in the relatively stable alliance relationship among clans, on the other hand. Such a system seems paradoxical but was in fact logical: although the ideal of warfare and equality led the clans to competition, conflicts, and wars, the flexibility of choosing the MBD or FZD in marital decision making offered possibilities of stability. As allies in war, clans perceived each other as equals, but in the competition for marriage partners, clans searched for harder bones when possible. It was through conflicts and alliances that Nuosu social values were expressed, summarized in the sayings "Where there are allies, there are enemies" and "It is goats that we cannot be short of; it is the clan that we find indispensable."

Since the clan is so important, the marriage choice of a clan member is far from being a choice pertaining only to his or her individual life: it is part of the larger interest of the clan. It is clan members who collect the betrothal gifts, hold the wedding, and build the new house for the bride. On the other hand, when a clan chooses spouses for its members, its considerations include not only the desire to increase the hardness of family bones through the marriage but also the overall political alliance of the whole clan. That is to say, if a man does not marry the daughter of his MB because her bones are not sufficiently hard, he may incur dissatisfaction of the MB's clan; if it is serious, it might cause military conflict or even war.

Another characteristic of Nuosu society is its mobility. The wide area of Liangshan provided space for the expansion of victorious clans, and it also offered alternative space for clans that lost wars and had to leave their own territories. Following this geographic mobility were changes in social spaces. A clan and its customary affinal clan might not only become distant in the geographic sense, their political interests also might not correspond. Therefore, a new alliance might be necessary. But a clan's oral history and genealogy always remind its offspring of the place of the clan's origin, the route of its migration, the lands it conquered, the places it settled, and the alliances it had. Oral history and genealogy also ensure that all clan members will find their consanguineal kin, *cyvi*, or affinal kin, *vusa*, in every corner of Liangshan. Mobility, which results from wars and changes in livelihood, injects a certain degree of flexibility in spouse selection and promotes changes and expansion of the political alliances of migrating segmented clans. In wars fought between *nuoho* clans, they had cooperation from their allies in combating their enemies; in dealing with the *nzymo* or the Han, all the Nuosu clans (including the "White" *quho* clans) would be united.

Marriage choice is not fixed, just as the interests of any clan are not always stable. The choice between the ideal marriage, the daughter of the FZ, and the actual preference, the daughter of the MB, is conditioned by the political and economic interests of the family or the clan. At the same time, as a system of exchange of gifts, marriage plays an essential role in balancing the social relationship among clans in a society constantly engaged in armed conflicts.

CHAPTER 5

Names and Genealogies
among the Nuosu of Liangshan

Ma Erzi

The Yi of Liangshan, who call themselves Nuosu in their own language, have a complex system of clan, birth-order, and personal names; terms of address; and clan genealogies. Research into names and naming, using Yi and Han language written sources, personal knowledge, and even archaeological data, can open an important window to understanding Yi history. This is a huge subject, one that cannot be treated comprehensively in a short essay. Here I will simply offer a classification of the Nuosu system of clan names, the various methods of choosing personal names, terms of address, and the topic of genealogies.

THE SYSTEM OF FAMILY AND PERSONAL NAMES

The Nuosu system of names is made up of three levels of organization: clan names, birth-order names, and personal names.

Clan Names and Surnames

In Liangshan there are only a few tens of large clans, but the clan names belonging to these large clans are innumerable. Naturally there are a few clans that have an all-clan surname, with no branch surnames below them, such as the Jjike clan. In the long course of history, the Jjike clan has produced a great many branches, and its steps have expanded to cover the whole of Liangshan, but historically and presently it has only the one surname, Jjike. The great majority of clans are not like this, however, and many large clans have produced within them a large number of branches that, because of natural, geographic, and environmental changes, have themselves become clans. The

Hxiesse clan, for example, has given birth to over forty subordinate clans, such as Shama Qubi, Jjisse, Jjimu, Mgebbu, and Ayie. These clans have all developed branch surnames under the overall Hxiesse surname. In the most formal activities, people usually do not use the branch surname, and in marriages and funerals people use only the whole-clan surname. In ordinary life people use the branch surname.

The names of birds and other animals, and their characteristics, that once were used to identify tribes have provided one source for all-clan surnames. For example:

Pohle Ssenge: *Pohle* is an onomatopoeic word for the sound of a bird's wings when taking off, and it represents a bird; *ssenge* refers to five sons, and the whole name means the five sons of the bird clan.

Mugu Sseggu: *Mugu* originally referred to a blue sky, but it was often suffixed by the term for eagle to denote "an eagle in the blue sky." *Sseggu* refers to nine sons, and so the full name means the nine sons of the eagle clan.

Amo Sseggu: *Amo* means "invisible," that is, flying very fast. It stands for a bird, and the full name denotes the nine sons of the flying bird clan.

Jjizze Sseshy: *Jjizze* means a wasp, clever and fierce. In Yi custom, it is not included in the category of insects, but rather in the category of winged creatures. *Sseshy* means seven sons, so the full name means the seven sons of the wasp clan. (There is another definition for *jjizze:* "noontime"; the story explaining this interpretation is too long to go into here.)

Hxiezzy Ssesuo: *Hxiezzy* means bird, and *ssesuo* means three sons, so this name means the three sons of the bird clan.

Bacha Sseshy: *Bacha* is an onomatopoeic word for the sound of an animal who is surprised and flees; this name denotes the seven sons of the animal clan.

Lahuo Sseshy: *Lahuo* is a gray tiger; this name means the seven sons of the gray tiger.

Asy Sseggu: *Asy* is the name of a particular kind of bird; this name means the nine sons of the bird clan.

In ancient times, when superior hunting weapons were not yet available, people had to rely on their quickness and bravery, and their catch was very small. Because of this, people disguised their arms as wings and walked as if flying. That some clans took their names from flying birds and running animals reflects their desire for such physical characteristics during a time of hunting and gathering. Branch clans evolved as the natural environment changed, developed as the forces of production developed, and chose appropriate names for themselves. For example, after the Yi came into contact with the Han, they often took Han names but did not give up their original Yi names; instead they took either the sound or the meaning of the original surname to form the Han name. For example, the Ga clan of Meigu also is called by its Han surname, Ga (standard Chinese: Gan). Some Yi surnames, such as Shamaqubi, are made up of four syllables. For Han surnames, there are those who have chosen Sha, Ma, Qu, Bai, and Qiu, and thus one surname has developed into five. Surnames that translate the meaning of the original surname are usually the names of plants, such as Yyhle, which means "poplar tree." When people with this surname adopted a Han surname, some of them chose Yang. Others of the Yyhle surname chose the sound of a syllable in the original surname instead: they chose He as their surname. Thus, choosing a surname was rather random. The Han names chosen are, however, used only in Han areas; in Yi areas people continue to use Yi surnames.

Birth-Order Names

In Yi names, the birth-order name is an intermediate name that stands between the clan name and the personal name. Men's and women's birth-order names are different, and traditionally were counted separately: the two sequences were not mixed together in the order.

This custom of birth-order names has been preserved intact in Tianba and other areas of Ganluo County in Liangshan. The order goes like this:

Male Birth-Order Names		*Female Birth-Order Names*	
Amu	First brother	Ayi	First sister
Munyi	Second brother	Aga	Second sister
Muga	Third brother	Azhy	Third sister
Mujy	Fourth brother	Agge	Fourth sister
Munyu	Fifth brother	Anyu	Fifth sister

The *a* in front of the *mu* syllable in the male names refers to the eldest son; the syllables that come after the *mu,* which expresses maleness, refer to the birth order. The *a* in the female birth-order names is a concise way of expressing femaleness, and the birth orders added after the *a* indicate second daughter, third daughter, and so on. If a child dies in any particular series of children, then his or her ordinal is not used again. If, for example, in a certain family there is a Munyi, a second brother, who dies, and a few years later another boy is born, then he is not placed according to the birth order of living brothers, but is called third brother, Muga, according to the order of brothers ever born to the family.

People in quite a few areas have destroyed this custom of birth-order naming by putting brothers and sisters together in ordering, and in fact the order that is used is not always the proper one. But the birth-order names are still separated by sex. For example, if the eldest child in a particular family is a son, then his birth order is written Muyi; if the second child is a girl, then they name her Aga (second girl), not Ayi (first girl). Another sort of variation is to reserve the first or even the second birth-order name, start with the second or even the third name, and arrange the rest of the names from there. In addition, often when the difference between the birth-order names of males and females goes past the fifth sibling, the birth-order names are doubled—such as Gaga, Jiejie, Gege, Nyunyu, and so on—to express that the person is even lower in the birth order. Birth-order names also affect terms of address between people at different places in the birth order, which I will discuss below.

Personal Names

Usually Liangshan Yi personal names are chosen by adults not long after the child's birth, and the names chosen bear the stamp of the development of Nuosu society, culture, and religion. The Nuosu proverb "If you raise a son for a whole generation, don't choose an improper name" shows the importance of naming children; the names given to children express the hopes and aspirations of the elder generation for the younger. For this reason, from ancient times to today Nuosu names have reflected definite aspirations and a definite timeliness, and are more than just a system of terms of address. Classifying and categorizing some names in actual use will, like the prismatic effect of seeing the sun in a drop of water, give us a different perspective on many aspects of Nuosu society.

1. Names taken from domestic animals:

Yonuo:	Sheep, black	Nyinji:	Cattle foundation
Yoga:	Sheep, rich	Nyiha:	Cattle, a hundred
Yoha:	Sheep, a hundred	Nyiddur:	Cattle, a thousand
Yopo:	Sheep lord	Nyibbu:	Cattle, many
Yose:	Sheep spirit	Nyiga:	Cattle, rich
Yuobbu:	Sheep, many	Nyida:	Cattle, strong
Nyipo:	Cattle lord	Nyijjo:	Cattle, has

The masculine suffix *sse* can be put after boys' names; the corresponding feminine *mo* can be used after girls' names.

2. Names that relate to slaves owned:

Lurbbu:	Slaves, many	Lurpo:	Slave lord
Lurda:	Slaves, strong	Lurha:	Slaves, a hundred
Lurshy:	Slaves, commander of	Jjiha:	Slaves, a hundred
Lurnji:	Slaves, origin of	Jjinu:	Slaves, a lot of

The masculine suffix *sse* can be put after boys' names; the corresponding feminine *mo* can be used after girls' names.

3. Names taken from gold and silver:

Shybbu:	Gold, a lot of	Shypo:	Gold lord
Shyqi:	Gold leaf	Quqi:	Silver leaf
Shynzy:	Gold lord	Qupo:	Silver lord
Shydu:	Gold digging	Quka:	Silver leap
Shyda:	Gold bars	Qubbu:	Silver, much
Shyvie:	Gold flowers	Quda:	Silver bars
Shymo:	Gold sand	Quvie:	Silver flowers
Shyha:	Gold, a hundred	Quha:	Silver, a hundred
Shyji:	Gold origin	Quji:	Silver foundation

A characteristic of names taken from livestock, slaves, or gold and silver is that after these nouns comes a descriptive or quantifying adjective, expressing the desire for even more of these things. Putting a verb after the noun expresses the hope of obtaining these things in the future. Using *livestock* as the root word for a name given to the next generation demonstrates that the Yi had entered the period of nomadic herding, and also that livestock had come to occupy a place in their consciousness. Having *slaves* as the root word for a name given to the next generation proclaimed the emergence of a Yi slave society; when gold and silver appeared in names, it demonstrated that Yi had already entered the period of metallurgy. Incorporating livestock, slaves, and precious metals into names clearly indicated some of the particular characteristics of Liangshan Yi society: its standard of wealth was generally determined by the quantities of slaves, precious metals, cattle, and sheep owned. If a family had a lot of slaves but no other wealth, people would still naturally count them as among the wealthy. In the same way, if they had a lot of gold and silver or a lot of cattle and sheep, this would also mark them as wealthy. Because of this, in Liangshan, slaves, stock, gold, and silver all belonged in the category of wealth. The masculine suffix *sse* can be put after boys' names; the corresponding feminine *mo* can be used after girls' names.

4. Names taken from mountains, rivers, and plants:

Ssuhuo:	Fir forest	Shuhuo:	Pine forest
Ssuha:	Fir, a hundred	Shuha:	Pine, a hundred
Ssuda:	Fir, strong	Shuda:	Pine, strong
Ssuqi:	Fir needles	Shuqi:	Pine needles
Ssusse:	Fir seeds	Shusse:	Pine nuts
Vahxe:	Cliff, surrounding	Yyke:	Water rushing
Vada:	Cliff, high	Yygge:	Water's edge

Vahuo:	Mountain reared	Yybbu:	Water, grand
Vasa:	Mountain content	Yyga:	Water, rich

I believe that there is not a people anywhere that is disinterested in landscape and forest, but at the same time I do not believe that every people's expression of their love of landscape and forest is the same. Some like peach forests and mountains full of orchards best; some are most fond of magnificent, limitless forests; some prefer little brooks and creeks; others are particularly respectful of great torrents. The Nuosu think that it is best to live at the foot of great cliffs in endless forests of verdant pines and luxuriant firs; only there can they nurture even greater good fortune and happiness. A Nuosu song expresses this:

> We come to raise sheep on the mountains behind our house;
> the sheep are like massed clouds.
> We come to the plains in front of our door to grow grain;
> the piles of grain are like mountains.
> We come to the stream at the side of the house to catch fish;
> the fish are like piles of firewood.

The names recorded above are a particular expression of this kind of thinking. The masculine suffix *sse* can be put after boys' names; the corresponding feminine *mo* can be used after girls' names.

5. Names taken from wild animals:

Jonuo:	Eagle, black	Ssybbu:	Leopard, many
Josse:	Eagle chick	Ssypu:	Leopard lord
Jomo:	Eagle, big	Ssyda:	Leopard, strong
Joddur:	Eagle wings	Ssyhuo:	Leopard, raising
Joha:	Eagle, a hundred	Ssyshy:	Leopard, yellow
Jojji:	Eagle flight	Ssymo:	Leopard, large
Laji:	Tiger foundation	Wonuo:	Bear, black
Lahxa:	Tiger's roar	Womo:	Bear, big/bear mother
Labbu:	Tiger, many	Wosse:	Bear cub
Lada:	Tiger, strong	Woke:	Bear leaping
Lapu:	Tiger lord	Woda:	Bear, big
Larry:	Tiger tooth	Woji:	Bear foundation
Lasy:	Tiger flower		
Ssyhxa:	Leopard, a hundred		
Ssynuo:	Leopard, black		

There are not many animal names that Nuosu like to take for their own; those commonly used are eagle, tiger, bear, and leopard, but many compounds can be formed from these names. The eagle expresses intelligence, the bear daring, the tiger and leopard bravery. This demonstrates the martial spirit of this people and expresses the hope that in war their descendants will enter the fray against the enemy with the bravery of the tiger, the leopard, or the bear, and will be able to capture their prey and dodge arrows with the cleverness of the eagle. The masculine suffix *sse* can be put after boys' names; the corresponding feminine *mo* can be used after girls' names.

6. Names derived from religious occupations:

Bimo:	*Bimo*
Bisse:	*Bisse* (apprentice)
Biti:	*Bimo's* chant
Bihxa:	Ceremonies, a hundred
Biga:	Rich in ceremonies
Biqu:	*Bimo* companion
Sunyi:	*Sunyi*
Susse:	*Susse* (child of *sunyi*)

Nuosu call the priest a *bimo; bimo* usually understand astrology, history, and law and can read Yi language religious texts. *Sunyi* are shamans. Choosing one of these names indicates two things: the first is respect for the *bimo* and hope that one's descendants will inherit the *bimo's* profession. The second has to do with people who have had many children die as infants: they believe that evil spirits are afraid of *bimo* and *sunyi,* and that by bearing one of these names the child can avoid misfortune. The masculine suffix *sse* can be put after boys' names; the corresponding feminine *mo* can be used after girls' names.

7. Names derived from compass directions:

Bbuddur:	East	Yyvu:	North
Bbujji:	West	Yyhmu:	South
Nyisi	Northeast	Keddi:	Northwest
Yosi:	Southwest	Luddi:	Southeast

The Nuosu in Liangshan have a kind of passive astrological outlook. Believing that life, death, and prosperity are to a large extent predetermined by heaven, they look at the mother's age and the birth animal of the child and thus determine the astrological direction the child could be expected to take. Accordingly, they give the child a name based on one of the compass points, which correlate with the cycle of twelve animals, thinking that this will bring contentment and good fortune. At the end of the name can be added *sse* for boys' names and *mo* for girls' names.

8. Names derived from power:

Nzypo:	Lord of power	Nzysa:	Power, content
Nzyda:	Power, great	Nzyhxa:	Power, a hundred
Nzyke:	Power leap	Geda:	Power, great
Nzyshu:	Power, recorded	Gehxa:	Power, a hundred

Putting a verb after the word *power* expresses the ability to exercise power; putting a quantifying or modifying adjective after the word expresses the greatness or breadth of the sphere of power. The appearance of this kind of name demonstrates respect for power in the society. The masculine suffix *sse* can be put after boys' names; the corresponding feminine *mo* can be used after girls' names.

9. Names derived from clans:

Vipu:	Clan lord	Vilur:	Clan included
Vihxa:	Clan, a hundred	Viji:	Clan foundation
Viqi:	Clan branch	Vimo:	Clan, big
Vika:	Clan leap	Vihxuo:	Clan, surrounding
Vidu:	Clan gathers		

The clan system of the Nuosu divides clan mates according to kin relationships into *cy* and *vi*. In general, those within seven generations are called *cy*, and after seven generations they are called *vi*. Intraclan marriage is strictly prohibited. *Cyvi* has become an enormous clan organization, but internally determined rules protect the equal status of every clan member. Nuosu say that, to a member of a clan, "It doesn't matter if you use a gold rod as a walking stick, or whether you use a wooden branch as a walking stick, your relative worth as a person is the same." This kind of internal solidarity of the clan pervaded Liangshan in the days before Liberation. Internal solidarity was uniform, as was reciprocal aid in troubles and difficulties; externally clan members formed a united force against invasion by outside forces. A Nuosu proverb says:

> That which you must rely on is the clan,
> that which you must raise is livestock,
> that which you must eat is grain.

10. Profane names:

Keqie:	Dog shit	Yoqie:	Sheep shit
Kenjy:	Dog skin	Voqie:	Pig shit
Vosse:	Piglet	Vaqie:	Chicken shit

People whose names are taken from animal skin or excrement almost always have been born after several elder brothers or sisters have died. Nuosu think that children's deaths are nearly always due to haunting by ghosts. Since they also believe that ghosts dislike dog and livestock excrement, they put aside their disgust and choose a profane name in the hope that, even though the child will be disgusted at his or her name, he or she may be able to avoid death at the hands of evil spirits and live a long life. As in other cases, a *sse* can be added after a boy's name and a *mo* after a girl's.

11. Borrowed names:

Changmao:	Long hair
Minguo:	Republic
Hongjun:	Red Army
Jiefang:	Liberation
Mingai:	Democratic Reforms
Chaoying:	Surpass England
Ganmei:	Catch Up to the United States
Jieyue:	Save
Geming:	Revolution
Wenge:	Cultural Revolution
Guoqing:	National Day
Sihua:	Four Modernizations
Baogan:	Land to the Household
Chaosheng:	Exceeding the Birth Quota

These and other names are borrowed from the Han language, and when they are used as part of the Yi language, some people do not understand what is going on. All are either political slogans or historical events that have happened in Liangshan, and people with these names are usually those born at the same time as the events or when the slogans were current. At the ends of these names, *sse* or *mo* is added to differentiate boys' from girls' names.

12. Names from weights:

A child who is born weighing a certain number of *jin* can be given that number of *jin* as a name, as in, for example, Ngejisse, Five-*jin* son. At the end of the number, the suffix *sse* is added to a boy's name and *mo* to a girl's.

13. Other names:

Many people use geographic names to name children. This occurs in two kinds of situations. The first has no hidden meaning to it: a child who is born at a certain place can conveniently be given the name of that place as a personal name in commemoration. In the second case, choosing the place of birth as the personal name indicates that this is a child of that place whose father is unknown. One might also ridicule or show prejudice toward an illegitimate child by giving it a name such as Potato, Buckwheat, Biscuit, Forest, or Basket, or a similar name. The suffix *sse* can be added to a boy's name and *mo* to a girl's.

In sum, the overall clan name and the branch clan name, along with the birth-order names, are the fixed portion of the system of naming; after a particular overall clan name becomes the name of a clan, it can, over the long course of history, spawn a lot of subordinate branch clan names; but all these branch clan names, as "little surnames," are subordinate to the overall clan name, the "big surname." In all of Liangshan society, the "big surname" is used in big contexts, and the "small surname" in small contexts, or the two are used together as a set. The birth-order names are fixed, though in some areas the order is no longer strictly followed.

In the case of the third level of the Nuosu system of naming—the personal name—if we compare the names used over the generations, as noted in the genealogies of various clans, as well as the names now in use among Nuosu people, we can easily discover that ever since the old days people have used this kind of name. If we investigate the repository of names, we can see roughly the general routes that Nuosu society has traveled: gradually evolving from a hunting and gathering to a nomadic pastoral society with an economy incorporating household slavery, in which money, slaves, and livestock occupied people's vision, to a society that is a peripheral part of the People's Republic of China. Nuosu names thus form a rough, simplified Nuosu history.

Terms of Address

A name is a term of address, and the three-level system of personal names examined here also forms the basis of a system of terms of address that clearly expresses the nature of hierarchy in personal relations in Nuosu society. For example, the full name of the late representative to the National People's Consultative Conference, Aho Lomusse, was Aho Vuga Lomusse. Aho is the name of his clan; Vuga shows that he is the second son, and Lomusse is his personal name. According to the rules, his grandfather's and father's generations, as well as elder brothers and cousins of his own clan, could directly call him Lomusse, but men and women of his own generation could only call him Vuga (second brother)—the birth-order name becomes a term of respect among his own generation. If people of the same generation called him Lomusse, it would be a serious discourtesy. (Naturally, expression of animosity is another matter.) The generation of his nephews would take the *ga* of his birth-order name and put an *a* in front of it, and call him Aga. The *a* put in front of the name is the *a* of *abbo* (father), so Aga means "second father." Classificatory sisters' sons would put an *o* in front and call him Oga, the *o* being a simplified way of saying *onyi* (mother's brother), and Oga thus meaning "second uncle." People with no kinship relationship to him, if they were of an older generation, could call him by name, and people of an age not much older or younger than he could call him Vuga. People of a younger generation could borrow the terms of address of people who had kinship relations with him. People who had none of the above relations with him would call him Aho Suyyi or Aho Mosu, using general terms of respect for an older person.

The various terms of address for a woman are basically the same as those for a man. For example, in the case of a woman called Aho Aga Quvie, the older generation would call her by her name, Quvie, while men and women of her own generation in her own clan, as well as children of her mother's sisters, would call her by her birth-order name, Aga. Children of her mother's brother's family would add Assa in front of her name, calling her Assa Aga, meaning mother's brother's daughter. Nieces and nephews of the same clan would have to add a *ba* before her birth-order name and call her Baga, with the *ba* being a phonetically altered simplified version of *abo,* or "father's sister." The children of her sisters, as well as the nephews' generation of her husband's clan, would put a *ma* in front of her name, calling her Maga, with *ma* a phonetically altered short version of *amo,* or mother, indicating a mother's sister. This term of address is related to the Nuosu marriage system, which is a preferential bilateral-cross-cousin marriage system, in which there is clan exogamy and prohibition of marriage with the classificatory mother's sister's children. So the terms of address used by mother's sister's children are the same as those used by members of her own clan.

To sum up, if a Nuosu person did not have a birth-order name, then there would be no way to express these kin relations. In the Liangshan Yi society, in which the clan corporation is the main structural form of society, terms of address have to fit with it, and the three-level system of naming—clan name, birth-order name, and personal name—realize it in a comprehensive way.

THE SO-CALLED YI FATHER-SON LINKED NAME SYSTEM

The idea that the Yi practice the system of father-son linked names has become a standard formulation that has made its way into a large number of authoritative reference works. On page 1495 of the *Concise Ci Hai* published by the Shanghai Dictionary Publishing House in 1979, it says, "Father-son linked name system (*fuzi lianming zhi* 父子連名制): A system of naming in which the name of the father and that of the son are linked over the generations. In China it still exists in some of the areas inhabited by several minority nationalities, such as Yi, Naxi, Lisu, Hani, Wa, and Jingpho. For example, among the Yi of Liangshan in Sichuan, Boshy Mugu (the name of the grandfather)—Mugu Jjiha (father)—Jjiha Vujjie (ego)." Wang Quangen, in his *Huaxia mingming mianmian guan* (An Overview of Personal Names among the Chinese), says,

> In the system of father-son linked names practiced by the Yi, the sound of the last character of the father's name becomes the sound of the first character of the son's name; in the same way, the sound of the last character in the son's name is used as the sound of the first character in the grandson's name. In this way, as names repeat themselves and continue for generations, the great interlinked genealogies of clan names have formed. In order to express a Yi person's birthright in the kinship system, and that person's place in the society of the Yi, the complete name of a Yi person is formed of the clan name (the original name of a tribe), the branch clan name (the name of a clan), the father's name, and the person's own name—four parts. Take, for example, the name of the deputy to the fifth National People's Consultative Conference Aho Bbujji Jjiha Lomusse (already seventy years old at the time). In this name, Aho is the original name of an Aho tribe; Bbujji is the name of his clan, Jjiha is his father's name, and Lomusse is his personal name; linking them together, the name says: Lomusse the son of Jjiha of the Bbujji clan of the Aho tribe. Within the Bbujji clan he is just called Lomusse. Within the Aho tribe, he is called Jjiha Lomusse (father's name and his own name). (Wang Quangen 1985)

Until now, all books that have referred to the naming system of the Yi have said that the Yi strictly adhere to the father-son linked name system, and thus that a Yi name is composed of the four levels: clan name, grandfather's name, father's name, own name. This is incorrect, and since it touches on the systematic evaluation of Yi society and culture, it is quite important that the mistake be corrected.

Why have so many experts and scholars stated that the Yi system of names is the father-son linked name system? This is connected to the genealogical system of Nuosu clans, in which father's name and son's name are linked across the generations. In the case of Aho Ddezze, the genealogical order is: Zuluo—Jjiha—Lomusse—Shuogge: when one recites the genealogy, one ordinarily leaves out the clan name and the birth-order name and uses only the third level of the system to link names together. In order to make the recitation easier and prevent omissions, one can change this to a recitation in a linked fashion: Aho Ddezze—Ddezze Zuluo—Zuluo Jjiha—Jjiha Lomusse—Lomu Shuogge. The example given in the *Ci Hai* is just this sort of genealogy. In addition, when Liangshan Yi are at war or in a formal situation, in order to amplify their ancestors and exalt themselves they often link together a relatively famous grandfather's name, father's name, and own name in a single recitation; for this reason people have mistakenly concluded that the Yi practice a father-son linked name system, and have seen this as an actual traditional pattern transmitted orally to today.

The Nuosu naming system thus provides us with insight into several facets of their society. The importance of clan organization is seen in the ubiquity of clan names and the pride of place taken by the clan name in the individual naming system. The importance of generational and age hierarchy is clearly reflected in the birth-order names and in the complex system of terms of address. And the economic and ecological bases of society are highly visible in the personal names people choose for their children.

CHAPTER 6

Homicide and Homicide Cases
in Old Liangshan

Qubi Shimei and Ma Erzi

Everybody who has done research on Yi society knows that in old Liangshan there was no organization holding coercive power and no military, police, courts, or jails to enforce social control, but nevertheless members of the whole society both strictly preserved internal social order and maintained social control in an orderly manner. What methods were used to effectively control social order and preserve it for hundreds or thousands of years? Few articles have discussed or investigated social control in Liangshan before the Democratic Reforms, and most of them have looked at this question from the standpoint of classes and social strata. Furthermore, although some of these articles have mentioned clan customary law, most have treated the issue only superficially.

This essay will examine customary laws used to settle cases of homicide within the patrilineal clan, along with a few case histories, in order to explain the stabilizing function of such customary laws in old Liangshan Yi society.

INTERNAL CLAN HOMICIDE CASES

Nuosu call homicide *coquo*, which means "smashing a person." Customary law defined a whole set of rules for settling homicide cases, which in Nuohxo are called *coquo dijie*, meaning "laws for settling homicide cases." These can be divided according to kinship relations into laws that settle cases of killing a clan mate, an affine, a woman, a maternal nephew, a husband or wife, or a nonrelative. According to occupation, they can be divided into laws that settle cases of killing a *ndeggu* (mediator), a *bimo* (priest), or a *jjojjo* (ordinary person). Homicide laws can also be divided according to social stratum into those that govern cases of killing an *nzymo*, a *nuoho*, a *quho*, a *mgajie*, or a *gaxy.* The judgment of and punishments for killing vary according to social circumstances. According to customary law, homicide includes not only deliberate killing but also causing someone to die by negligence, as well as causing someone, as a result of a quarrel, to use one of various methods to commit suicide, such as taking poison, hanging oneself, jumping into a river, or jumping off a cliff. The rules for settling a murder of someone within the clan are the most thorough, with absolutely no contingencies left unconsidered and no room for anyone to alter the methods of settlement.

Historically, it was absolutely necessary to carry out these laws according to a strict standard of justice. These were different from other kinds of homicide cases, in that other cases had definite temporal and spatial constraints on their settlement, and more lenient results could be sought through employing the power of the clan as a group or though various economic measures. Even those guilty of the most serious types of homicide could, if they had power or money, arrange a behind-the-scenes way to be spared. Homicides internal to the clan vitiated the usefulness of power or money and transcended the limits of space and time. It was just as the Nuosu proverb said: "Anyone who on earth has killed a clan mate will not be received in heaven by the ancestral spirits."

In the process of determining the legal rules for settling an intraclan homicide according to Liangshan Nuosu customary law, people did not think systematically about the justice of the rules. Nuosu believed that as long as they employed the principle of "those who hold the child do not cause the child to cry," that was satisfactory. When homicide occurred among members of the same clan, and a settlement was reached through negotiation between the close relatives of the killer and the victim so that there was no further trouble, then afterward people would naturally respect this method of settlement. Like a legal precedent, it would be transmitted from generation to generation and would gradually become a general and systematic rule. This is what is meant by the Nuosu proverb "If there are no precedents, how can there be legal rules?" In many respects Nuosu in Liangshan did not settle cases according to concrete legal statutes, but rather settled them according to like precedents. Still, the application of such precedents gradually extended until they became habitual customary laws or compacts, which everyone was compelled to obey through customary, moral, and religious strictures.

Liangshan intraclan homicides were divided according to their severity into *anuo, azzi,* and *aqu:* respectively, "black," "colored," and "white." Black refers to very serious cases, colored to semiserious cases, and white to not serious cases.

Black Cases

Cases of clan mates who, due to lack of respect for each other or for other people's lives or safety during quarrels or other discussions of differences, deliberately killed other members of their clan were black cases. Among these, if we divide them according to the method of killing, the most serious of all involved bashing with a rock, hitting with a club, or using metal tools or other blunt instruments to beat someone to death. These were called "jet black beating to death." Using a gun or knife to kill was the next most serious, called "blood-dripping killing." In black cases, all that could be done was to give the killer a time limit in which to take his own life. Before he died (most killers were male), it was impermissible to hit him or kill him or even to insult him. Close relatives and friends were to use gentle words to encourage him to kill himself: "The crime that you have committed, which shakes the heavens, was perhaps brought about by evil spirits from heaven. Even though the ultimate blame for the wrong lies with heaven, the two hands that perpetrated the crime are yours, so the life that has to be taken in return must be yours. Go ahead, don't be afraid—the ancestors have made the rules and the descendants have to follow them. Only this way are you a wise person, and otherwise you will have sullied the souls of the ancestors, as well as ruined the face of their descendants." As they were urging him, his close relatives and friends also prepared fine food for him, called sendoff feasts. When the time came, he could choose his own method of death—poisoning or hanging. When he died he was cremated immediately, without any solemn funeral proceedings. If he was not willing to kill himself to replace the life of the slain, clan mates would continuously urge him to kill himself, while at the same time keeping watch over him, offering him deadly poisons, ropes, and other means of committing suicide, until he finally capitulated. If he fled for his life and there was no means of capturing him and bringing him back, all nearby clan members were brought together, and a religious ceremony was held to expel him from the clan. All his property was confiscated and distributed among the close relatives of the deceased and other clan members.

If the killer was an only son, and his parents were already past reproductive age, and he was either unmarried or without sons, and he was not willing to kill himself, claiming destitution, in a few cases the death penalty could be voided by a meeting of clan members, and blood money paid as a penalty instead. Every clan had its own specific standards for blood money; there was no universal level for all of Liangshan. There were local and social stratum differences. Even so, the amount of blood money paid in compensation was basically the same everywhere and had to come entirely from the murderer's direct relatives, with no contributions allowed from other clan members.

For all of Liangshan, the commonly paid amounts of blood money in a black case varied according to stratum. A *nuoho* killer was required to provide three large pieces of good land, three large households of agricultural slaves, a horse to carry the ashes, a person to carry the ashes on his back, and a piece of silk to wrap the ashes. In addition, the blood money for the dead man was 1,700 ounces of silver, with an additional 1,200 ounces to the victim's mother's brother's family. A horse went to the victim's father's mother's brother's family. If the victim had children, they were to be provided with economic support while they were young; if they were unmarried they would receive money for bride-price and dowry. The price for hiring a *bimo* to exorcise evil spirits and send the soul on its way was 9 ingots of silver.

After all the above-mentioned compensation was paid, the killer knelt on the ground and used a drinking vessel made of a pig's foot or an ox or ram's horn to drink to the close relatives of the deceased. After the settlement was made, the killer and his generation could not live together with the other members of the clan, but had to move to a place near their mother's brother or to some other place. Nuosu called this "having enmity with their own clan, and so living with the mother's brother." After the killer died, if his children wanted strongly to return to the original clan home, recover their original clan membership, and receive the protection of the clan, they could do so— if they obtained the permission of the leaders and elders of the clan who discussed the matter—after undergoing a solemn religious ceremony. They would ask a *bimo* to perform the ceremony of "exorcism and reconciliation of a parricide," kill an ox, buy some liquor, offer them to the clan members living in the original home, and give some money to the relatives of the original crime victim; this was called drinking reconciliation liquor, eating reconciliation beef, and giving reconciliation money. Only after these procedures were carried out could the children of the killer be restored to their full clan membership. Otherwise it was said that misfortune would come to both sides. At the same time, the relatives of the original victim could still seek revenge, because in Nuosu thinking, the saying "If the grandson is strong, he will avenge his grandfather" describes a dignified way to behave. However, through the performance of religious ceremonies of reconciliation, people could eliminate this layer of enmity left by previous generations.

The blood money paid for a black-case homicide in a *quho* clan was a little bit less than that paid by *nuoho*. Usually the killer was required to provide 1,700 ounces of silver, a horse to carry the ashes, a man to carry the ashes on his back, and a piece of silk cloth to wrap the ashes. In addition, he gave 1,200 ounces of silver to the victim's mother's brother's family and a horse to the victim's father's mother's brother's family. If there were small children, he was required to give enough money to cover the cost of raising them, and if there were children not yet married, to contribute to wedding expenses. When a *bimo* was called to read scriptures to send off the soul of the deceased, he was given 9 ounces of silver. The murderer would kneel on the ground and, using a cup made of a pig's foot or an ox or ram's horn, drink individually to each relative of the victim and to each member of the ascending generation who was present. Members of the murderer's own generation were not allowed to live in the same place as the rest of their clan, and had to move to a place near their mother's brother's clan or to some other place. After the murderer died, if his children had a strong desire to return, they would have to seek general agreement, and then kill an ox of reconciliation, drink reconciliation wine, and pay reconciliation money before they could restore their original clan membership.

Colored Cases

If members of a clan ordinarily had no disputes between them, but one slipped unintentionally—for example, if a gun went off accidentally, or if one killed another accidentally during a battle, or if while working one rolled a rock or felled a tree that killed a fellow clan member, or if after a quarrel one committed suicide by jumping off a cliff, hanging himself, jumping into a river, or taking poison out of spite—then the perpetrator was guilty of a colored case. In a lot of colored cases, the perpetrator killed himself voluntarily at a time he himself decided, but generally not more than a month after the original death. During this time relatives and close friends could entertain him as much as they liked and encourage him to visit friends and relatives and to call together relatives and friends to make a parting statement. Everyone would praise his resolution and call him a man of courage. If the victim had said any last words expressing the fact that the two sides were the best of friends or exhorting the members of the clan to exercise lenient treatment or not to pursue the affair, then a meeting of the clan could authorize the loosening of certain conditions. But usually someone who had previously had this degree of closeness with the deceased would be determined to follow his friend to death without hesitation, so there would be no need for anyone to apply customary law.

If someone guilty of a colored-case killing did not want to take his own life, then usually the members of the clan would not coerce him to commit suicide, and he could pay blood money to compensate for the death. But in a case like this, people would not respect his actions. The amount of blood money paid varied from place to place and clan to clan. In general, among Nuosu in Liangshan there were two kinds of situations, as the following describes.

First, in a case of accidental death of a clan mate among *nuoho* living in the core areas of Liangshan, the blood money was 1,700 ounces of silver, plus the killer provided a horse to carry the ashes, a man to carry the ashes on his back, and a piece of silk to wrap the ashes. In addition, 1,200 ounces of silver went to the victim's mother's brother, a horse to the victim's father's mother's brother, and 9 ingots of silver to the *bimo*. The killer would pay a portion of the cost of animals sacrificed at the funeral. The blood money for

a person who killed himself by jumping into a river or off a cliff in consequence of a quarrel was 1,200 ounces of silver, along with 900 ounces for
the mother's brother's family, a horse for the father's mother's brother's family, 9 ingots for the *bimo*, and a portion of the cost of animals sacrificed at
the funeral. The blood money for one who took poison or hanged himself
was 900 ounces, along with 700 for the mother's brother's family, a horse
for the father's mother's brother's family, 9 ingots for the *bimo*, and a portion of the cost of sacrificial animals. For a poisoning, one horse was added
to the penalty.

The blood money for a colored case among the *quho* stratum in the core
areas was 1,200 ounces of silver, plus the cost of a horse to carry the ashes
and a man to carry the ashes on his back, 900 ounces of silver for the mother's
brother's family, a horse for the father's mother's brother's family, 9 ingots
for the *bimo*, and part of the cost of funeral sacrifices. For one who killed
himself by hanging, taking poison, or jumping off a cliff, the blood money
was 700 ounces, along with 500 ounces for the victim's mother's brother's
family, a horse for the father's mother's brother's family, 9 ingots for the *bimo*,
and a portion of the cost of sacrificial animals at the funeral. Another horse
was added in cases of poisoning.

In the second variant for colored cases, the accidental killing of a clan
mate among *nuoho* in peripheral areas where the Nuosu were in contact with
other peoples, the blood money was 1,200 ounces of silver, along with 600
ounces for the victim's mother's brother's family, 9 ingots for the *bimo*, and
a portion of the cost of the funeral sacrifices. For one who committed suicide by taking poison, hanging, jumping into a river or off a cliff, the blood
money was 600 ounces, along with 300 for the victim's mother's brother's
family, 9 ingots for the *bimo*, and a portion of the cost of the funeral sacrifices. Hanging added an extra horse. For *quho* in these areas who accidentally killed a member of their clan in a colored case, the blood money was
600 ounces, along with 300 for the mother's brother's family, 9 ingots for
the *bimo* and a portion of the cost of funeral sacrifices. For a suicide who
jumped into a river or off a cliff, took poison, or hanged himself, the blood
money was 300 ounces, along with 150 to the mother's brother's family, a
bimo's fee of 9 ingots, and a portion of the cost of funeral sacrifices. Suicide
by poisoning added a horse to the compensation.

White Cases

These usually referred to cases in which an individual committed suicide by
jumping into a river or off a cliff, took poison, or hanged himself, and in
which—even though no particular clan mate was directly implicated in pro-
voking the suicide—a certain clan member might have indirectly participated
by maligning or insulting the victim or by some other activity. The regula-

tions for settling white cases were generally the same across areas and social strata: compensation was usually a horse, a vat of wine, and hosting a feast for the relatives, for which the perpetrator sacrificed an ox or a pair of sheep; after this it was considered settled.

CASE HISTORIES

Cases in Nuoho Clans

In the Hxobulieto area of Meigu there was a man named Aho Gezuo Lahxa. Ordinarily he cared for nobody, and he was known for selfish behavior, which gradually developed to the point where he traveled around irresponsibly creating trouble, causing his close relatives to apologize right and left, pay fines left and right, and be extremely ashamed of his behavior. One time he was dragged back home by his nephew Aho Tidu Lati, who used iron fetters to lock him up in his house, where people had the idea that they could gradually educate him and cause him to give up his bad habits and become a moral person again. But a few days later, he took advantage of his attendants' lack of attention and managed to secretly unlock the fetters and flee. When he was discovered by Tidu Lati, and Lati yelled at him to come home again, he did not listen. Lati chased him but could not catch him, and in anger took up his gun and shot him dead.

Leaders of the Aho clan quickly gathered at the scene from all over. At their meeting they decided, after going over all angles of the case, that Lahxa's misbehaviors were real, but that an action must be requited with a like action, and a death with a death. They determined that for Lati, a member of a younger generation, to shoot to death his uncle Laha should surely be classified under the precedent of "plucking the feathers to kill the bird," and for this reason Lati would have to compensate with his life. When this decision was made, Lati was unwilling to commit suicide and he immediately fled. All the members of the clan chased him, but they were unable to catch him and he got farther and farther away from them. They decided they would all get their guns and shoot him simultaneously (so that if he were hit, the whole group, rather than an individual, would be responsible). But after a few volleys of shots they quickly lost the resolve to shoot, and Lati again fled into the distance.

After a short time, they heard that Lati had come back to settle at his mother's brother's house. The Aho clan gathered together again from an even wider area to hear the opinions of clan members. All agreed that Aho Lati had seriously violated clan rules, and that they could only allow him to take his life, that the case could not be settled by other means. After a few years, Aho Lati had no other recourse but to return to his original home and take his life. Before he died, they held a feast for him and prepared his funeral clothes, and he chose hanging as his method of taking his life. This case happened five generations ago.

In another case, the Hma clan living in Meigu sent out fighters to battle the Alu clan. On the road they ran into Alu Ggehxa, who took up rocks to pelt the Hma fighters. When Hmasse Shyha arrived to mediate, he was accidentally killed by Hmasse Zhybuo. The two were cousins twelve generations removed, so Zhybuo was not willing to take his own life to atone for this. The Hma clan who discussed the matter decided that "a hen laid an egg by mistake; it's not the case of the hen eating her own egg; it's a sow mistakenly giving birth to a piglet, not a sow eating her own piglet." Zhybuo mistakenly killed Shyha while he was serving his clan in a confusing situation, and because of this if he were unwilling to take his life, then it was permissible to pay blood money in compensation. In the end, he paid 1,700 ounces of silver in blood money, along with 1,200 to Shyha's mother's brother's family, a horse to his father's mother's brother's family, and 9 ingots to the *bimo*. In addition they killed a reconciliation ox, drank reconciliation liquor, and paid reconciliation money. Zhybuo knelt and drank to each member of the senior generation one by one, and so this case was resolved.

Cases in Quho Clans

At Hxtobulashy in Meigu, there was a conflict between Jjiemu Lyhuo and Jjiemu Abi, and one day during a quarrel Lyhuo killed Abi. After killing him, Lyhuo was not willing to kill himself, so his relatives built him a simple lean-to and killed an ox for him to eat. After this, his brothers and his children all urged him to commit suicide, telling him clearly that, since he had killed a clan mate, if he did not give his life they would give their lives in his place. They asked how he could go on living after that. After five days, Lyhuo took poison to kill himself, and after this the relatives on both sides got along very well. This case happened four generations ago.

In 1939 at Zala Shan in Yanyuan, in the ordinary course of discussion between Ddisse Shuosse and his uncle Ddisse Nyinyi, both of the Bacha clan, there had emerged a few small conflicts. One day Nyinyi's son Xifasse was out looking for a stray ox, carrying a gun on his back, and when he was partway there he ran into Shuosse's two sisters digging potatoes by the roadside. When their dog came over and bit Xifasse, he asked the sisters several times to chase the dog away. Perhaps because the two of them did not hear him, he became angry and picked up his gun and shot the dog dead. When Shuosse heard about this, he quickly ran after Xifasse, threatening to kill him. Xifasse, thinking he was no match for Shuosse, kept running in fear of his life. After running for quite a long stretch, thinking that Shuosse was too much of a bully, Xifasse turned around and shot Shuosse dead with one shot, after which he fled to his mother's brother's house to hide.

Upon hearing this, members of the Bacha clan from all over gathered at Nyinyi's house. Some felt that Xifasse would have to kill himself, because if he did not, order in the Bacha clan would be ruined. Others felt that since Nyinyi had just one son, and because he was already old and unable to have more children, it would be best if they paid blood money according to custom. One of the leaders of a *nuoho* clan, Luoho Nyidu, used his long-standing good relations with Nyinyi to urge the leaders of the Bacha clan to settle the case by paying blood money according to custom. After going back and forth considering the question, it was settled that blood money appropriate to a black case would be paid. All of Nyinyi's family's land was given to the relatives of the deceased, and half their oxen, sheep, horses, and domestic slaves were given to the relatives of the deceased (at that time, Nyinyi's family was among the first rank of wealthy families in this area, and thus the amount given was not small). The family also paid 333 ounces of silver, a rifle, sacrificial goods for the funeral, and the fee for the *bimo*. Every one of the leaders and elders of the Bacha clan who took part in the settlement of this case got an ingot of silver. At the time of the settlement, Xifasse knelt on the ground and drank to all the elders out of an ox-hoof cup. He killed a settlement ox, bought settlement liquor, and feasted members of the clan. As soon as the process was completed, Nyinyi's whole family immediately moved to live at a place about ten kilometers away.

CONCLUSION

The clans of the Nuosu in Liangshan are organized kinship groups based on patrilineal descent through genealogical links from father to son over the generations. These lineages are called *cyvi* in the Nuosu language and are divided into two kinds of relationships—*cy* means relatively close descent relations, usually within seven generations; *vi* refers to relations separated by more than seven generations. Whether between the *cy* within seven generations or between the *vi* separated by more than seven generations, there is a strict prohibition on intermarriage. In the Nuosu society of old Liangshan, the clan organization guaranteed the basic social existence of the individual; in customary terms, an individual who was not a member of a clan in old Liangshan would not survive long. The strength or weakness of a clan usually was closely connected to the satisfaction or dissatisfaction of the individual. A Yi proverb says that in being a man, "it is best to be a tree that forms part of the fence protecting the clan; next best is to be part of the earth that supports this fence; after that one wants to receive the attention of clan members." This means that if one cannot be one of the organizers of his own clan, he will still want to be one of its vanguard. In the Nuosu language *Hmamu teyy* (The Book of Knowledge), it says, "For nine generations you should under no conditions leave the clan; if you do leave the clan you should under no conditions incur any enmity; if you leave the clan and incur enmity, then you will have enemies and have nobody to help you; you will float lonely and alone in other peoples' homes, acting as their slave." We can see the importance of the clan in Liangshan Nuosu society.

We can say that a particular social environment produced a particular social system, and the customary law of the Liangshan Nuosu developed continuously and completely on the primary basis of clan law. The warp of clan customary law extended to produce the law for settling disputes between affines; the woof extended to produce the law on settling disputes between elders and juniors according to generational position and the law of relations between social strata on the basis of descent relationships. The enforcement of these various customary laws was carried out by the clans; apart from the clans a lot of customary laws would become worthless checks, not excepting the law of social strata. By examining the laws governing intraclan homicide and several case studies, we can broadly discern that paying with one's life and compensating with blood money were, ultimately, ways of unraveling the myriad threads of vengeance woven into the term *relative*.

In the discussion of how a case would be settled, there appear around the central figure of the victim two kinds of kinship relations: the inner circle consists of clan relations (close relatives and clan mates); the outer circle consists of affinal relations (the mother's brother's family and the father's mother's brother's family). The mother's brother's family referred to here is not just the mother's brother himself: for the Liangshan Nuosu, all men of the mother's clan are considered part of the mother's brother's family. The blood money paid to the mother's brother's family is equally divided, so that collateral uncles also get a share.

Many clans' internally determined customary laws are continuously legitimated versions of cases that have settled disputes within the clans. Their style of management is democratic, in that nobody is allowed to take his own measures against the wishes of the majority of clan members. The autonomy of the clan is very strong, as is the autonomy of the individual. Commonly, in the course of regular life, many able individuals have emerged and established their own particular reputations, such as the *ndeggu* and *suyyi,* who had an acute sense that allowed them to settle disputes; the *ssakuo,* who bravely stood at the vanguard in war; and the *suga* who accumulated great wealth without setbacks. But none of them could act arbitrarily within the clan group. The clan determined customary law, and customary law united the group very closely. Within the warp and woof of clan customary law, a whole set of Nuosu customary laws was developed, and this set of customary laws made an overriding contribution to social order in the Nuosu area of old Liangshan.

CHAPTER 7

Searching for the Heroic Age of the Yi People of Liangshan

Liu Yu

Liangshan before the revolution of 1956 was a contradictory society full of the spirit of the Heroic Age. Competition and development, conservatism and stagnation, slave levies and exploitation: all were interwoven here. Of course, most of those able to take part in competition were *nuoho* (Black Yi) of noble rank, and after them *qunuo* (commoners). As for the slaves—*gaxy,* people of other nationalities who had been captured—they were deprived of all rights. For them there was no equality on which they could depend, only exploitative enslavement. It is a common element of class societies that the freedom of some people is sacrificed in order to bring about other people's development; in Liangshan society this circumstance was more nakedly displayed. In discussing the Heroic Age, Qian Mingzi has stated: "This is an age of rebellion, and also an age of hope; it is an age in which boundless evil is brought about by private desires between people; and it is an age in which the human race has, from the barbarous state, entered a stage of civilization. In these times, the standard of justice and wickedness is whether or not something benefits one's own tribe. People depend on courage and force of arms to protect themselves, and warfare is an important means of increasing the wealth of oneself and one's own group. Martial prowess is seen as the highest virtue" (1982, 91).

If we ignore Toynbee's criticism of the Heroic Age from the standard of civilization, then his characterization of the Heroic Age matches Qian's. Toynbee wrote, "The sociological explanation is to be found in the fact that the Heroic Age is a social interregnum in which the traditional habits of primi-

The author is grateful for the kind help and guidance of Professor Stevan Harrell of the University of Washington, and Professor Wang Qingren and Associate Professor Leng Fuxiang of Central University of Nationality. The manuscript draft was translated by David Prager Banner.

tive life have been broken up, while no new 'cake of custom' had yet been baked by a nascent civilization or a nascent higher religion. In this ephemeral situation a social vacuum is filled by an individualism so absolute that it overrides the intrinsic differences between the sexes" (1957, 1422–23).

Of course, a heroic age is a special period in which an ethnic group can concentrate its own power and stimulate its own sense of pride. It is also a turning point for an ethnic group on its way to unity and maturity. For those peoples who have experienced it, even though their heroic ages took place at different times, the patterns were quite similar. War was pervasive, and the major cause for war was pressure from both inside and outside. However, this does not mean that a heroic age can appear at any time; that is, without the occurrence of specific historical conditions. Generally speaking, a heroic age would appear only when an ethnic group was still in separated tribal society, a circumstance that could unify the group, complete its character, and make it a powerful nationality. But the warlike style of a heroic age leads to the fact that the period must be short. If a society long remained in its heroic age, it could not exist in the civilized world or, at least, could not develop sufficiently.

The Yi people of Liangshan were a typical example in this regard. Ceaseless war in Liangshan during the Heroic Age of the Yi destroyed local productivity, hampered the growth of the economy, and restricted political development. One reason that Liangshan Yi society could exist in a special environment surrounded by class society might have resulted from its heroic spirit, which became the ideological prompt that caused the Liangshan Yi people to unify consistently and fight bravely against outside invasions. For us today, it is the living scene of Liangshan Yi people that turns the Greek myths and the poems of Homer into reality and shows a lifelike picture of the Heroic Age. Reading the Greek myths and the poems of Homer I have felt this heroic spirit most deeply. But these are merely myths and old poems. The Liangshan Yi view of life seems to exhibit before my very eyes the vivid image of another heroic age. I feel the strong ethnic pride and cohesion of the Yi, and the great value of their customs, culture, ornamentation, and all the rest. These things are inseparably bound to the heroic temperament that perpetuates this age, deeply enticing me to explore.

A wealth of research has been conducted about the Yi people of Liangshan and their society as they were prior to the 1950s. By and large almost all researchers have fixed their sights on the "cruel and bloodstained" slave system. Judging from the materials in my possession, there was doubtless a significant element of "cruelty and blood" in Liangshan society, yet many scholars have never deeply explored other elements: the society's spirit of valor, resourcefulness, eloquence, and competitiveness—all of which are characteristics of a heroic age. In my opinion, it is necessary to research this aspect in detail if we want to thoroughly understand either the society or the Yi people of Liangshan.

I. THE HEROIC AGE—ANOTHER ASPECT
OF THE YI, SEEN THROUGH THEIR SAYINGS

Toynbee wrote:

> From the scientific standpoint, it is a mere accident of no scientific significance that the material tools which Man has made for himself should have a greater capacity to survive, after they have been thrown on the scrap-heap, than Man's psychic artifacts: his institutions and feelings and ideas. Actually, while this mental apparatus is in use, it plays a vastly more important part than any material apparatus can ever play in human lives; yet because of the accident that a discarded material apparatus leaves, and a discarded psychic apparatus does not leave, a tangible detritus, and because it is the métier of the archaeologist to deal with human detritus in the hope of extracting from it a knowledge of human history, the archaeological mind tends to picture Homo Sapiens as Homo Faber par excellence. (1939, 156)

In the case of the Liangshan Yi, it is merely a result of certain historical circumstances that their transition from a clan society to a political society was especially drawn out. It is exactly for this reason that the psychic artifacts of the Heroic Age—institutions and feelings and ideas—are not only preserved by Liangshan Yi society but also, as Toynbee said, play a more important role than any material tool in the society. The great numbers of proverbs in the Yi language, along with the patriclan system, are the psychic artifacts of the Liangshan Yi Heroic Age that do remain. The Yi people are a nationality with a profound culture, and the Liangshan Yi demonstrate this profundity in their corpus of proverbs, full of wisdom, experience, and customs. These proverbs are the crystallized life experience of the Yi, the flower of the Yi language, the very measure of their life and deportment. Many proverbs fairly overflow with heroic sentiments.[1]

> In battle one thinks not of life; in the field one thinks not of death.

> One thinks not of thrift when entertaining a guest; one thinks not of one's life when fighting or killing enemies.

> No one gives way when wrestling; no one flees when caught in a hold.

> There is no boy that does not wish to be brave; there is no girl that does not wish to be beautiful.

> When one goes into the forest one does not fear leopards; when one guards the crops one does not fear bears.

> When one climbs high cliffs one does not fear vultures; on the battlefield one does not fear sacrifice.

---

1. Translator's note: These proverbs are all translated from the Chinese shown in the author's draft, not from the original Yi.

Yi men from the mountains are brave; Yi women from the mountains are beautiful.

To wrestle is to want to win; to win is to want to be famous.

If I am not strong, other people are not weak.

What these deceptively simple expressions of heroism show is the very soul of the Yi. Once you remove the pettiness and degradation of the people involved in the slave society, what are revealed are the value and pursuit of life.

Scholars in the past have paid attention only to certain particular features of this slave society, have researched only the four castes of this society within the framework of class oppression; naturally, what they have seen is the misery of the *gaxy* and the overbearing character of the *nuoho* nobility. But if we take the Yi clan system as our viewpoint, we will see that within clan society the *nuoho* and *qunuo* are actually living in a society of egalitarian competition, and that within their clans not only does oppression not exist, but there is no personal authority above that of the clan as a whole. In fact, up until the beginning of the 1950s, there were no administrative divisions equivalent to the township *(xiang)*, district *(qu)*, or county *(xian)* among the Yi; much less had they evolved a unified regime. Of the Lolo Xuanwei Authority set up under Mongol rule—and even the Jianchang *tusi* (local ruler) who was the highest authority in Ming-era Liangshan—it was said that "although in name he is the administrator in chief, he doesn't even have fixed fortified village sites" (Gu 1831, chap. 65, 26a). That is to say, the famous Lili *tusi* who served as Jianchang headman did not even supervise property and people by *zhai* (village) territorial units; he imposed levies and exacted tribute not by geography but by the traditional system of clans. For instance, he exacted tax and tribute according to the social position of the various *nzymo* and *nuoho* clans of Adu *tusi*, Azhuo *tusi*, Jiejue *tumu* (local government officers), Alu, Aho, Ezha, Hma, Ga, and so on. If even the Lili *tusi* did things this way, then there is no question about the other *tusi* and *tumu*. Actually, the titles *tusi* and *tumu* applied only to the people who lived near Han areas, the so-called familiar, or cooked, barbarians *(shouyi)*. As for the uncontrollable Nuosu in the heart of Liangshan, the so-called alien or raw barbarians *(shengfan)*, the *Annals of Mabian Sub-prefecture* written during the Jiaqing period of Qing Dynasty has this to say: "Although the Black-Bones *[heigutou]* family belongs to the same clan as the *tubaihu* [local government officers], it looks to the strength of its own people, it has its own subdivisions, and it governs its own clansmen; the *tubaihu* cannot give it orders."[2] Again, "those that live in the Han area and are under the administration of the *tusi* and *tushe* [local government officers] are the friendly barbarians, numbering some three or four thousand households; those in [the heart of] Liangshan are alien barbar-

---

2. *Tubaihu* means a low-ranking *tusi* or native official.

ians, and number in the tens of thousands of households" (Leibo 1796–1820). For the members of the Yi clans, it is absolutely true that "as eggs are all the same in size, every *nuoho* is equally important." For other clans, "horsemen are all of one clan, infantry are all of one clan, farmers are all of one clan, those who hold the golden staff are all of one clan, those who hold the wooden staff are all of one clan; and the farmers' clan is not afraid of the clan with golden staves." The Chinese feudal dynasties enfeoffed local officials in Yi society with the idea of "raising up the best men and ruling all the others," with the purpose of "ruling Barbarians by means of Barbarians," but this ran exactly counter to the Yi principle of "every *nuoho* is equally important." And so the officials chosen by the Chinese court often met with united resistance by *nuoho* clans.

For example, two hundred years ago, the Alu and Hma clans joined forces to defeat the Jiejue *tumu,* driving the Shama *tusi* from Meigu district to Wagang and dividing the land and slaves they captured. Only a generation before this, the Aho clan had crushed the Xinji *tusi* (Sichuan Sheng bianji zu 1987, 67). That the *nuoho* dared to rebel and attack the *tusi* and *tumu* was no doubt because they could not bear the heavy taxation and because they were greedy for the slaves and land of the *tusi* and *tumu.* This illustrates even more fully the true feeling of the Yi that "Nuoho have no masters; they speak and act of their own will." This feeling is a psychological portrait of a heroic age.

The experiences of the Yi through history have taught them that "a strong clan can defeat a strong enemy." Indeed, their strong clans, linked by blood bonds, became the "hundred-armed giants" of Greek myth. In the face of these hundred-armed giants, the 93 percent of the population that was ruled (including ordinary *quho* and true slaves) had no means of resistance. One *nuoho* has described things this way: "If a *gaxy* belonging to a *nuoho* household ran away or did something serious, the household merely got in touch with the head of their branch of the clan, and the news quickly reached the heads of all the individual families of relatives. All the branches could get in touch with each other to coordinate or research means of dealing with the problem. No matter where the *gaxy* was sold, just like a frog that has fallen into a basin he or she would have great difficulty going back." Imagine if the Nuosu clans had not had this clan blood bond—it would have been much easier for slaves to abscond, and the *nuoho* would have lost their mighty network of rule. By governing separately, using only the chain and the whip, it would have been impossible for the minority *nuo* (*nuo* means noble; *nuoho* indicates a specific group of nobles) nobility to rule the slave majority. That is why the Yi proverb says "The horse's strength is in its waist, the ox's strength is in its neck; the *nuoho's* strength is in his clan."

Nuoho clans, linked by blood ties, could not only deal with slaves who were ideologically shackled, whose clans had dispersed, or who lacked a clan altogether, but even the Kuomintang (KMT) army was once routed abjectly before them, as when the old KMT Twenty-fourth Division sent heavily armed troops to attack Puxiong. The Aho clan called a meeting of family heads and through consultation managed to stop internal feuds and squabbling among the branches. Next, the Aho and Guoji clan heads held a meeting and stopped the armed feud between those two clans. Finally, separate clans convened and mobilized their respective members to fight. In the end, a whole regiment of the Twenty-fourth Division was destroyed by the combined fighting strength of the Aho and Guoji clans, the KMT army was driven out of Puxiong, and hundreds of its troops fell into slavery (became *gaxy*) (Sichuan Sheng bianji zu 1987, 69).

It was precisely this summoning of clan power that allowed the *nuoho* to rule within and resist attack without. The clan system was a powerful social organizing force for them, whether politically, economically, or militarily. Under the flag of one's own blood clan, everyone had a common enemy and everything was directed outward. And so a Yi saying compares the clan to indispensable necessities of life like food and clothing: "What you must own are cattle and sheep; what you must eat is food, what you must have is your clan."

The clan could also make a stand for the sake of one member or for the benefit of one family. For instance, when the Ssehxo subclan of the Vulie clan killed Aho Sseha, Sseha's elder brother sought help from the subclan to take revenge for the dead. At the clan meeting, it was agreed that if one person's murder were not taken seriously, then the safety of the whole clan could not be guaranteed, and so they launched a revenge party. In another example, Aho Degie was so poor that he didn't have enough to eat. People in the clan pooled grain to give him, while others invited him to eat with them. After he died, all his burial expenses were paid by people in the clan (Sichuan Sheng bianji zu 1987, 68). Conversely, the clan demanded the willing sacrifice of individuals for the benefit of the whole clan. Take the example of the Suxie and Ashy branches of the Jjidi clan, which were having a feud. For the sake of peace negotiations, the Suxie forfeited the lives of two of its own members, which put an end to the feud (ibid., 152). By doing so, the Suxie branch preserved itself from the brink of destruction and upheld the entire clan's rule of the *qunuo* and the castes below them. A proverb says "If you fail to protect one household, the whole clan is in danger; if you fail to protect the clan, the whole thing will be picked bare." On this basis stood both the protection of an individual and the demand for sacrifice of an individual—both were done for the sake of the whole. Otherwise, both the clan and its individual members would have been weaker; they were bound together, sharing whatever life brought, for better or for worse. Because every Nuosu grasped this, there were countless souls willing to volunteer to die for the good of the clan. In autumn 1931, for example,

Ssenra Mushu, head of the Ssenra branch of the Luohxo clan, willingly offered his head to the KMT warlord Deng Xiuting in order to preserve the collective of his own branch (ibid.). Bronislaw Malinowski said that one of the duties of culture is to ensure the safety of humanity: "Safety refers to the prevention of bodily injuries by mechanical accident, attack from animals or other human beings. . . . Under conditions where most organisms are not protected from bodily injury the culture and its group will not survive" (1942, 91–92).

It is true that the clan system of the Nuosu of Liangshan offered protection to each member; therefore Liangshan people sigh, "For Yi to have kin is more important than anything; lack anything, but do not lack kin" (Sichuan Sheng bianji zu 1987, 69). In Liangshan, clan heads merely attended to common activities of the society when required or at the request of clan members. In daily life, Liangshan people attended to their own affairs—*nuoho* ruled their slaves of different classes, using the power of their blood bonds within the district where they lived. And so the saying goes: "The *nuoho* have no master; the clan is their master." Indeed, one single phrase sums up the true meaning of Liangshan society—the individual belongs to the clan.

II. UPBRINGING AND LIFE AMONG THE LIANGSHAN YI

In Liangshan, *nuoho* clan structure was a tool for protecting the privileges of the *nuoho* nobility and oppressing the ruled ranks. Common hero worship stimulated individual ability and molded the spiritual vigor of those who possessed the talent needed by society. As for the ruled *quho* ranks, they depended on clan structure for protection and took *nuoho* hero worship as their model. Both *nuoho* and *quho* wanted their own clans to be powerful and to produce heroes, generation after generation. To achieve this, the society formed a whole set of norms for raising and training the young, including the following.

1. Reciting One's Family Tree

"All Kachins recognize the existence of an elaborate system of patrilineal clanship elaborately segmented. The lineages of this clan system ramify throughout the Kachin Hills Area and override all frontiers of language and local custom" (Leach 1954, 57). Similarly, the Nuosu also understand their genealogies and use them to confirm their kinship relations. Nuosu, regardless of whether they are *nuoho* or *quho*, must have from a young age a complete understanding of the environment in which they live. This environment consists foremost of a network of blood relations, on one hand, and interpersonal relations, on the other. Children come to comprehend their place in the clan by reciting their genealogy. Someone who can recite this genealogy can find an advantage in any situation and escape from danger. Vice Party Secretary Asu Daling of Lijiang Prefecture in Yunnan (who is Yi) has said that, prior to the 1950s, if a Yi person who belonged to a clan had the misfortune to be taken into bondage somewhere unfamiliar, as long as that person could recite his or her genealogy he or she could find relatives or kinsmen and obtain their help or protection. This is why people who were captured from other nationalities or other Yi outside Liangshan and then enslaved would link their genealogies to a *quho* family tree. In Liangshan, only if one had a place in Nuosu genealogy, and had thus become recognized as a full member of Nuosu society, could one use this identity to get a certain security within society for oneself and one's family. Only then would the clan offer solicitude and protection for one's living conditions and personal security.

Even in contemporary Liangshan society these functions of genealogy continue to play vital roles. In the early 1990s, when my father Liu Yaohan was doing a survey in Lesser Liangshan on the Sichuan-Yunnan border, Ma Xudong, a cadre of Ninglang County, paid him a courtesy visit. It was chilly weather in early spring, but Ma came wearing only an unlined jacket. It turned out (when my father inquired) that Ma had run into someone on the way, and upon reciting their genealogies they discovered that they were kin. The other man was in difficulty and had come to ask for help from his relatives; Ma not only gave him all the money and property he had on him but he even took off his coat and gave that to the man. If the man had not been able to recite his genealogy, things would have turned out as described in a Nuosu saying: "If you can't say your father's genealogy, your clan will not acknowledge you; if you can't say your mother's brother's genealogy, your kin will not acknowledge you." It is without doubt that in the Liangshan of forty-odd years ago, with all its incessant conflicts, genealogies linking the names of fathers and sons—serving as the direct manifestation of the blood ties in one's patrilineal clan—bore a heavy responsibility for the social security of every single person in this society. To put it another way, the network of connotative blood ties of a genealogy had in fact already become a social insurance system. Genealogies could even serve as individuals' "safe conduct," because with them, they could "carry no provisions when traveling among one's clan, and [still] have safety for one's parents, children, and spouse by relying on the clan."

2. Cultivating Intelligence and Physical Prowess

Liangshan did not develop specialized schools for training youth like those in Sparta, but Liangshan children were cultivated by their fathers and elder brothers, knowingly or not. When *nuoho* Guoji Kenyu was young, his father taught him to be brave and resolute, to swim, and to surmount all obstacles when carrying out a feud. He told him that if he wanted his family to have a good livelihood, then in addition to being frugal he must seize extra grain, slaves, and livestock from his enemies. He also considered himself to have the most prestige of anyone in his clan and to be an example for imitation (Sichuan Sheng bianji zu 1987, 67). The sort of education that Guoji Kenyu received was exactly the kind ordinarily given to the children of *nuoho* and even *qunuo* by the clan organization. Just as the Nuosu saying has it, "There is no boy that does not wish to be brave," so in fact there were no Nuosu that did not wish their sons to be brave. Because feuding between enemies had gone on for such a long time without abating, militaristic thinking had had an influence on all ordinary Yi and an especially profound influence on the *nuoho*. Hence, when they taught their children, they subconsciously stressed athletic training and mastery of weapons. Yi children learned to throw pebbles, swim, and compete in running races at the age of five or six; at seven or eight, boys could already ride horseback—a Yi saying goes, "At seven, *nuoho* lead horses to ride."

There is one more skill they learned from an early age: wrestling, a form of exercise that Nuosu take when they are happy. It is also a game played when male cousins of different surnames meet, to vie with each other in strength. *Nuoho* not only stressed the training of the bodies and wills of their children but also took great care in training them in ideology and self-expression. In their view, "If one doesn't guard the clan, the whole area will be robbed bare." The supremacy of the clan was something over which they brooked no doubt, and it is for this reason that elders often exhorted the young to recognize that "toward family members one must be obliging, toward relatives by marriage one should smile effusively, toward kin and friends one must be kind, toward enemies one must be malicious." Thus they constructed in the minds of children and youths a firm sense of clan. In this mindset, someone who stole slaves or livestock from a rival clan became the subject of laudatory tales, while someone who stole property from his own clansmen was viewed as lacking in moral values. Therefore a saying warned that "one who deceives his own kin will be fined nine armloads of arrows; one who deceives his own family will be fined good horses."

Elders often narrated to the young the deeds of their ancestors on the battlefield and boasted about their own battle prowess: how many people they killed, how much loot they plundered from the enemy. This sort of informal education could take place at any time and in any circumstances. For example, at a funeral, people would always sing about the glorious deeds of the departed person: "When you were alive, Grandfather, none could rival you in swift riding on the battlefield, and you exposed yourself to danger without fear. In charges you were at the very front, and in withdrawals you were at the very rear" (Butuo County n.d., 275). This manner of taking advantage of important occasions such as weddings and funerals to educate and inspire young people in story and song was one of the most effective teaching methods in the days before there were schools, and it has been used by all ethnic groups at one time or another. In evaluating Nuosu education, one may consider the words of Robert H. Lowie: "All this was capital vocational training. . . . Above all, the natural way of letting play and imitation largely take the place of deliberate and formal precept is quite up-to-date" (1929, 176–78).

The Nuosu were not alone in using these methods. The method of training children in ancient Sparta evolved into an entire system. Although Liangshan Yi did not yet have the same system as ancient Sparta, the goals and many of the training methods of Yi were very similar to those of Spartans. To the Spartans, only by becoming an out-and-out warrior could one fully be a Spartan. To this end, newborn infants were subjected to strict inspection, which only the fit survived. Spartan children stayed with their mothers only until the age of seven. Even though the mother and child were together only a short time, the mother never pampered her child but instead used every means to cultivate a brave and cool-headed character in her child that would be uncomplaining, not picky about food, not afraid of the dark, and not afraid to be independent. At the age of seven, a boy would leave home and join a national corps of children, which would receive a strict, unified education. This education stressed physical training, mock battle, and debate. Sparta actually encouraged children to steal from a young age, with the aim of fostering in them craftiness and bravery. Aside from making children into fit warriors by training them in strength, courage, discipline, and deceit, elders also inculcated them with the stories of heroic figures and boasted about their own deeds (Liu Jiahe 1963, 26–28).

Compared with the Nuosu, though, the Spartans were almost cruel to children; and they were openly threatening to the helots. This is because at that time, Sparta was already a highly developed country with a slave system; the main reason it trained its children in this way was to suppress the resistance of the helots. But though the original heroic spirit of the Spartans had already been utterly sullied by the slave master's cruelty, they had only recently passed through a heroic age, and through selfless training they were still able to demonstrate a heroic spirit. The training the Nuosu put their children through also had an aspect aimed at slaves; but in Liangshan, bursting as it was with the glory of the Heroic Age, the slaves utterly lacked the ability to put up resistance and were certainly not the main targets of the heroism demonstrated by the *nuoho*. The *nuoho* saw slaves as their property, indeed as their subjects of their guardianship. For example, since they expected the slaves to do their bidding, should anyone cheat their slaves they had the responsibility to take vengeance, lest they fail to be good masters and their slaves run away or be stolen. The *nuoho* nobility had to be like "the stout tree on the mountaintop that blocks the wind and storms; the firm rock on the river shore that blocks the harsh waves and storms." While this had a deterrent effect on the slaves, it also gave them a sense of security. A saying goes, "If the master is as big as a tiger, the slave can be as big as a leopard." The slave master used this technique of "hard and soft fists" to keep his own slaves firmly tethered while enticing other people's slaves to come to him. This latter technique was something even more commendable in Liangshan. Unlike the Spartans, the *nuoho* aimed their martial spirit mainly at enemies and interlopers of the same class. Hence they educated their children to be "tough to those outside, and amiable to those within." One had to become a hero who "is a hero because of what he can do."

Naturally, in Liangshan talent was not limited to military prowess; this society valued resourcefulness and eloquence even more, and people with these qualities were even more greatly esteemed and respected. There are Nuosu proverbs to prove this: "A fist can break through one layer; the tongue can break through nine"; "Property can fill a cubbyhole; the tongue can fill nine cubbyholes."

It was just for this reason that in Liangshan society everyone—men and women alike—were articulate and eloquent, and plenty of women became *ndeggu* (mediators). A proverb says, "Ten people without brains cannot beat one with brains." That a society values intelligence to such a high degree is one indication that it is experiencing a vigorous heroic age. By contrast, consider the endless stifling of human talent in feudal societies, which deprecate knowledge by saying things like "Three stinky tanners are better than one Zhuge Liang." All in all, the young were trained by participating in society: they looked to heroes, or indeed became heroes themselves, whether by using intelligence—that is, eloquence and ability to mediate quarrels—or skills, such as riding and archery.

3. Counting Time by Battles

In olden times, the frequency of armed feuds made going into battle one of the main elements of life. This was because "the enmity of the Nuosu cannot be forgotten, and the joints of the fir will not rot." And it was because "only the son who seeks revenge for his grandfather counts as number one; only the son who seeks revenge for his father counts as number two." Thus wars and pillage took place incessantly and over a long period of time. The eminent late-Ming thinker Gu Yanwu wrote that the Nuosu "think of battle as an everyday occurrence and of pillage as a way of farming" (1831, chap. 68, 25b). And this epitomizes perfectly the whole heroic air of Yi life. Up to the sixth decade of this century, warfare continued to play an important role in Yi life. Their behavior and attitude in battle fully expressed their heroic mettle. Before going out to fight, men ate the best foods and put on their best clothes in order to concentrate their energy and raise their spirits to high pitch. This shows what they thought of the value of human life: if you must die, die splendidly and without regret. The ancient Qiang, who share their origins with the Yi, held that "to die of old age is misfortune; to die in battle is glory." At the end of the last century, the gun had not yet arrived in Liangshan, and the Yi still wore their exquisite helmets and armor of lacquer with leather padding, their arm greaves and elbow guards; they still had their bows and arrows tucked into their waistbands, swords and spears in their hands, and yak tails flying from their backs. Their whole appearance exuded the very ideal of the saying "Sallying into battle, there is no one who does not want to be brave." In order to give this impression, they would sometimes hold pledging ceremonies or horse races.

Lowie said, "Primitive man wants, above all, to shine before his fellows; he craves praise and abhors the loss of 'face.' . . . He risks life itself if that is the way to gain the honor of a public eulogy" (1929, 156–58). And these hallmarks have been extremely prominent among the Liangshan Yi. A *nuoho* injured on the battlefield "must clench his jaws shut and not let out so much as a gasp, lest he be ridiculed by the other *nuoho.* Losing face in view of slaves—for instance falling captive to the enemy—is worse still, and he will by all means rather commit suicide than surrender." When *quho* clans fought their enemies, both sides invited their masters, who professed to be the "protectors" of the *quho;* not to take part would mean being laughed at, being thought timid. In battle, the masters would display valor in order to win over slaves and make themselves look good. Someone in the Buji clan once said, "He is *nuoho;* I am *nuoho;* why should I fear him?" This kind of thinking is precisely why Liangshan was the stage of so many wars—armed feuds! And so Qumo Zangyao has said, "Within the 360-odd days of one year, there is no one in all of Luoyi who will not take up arms and do battle" (1933, 55). The idea of "taking up arms and doing battle" had a high *aesthetic* appeal to Nuosu. A Nuosu saying goes, "*Nuoho* are most beautiful with the smell of gun smoke all around them; women are most beautiful with the smell of gold and silver on their bodies." Clearly, courage and wealth were what Liangshan society esteemed. And courage had to be embodied—wealth had to be obtained—through "the smell of gun smoke." So Liangshan society was one in which "the land does not have feet, but masters are often changed; the enemy does not have wings, but the sky is filled with them in flight"; and "there is no kin who is not enemy; there is no enemy who is not kin."

4. Peacemaking

In a political society, war is the highest form of politics. In Liangshan, however, war was the bread of everyday life, and peacemaking was the "highest form of politics." In Liangshan, the way to bring an end to a matter was not through arms but through serious mediation. Only by counting up the number of dead on both sides and paying death compensation to the side with the larger number of dead could peace be reached and a final end put to a war. Otherwise, neither side's members would dare cross into their enemies' lands. A proverb has it, "If you meet an enemy you must fight; if you don't fight you will come to regret it." In other words, as long as the feuding parties had not gone through a peace process, they would both—especially the losing party—feel obliged to seek revenge by war. If someone abandoned a war for no reason, he would not only meet with ridicule from his clansmen, but the enemy clan would view him with disdain. But let them go through mediation with their headmen and drink blood-liquor (liquor with the blood of livestock or domestic fowls dropped into it for mediation purposes) together, and even though there was nothing in writing they could melt down their weapons into ornaments, and no one would go back on his word or resist the peace. To the Nuosu, "One man is worth only one horse, and one horse is worth only one cup of liquor." That is to say, they viewed liquor as equal in value to "duty" and life. Thus, people who had drunk together could not possibly go back on their word; to go back on one's word would have been to treat one's life as a plaything.

During peace talks, the cost of death compensation was an enormous monetary burden. But, as Aho Lomusse said, "If there are too few people in this branch of the clan and they cannot shoulder the cost of paying death compensation, what kind of clan branch are they?" By implication, a clan like this lacked the ability to hold its own in Liangshan society. Having a feud meant paying compensation: without paying compensation there could be no peace. Hence, for a clan, being unable to bear any and every function was ignominious. Compensation and the ending of a war had to be mediated, thus the saying "Peace talks lay a foundation, concluding the peace saves lives."

5. The Headman

A proverb says, "For drying grain we have the sun; for resolving problems we have the headman." Headmen were obviously key players in Liangshan society. Liangshan Yi call them *suyy, ndeggu,* and *ssakuo.* Actually, these three terms do not mean "headman" at all, but merely express the intelligence, talent, and courage of these three kinds of people. Nor were there hereditary headmen; people won these titles by exhibiting certain qualities. Headman is not an office of power, but one of honor—a kind of honor highly valued by the Yi of Liangshan—and it embodies the Liangshan idea of a hero. A person's courage and wisdom are fully displayed spontaneously in living practice, and only people who are valued and trusted by the clan membership can obtain these honors. Otherwise, not even the son of a headman can be a headman; as the proverb says, "The elder was wise and became a *ndeggu;* the son is a nothing and tends horses." But the nurturing influences in the environment of a headman's home gave his descendants more advantages in becoming headmen themselves. Hence the saying goes, "If the children and grandchildren are at all capable, they will always become *ndeggu.*" What is more, the opportunity to become a headman was not restricted to *nuoho,* nor to men: anyone who had sufficient qualifications in ability and fairness could be a headman, whether *nuoho* or *quho,* including women. The responsibilities of the headman were to solve problems for other people and arbitrate in disputes. If a problem arose in a clan, the headman would show up without being summoned and try to resolve it, lest matters get out of hand and he or she bear the blame. And if a headman failed to be evenhanded in resolving a dispute, he or she would lose the confidence of others and would not be asked to handle things again; and then he or she would not be regarded as headman anymore. There were no distinctions or ranks among headmen, nor was there a sense of difference in rank between headmen and ordinary clan members. Liangshan heroes did not recognize any authority, did not recognize one person as being higher than another— just as in the saying "As eggs are all the same size, every *nuoho* is equally important." But if someone had resolved several disputes impartially, his or her name would travel, and people from other clans would come forward in admiration to ask him or her to solve their problems. This is how someone would become a famous *ndeggu* whose prestige and influence went well beyond his or her own clan. In recent times, the influence of the headman's functions has grown smaller and smaller, but the repercussions of those functions are still evident in Liangshan society even today. For instance, in April of 1989, a *ndeggu* in Gewu Township, Zhaojue County, considered the brawls that had been taking place in recent years at a great cost in property and time. Without any prompting, this *ndeggu* organized more than a hundred representatives of the *nuoho* and *quho* clans and called a rally, formulating a set of rules and agreements among the township government and the population. In Liangshan, even today the *ndeggu* still has this kind of power to make an appeal to people. It makes one sigh.

Today, the Liangshan Yi have entered a new stage of development. As China's reforms continue and the country opens further, more and more people will win the opportunity for equal competition. As for research on Yi culture, people have done a great deal of analytical research from a macroscopic angle and obtained gratifying results. But far less research has been done from a microscopic angle. Research on Liangshan Yi society as one experiencing a heroic age is precisely such microscopic research. The present article is merely a first attempt with inevitable biases; I look to the learned scholars who read it to give me guidance and correction.

CHAPTER 8

On the Nature and Transmission of *Bimo* Knowledge in Liangshan

Bamo Ayi

In the mountain fastness of Liangshan, the traditional clan society, which had no centralized government, adopted a slaveholding system that persisted until 1956; the efforts of successive dynasties to control the area ended in failure. Because of the geographic barriers and the special characteristics of the slave system, foreign scholars referred to Liangshan as an independent area and to the Nuosu people as the "Independent Lolo."

In 1956, Liangshan began to undergo the Democratic Reforms and the slave system was abolished. Since then, there have been great changes in politics, economy, and culture, particularly during the Great Proletarian Cultural Revolution (1966–76), when traditional Nuosu culture and religion became targets of campaigns to "smash the Four Olds" and "root out superstition." Clan leaders *(suyy)*, respected mediators *(ndeggu)*, and priests *(bimo)* were scorned, and all were subjected to socialist reeducation. Clan meetings and other clan activities were forbidden, religious texts were confiscated and burned, and all kinds of ritual activity were prohibited. Nevertheless, in remote mountain villages in the core area where Nuosu are concentrated, Nuosu people preserved many aspects of their original way of life, and traditional religious beliefs and rituals continued in secret at that time.

Since the early 1980s, when minority policy turned away from promoting assimilation of Han ways, Nuosu people from the countryside and the cities have been spontaneously working toward the revitalization of traditional Nuosu culture. In the villages, the movement for cultural revitalization is characterized by the resurgence of the clans and the revival of traditional religious activities. With the redistribution of the land to households in the early 1980s and the administrative reforms of the 1990s, government power in the villages has been severely weakened. Agricultural cooperation is now undertaken on a clan basis. Clans unite to face natural disasters and human misfortunes and intervene to settle disputes and legal cases. Large and small clan meetings and other activities take place often, and *suyy* and *ndeggu* are busy once again with clan and community affairs. This resurgence of clans has provided the conditions for the continuing revival of religious and ritual activities. *Bimo* have begun to be active again in almost all villages. Even Nuosu cadres and intellectuals invite *bimo* to come to the cities to perform rituals. More and more boys and young men from *bimo* clans are studying the priestly vocation. In some villages inhabited by *bimo* clans, all males in these clans are either practicing *bimo* or are learning the trade, and some boys as young as four years old can already recite simple ritual texts. According to 1996 statistics from Meigu County, about sixty-eight hundred men and boys, or 8 percent of the male population of the county, were practicing or training to be *bimo*, and over two hundred types of rituals were being performed (Gaha 1996, 21–22).

The *bimo* are religious professionals who guide the spiritual life of mountain Nuosu villages. In the Nuosu language, *bi* means to recite or chant a scripture or to perform a ritual; *mo* is a person of knowledge or accomplishment. *Bimo* are the bridge between people and spirits. They perform and direct all kinds of rituals, perform ceremonies to spirits and ancestors, exorcise ghosts and evil spirits, and cure illnesses. In the course of the historical development of Nuosu religion, the ranks of the *bimo* have developed their own system of reproducing themselves and of recruiting and training new members through a combination of inheritance and education.

BIMO AND THEIR PLACE IN SOCIETY

As religious professionals, *bimo* perform and direct all kinds of rituals to propitiate gods and ancestors, exorcise ghosts, call spirits, appease spirits, and cure illnesses. In traditional Nuosu belief, the human life course, wealth and poverty, peace and conflict are all the result of the influence of gods, ghosts, ancestors, and spirits. *Bimo* are the mediators between human beings and these supernaturals, representing their clients in their ceremonies and prayers to the supernaturals and even controlling people's access to health and wealth through supernatural intervention. As a Nuosu proverb says, "Where the crane flies over, the sky will be clear; where the *bimo* arrives, people will be fortunate."

As village intellectuals, *bimo* were formerly the only literate group in Nuosu areas; even today, they are the only ones who can read and understand traditional scriptures and old documents, compile historical scriptures, and write new texts relating to philosophy, literature, history, astronomy, medicine, agriculture, arts and crafts, rituals, religion, and ethics. There is a proverb that says, "The knowledge of a *bimo* is limitless." The *bimo* are the strength of traditional knowledge and the most important carriers of traditional culture.

Suyy, ndeggu, and *bimo* are like the three stones that hold up the cooking pot over the fire pit in a Nuosu household: they are the triple pillars of Nuosu traditional society. *Suyy* are secular political leaders; *ndeggu* are like judges, specialists in mediation and dispute resolution between individuals and between clans (Ma Erzi 1992). But *bimo* are both leaders and mediators. As spiritual leaders, *bimo* deal with people's faith and guide the spiritual life of mountain Nuosu villages. As religious mediators, they are the bridge between people and supernaturals. Because of their complex role in Nuosu society, *bimo* became a distinct professional stratum very early in history. Their professional activity was not subject to control by secular authorities, but they sometimes joined forces with secular authorities, using the power of gods and ancestors to help solve or deal with otherwise insoluble questions; they thus became an important bulwark of the Nuosu clan system. For example, if a clan wants to divide into two because it is too large, or so that distant clan mates may marry, it is necessary to have a *bimo* perform the ceremony called *nimu ajie;* if two clans who have divided want to combine again after their strength has been reduced by natural disasters or wars, a *bimo* must perform the ceremony called *nimu ate.* When two clans form an alliance, a *bimo* performs the ceremony called *lendu* (bashing an ox) to consecrate the alliance and emphasize its permanence; when someone who had committed a serious violation of customary law is expelled from the clan, a *bimo* will perform the ceremony of *loyycy* (expulsion from one's clan), which calls on the ancestors to witness the expulsion. And when a case is so difficult that a *ndeggu* cannot solve it, a *bimo* may be called upon for an oracular solution.

Because of the services they offer to the population, *bimo* have a distinct and honored place in society. In the past, there was a custom described as *nzy la bi a de,* or "even when a *tusi* arrives, a *bimo* does not have to get up," and even today when a *bimo* arrives the best seat is given up for him. In the course of Nuosu history, the ranks of the *bimo* have developed their own system of reproducing themselves and of recruiting and training new members through a combination of inheritance and education.

SUCCESSION TO *BIMO* STATUS

The status and social role of *bimo,* particularly in relation to religious activities, are inherited. It is a natural law that senior *bimo* will become old and eventually die. To whom will the *bimo* pass on their status and social roles? Who may qualify for the *bimo* profession to receive training and to carry on the tradition? Let us look at the principles and customary rules for the succession of the *bimo.*

Succession by Males Only

The *bimo* social stratum is a male social group, one whose inheritance is passed on to males only. Females have neither the right nor the opportunity to receive *bimo* education or engage in *bimo* professional activities. The notion of "polluted females" is internalized in religious beliefs of the Nuosu people, so females are prohibited from becoming priests, touching religious instruments and texts, or participating in certain religious ceremonies. Thus, the *bimo*, as sacred interlocutor between humans and supernatural beings, naturally exclude the "polluted" females. The Yi classic *The Origin of Ghosts* links the origin of ghosts to a beautiful girl. And it is said that there was only one female *bimo* in Yi history—Lazzi Shysi, a daughter of the eminent *bimo* Ashy Lazzi.

Even though Lazzi Shysi learned the highest-level magic from her father, understood the most powerful and complicated classics, had unusual talent—a horse she painted could fly; a bird she painted could sing; a dragon she painted could dance—and was able to suppress demons, banish ghosts, and rescue people from dangerous accidents, she still had to dress in male clothing when she performed as a *bimo*, so that no one knew she was female. This example shows the principle that the inheritance of the *bimo* excludes females.

Two Ways of Transmitting Bimo Status

The Primary Method: Inherited Status.   Some Nuosu clans—for example, the Jjike, the Shama, the Ddisse, and the Jynyi—have produced *bimo* for many generations, as indicated in their genealogical documents, which demonstrate that their clans have practiced the rituals of *bimo* for dozens or even more than one hundred generations. In my own fieldwork, I discovered one clan in Meigu that claims to have practiced *bimo* arts for about 136 generations. According to customary rules of *bimo* succession, *bimo* status is inherited within one clan, particularly among nuclear family members, usually patrilineally from father to son. This kind of inheritance is conservative and thus has some limitations.

This type of succession within a clan that has traditionally produced *bimo* is statistically much more common than extraclan inheritance, for several reasons. First, hereditary *bimo* retain privileges when they offer services in the religion of ancestral worship. Nuosu people believe that ancestors are the source of disaster, fortune, prosperity, and disease, and thus they often require that ceremonies be performed to propitiate the ancestors. They cannot do these ceremonies themselves; the *bimo* must perform them. Usually a hereditary *bimo* will be asked to accept the honored and privileged position of performing such a ceremony. In addition, a hereditary *bimo* also dominates in other major ceremonies, such as calling souls, pronouncing curses, and ghost-cursing. In contrast, any nonhereditary *bimo*, no matter how intelligent he is, can perform only small-scale ceremonies such as lifting curses, dealing with pollution, housecleaning, and ghost exorcism.

Second, because hereditary *bimo* are protected by their *bimo* ancestors and possess inherited ceremonial books and instruments, the Nuosu people believe them to have powerful abilities, and they trust them. They, as a dominant force in the *bimo* social group, are also very influential in Nuosu society generally.

Finally, hereditary *bimo* receive the highest compensation for performing a ceremony. They are the most authoritative, and their position in the *bimo* social class is the highest.

In order to preserve the status and the profession of the *bimo* within one's clan, a hereditary *bimo* is responsible for training younger generations; every male who is born in the nuclear family of a hereditary *bimo* is also responsible for learning *bimo* knowledge and associated skills and engaging in the *bimo* profession. Normally, if there is a *bimo* in the father's generation, there should be at least one *bimo* among the sons' generation. Thus the profession and status of *bimo* are continuously transmitted according to this customary rule.

A Secondary Method: Apprenticeship.   Nonhereditary *bimo* are apprentices, called *zzybi* in Nuosu, of hereditary *bimo*. *Zzy* means "mixed" and "impure"; *bi* means *bimo*. *Zzybi* indicates that apprentice *bimo* are not pure and not authentic. There are two ways of becoming an apprentice *bimo:* the path may be determined by oneself or determined by divination. When a son is born, if his mother's rotating horoscopic compass currently points toward the east or the west, this indicates that he meets the *bimo* spirit and the *bimo's* protective eagle spirit, and thus is qualified to become a *bimo*. In fact, he *should* become a *bimo*, otherwise the *bimo* spirit and *bimo* eagle might become angry with him and cause diseases and disasters. If he becomes a *bimo*, the spirit will protect him and ensure his success in learning and performing ceremonies. Some parents voluntarily send their son to a *bimo* family to study; others do so after they get sick or after a disaster occurs: these parents, by means of divining, realize that the *bimo* spirit and the *bimo* eagle have caused the disease or disaster. This seems to imply that every Nuosu male has the opportunity to become a *bimo*, but because nonhereditary *bimo* or apprentice *bimo* can perform only small-scale ceremonies and have limited income, and because these *bimo* are not protected by their ancestors and do not inherit ceremonial books and instruments, they are not completely trusted and authoritative; thus they can perform only certain ceremonies. Apprentice *bimo* do not play an important role in transmitting the *bimo* status.

What accounts for this pattern of succession by males but not by females, and of limited powers for those who learn their skills by apprenticeship? It seems to me that the system of *bimo* inheritance is determined by blood relationships and their associated perceptions. As we know, in Nuosu society clan organizations and perceptions about blood relationships play an extremely important role. In such a kin-based society, agnatic relationships and their traditions have long existed and have come to pervade every aspect of Nuosu thought and behavior. These perceptions about blood relationships and their connection to Nuosu cultural identity also determine the system of *bimo* succession. For example, on the surface the rule of male inheritance indicates professional prohibition because of the perception of "polluted females." It is in fact closely related to the patrilineal system of Nuosu society. A Nuosu proverb tells us: "An egg is both meat and not meat; a daughter is both family member and not." A Nuosu girl normally gets married when she is seventeen or so. She usually does not immediately move to her husband's household, but she does become a member of her husband's family. Even if a girl is not married when she is seventeen, she will attend a fake "wedding ceremony," in which she is symbolically married to a stone or piece of wood. From that point on, she is no longer regarded as a member of her father's family—even though she still lives with them—and is not allowed to attend religious ceremonies of her father's family.

From the Nuosu point of view, the *bimo* profession is sacred: the profession and its social status can be inherited only within one clan so that the clan will maintain its respected status as a hereditary *bimo* clan. The respected *bimo* status cannot be transferred to one's affines. This is the essential reason for the rule of male inheritance.

The *bimo* social status group is partially open to those males whose do not come from hereditary *bimo* clans, but this is only possible under the condition that it does not cause any damage to the principle of agnatic relationships. There is a clear line between hereditary and apprentice *bimo*. An apprentice *bimo* cannot be in charge of ceremonies such as ancestral worship, human-cursing, ghost-cursing, or soul-directing. Furthermore, an apprentice *bimo* cannot have his own *bimo* genealogy and transform his family into a hereditary *bimo* family. In Liangshan, we can often hear hereditary *bimo* families distinguish themselves by saying, "We have proof of being a *bimo* family" or "Our ancestors were *bimo*." An apprentice *bimo* does not pass his status on to his sons. In my own fieldwork, I found that the greatest number of *bimo* generations in an apprentice *bimo* family occurs in the Hielie family in Chengmendong Village, Yanyuan County, which has four *bimo* generations. Even this family, however, still lives in the shadow of inauthenticity and cannot perform ancestral worship ceremonies, and each generation must acquire priestly knowledge anew from a hereditary *bimo*. Therefore, the *bimo*— as a self-perpetuating professional stratum—are limited to blood relationships.

In sum, not only does the system of *bimo* form its own inheritance mechanism, but it also clearly shows its conservativeness and exclusiveness. This closed inheritance system is produced on the basis of *bimo* ancestor worship, the concept of blood relationships in a patrilineal society, and the practice of the *bimo* traditional culture. The inheritance network to a large extent conditions the *bimo* social stratum and regulates the constitution and development of this group.

THE CONTENT OF *BIMO* EDUCATION

If the system discussed above regulates succession to the *bimo's* social position and roles, the *bimo* education constitutes the process of transmission. *Bimo* education aims to produce qualified *bimo* to take charge of religious ceremonies in order to avoid disasters and bring fortune. As we know, Yi religion is a complicated system that focuses on ancestral worship and incorporates nature worship, spirit worship, and belief in ghosts. Because of the numerous sacrifice and magic rituals, the complicated nature of ceremonial procedure, and the difficulty of ritual texts in the Nuosu language, in order to become a qualified priest one must have specialized knowledge and the ability to communicate with supernaturals. Let us examine the *bimo* education.

Bimo education focuses on the specialized knowledge and skills of *bimo* practice. As a professional priest, a *bimo* is in charge of practicing sacrifice rituals, medicine, and divination. He conducts ceremonies such as peace-making with ancestors, escorting ancestors, preventing disasters, expelling ghosts, treating disease, asking for fertility, guiding souls, praying for fortune, divining, making alliances, passing judgment in the name of the gods, and so on. As an intellectual, a *bimo* is the repository and disseminator of ancient Yi history and cultural heritage. In order to ensure that a *bimo* is able to perform his duties, *bimo* education covers the following subjects.

Knowledge about Ancestors, Gods, Spirits, and Ghosts

Nuosu generally believe that everything has a soul, or *yyrhla*, and commonly believe in *apu abo* (ancestors), *mulumuse* (nature gods), *jjylukuhxo* (spirits), and *nyicy hamo* (ghosts). Belief in the ancestors is the most important. Nuosu believe that anyone, male or female, who has sons becomes an ancestor after death, returning to the world of the ancestors, where they should receive offerings of their patrilineal descendants in perpetuity and where they take on the responsibility of protecting their descendants. People who are childless or have only daughters become only ghosts after death, cold and hungry without a permanent abode. Gods are primarily the spirits of the natural world, such as spirits of heaven, earth, mountains, bodies of water, rain, cliffs, and so on. Different gods influence people's livelihood in different ways. Spirits belong to particular individuals or households, and they influence them in different ways. For example, a *qosi* is a protective spirit; if a man's *qosi* is very strong, he is bound to be successful in war or business. One's *kepo* is a spirit of luck or fortune; if a *kepo* stays with you, you will be lucky; if the *kepo* deserts you, you will have bad fortune. Ghosts often attack people, bringing them disaster, sickness, or death. There are many kinds of ghosts; for example, twenty different kinds of ghosts cause twenty different kinds of rheumatism.

Because *bimo* mediate between humans and supernaturals, they must know great amounts about these supernatural beings, and they often portray them as having diverse images. The hero-ancestor Zhigealu, who assists a *bimo* in treating insanity and in cursing humans or ghosts, is portrayed as wearing an iron helmet, carrying the sun and the moon on his shoulders, holding an iron bag in one hand and an iron fork in the other. The ghost Tusha, who haunts domestic animals until their death, is portrayed as having a long jaw, carrying a cutting board on the top of his head, wearing sheepskin, holding a small ax in his hand, and carrying an old bamboo basket on his back. In addition, spirits and ghosts have diverse personalities. The spirit Gefi, who is in charge of fertility, enjoys playing in forests and on lakes, which sometimes permits difficult birth and early death. Thus the ritual for directing Gefi symbolizes calling the spirit back from forests and lakes. The rheumatism ghost loves to dress up. In the ceremony of deporting the ghost, the ghost will not leave until he receives colorful clothes, a comb, hair pins, and a pretty triangle wallet. A *bimo* student should understand the images of supernatural beings, their personalities, and the disasters, diseases, and benefits caused by them in production, life, and health. As a result, a *bimo* can make his religious service smoother and control gods and ghosts in rituals when he prevents disasters and brings fortune.

Knowledge about Ceremonial Texts

The Nuosu have their own variety of Yi writing and have produced numerous classic documents. The *bimo* control Nuosu-language documents and ceremonial books. Although most books are religious, some of them deal with philosophy, literature, ethics, and morality. These books tell a *bimo* how to perform a ritual. "Narrating the origin" is an important part of a ritual, based on *The Book of Origins (Hnewo teyy)* (see Wu Jingzhong, chapter 2 in this volume). This book discusses many issues, from the formation of the universe to the creation of the sky and the earth, from the origins of objects to the origin of humans, from the development of a society to the formation of human activities, from natural phenomena to human ones, and so on.

As a key to the *bimo's* education, his ability to understand ceremonial books is related to his cognitive ability and knowledge structure. The content of a *bimo's* recitation in a ceremony determines how the ceremony is arranged and how it progresses. That is, a ceremony is performed during the process

of recitation by a *bimo* because reciting dominates the process of the ceremony. From the *bimo's* point of view, ceremonial books are religious instruments and have special magic power. There are rules and taboos regarding
copying, binding, cataloging, circulating, and collecting ceremonial books.
A qualified *bimo* should master the Nuosu script, be extremely familiar with
the contents of ceremonial books, and understand how to use each book.
Acquiring these skills is a major aspect of *bimo* education.

Knowledge about Genealogies, History, and Geography

A *bimo* must be familiar with genealogies of all families, lineages, and clans,
the migration direction of their ancestors, and all associated important
events, as well as the natural environment and topography of the Liangshan
region. During a large-scale ancestral worship ceremony, a *bimo* usually has
to narrate the origin of the group and its history. All *bimo* conducting ancestral worship rituals in different Yi regions have to narrate the history of
their remote, original ancestor, Apudumu, and the history of the tribes of
the "six ancestors." In addition, historical documents such as *The Division of
the Six Ancestral Tribes* and *The Enlightenment of the Six Ancestors' Souls* are important in *bimo* education. During a death ritual, a *bimo* has to narrate the
text *Soul-Directing* in order to lead the soul of the dead to pass all places the
family (and their ancestors) lived and eventually to arrive at the original ancestral home. In order to lead the soul to pass places easily, a *bimo* must describe the natural environment and typology of every site the family has lived
in; he also has to tell the soul of the dead about important historical events
associated with each place and its name, and about achievements of ancestors. In addition, a *bimo*, in every ritual, has to narrate the text *Inviting Gods*
to assist his performance. Most spirits in this text are mountain spirits, each
of whom is associated with one particular natural environment.

Knowledge about the Calendar and Astrology

The *bimo* excel at controlling supernaturals in a given time and space. The
Yi calendar and the Yi people's knowledge about the universe are very closely
related to the cycles and rules of religious rituals. The Yi calendar is clearly
shaped by the ritual calendar. When Yi people observe the universe, they in
fact predict what happens in the world of humans. Knowledge about the calendar and astrology, as an important aspect of the *bimo* education, provides
a powerful means for a *bimo* to communicate with supernatural beings in
ceremonies.

Knowledge about Medicine and Disease

Bimo medical practice is characterized by a combination of treatment and divination. Nuosu believe that diseases are caused by disease ghosts. Diseases are

named after ghosts: for example, *nusi* (leprosy ghost), *nuna* (pulmonary tuberculosis ghost), *dimu* (sore ghost), and so on. Medical treatment is also part of rituals such as cursing disease ghosts and expelling disease ghosts. *Bimo* medical treatments include oral medication, acupuncture, and moxibustion. The most important medical books are *The Book of Pharmaceutical Identification, The Book of Making Pharmaceuticals, Treatment and Detoxification*, and *The Book of Medical Calculations*. In training his students, a *bimo* teaches about medicine and treatment, such as how to diagnose symptoms, how to gather plant and animal medicines, and how to make medicines and give a correct prescription.

Knowledge about Arts and Crafts

One important aspect of *bimo* education is arts and crafts: drawing, straw weaving, sculpture, carving, and paper cutting. Yi books usually include drawn images of ghosts and illustrate the skills of gods. In some books, drawings illustrate text, while in others text explains drawings. Straw weaving and sculpture are normally used to portray the ghost to be displayed in rituals such as escorting ghosts and cursing ghosts. Paper cutting is a basic skill used to make images of objects to be sacrificed symbolically, such as the sun, moon, stars, animals, plants, objects used in everyday life, and domestic animals. When a *bimo* makes religious instruments and ancestral totem figures, he also needs to be a skilled wood carver.

Knowledge about Ritual Procedures

The ultimate goal of *bimo* education is to train a student to take independent charge of a ritual. One characteristic of Yi religious ceremonies is the combination of sacrificing and controlling, or the combination of sacrificing and black magic. The procedure of a ritual is formalized; all customary rules must be strictly followed. Choosing the time for a ritual, for example, one must pay attention to the year, month, date, and specific time. A sacrificed animal must be chosen according to its sex, hair color, age, and quality. An animal used in a sacrificing ceremony may be living, slaughtered and cooked, slaughtered but not cooked, and with or without blood or horns. A qualified *bimo* should know all the rules and procedures of rituals.

Knowledge about Folklore

In order to perform rituals, a *bimo* should know Yi folklore and oral traditions included in rituals, such as mythology, traditional songs, epics, folktales, and proverbs. Many *bimo* in Yunnan and Guizhou, as well as in Nuosu country, are famous for their singing; they are very knowledgeable about Yi folklore and oral traditions. They absorb folklore and oral traditions in order to enrich the content of their narration in rituals.

In sum, the content of *bimo* education derives fundamentally from Nuosu rituals and includes knowledge about supernatural beings, Nuosu language and texts, genealogies, history, geography, the Yi calendar, astrology, arts and crafts, ritual procedures, and folklore. Such systematic knowledge is required for a *bimo* in conducting rituals.

PEDAGOGY

There is no formal institution for *bimo* education in traditional Nuosu society. A junior *bimo* is trained by a senior *bimop*.[1] A senior *bimop* is an experienced and knowledgeable elder who knows how to conduct a ritual, while a junior *bimo*, or *bisse*, is an inexperienced student. A *bisse* can be called *bimo* only when, after a few years, he completes his study and can independently run ceremonies. A *bimop* may teach either one or many *bisse* at one time. Whether or not one comes from a hereditary *bimo* family, one has to study under a *bimop*. The relationship between a student and a teacher or between learning and teaching has the following characteristics.

First, there are no fixed time and place for teaching and learning. The most important duty for a *bimo* is to conduct rituals. Other duties cannot interrupt religious activities. Rituals are numerous in Nuosu regions, and a *bimop*, when summoned by a host family, takes his *bisse* with him, from one family to another and from one village to another, to conduct rituals. Thus the time and place are not fixed for a *bimop* to teach his *bisse*.

Second, teaching is mixed with performing rituals. A *bimo* often has to teach his student(s) at intervals between rituals, but more important, he teaches his student(s) during ceremonies, when a student may become his teacher's assistant. As a student, a *bisse* should ask questions of his teacher, observe the procedure of a ritual, understand the meanings of a ritual, and practice it sometimes. Not only does each ritual become an opportunity for a *bimop* to teach, but it also becomes a process of learning for a *bisse*.

Third, the relationship between teacher and student is also shaped by other factors. In the Yi region, some students take the initiative to study from a particular teacher; some learn from their fathers, grandfathers, or uncles. A *bimop* teaches without being paid. A teacher takes care of his student, while students respect their teachers. The quality of a student's work affects the future of both the student and the teacher. Therefore, both teachers and students work very hard in teaching and learning.

In such a master-apprentice relationship, a *bimo* normally teaches on an individual basis; he does not have formalized pedagogy. He teaches accord-

---

1. The term *bimop* (with the last syllable pronounced *mop*, in the low tone) refers to a master *bimo* who can teach students, as opposed to *bimo* or *bimox* (middle or middle-high tone), which is a generic term.

ing to the level of his student and his schedule for conducting rituals. Thus, a teacher decides what, how, and when he teaches his student. Even if a *bimop* teaches many students at one time, he always concerns himself with individual needs. In fact, focusing on individual needs makes his teaching more effective.

Bimo texts are also important in the *bimo* education. Learning them starts with the Nuosu script. Each Yi character represents both one word and one sound. There are many variations for a word in traditional Nuosu writing, making it difficult to learn.[2] An experienced *bimop* trains his students to show interest in discovering the relationships between a written word and a sound, between a written form and the meaning, and between one written word and another. After learning some basic writing, a student begins to study *bimo* texts. The study of a *bimo* text includes reading, reciting, and copying. There is no punctuation, and there are many specialized and archaic religious words and phrases in Nuosu texts. Literary words used in texts are different from words used in ordinary speech. These make reading a *bimo* text quite difficult. Therefore, when a teacher performs a ritual he usually reads a text first, then his students follow. Recitation is very important because it makes communication between a *bimo* and supernatural beings smoother and easier. If a *bimo* cannot recite everything from a text, the ritual is ineffective. After a student can read and recite a text, he copies the text so that he can learn the format and writing style. At the same time, he also has to learn how to make a brush and ink and how to make a scroll-style notebook. Because what he reads, recites, and copies is what he will use in the future when he conducts rituals by himself, a student usually is very serious about his study. One major problem for *bimo* education today is that some teachers require their students only to recite texts and do not pay enough attention to the explanation of their contents and sociohistorical contexts. This has caused some students to learn to read and recite texts without understanding their meanings clearly.

In addition to the religious scriptures are some textbooks written especially for students, which have emerged in the course of *bimo* education. These include the *Suosi teyy,* a compilation of the names, natures, and characteristics of various ghosts and spirits; the *Bijie teyy,* which narrates the order of various rituals as well as the ritual instruments texts and charts use, and the *Mguvangeyima,* which is a collection devoted especially to charts of the ritual space of various ceremonies. These textbooks are designed especially for students and are concerned with the effectiveness of pedagogy. Taking language as an example, religious texts are usually written in poetic language,

2. This refers to the traditional script used by the *bimo*. The new, standardized script is based on a one-to-one correspondence between the sound of a syllable and the sign used to write it. See David Bradley, chapter 12 in this volume.

but textbooks are written in oral language, which makes it easier for students to understand the contents. Because these newly compiled textbooks are carefully edited and more scientifically organized and precise, *bimop* and their students have taken them as the basis for knowledge. In order to ensure that these books may be preserved for learning and instruction, and to prevent damage to them, many have been written on white cloth and are therefore called "cloth books."

Some *bimo* teachers are good at using proverbs and pithy formulas in teaching. In their long history of ritual practice, the *bimo* have accumulated many proverbs and formulas of *bimo* knowledge and used them in education. For example, in selecting animals for sacrifice, we have "For exorcising ghosts, a black hen; for calling souls, a brown hen"; "For cursing ghosts, a black billy goat; for presenting offerings, a white ram"; and so forth. In these sayings, "exorcising ghosts," "calling souls," "cursing ghosts," and "presenting offerings" are all different steps in the ritual of sending off the ancestral soul; the sacrificial animals used in each stage are different species and different colors. In another example, in planting spirit branches, there are sayings such as "A spirit branch has to be peeled at the base; if you don't peel it, it can't become a spirit branch"; "In *mge ndi* [the name of a ritual], seven *bimo* [plant seven spirit branches to represent seven *bimo* ancestor spirits]; in *chy ke*, twelve *bimo* [plant twelve spirit branches] above the Heavenly God White Father, below the Earthly God Black Mother, in the middle of all the Star Ancestors," and so forth. There are also formulas for choosing auspicious days for rituals: "Sending off the ancestor in the first half of the month; wedding in the second half of the month"; "Send off the ancestor on a dragon day; conduct a wedding on a rat day"; "On a horse day, don't build a house; if you build it, don't move in"; "On a sheep day, don't perform a cure; if you perform the cure, the sickness won't be over with"; and so forth. Proverbs are also a way of educating students in the principles of *bimo* education, such as "No matter how poor the person who invites you to perform a ritual, you must still go happily"; or "The rule of a *tusi* is the same inside and outside the city walls; when *bimo* perform rituals, it is the same for relatives or nonrelatives"; "You can kill a *bimo* who fails an appointment to perform a ritual"; and "A *bimo* should listen in back of him for three days [after a ritual]; is there really peace and content?" Using proverbs and aphorisms helps students more effectively master *bimo* knowledge and ethics.

Demonstration and practice are often a part of *bimo* education. A teacher demonstrates how to carve a ghost statue, cut paper, make mud figures, draw ghosts, and sing different tunes. During his demonstration, a teacher explains key skills and procedures. A student practices: under guidance he copies and repeats what his teacher did. When a student is skillful, he will be allowed to perform and practice in a real ceremony. Demonstration and practice are essential for students to apply what they study.

In sum, the *bimo* educational style and its pedagogy are based on the master-apprentice relation. *Bimo* education is practice-oriented. In teaching, not only does the method focus on the guidance of the teacher, but it also pays attention to the participation of the student. This method deals with both knowledge and its application. This practice-oriented, master-apprentice education is an effective way of training younger generations to succeed elder *bimo* and is essential to reach the goal of *bimo* education.

In the course of historical development, the persistence of the *bimo*—as both practitioners of a religious profession and as intellectuals among the Yi—is possible only through inheritance of the *bimo's* religious status and social roles, and through teaching successive generations the *bimo* knowledge and skills. It is in their educational and religious activities that the *bimo* preserve and disseminate their indigenous religion and, at the same time, enrich the traditional Yi culture.

PART III

Yi Society in Yunnan

CHAPTER 9

The Cold Funeral of the Nisu Yi

Li Yongxiang

The Nisu, whose population exceeds one million, are one of the seventy-odd branches of the Yi and are scattered in wide areas of southern Yunnan and some countries in Southeast Asia. The language of the Nisu is a southern dialect of the Yi language, has its own ancient scripts, and is rich in literature (see David Bradley, chapter 12 in this volume). The famous creation myth *The Chamu Epic* and *The Shuangbo Yi Medicinal Gazetteer,* which has been praised as "a jewel of the Yi nationality," were actually translated from ancient Yi documents of the Nisu. Because this Yi branch is concentrated in the Ailao mountain range and the Hong River basin, it is known to scholarship as the Ailao Yi.

Specifically, the Nisu are distributed in Kunming Municipality and nearly thirty counties and cities in Chuxiong Yi Autonomous Prefecture, Honghe Hani-Yi Autonomous Prefecture, Yuxi Prefecture, and Simao Prefecture of Yunnan. Because of geographic differences and influences from ethnic interaction, there are variations and differences in culture, customs, and language among the Nisu of different areas. This essay examines the Nisu of Zhuyuan Village in Laochang Township of Xinping Yi-Dai Autonomous County in Yuxi Prefecture and analyzes a characteristic ritual sequence called *ka-dji-da-le,* or "cold funeral," and related cultural phenomena.

THE CONCEPT OF THE COLD FUNERAL

There are two varieties of funeral rituals among the Nisu: *cha-ma-da-le* (the warm funeral) and *ka-dji-da-le* (the cold funeral). In the warm funeral, as soon as a person dies a day is selected for the funeral to send the soul across to Ngomi, the spirit world, back to where the Yi's ancestors used to live. The cold funeral, however, is selected in circumstances where it is not possible to conduct the funeral right after death—for various reasons, such as economic hardship—so it is conducted some years after the burial. This rite is restricted to the dead who did not undergo the warm funeral ritual; if a person has already undergone a funeral ritual, it is not possible to perform the cold funeral rite for him or her.

Why do people perform the cold funeral ritual? The Nisu believe that there is only one spirit attached to one's body when one is alive, but that after one's death the one spirit turns into three: one spirit returns home to become an ancestor, one stays in the graveyard to watch the tombstone, and the third is sent by local priests, or *bema* (equivalent to *bimo* in Liangshan), to Ngomi, the World to Come, to be reunited with ancestors. There are no human beings in Ngomi, which is inhabited only by ancestors' spirits. But if no funeral rite is performed after one's death, the third spirit will not be reunited with those of the ancestors, and this is a taboo. Therefore, as long as a dead person has not yet undergone the funeral rite, the cold funeral rite will be performed, no matter how long ago he or she died. According to Zhou Juzhang, the *bema* of Zhuyuan Village, *ka-dji* means "cold" and *da-le* means "performing the funeral ritual." *Ka-dji-da-le* means a ritual that is "left to be cold," that is, a "cold funeral." This name originates in the idea that people think this activity is comparable to eating cold rice and cold dishes.

It is not possible to perform the cold funeral ritual for a dead person who has undergone a funeral rite, because the third spirit has already been sent to the land of the ancestors. What is there to send off? Therefore, *bema* Zhou said, one dead person cannot experience two funeral rituals, and such a thing has never been heard of. Both warm and cold funerals are funeral activities and they have many things in common. Moreover, the important rituals— *ngo-dzo-de,* fighting off demons; *dzo-mo,* showing the way to Ngomi; *lo-she-dzuo-duo,* trampling the grasses; *chi-dza-dzo-chuo,* eating a small nighttime meal; and *mi-sho,* obtaining a grave site—are all performed the same way in both types of funerals. But the cold and the warm funerals are each of a piece and have many different characteristics. First, the site of the ritual is different: the great majority of warm funerals are held in the home of the dead person, and only rarely are they held at the grave site; almost all cold funerals take place beside the mountain grave, and the participants eat and sleep on the mountain, with only one ritual, that of calling the soul, taking place in the home. Second, the numbers and points of emphasis of the rites are different: warm funeral rites are numerous and detailed—there are rites for ablution of the corpse, dressing the corpse and laying it in the coffin, and cremation. During a cold funeral, these rites are not performed because the person has already been dead for some years; but many rites that the warm funeral does not have are added, such as the *she-ka-tsi,* which re-creates the circumstances of the time of death. Third, when three years have passed since a warm funeral, there is a "three full years" *(sa ku de)* rite, whose purpose is to end all kinship connections between the living and the dead—in the Nisu view, three years marks the end of the human part of the matter. The *sa ku de* rite represents a demarcation between the dead person and humankind. After *sa ku de,* no other rite is performed for the dead person. But in a cold funeral, after the rite of sending the soul to Ngomi, a "three full years" rite is also performed—it is actually a part of the cold funeral, although it is carried out separately. It involves hanging pepper and sacrificing animals, and the fees of the *bema* have to be tallied up separately.

There are many reasons for holding a cold funeral—for instance, when a person dies, it may take several years before a funeral can take place because an auspicious day cannot be found. Or the family may be experiencing economic hardship; after having waited for some years, they will have made financial preparations and will perform a cold funeral.

THE BOUNDARY BETWEEN DIMI AND NGOMI, AND THE LAND WHERE THE ANCESTORS LIVED

In the traditional view of the Nisu, the cosmos is divided into two worlds: Dimi and Ngomi. The former is inhabited by living human beings and is where they live and reproduce; the latter is inhabited by spirits, who must go there. This concept is similar to the division of the *yin* world and the *yang* world in the Han cosmology. Certainly there are some differences, because the Nisu have a very vague idea about Ngomi, and *bema* cannot clearly explain what that world is like. But *bema* know that there is a land in that world, where Yi ancestors used to live. Therefore, the core of funeral activities is the act of escorting the spirit from the place where the dead person lived to the place where the ancestors are said to have lived. The cold funeral is no exception: held at the grave site, it entails sending the spirit from the grave site to the land of ancestors. It is said that the spirit will meet with many difficulties on its journey, and so it is necessary to have the advice and assistance of the *bema*. And how does the *bema* know when the spirit has entered Ngomi and reached the land where the ancestors lived? How does the *bema* know where the boundary is between Dimi and Ngomi and the location of the place where the ancestors lived? The *bema* has an array of methods and thought models.

On the matter of the boundary, the Yi classical books are full of material. For example, the Ngo-dzo-de Prayer (Fighting the Demons Prayer), which is read during the rite of what is called "fighting off demons," mentions a place called the Street of the Intermingling of *Yin* and *Yang* Forces (*she-shu-tsi-li-dze*). This street is the boundary of the two worlds; beyond it is Ngomi and this side of it is the world of the living. And the two are opposed worlds in the Dzo-mo Prayer (Prayer of Showing the Way). Human life is Dimi and existence after death is Ngomi. Even if the spirit is still at home, it is, according to classical texts, nevertheless in the other world. And it is only because of this that the *bema* is able to eat a small nighttime meal *(chi-dza-dzo-chuo)* with the spirit and express feelings of nostalgia.

However, in actuality the boundary perceived by the *bema* is not too consistent with the one described in the classical texts. They believe that the top of *ngo-di-dje,* meaning "the tree of entering Ngomi," an enormous paper tree used in the cold funeral, is the very boundary. Inside the *ngo-di-dje,* there is a piece of blue cloth (in some places white cloth) hanging vertically, and this provides the way across. The spirit climbs up along this piece of cloth, and when it crosses the top, it has reached Ngomi. The construction of the *ngo-di-dje* is very particular and precise. It is divided into twelve platforms, symbolizing the twelve months of the year. Its "body" is covered with little openings, which are "windows" through which the spirit takes leave of its friends and relatives; as the spirit climbs up the cloth, he or she can see the living world through these windows, but the world of the living cannot see the spirit. And when the spirit has crossed the top, he or she enters Ngomi.

On the matter of the boundary, the shamans have their own set of explanations. They believe that the points of interconnection between the two different worlds are located just below their own ears. Shamans claim that they can call out to spirits to communicate with the human world through themselves, and that the spirits they summon are located just below their ears, so that only they can hear what the spirits say. Similarly, they can relay people's requests and hopes to the spirits.

As for the land where the ancestors once lived, the *bema* refer to it generally as "the place where the King of the Underworld of the Universe *[mu-mi tze-lo-wa]* resides." The path described in the classical Yi Dzo-mo Prayer leads from the grave toward Mount Ailao, to Xinping City, to Mount Lukui, to Eshan City, to Yixi City, to Mount Xi, to Kunming, and on northward. Regardless of who has died, the Yi invariably direct the spirit to take this route back, which dovetails neatly with the belief among scholars that the Yi came from the north. Clearly, the Nisu funeral rites contain much that reflects their history.

As for how the rite of showing the way *(dzo-mo)* in the cold funeral relates to the place of the ancestors: one takes the head, skin, limbs, and tail of the ox used in the ritual of fighting off demons *(ngo-dzo-de)* and presents them completely intact at a spot some fifteen meters from the grave; two sticks of incense are stuck into the ox's nostrils, with the whole head facing the sky; the *bema,* holding a golden-bamboo staff and wearing a *bema* headdress, and starting in front of the grave, recites the Dzo-mo Prayer while walking slowly toward the ox's head. When the *bema* reaches the head, the prayer is finished, and the *bema* pokes the head with the staff so that it faces the ground. This poke signifies that the spirit has reached the land of the ancestors; and then, while calling to the spirit, the *bema* walks back toward the grave and returns to the world of the living.

The Nisu believe that in Ngomi there are also mountains, waters, a sun, a moon, rice, cows, sheep, chicken, pigs, and so on. The spirits work and produce subsistence materials for their living.

SACRIFICE OF ANIMALS, MONEY, AND OBJECTS

Regardless of who passes away, the Nisu must send that person's spirit back to the land of the ancestors to be reunited with them. The spirit, of course, needs advice and assistance from the *bema*. But according to etiquette, the *bema* cannot send back the spirit empty-handed. Furthermore, the Nisu believe that the spirit needs an assortment of things in order to live in the other world, such as livestock, money, and tools, and that if the living do not give them to him or her, there is no way for the spirit to obtain these. Hence people make sacrifices of livestock (such as cattle, goats, pigs, chickens), money (paper money or various paper trees), grain, and tools. Superficially these things are used in sacrifice, but in fact they are given to the spirit.

The question of what things should be given to the spirit is decided by the host family, based on what resources are available; once decided, this cannot be changed, especially with gifts of livestock. It once happened that the host family had decided that a few chickens were to be sacrificed, but then changed their minds; all the chickens died anyway. The *bema* explained that the spirits of those chickens had been snatched away by the soul. In today's cold funeral, decisions of this kind cannot ordinarily be altered.

In the cold funeral there are two rituals related to gifts of livestock—cattle, goats, pigs, or chickens—that are offered to the spirit. First comes the *shu-pu* in the second part of the ritual. The expression *shu-pu* is translated as "handing over alive" by some, as "sacrifice" by others, but in any case the meaning is the same: the livestock are offered to the spirit. The *bema* recites the Shu-pu Scripture, which must be finished before the animals can be killed. The prayer tells where these livestock came from, where the knife came from, and the difficulties of killing the animals. The other ritual is called *dji-ti*, which is difficult to translate neatly: *dji* means "everything, all things," and *ti* means "to inform"—that is, to inform the spirit about all the activities taking place as part of the cold funeral, including who is taking part and their kinship relation to the dead person, what gifts they have brought (livestock, money, objects, and so on), and such matters.

Money given to the spirit is made of paper; and of the five large paper trees used in the cold funeral activities, four represent money. These four trees are the *baitian wang*, the *ertian wang*,[1] the "gold tree" *(she-dze)*, and the "silver tree" *(tu-dze)*. The *baitian wang* is given to the King of the Underworld

---

1. These terms are of Han origin and have no Yi language equivalents. The Han terms are used in the ritual.

(mu-mi tze-lo-wa) as the price of some land; the *ertian wang* is used by the spirit to do business in Ngomi. It is said that if the spirit gets rich in Ngomi, he or she will give money to the world of the living. The gold and silver trees serve as spending money for use in Ngomi. The *bema* even gives the soul a little paper tree called a *gu,* and when the money has run out the soul can shake the *gu* and more money will fall out.

Grain and tools are also a part of the offering to the spirit. First, the *bema* gives the spirit a pair of *chi-che* (gourd ladles) as tools for drawing water in Ngomi. The *bema* also represents the spirit in the "trampling the grasses" *(lo-she-dzuo-duo)* rite and asks for things from the daughter of the dead person—things such as money, towels, clothes, shoes, tobacco, liquor, grain, and meat. She must hand over immediately the gifts she has prepared. Only after the *bema* has the requested items can the "trampling the grasses" rite begin.

Not only does the *bema* give things to the spirit on behalf of the host family, he even instructs the spirit in their use. With the *gu,* for instance, the *bema* tells him or her, "The *gu* is important in the Underworld: in hot weather merely put the *gu* on your head and you won't feel hot, but cool; in the rain, hold up the *gu* and your clothes will remain dry while other people are getting drenched; in the winter, the *gu* can be worn as clothing, so that when other people are cold, you will be warm." The same thing happens with the *ngo-di-dje*—the *bema* tells the spirit, "There are seas, rivers, and mountains in Ngomi just as there are here; when you come to the sea, the *ngo-di-dje* will turn into a boat; when you come to a river, into a bridge; when you come to a mountain, into a ladder; as long as you have it, you can overcome any difficulty." Of course, the spirit cannot take all the gifts with him or her; a portion is left as inheritance for his or her descendants.

The purpose for holding the cold funeral is to offer paper money, livestock, and objects to the spirit. It seems very normal for the Nisu—things that the spirit needs in Ngomi have to be brought there from Dimi. It is the same with the birth of a person—all he or she needs in the living world, such as money, livestock, grain, and clothes, are brought from Ngomi.

THE RITE OF FIGHTING OFF DEMONS

When the *bema* escorts the spirit to the land of the ancestors, it is by no means smooth sailing all the way. It is necessary for the spirit to be psychologically prepared in order to complete a successful journey. Aside from having to climb steep inclines, cross seas and rivers, be buffeted by the wind and rain and baked by the sun, the spirit also has to fight off all sorts of demons along the way. These demons include some in human form and some in animal form. They hold areas in the road, and the spirit can reach its destination only if they are fought off.

As in other rites, it is mainly the *bema* who drives them off, because it is the *bema* who escorts the spirit from start to finish. There are two varieties of this rite—fighting off demons in human form, which is called *ngo-dzo-de*, and fighting off demons in animal form, called *ngo-dzo-xo*—though in the cold funeral the two varieties are performed simultaneously.

While fighting off the human demons, the *bema* chants the Ngo-dzo-de Prayer, which tells of a girl named Gu-dji-ni-pa who could not enter Ngomi because she had not been married in the human world. She does nothing but wait by the road to grab men's spirits and make them marry her, and the *bema* must drive her off in order to give the spirit free passage. This prayer is not read for the spirit of a dead woman, nor are demons in human form driven off.

It takes two *bema* to fight off demons; the two represent Aji and Ajuo, who are brothers. They were orphaned as children and grew up together. After they grew up, Aji married and began to change. He forced his younger brother to divide their family property, of which he took eight of the nine parts, leaving the least desirable ninth for his brother. Ajuo sent the goats, cattle, pigs, and chickens that had come to him off into the mountains, sent the ducks into the sea, and then ran off to the Street of the Intermingling of *Yin* and *Yang* Forces (*she-shu-tsi-li-dze*) and indeed to Ngomi itself. When Aji, the elder brother, learned of this, he grieved beyond all reason, but it was too late. Three years later, after Aji eventually died, he still had not entered Ngomi, and his brother, Ajuo, finally came forward to drive off demons, allowing Aji to enter.

The rite of driving off animal demons is necessary because, in addition to the female demon, there are all manner of animal demons on the road to Ngomi, such as the Red-Tailed Tiger (*lo-nu-mo*), Long-Necked Leopard (*tsi-mo*), Short-Tailed Dog (*tsi-me-du*), and Great White Fowl (*ji-tu*). The only way for the spirit to reach the land of the ancestors in peace is for the *bema* to make all of them disappear.

When the rite of fighting off demons begins, some people beat gongs and drums and begin doing a dance of offering. One of the two *bema* holds a beef rib pierced by a sharp-tipped knife: the knife is for killing human demons, and the bone is for the tiger and leopard to eat. The other *bema* holds the golden-bamboo staff (*vu-du*). The *bema* with the knife plays the part of Ajuo, the one with the staff, Aji. The ritual starts at the grave with the *bema* playing Ajuo saying the Ngo-dzo-de Prayer and then breaking into wild dance. The *bema* playing Aji immediately starts saying the Ngo-dzo-xo Scripture. While this is going on, the daughter of the deceased pretends to be a tiger trying to seize the beef bone to eat, and the other *bema*, watching the time closely, does the ritual for driving off demons in animal form. The whole demon-fighting rite goes on for half an hour, and then beside the ox skin the *bema* breaks a small white bowl that has been offered, signifying that the demons have all been dispersed.

There is another demon-chasing ritual in the funeral ritual, called *ni-mi*. The *ni-mi* is different from the *ngo-dzo* in that it chases away all unpropitiated ghosts not connected with the cold funeral, "sweeping clean" the funeral area. With demons of somewhat greater power or importance, one uses a spirit horse *(sa-mo)* to escort them away.

PEOPLE'S IDEAS ABOUT THE COLD FUNERAL

In the funeral ritual, various participants—the *bema,* host family, and members and assistants of different troupes of mourners—all present different states of mind. Here I will discuss two common states of mind in the ritual.

The first of these is found in dancing reverential dances. Ritual dancing is an important constituent of the cold funeral; not only are there sections consisting only of reverential dancing, but many other sections also involve ritual dancing. Rituals made up entirely of dancing generally begin at 7 P.M. or later and last until 3 A.M., with as much as eight hours of continuous dancing. What is more, the mourners compete to see which troupe can dance the longest and most beautifully. According to the custom, the longer and grander the dancing, the more successful the cold funeral ritual.

But why dancing? There are different explanations. The *bema* believe that reverential dancing shows the King of Ngomi that the world of the living still needs people to go on multiplying. The dancing in a number of specific rituals signifies the greeting or sending off of divine entities—as for instance when the *bema* protects a god. Ordinary Nisu people say that ceremonial dancing boosts courage for the participants. They believe in the existence of ghosts and spirits, and the idea of ghosts and spirits is constant throughout the ritual. The fear of spirits is so deeply embedded in people's minds that they almost turn pale at the mention of them. In their view, ghosts always follow people—in fields, at the edges of fields, on roads, and so on. Ghosts throw sand in the woods and make one hear the noise; or they make strange howls (they howl only once on a mountain, traveling to a different mountain to howl again; day breaks after they howl three times); or they imitate cries of children or women; or they follow humans or livestock at some distance behind. The Nisu who walk outside at night feel very nervous. They point the flashlight backward and turn the radio on really loud. And they believe that by doing so, ghosts and spirits dare not follow them. Every time someone dies in the village or in a neighboring village, people usually do not go out in the evening, women and children especially. In the ritual, people are involved with ghosts and they get edgy during the night. But after the reverential dancing, their courage is boosted and they feel more relaxed.

The second type of psychological state is found in calling spirits. The *bema* is the person who communicates between the Dimi and Ngomi worlds. But even with the protection of the *bema's* spirits, the *bema* are still in a state of terror; as they escort the departing spirit to the land of the ancestors, the implication is that their own spirits are traveling off with the departing spirit. If they should fail to return, they will also die. In some rituals, such as fighting off demons and showing the way, the *bema* who is not taking part will greet the other on his way back, meaning that the *bema* has already returned among them. Not only the *bema* but also Nisu people in general hold this folk belief about the importance of the spirit in one's body. If one is startled at some place, he or she will return to that place to call back his or her spirit. A sick person will often have his or her spirit called. The author witnessed such an incident in his childhood: It happened that a child fell while climbing a tree and was seriously injured. People took the child to the clinic in the brigade headquarters of the rural people's commune. While the doctor was treating the child, the mother said, "My child, don't go to other places; don't go around to play. Mother is at your side." She was calling the child's spirit. Nobody present, including the doctor, found this strange. In the Nisu areas, it is firmly believed that if one's spirit leaves one's body, one will die. This applies not only to human beings but also to livestock. Therefore, in funeral rituals the *bema* calls not only his own spirit, but the spirits of all the participants. In addition, he calls "souls of the five grains and six types of livestock." The importance of calling them is that what is supposed to depart departs and what is supposed to come back comes back. Before the funeral rituals, people's minds are blank; afterward, they are at ease and free from worry.

CHAPTER 10

A Valley-House: Remembering a Yi Headmanship

Erik Mueggler

In 1953, a team of ethnographers taking part in the nationwide Nationalities Classification *(minzu shibie)* project visited the village of Yijichang in Yongren County, Yunnan.[1] Their report analyzed patterns of land use, relations of exploitation, and local government structure in this area before Liberation and classed its people as members of the newly constituted Yi nationality. The pre-Liberation local state hierarchy, it stated, had here as elsewhere been an instrument of direct oppression, designed to extract wealth from the people through taxes and corvée labor. In the Qing dynasty and the Republic, the first level of this oppressive hierarchy had been an institution unique to this part of Yunnan. It was called a *huotou* (伙頭), and it administered a small group of Yi villages. Of the Yijichang *huotou* the report declared:

Grants from the Committee for Scholarly Communications with China and the Wenner-Gren Foundation for Anthropological Research supported the field research for this chapter. I am indebted to Professor Liu Yaohan of the Chuxiong Yi Culture Research Institute and Professor He Yaohua of the Yunnan Social Sciences Academy for their indispensable aid in setting up this project, and to Luo Wengao for his patient help in gathering every aspect of this material. I also owe thanks to William Rowe, Emily Martin, Gillian Feeley-Harnik, Laury Oaks, Katherine Verdery, Sara Berry, Stevan Harrell, and the participants in the First International Conference on Yi Studies for their comments on earlier drafts.

1. Some of the colloquial terms here are in standard Mandarin or its Yunnan dialect variation. These are rendered in Hanyu pinyin. Many are in a language generally considered a subdialect of the Central dialect of Yi, a Loloish Tibeto-Burman language (Bradley 1979; Chen, Bian, and Li 1985). Following local usage, I call this dialect Lòloŋò. For transcriptions of Lòloŋò, I have modified the version of the International Phonetic Alphabet employed by Ma Xueliang to transcribe Yi languages (1951, 1992). Acute accents indicate high, level tones; grave accents low, falling tones; and mid-range level tones are unmarked. Underlining of vowels indicates laryngalization. On the Nationalities Classification project, see Fei 1981; Jiang 1985; Lin 1987, 1990; Lin and Jin 1980; Guldin 1994.

It is said that in Yijichang in the late Qing and early Republic, the positions of *huotou* and so forth [in the hierarchy of local government] were dominated by local tyrants and evil gentry. After the county reform [in 1925], corvée and grain tax gradually increased, and the *baozhang* [the local leader of the community self-policing organization] and *huotou* seized every opportunity to blackmail the people. After 1935, corvée and grain tax grew ever deeper. . . . The suffering of poor laborers and peasants was extremely heavy. Each change or continuity at this basic level of the puppet state followed its need to oppress and exploit the peasants. (YSB 1986, 109)

In the early 1990s, the view that *huotou* had been the lowest level of an oppressive administrative hierarchy dominated by "local tyrants and evil gentry" still prevailed among government and Party officials in Yongren County. People in the county's minority areas, however, had begun to use a very different vocabulary to speak of the former *huotou*. In Zhizuo, a long day's walk from Yijichang, an elementary schoolteacher told me, "If you really want to study our nationality's religion, you should begin by studying the *ts'ici* [the local term for *huotou*]." "Even though it was discontinued a long time ago," another Zhizuo resident frequently asserted, "the *ts'ici* still exists in people's hearts. It is the heart of our nationality." A budding entrepreneur, who would have made an excellent candidate for the *ts'ici*, was more explicit: "If the Communist Party were serious about restoring national customs, they would allow us to reinstate the *ts'ici*, because after all it is our nationality's most important custom."

In the 1980s, the post-Mao regime had granted such terms as *nationality (minzu), nationality religion (minzu zongjiao),* and *nationality customs (minzu fengsu)* new legitimacy. Three decades before, the Nationalities Classification project had assigned 95 percent of Zhizuo's population to the Yi nationality. Zhizuo residents used this label when traveling in the largely Han lowlands or dealing with officials at the county level or above; but among other inhabitants of Zhizuo or the surrounding mountains, most preferred the term *Lòlop'ò*. By the early 1990s some had begun to assert that their official "nationality" should be Lòlop'ò. These claims were always founded on statements about the old *ts'ici*. The territory of the "Lòlop'ò nationality" was the region that had been governed by the *ts'ici*, its language was the language spoken in this area, and its distinguishing "religion" and "customs" were the rituals associated with the *ts'ici*.

When I took my hosts' advice and began to investigate the Zhizuo *ts'ici*, I found that these claims were only the most recent development of a prolonged and complex struggle over collective memory, in which recollections of the *ts'ici* were central. This chapter is part of a history of this struggle. It describes memories of the *ts'ici* system in the two decades preceding Liberation. In the early 1990s, Zhizuo Lòlop'ò spoke of the *ts'ici* of the 1930s and 1940s as their ancestors' cleverest invention, designed to protect their community from the state's least predictable excesses. Most important, it was a practical solution to the difficulties of feeding and entertaining visiting officials, soldiers, and other influential outsiders. Systems like the *ts'iɐi* existed where speakers of what is now known as the Central dialect of Yi resided along important trading routes or in close proximity to administrative centers. When officials traveled through these areas, they descended, often with large entourages, on relatively affluent households and demanded their most lavish hospitality. In mountain communities, where even the wealthiest had few resources, such hospitality might well ruin the host. Zhizuo's *ts'iɐi* system rotated the responsibility for hosting outsiders among the community's most prosperous households, supplying them with the harvest of a large parcel of irrigated rice land to help offset their expenses. In the early 1990s, residents described such responsibilities as services to the community. If the *ts'iɐi* system could do little to diminish the force of the local state's demands, it could at least distribute them evenly among those best able to bear them.

In speaking of the *ts'iɐi*, people in Zhizuo often exhibited a "virtuosity in self description" that, as Keane (1995, 102) has noted, seems to characterize societies where ritual oratory and formal discourse are strongly valued. Much speech about the *ts'iɐi* was formalized, consisting of lists of "rules and procedures" (*ɕipe mope*), poetic phrases from ritual chants referring to these rules' ancestral origins, and reflexive exegetical commentary. While many people in Zhizuo enthusiastically agreed to talk about general aspects of the *ts'iɐi* system and its relation to present concerns about "nationality," most deferred my more specific questions to a small group of elderly ritual specialists and former members of *ts'iɐi* households. Like many anthropologists blessed with highly articulate informants, I often listened to these experts' fluent discourse on "rules and procedures" with a sense of unease. This talk often seemed to refer to a bounded, timeless world that could have had no real existence in the violent, conflict-ridden, and rapidly changing context of early-twentieth-century China. In this talk, the *ts'iɐi* system took on a text-like legibility, eminently readable but divorced from the confusion and ambiguity of daily life. I soon learned, however, that its formal qualities were precisely what gave this talk the unifying potential that made it politically potent in the real world. As Keane (ibid., 103) argues, such "expansive self-consciousness . . . should neither be taken for granted as a straightforward expression of autonomous cultural meanings nor dismissed out of hand as merely the product of 'officializing strategies'" (Bourdieu 1977 [1972]). Talk about the *ts'iɐi* system amounted, to the contrary, to a powerful strategy of self-representation, which drew its force from the capacity of formal, reflexive speech to frame a coherent, synchronic world removed from present conflicts and ambiguities. A "strategic essentialism" (Spivak 1988), this was an effort to seize control of collective self-representation from those who promoted and distributed the official revitalization of "nationality customs" and "nationality religion."

The aim of this chapter is to re-present the picture of the *ts'ici* system that ritual experts and former members of *ts'ici* households presented to me as an outsider.[2] These specialized accounts were at the heart of struggles over memories of the *ts'ici* after 1950. They gave such memories continuity and coherence, kept alive the possibility that the *ts'ici* system might be reconstructed should local officials accede, and created a foundation for the politically powerful claim that the area once administered by the *ts'ici* should be the territory of a distinct nationality. Much of this systematically ordered knowledge concerned the yearly cycle of rituals sponsored by the *ts'ici* household (Mueggler 1996). Here, though, I have chosen to organize accounts concerned with the responsibilities, ideal moral character, proscribed activities, and prescribed compensation of the major players in the *ts'ici* system. I show how these recollections employ procreative metaphor and moral ideas about speech, sexuality, and sociability to create an imagined unity for all who lived in the former *ts'ici* and claimed to be Lòlop'ò. This talk employed elaborate spatial and temporal homologies to associate the *ts'ici* with procreative force. In temporal terms, it drew parallels between giving birth and nurturing children and the communal work of farming rice to pay for the *ts'ici*'s social and ritual obligations; in spatial terms, it compared the bounded territory of Zhizuo to the *ts'ici*'s house, with a productive unity of ancestral spouses at its center and a crowd of honored but potentially threatening guests at its margins.

As Lévi-Strauss pointed out, house images frequently display the capacity to integrate diverse or mutually contradictory ideas and principles (1983, 1984; cf. Carsten and Hugh-Jones 1995). Following this suggestion, I argue that recollections of the *ts'ici* system used a series of interrelated house images—a reliquary box, the *ts'ici*'s house, the houselike valley—to fashion an inclusive unity imagined to embrace all Zhizuo residents and to exclude from internal household matters the powerful outsiders the system ostensively served. From within this domain, people in Zhizuo could expand in apparently contradictory ways the principles of descent and affinity that structured social relations within their own households. People of diverse origins, including many with Han forbears, could speak of each other as descended from a single ancestral couple. People from households that had not experienced intermarriage could speak of each other as linked in a circle of affinal relations and mutually engaged in the intimate processes of household reproduction. This formal and reflexive talk of a long-defunct institution could

2. Published material on *huotou* systems is thin, consisting in a few scattered references by 1950s investigators (such as the one quoted above) some brief descriptions in local gazetteers (see, e.g., Guo and Xi 1924, 1:16a), and a few articles in local history journals (see Su 1989).

thus take advantage of long-standing associations of the concept of "nationality" *(minzu)* with origin, inheritance, and descent to become a powerful strategy of self-representation, making possible the demands for a separate nationality status for the *ts'ici's* former inhabitants.

"THOSE WHO CAN BEAR IT"

In the last two decades of the Republic, about fifteen hundred people lived in Zhizuo's twenty-four villages and hamlets. The largest villages formed a rough oval around a stretch of irrigated rice paddy land on the floor of the biggest valley. A footpath, paved with stone in the steepest places, ran through this valley, linking the two county centers of Dayao and Yongren (or Zuojie).[3] In the first half of the twentieth century, these mountains were frequently awash with armies, which forcibly recruited soldiers and requisitioned grain, livestock, money, and corvée labor (see Map 10.1). Between 1915 and 1929, warlord armies from Sichuan and Yunnan entered through the tiny county of Yongren on Zhizuo's northern border at least eight times, requisitioning grain worth over eight hundred *liang* of silver and nearly two million yuan (CYZZ 1993, 148). The People's Liberation Army passed through twice on its long march, attacking and briefly occupying the town of Dayao early in 1935, and returning in 1936 (ibid., 150). In 1938 the Burma road, passing to the south of Zhizuo, became South China's only conduit for supplies from the West to keep alive the Guomindang's resistance against the Japanese. New roads were constructed through Dayao and Yongren Counties to link the Burma road to the Guomindang bases in Sichuan (ibid., 149), and its heavy military, administrative, and civilian traffic on this road often spilled onto the footpath through Zhizuo. In the 1940s, the nationalist government's regime of forced military conscription bore heavily on both counties, as groups of soldiers ranged through their mountains hunting down youths evading the draft. Finally, in 1948 and 1949 the Communist Party underground carried out a series of armed rebellions in the area, and "Communist bandits," Guomindang regulars, and militia units fought pitched battles in Zhizuo and the surrounding mountains (ibid., 151).

In addition to this formidable military traffic, local officials and police stopped in Zhizuo to oversee conscription and tax collection, recruit corvée

3. Before 1925, Dayao County was divided into administrative units called *fensi*. In 1925, a separate county, Yongren, was formed out of Dayao's northernmost *fensi*, and both counties were divided into smaller units called *qu*, or districts. Zhizuo was part of Dayao's Zhonghe *qu*, controlled by the Xia family of hereditary officials. In 1958, when the political lines of China's rural areas were redrawn to form communes, most of Zhonghe district, including most of Zhizuo, became part of Yongren Commune (which later reverted to Yongren County). This redivision left a few, outlying villages of the Zhizuo *ts'ici* in Dayao County (YSB 1986, 109; YSRTB 1990).

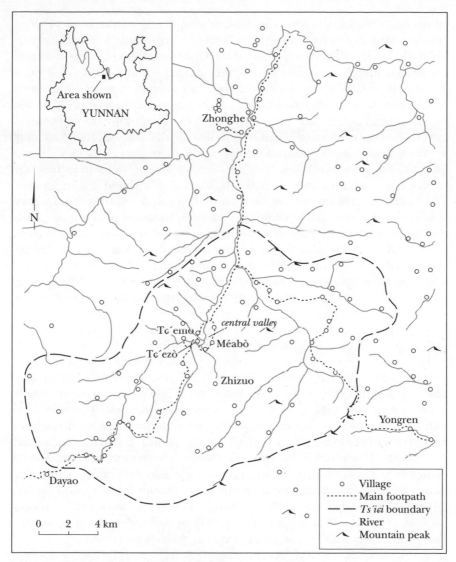

Map 10.1. Zhizuo and surrounding area

labor, settle disputes, arrest criminals, or simply rest on the road between county towns. Zhizuo was located in Dayao's northernmost district *(qu)*. In the period of instability that preceded the Qing dynasty's fall in 1911, an ethnically Han merchant named Xia had seized control of this district and given himself the title of *tusi*. (*Tusi* were hereditary officials in regions occupied by non-Han peoples, who maintained varying degrees of independence from provincial and central state bureaucracies.)[4] The Xia family retained control over this region until 1949. Their district was divided into *bao,* for which they appointed *baozhang* to conscript soldiers and collect taxes and levies. Zhizuo formed a single *bao,* and its *baozhang* appointed a *jiazhang* (until 1938, *luzhang*) to take responsibility for each small village or neighborhood of a larger one. The Xia family allowed *baozhang* to retain about two *dan* of the tax grain they collected as a yearly salary,[5] while *jiazhang* drew pittances of about .26 *dan* a year for their thankless task of convincing their fellow villagers to pay their taxes (YSB 1986, 109). In the 1940s the power of the Xia family in Zhizuo was rivaled by that of Zhizuo's militia commander, Luo Guotian, a local who sold guns to men in Zhizuo and organized them into a formidable fighting force. Tension with Luo Guotian, the pressing need to keep an eye on revenue collection, and Zhizuo's convenience as a rest stop on the road to the county capital frequently brought members of the Xia family to Zhizuo, along with large retinues of guards, servants, and runners.

Each year, Zhizuo residents selected a *ts'ici* household from among the community's most affluent families. The most expensive and time-consuming obligation of this household was to lodge, feed, and entertain the stream of soldiers, officials, police, merchants, and other influential visitors who walked the stone path through the valley. In addition, the host household and its staff of five maintained a prison cell for locals arrested for crimes and youths held to be forcibly conscripted. They carried letters from the district center to the next group of villages on the route to the county seat, maintained the stone footpath that made this route easier to travel, and buried all outsiders who died within Zhizuo and had no nearby kin. Finally, they organized a yearly cycle of communal rituals intended to draw fertility, wealth, and good health into Zhizuo and drive away poverty and disease.

Unlike *baozhang* and militia commanders, host households in the *ts'ici* system were not appointed by the Xia family. Instead, they were elected by a group of the community's most influential or affluent men, who met yearly

4. The ethnically Han Xia family took the title of *tusi* several decades after the Qing state had replaced previous hereditary officials in this part of Yunnan with ordinary appointed magistrates. On the history of the *tusi* system see Herman 1997; Hu 1981; Huang 1968; Li Shiyu 1990, 465–94; She 1947; Smith 1970.

5. Units of measure used in this chapter are as follows: a *mu* was about one-fifteenth of a hectare, a *sheng* about 1.08 liters, and a *dan* about 50 kilograms.

during a festival on the first day of the lunar year, in which much of Zhizuo's population gathered in the courtyard of the previous year's host household to celebrate the transfer of the title of *ts'ici*. The most powerful members of this group were the *baozhang* and, in the 1940s, the militia commander Luo Guotian. Representatives from all the other relatively wealthy families of the area, *jiazhang*, and former *ts'ici* also participated. The only affluent households excluded from this group, and from serving as host households, were the few that insisted on their Han ethnicity. On new year's day, the outgoing *ts'ici* ushered these most important of his guests—between twenty and thirty in number—into his barn loft. This room—now cleared of hay and furnished with two low beds and a fire pit—had been the cell in which the host household had held those arrested by agents of the local state. The *baozhang* and the militia commander usually took the seats at the upper ends of the beds, while others crowded in next to them. Those who did not wish to assert a claim of status or participate in the discussion squatted on the floor at the foot of the beds, or near the door. Over a meal of meat, sticky rice, and alcohol, the guests reviewed the names of two households chosen the year before to serve as hosts for the next two years and added a third name to the list.

The "rules and procedures" of the *ts'ici* system mandated that the title of *ts'ici* should rotate around the oval of villages on the slopes of Zhizuo's largest valley "toward the right hand" (counterclockwise). For this reason, households of only one village were considered each year. Zhizuo residents insisted that the *ts'ici* household should be free of deaths for the year previous to its service (except for miscarriages and deaths of infants without teeth). If the household already selected for the following year had experienced a death, another choice should be made. Households with widows or widowers of any generation were unacceptable. Most important, the household should have a healthy resident elderly couple who could take on the *ts'ici's* ritual duties. This couple should have raised several children to adulthood and preserved the habit of wearing old-style Lòlop'ò clothing: hemp sandals rather than the more common straw ones, hempen shirts and trousers, and robes that buttoned down the side instead of the front. Finally, and crucially, the household had to be wealthy enough to bear the financial burdens of the *ts'ici*.

The formula "give it to those who can bear it [on their backs] or carry it [in their hands], *bù dù vé kɔ́ sṳ t'ɛ̀ gɔ̀*, was supposed to guide the *ts'ici's* selection. Every year, the host household drew an income of about thirty *dan* of grain from a ten-*mu* parcel of land that rotated with the *ts'ici*, but it often expended as much as sixty *dan* of grain and forty to fifty goats. Zhizuo residents remembered some years in which hundreds of officials and soldiers traveled through the valley, staying days or weeks at a time and plunging the *ts'ici* household into serious debt. For this reason, most prospective *ts'ici* were said to be desperate to evade the responsibility. A member of the outgoing *ts'iɐi's* staff (the *lòrʑ*), chosen for his ability to speak and entertain, attended the meeting to persuade candidates to accept the position. Face-to-face with the most powerful members of the community, most of those selected found themselves accepting. Yet after the meeting, or so former members of *ts'iɐi* households maintained, those chosen would seek a patron among the meeting's most influential members—the militia commander and a certain former *baozhang* were said to be the favorite choices. Those chosen would borrow from kin and call in debts to offer the patron a massive bribe of money and livestock, following this up with a young goat or chicken on the first day of the month every month for a year. If the bribes were sufficient, the patron would speak for the family at the next year's meeting, claiming that its situation had changed, and it could no longer bear the burden. As a daughter of a former *ts'iɐi* commented, having one's name mentioned at the meeting might easily mean ruin, either from the expenses of the *ts'iɐi* or from the bribes paid to avoid it.

Though few would willingly take on the burden of the *ts'iɐi*, this service compensated a household's members with prestige they could obtain no other way. Selection was public affirmation that a household had attained the most enviable of states. Relations between its eldest married couple were harmonious and fruitful, attended by neither deaths nor quarrels; they had produced several sons and daughters and their fertility had successfully blossomed into wealth. A passage from a mortuary lament, in which a daughter sings of happy times before her parents' deaths, describes this ideal state of fortune.

wú nɨ̀ k'ə pɛ̠́ zò
kà dù mi pɛ̠́ wo
ló dù mi pɛ̠́ wo
tcí lu tcè tca ga
kà lu tso tca ga
zò ho né yi t'ù tsɔ ga
né ho lò tce ka̠ tsɔ ga
tsò mi sɨ́ zò tsɔ du̠ lɔ
dɔ mi ló zò tsɔ du̠ lɔ

like rings on a buffalo's horns
our fields widened
our pastures expanded
every kind of livestock grazed for us
every kind of grain grew for us
our sons raised a sea of wealth
our daughters filled the granary
our bowls overflowed with grain
our cups filled up with broth

Those who selected such a household expected that if it fulfilled its ritual obligations correctly its harmonious productivity would saturate Zhizuo. In addition to this prestige, having served as *ts'iei* made one a permanent member of the inner circle that controlled the *ts'iei* system. Finally, many in Zhizuo insisted that though some former *ts'iei* may have been ruined financially, and though some were persecuted harshly during the Cultural Revolution, with few exceptions they lived long, healthy lives as a result of their year of service.

In some ways Zhizuo's *ts'iei* system bears comparison to Maya cargo systems. Eric Wolf once suggested that service in such systems tended to impede the mobilization of wealth as capital within the community in comparison to the outside world (1955, 458). This suggestion stimulated a debate about whether cargo service tended to level a community economically by creating the incentive for the most prosperous to expend their wealth within the community or to stratify it socially by creating avenues for the rich to accumulate social prestige (Cancian 1965, 1992; Haviland 1977; Nash 1964; Wolf 1957, 1986). While Zhizuo residents' reminiscences of the 1930s and 1940s do not provide enough evidence to indicate whether the *ts'iei* system impeded the mobilization of wealth as capital, they do leave room for some informed speculation. Of the four Zhizuo households classified as "landlords" during the Land Reform Movement, one was Han and thus excluded from service. In the mid-1940s, the Han family opened a hostel in Zhizuo for travelers with mule trains. Using profits from this hostel, the family purchased land to farm with hired labor and mules to haul salt, sugar, and opium, expanding its fortunes considerably. The two Lòlop'ò "landlord" families whose location made them eligible for service were those of the militia commander Luo Guotian and of a former *baozhang* whom Zhizuo residents considered to be "gentry" *(shenshi)*. These were among a very few Lòlop'ò households powerful enough to forestall their own selection as host household. They not only avoided the enormous drain on their resources that service would have entailed but also received flows of bribes from families wishing to evade service. By the end of the 1940s, each of these households was heavily engaged in the salt, sugar, and opium trades, while most Zhizuo residents benefited from this trade only by hiring out as porters or muleteers. One might speculate that the *ts'iei* system helped free a few of the politically or militarily most influential to make use of Zhizuo's location along a trading route, even as it limited the capacity of prosperous community members to mobilize their wealth for trade.

A PRODUCTIVE EMBRACE

The titles of *ts'iei* and *ts'ieimo* (*ts'iei's* wife) were granted the household's eldest married couple. This pair was spared the mundane duties of hosting visitors, carrying baggage and letters, guarding prisoners, and burying dead outsiders, tasks left to other household members and a staff of aides. They were expected to live a life of quiet seclusion in the service of a group of ancestral spirits, the souls of a mythological family believed to have founded Zhizuo. These were said to have been not Lòlop'ò but Líp'ò—Central-dialect speakers who lived in the adjacent mountains, mostly in Dayao County. Every account of the *ts'ici* system included a tale in which these ancestors, a father and his sons, traveled every year from their home in the nearby Baicaolin Mountains to Zhizuo's wide, pleasant valley in search of wild pigs. At the center of the valley was a marsh, where they drove the pigs into the mud to be clubbed to death. On one occasion, as one ritualist in Zhizho told the story, the father looked around him and liked what he saw: "At that time, the forest was very thick, and water gushed and spurted from the spring down there. When one of them dropped his knife sheath to drink water, two rice grains rolled out. He shook more seeds out of the sheath. 'Can one plow and plant in this place? It looks like a fine place to live. If this is a good place to plow and plant, let the heads of these rice plants grow as long as horse's tails; let the rats not eat them or the insects climb them; let them be truly excellent.' After saying this, he sowed the seeds in three places." After planting the marsh, father and sons went home. They returned nine months later to discover the rice growing tall and thick, untouched by rats, birds, or insects. Understanding that this was indeed a fine place to live, they brought their families to settle. Initially, all the obligations of the *ts'ici* were undertaken by a single family living in the center of Zhizuo's largest village of Tc'emo in a house called "little *ts'ici*." After several generations, as the numbers of visitors to the valley swelled, this family found its burdens too heavy, and with a large parcel of the valley's best land it created an ancestral trust that would rotate from village to village with the obligations of the *ts'ici*. In addition, the family established several resting places for the souls of the founding ancestors. One was a wooden reliquary box, passed with the title of *ts'ici* from one household to another. This box was rectangular, a little larger than a shoe box, with a protruding, scalloped rim on its lid (Figure 10.1). It held (in different accounts) two, six, or twelve ox, tiger or human bones, a few seeds of buckwheat, six or twelve copper coins, and the legal title to the ten-*mu* ancestral trust that supplied the *ts'ici* household its income. It was shaped like the earth of Lòlop'ò mythology: a rectangular valley, surrounded by mountains (the lid's scalloped rim), beneath which were seeds, buried wealth, and the bones of ancestors.

Another resting place was on a hilltop behind the village of Tc'emo. Even in the early 1990s, many mountain villages in Líp'ò and Lòlop'ò areas had preserved a patch of old-growth forest on the mountain slope behind and above the houses (cf. CYZZ 1993, 376). One large, old tree was a Misi, said to govern the earth, weather, crops, animals, and all other living things in the area around the village. Others were sometimes called Mitṣù (or Mitsï),

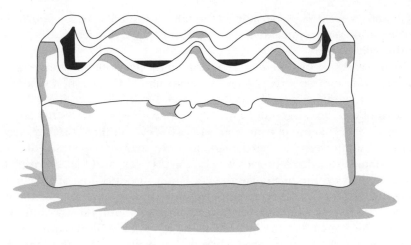

Figure 10.1. The reliquary box, containing the souls of the founding ancestors, shaped like the earth of Lòlop'ò mythology.

the spirit of "earth veins," which governed weather; Sr̀mògù or Amùt'anè, the lightning spirit; and Lebùnè, a hunting spirit. Zhizuo's Misi was formally called Agàmisimo (great earth spirit behind the house), and it was a residence for the souls of the founding ancestral couple. It inhabited a giant pine tree surrounded by a low stone wall in the center of a dense patch of forest on the peak of a hill several hundred yards higher than the village's highest house, but much lower than the surrounding mountains. Beside it stood an equally tall tree inhabited by Sr̀mògù, the lightning spirit. From the top of this hill, Agàmisimo could survey the entire central valley of Zhizuo; but its influence was said to extend much further, to all twenty-four villages and hamlets of Zhizuo.

The souls of this founding couple's children inhabited other places in the valley. The eldest and his or her spouse (Lòhə) occupied a small round stone beside the ancestral trust fields. In the spring, the host household organized a festival to transplant rice seedlings into the ancestral trust land and to propitiate this spirit. It was said to regulate the sexuality of women, which bloomed to threatening proportions in this season. Another couple (Lɔmælòhə) resided in a small stone shaped "like a little person" or fetus, curled up inside a close, stone shelter just below and outside the valley. The host household sponsored propitiations for this spirit when drought threatened the rice crops. A third (Tɕ'a) rested on a small wooden shelf within the doorway of a private house in Tɕ'emo and was propitiated yearly in the summer to counter the threat of epidemic disease. A fourth (Mitṣù) occupied a giant pine on a hilltop across the valley from Agàmisimo's tree and regulated the weather, especially on the valley's drought-prone eastern side. A fifth, no longer propitiated in the 1930s and 1940s, rested in another stone on the valley floor.

In the early 1990s, these spirits were still a live topic of conversation. "Here's what some people say about Agàmisimo," Qi Degui, a teacher at Zhizuo's elementary school once remarked. Qi and I were sitting outside the school gate, looking out over a ravine toward Agàmisimo's hill and the large village of Tc'emo in front of it, where the ever-diligent Li Zhidong was planting walnut trees. "He has a head, up there near the top of the hill," said Qi, "a stomach in the center of Tc'emo, arms, legs, and feet down by the river. Families on the head, like the Gu family, produce lots of college students. Those who live on his stomach never go hungry. And people who live on his feet, like Li Zhidong, are always running about, busy, wishing they were on the stomach or the head." Poking fun at Li Zhidong's industry, Qi Degui imagined Agàmisimo to be like the ox (or tiger) of Lòlop'ò mythology, distributed over the land at the creation of the world, his veins becoming the rivers, his hair the forests, his teeth the cliffs, and his lice the goats. Agàmisimo's body, sprawled out over the village of Tc'emo, could as well be said to cover all of Zhizuo, encompassing its spirit progeny as it encompassed its own head, stomach, and feet.

Qi Haiyun, a man in his late twenties who was soon to become Zhizuo's Party secretary, used a different set of idioms to describe the relationship between Agàmisimo and Miṭṣù, a second child of Agàmisimo, who occupied a pine tree on the opposite hilltop:

> Miṭṣù is over there on the shady side because he is only a branch of Agàmisimo. Agàmisimo sits where the sun shines first because he is like the king of a country. He governs Miṭṣù and all the rest, as well as the little *həbə* [spirits that watch mountain passes], which are like customs officials guarding the doors: you have to have their permission to pass or things go badly for you.
>
> [But why are they on opposite sides?] It's like in a house, where older and younger generations don't sit together. Spirits are like that, too; if they sat together, they would be equal. Agàmisimo takes the best seat. Analyzing it with modern thought, we could say that Agàmisimo is like a township *[xiang]* government and Miṭṣù is a village government *[cungongsuo]* in the township. Or better, it's as though Miṭṣù is the land-management office *[tudi guanlisuo]* of the township government: the territory they govern is the same, but Miṭṣù has more specific duties. He manages the rain and the insect infestations while Agàmisimo governs everything.

A body divided among head, stomach, and feet, a country with customs officials at the borders, a household where the elder generation takes the upstream seats, a township government organized bureaucratically into departments: each metaphor evokes an entity with a definite boundary, internally differentiated into organs encompassed by, and subordinate to, the whole. Lòlop'ò seemed to imagine Agàmisimo as a presence that, while anchored to the hill above Tc'emo, saturated the territory of Zhizuo to its outermost boundaries. Agàmisimo's spirit offspring took up specialized tasks associated with their own local anchorages but, because they were encompassed within this body, their influence also reached to its borders.

All in Zhizuo who called themselves Lòlop'ò, whether they believed themselves directly descended from Líp'ò immigrants from the Baicaolin Mountains or from Han immigrants from nearby parts of Yunnan or Sichuan, claimed Agàmisimo as their own ancestor. This claim was based not on genealogy but on this principle of spatially encompassing hierarchy. In saying, "It's like in a house, where older and younger generations don't sit together," Qi Haiyun referred to a spatial hierarchization that informs all Lòlop'ò notions of descent. The mortuary lament quoted above also eulogizes this hierarchy by describing a happy, unified family eating together in a house's upstream room, properly distributed by generation and gender:

> mo tsɔ gə̀ wú ti
> p'ò tsɔ gə̀ wú ti
> né tsɔ gə̀ tsò ti
> zò tsɔ gə̀ tsò ti
> lí tsɔ le tsɔ ko tə ti
> væ yi p'à la té ne tsò
> væ cí væ ha tsò

> mother sat at the bed's head
> father at the [opposite] bed's head
> daughters sat on the bed's center
> sons on the [opposite] bed's center
> grandchildren and great-grandchildren near the door
> we ate with laughing faces
> lifted bowls with smiling faces

The notion of descent evoked here is informed by the spatial disposition of bodies in a house's upstream room, where food is cooked and household members eat together. Authority and responsibility descend the two parallel beds from head to tail, from mothers to "daughters" (including daughters-in-law) to granddaughters, and from fathers to sons to grandsons. The parents' property and burdens descend to their children, as the latter move up to take their places. This is an encompassing hierarchy like that of Agàmisimo and his spirit progeny. The upstream room in which the happy family eats is the sleeping room of the mother and father; the beds on which the family sits are their sleeping beds from which the sons, daughters, and grandchildren are imagined to have sprung. The room enclosing the family is the receptacle for the parents' procreative union, in which all those who sit below them on the beds are imagined to have been generated.

A similar image of an encompassing domain in which titles, property, and burdens descend a spatially conceived hierarchy allowed those who claimed Lòlop'ò identity to speak of themselves as descended from the original Líp'ò ancestors. Lòlop'ò did not keep written genealogies, and they disposed of their version of ancestral tablets (a pair of wooden figurines bound together in conjugal union on a tiny woven-bamboo bed) after three generations. The absence of concrete evidence of genealogy gave Zhizuo residents great flexibility in imagining their descent. I frequently heard people who traced their ancestry through Han settlers from Sichuan or other parts of northern Yunnan refer simultaneously to the myth of origins quoted above as the arrival of their own ancestors in the valley. This claim was founded on their residence within Agàmisimo's sprawled and differentiated body, like sons and daughters sitting below their parents and within the embrace of their room.

WARDEN, SPEAKER, BEARER

Ritual experts remembered *ts'ici* and *ts'icimo* primarily as servants of these ancestral spirits: hosts to the wooden reliquary and sponsors of a cycle of rituals for the Agàmisimo's spirit progeny scattered through the valley. Their union was imagined to enfold all of Agàmisimo's descendants like the skin of that spirit's extended body or the walls of a parental household. Like the still, conjugal, but asexual union of the founding ancestors in Agàmisimo itself, this union was a source of procreative force for all those it embraced. In service of this force, the *ts'ici* couple was expected strictly to avoid everything associated with their influential visitors from the lowlands. They were to wear only the clothing thought to have been worn by the original ancestors, eat and drink from wooden bowls and clay jugs, rather than factory-made ceramic bowls, and eat no meat of dogs, horses, cattle, or any animals that had died rather than being slaughtered, all associated with lowland Han and considered filthy and insulting to ancestors. They were not to drink anything but homemade wheat beer, and were not to smoke. They were to be restrained in speech, never referring to death, violence, or conflict and to speak no Chinese for their entire year of service. It was understood that as an elderly couple they would not sit or sleep on the same bed or have sex. The *ts'icimo* should be past menopause so menstrual pollution would not compromise her ritual purity. And they were to be socially restrained, rarely stepping outside of their inner, upstream room and letting their staff and other members of their household serve as intermediaries between them and their important guests.

These proscriptions were intended to seclude the procreative union of *ts'ici* and *ts'icimo* from polluting influences associated with Han outsiders, but the household's influential visitors nevertheless concentrated within its walls everything the *ts'ici* couple was constrained to avoid. A staff of five kin and friends, selected by the *ts'iɛi* a few days after the new year (on the year's first day of the tiger), managed these threats. The "rules and procedures" of the *ts'iɛi* system mandated that this staff had five positions: *bôtṣə, lôrə, k'ələ, fumo,* and *fuzô*. In the recollections of ritual experts and members of former *ts'iɛi* households, the prescribed duties and ideal personal qualities of these staff members exploited ideas about speech, sociability, sexuality, and procreation to manage the margins of the *ts'iɛi's* household and negotiate the boundaries of the *ts'iɛi* territory. This staff guarded the still center of ancestral procreative force in Zhizuo by expediting the smooth passage of potentially threatening outsiders through and away.

Those who described the *ts'iɛi* system to me compared the *bôtṣə* to a prison warden. He helped the household with its least pleasant duties: caring for prisoners arrested by the *tusi's* guards or by police from the county town. In keeping with its role as host for troublesome guests, the *ts'iɛi* household kept, clothed, and fed all such prisoners until they were led out of the valley in chains. Prisoners were kept in a room in the barn's loft, which was furnished with a pair of low beds, strong lock, an iron collar, and chains. Few spent more than a few days in this cell, for all serious cases were tried either at the residence of the Xia *tusi* or the county seat. However, minor cases such as livestock theft and disputes over boundaries between adjoining fields were handled in the *ts'iɛi's* courtyard. In such cases, the offended party made a formal complaint to the *baozhang,* who forwarded a written report to the *tusi,* who then decided whether to order a hearing. To conduct a hearing, the *tusi* traveled to Zhizuo and summoned the *baozhang* and the militia commander to the *ts'iɛi's* house. After eating a full meal at the host household's expense, the *tusi* sent the warden to bring in both parties to the dispute. These knelt in the courtyard while the *tusi* and the militia commander, seated on the porch, questioned them and delivered judgment. Zhizuo residents claimed that the host household paid the fees associated with the hearing, although the officials probably also exacted additional fees from the accused party. In contrast to most agents of justice, some in Zhizuo maintained, the warden and *ts'iɛi* treated prisoners as guests, feeding them adequately and neither beating nor cursing them. In the last decade of the Republic, many prisoners were local youths arrested to be forcibly conscripted into the Guomindang armies, and most of these would have had ties of kinship with both the warden and the host household.

Zhizuo residents recalled that the *ts'iɛi* cell was put to its final use in May 1949, after a battle with a "Communist bandit" named Ding Zhiping. According to official histories, Ding Zhiping was a Party member and a staff officer in the People's Liberation Army's Eighth Route Army. Six years previously, he had returned to his hometown in nearby Huaping County to begin underground work. By 1949, he had gathered an army of several hundred, which he called the "People's Liberation Army, Western Yunnan Column." In March, he attacked a Huaping County town and from there marched on Yongren. There, the Yongren militia and troops of sympathizing local military commanders from Sichuan and northern Yunnan swelled the numbers of Ding's column to over ten thousand. From Yongren, the column divided to attack the northern Yunnan towns of Yuanmou and Dayao (CYZZ 1993, 190; ZYSZY 1988, 204). Reports of the battle at Dayao that drifted to Zhizuo described it as a terrifying cataclysm, in which tens of thousands of Guomindang soldiers, accompanied by tanks and cannon, defeated Ding's army. More terrifying yet, Ding's forces fled Dayao back toward Yongren on the mountain road that passed through Zhizuo. Ding and over a hundred troops holed up in the massive new house of the militia commander Luo Guotian, threatening to burn it down if attacked. Unable to stomach the idea of his new house in ashes, Luo offered Ding peaceful passage out of Zhizuo. After the "Communist bandits" filed out of his front door, Luo Guotian and his Zhizuo militia attacked them, killing over twenty and sparing none of the wounded. For the next few months, Guomindang troops hunted those who escaped through the surrounding hills, locking them up in the host household's prison cell until they could be taken to Dayao for punishment.

Stories of this battle were also the occasion for recollections of the host household's most onerous of duties, burying outsiders who died within Zhizuo's boundaries and who had no kin to care for their corpses. Elderly men and women in Zhizuo remembered that after the battle with Ding Zhiping, over twenty corpses lay in the sun for days while the elderly *ts'iɕi* and his son dragged them one by one into a gully near the battlefield and buried them. No one else would touch the corpses, dangerously polluted by their violent deaths. For forty years after this incident, people passing this mass grave reported spotting the ghosts of Ding Zhiping's defeated army wandering headless about the rocks, with bullet holes in their bodies or spears through their chests.

Another member of the staff, the *lòrɔ*, or speaker, was expected to help the household with its formidable task of feeding and entertaining important visitors. Former members of *ts'iɕi* families spoke of enormous trouble and expense. "These days officials come in groups of two or three, stay a day, and leave," recalled a woman who was twelve when her household was *ts'iɕi*, "but back then, they came in groups of twenty or thirty. They came in litters with bearers and someone out front to wave the flies away." These processions of officials, clerks, and runners would demand meat, bean curd, and alcohol and would stay for days to eat and drink. The worst years in living memory were 1935 and 1949, when soldiers from the People's Liberation Army and the Guomindang armies visited Zhizuo in quick succession. Residents of the large village of Tɕ'emo recalled that in the summer of 1949, four hundred soldiers of the Guomindang's 26th Division lodged in the host household's courtyard in that village for a month, hunting down the remnants of Ding Zhiping's army of "Communist bandits" and eating meat daily. Later that year, soldiers of the People's Liberation Army came through and stayed with the same host household for several weeks. The family, among Tc'emo's most affluent, was ruined just in time to be classed as "lower-middle peasants" during the Land Reform Movement and to enjoy the relative safety from persecution this status afforded for the next thirty years.

These powerful outsiders rarely showed the civility that hosts could expect from local guests. Another child of a former *ts'ici* recalled how on one of his frequent journeys through Zhizuo, the Xia *tusi*, dissatisfied with the quality of his dinner, beat the *ts'ici* with a board. The speaker's job was to prevent such incidents by contributing witty conversation to the *ts'ici's* hospitality. He stayed in the *ts'ici* household, at its expense, for his entire year of service, eating, drinking, and chatting with the guests. Experts on the *ts'ici* system maintained that a good speaker should be a gregarious personality, a good drinker, and an accomplished conversationalist. He should be fluent in Chinese, dress fashionably, and have cosmopolitan manners that would not draw scorn from the sophisticated guests. In a well-run *ts'ici* household, the speaker should greet the guests as they entered the valley, lead them to the host household, seat them, and call for food and drink. The elderly *ts'ici* and *ts'icimo* should only have to make a brief appearance to welcome the guests before retiring again.

Another aide was the *k'ɔlɔ*, or bearer, whose primary responsibility was to carry the luggage of visiting officials as they left the valley. As most officials traveled with more belongings than one man could carry, the bearer often pressed his and the *ts'ici's* kin to help. He and his crew accompanied officials twenty five kilometers to the next convenient stop on the way to the county seat or twenty kilometers to the residence of the *tusi*. Once on the road, officials sometimes forced bearer and company into service for the seventy kilometers to the county seat, or even beyond. The bearer was also responsible for carrying letters that arrived in Zhizuo onward to the next group of villages or the *tusi's* seat. Because he was usually busy with parties of visitors, this task often fell to the younger members of the *ts'ici's* own household. The youngest son of a former *ts'ici* recalled that during his father's year of service, he delivered letters after school. He was only nine years old and shoeless, but on the days letters came in, he packed them in his school bag and walked twenty-five kilometers to the next group of villages, returning in the dark.

The bearer also had a ritual obligation: at the new year, he carried the reliquary box from the old to the new *ts'ici* household. This duty required of the bearer a ritual purity similar to that of the elderly *ts'ici* couple. Experts on the *ts'ici* system said that the best candidate for bearer would be unmarried, would wear only clothing associated with the original Líp'ò ancestors, and would be an "honest" man who spoke seldom and displayed little agility or wit. One expert put it more bluntly. The ideal bearer he said, was an idiot *(bomi)* who spoke slowly if at all and was naive about sexual relations.

In addition to warden, speaker, and bearer, the *ts'iɕi's* staff included two assistants (*fumo* and *fuzò,* combining the Mandarin word *fu,* deputy or assistant, with the Lòloŋo suffixes *mo* and *zò,* big and small). Several villages in Zhizuo selected responsible men to greet and host important people passing through from other villages or regions. Those selected in the *ts'iɕi's* village became general assistants to the *ts'iɕi* household and helped organize and prepare food for rituals. At most, they expended several days of labor and two chickens, and their only compensation was the prestige of their jobs.

THE "PRICE OF HORSE FEED"

The "rules and procedures" recounted by ritual experts and former members of *ts'iɕi* households gave warden, speaker, and bearer rights to collect recompense for their duties. In exercising these rights, they extended the personal qualities associated with their practical duties to participate in the imaginative work of constituting Zhizuo as a house and household. Some of these "rules and procedures" were listed in chants performed during collective rituals for Agàmisimo and his spirit progeny. One chant outlined the warden's right of compensation:

> tɕ'e wú nï mæ ʂo
> tʂú zò tɕ'ï lɔ tʂɔ
> ts'i ɕi tɕ'ï lɔ tʂɔ
> mò tɕí mò tsæ ga
> mò tɕí mò go lɔ gɔ . . .
> tɕ'ï vɛ ʂo tɕ'ï ni
> nï ʂǎ ŋo lɔ ʂo
> sá vɛ ʂo tɕ'ï ni
> tʂ'o ʂǎ ŋo lɔ ʂo
> mò lu ŋo ņ ʂo
> ní lu ŋo ņ ʂo
> mǜ ni tɕ'ï hæ̱ tɕí
> me ne tɕe wò tɕí
> p'ò tʂɔ zò tʂɔ tɕí dó ŋɔ ŋɔ
> p'ò p'ò sa ts'i tɕe̱
> zò lí sa tsi tɕe̱

> receive from the village's head and tail
> from all who live in Zhizuo
> all who live in this *ts'iɕi*
> who breed fine horses
> who breed horses smoothly . . .

from one family
take two *sheng*
from three families
take six *sheng*
take no more
take no less
from the sky's creation
from the earth's origin
fathers and sons have bred horses together
thirty generations of fathers
thirty generations of sons and grandsons

At the end of his year of service, the warden was said to visit every household in Zhizuo that owned a brood mare to collect the "price of horse feed" *(mò tsò ṣo)*. Each family with a productive mare was expected to contribute two *sheng* of grain. In this mountainous region, horses and mules were the sole mode of transport besides human backs. They were especially valuable along the salt- and sugar-trading route that passed through Zhizuo, and their price was very high. Mules were particularly prized as the strongest and most agile of pack animals. Zhizuo residents estimated that just before Liberation a decent horse cost 200 to 300 yuan and a good mule up to 500, while cattle cost only 40 to 50. Raising horses and mules could be lucrative for those who could afford a brood mare, and residents estimated that in the late 1940s Zhizuo had a population of about five hundred to six hundred horses concentrated in the most prosperous households. An enterprising warden might thus collect a thousand to twelve hundred *sheng* of grain after his year of service. The "price of horse feed" was a sort of tax, people recalled, but unlike the taxes collected by the *baozhang*, it was levied only against the most prosperous.

As a tax on the fertility of horses, the "price of horse feed" was appropriate remuneration for the warden, whose duties became increasingly associated with compulsory military service in the Guomindang armies. The Republican government instituted a draft system of military conscription in 1933, which targeted men from eighteen to thirty-five years of age. Initially, the military conscription law stipulated that only sons would not be drafted; one son in families with two or three would be drafted; two in families with three to five (CYZZ 1994, 298). As the Guomindang struggled to prosecute the war against the Japanese, military conscription in rural Yunnan expanded dramatically in scope and intensity. Conscription quotas for the neighboring county of Yaoan, for instance, increased from 120 men in 1935 to 800 in 1942.[6] During the civil war, the military conscription law was revised to

---

6. CYZZ 1994, 299. Similar figures do not exist for Dayao and Yongren Counties.

stipulate that one son in families with two would be drafted; two in families with three; three in families with five (ibid., 298). The words "from one family take two *sheng*, from three families take six *sheng*, take no more, take no less" seem to mimic this harsher injunction, which Zhizuo residents chanted thus:

nǐ zò tɕʼì zò ṣo
sa zò nǐ zò ṣo
ŋó zò sa zò ṣo

of two sons harvest one
of three sons harvest two
of five sons harvest three

Youths were drafted from their villages in October and November of each year so their official term of service could begin in January. Each autumn of the Republic's last decade, some in Zhizuo recalled, the *baozhang* employed two local Lòlop'ò men to capture conscripts. Carrying guns, iron neck bands, and chains, they apprehended youths, secured their necks with chains, and led them to the *ts'iɛi's* prison cell, where it was the warden's responsibility to guard them. These two men were roundly despised by their neighbors, who called them "dog's legs" *(ánò tɕ'i)* and sometimes spat on them when passing on the paths. When these police were spotted near their villages, youths from poor households fled or went into hiding. Some ate a certain wild fruit to give themselves a permanent goiter or cut off two joints of their trigger finger. Those who could afford it paid the *baozhang* a bribe when their sons reached the age of sixteen and followed this up with more bribes each autumn. After being gathered in the *ts'iɛi's* house, conscripts were chained together and led from the valley at gunpoint. War and the execrable conditions suffered by ordinary soldiers of the Guomindang armies ensured that few returned. The warden's chanted words, "from the sky's creation, from the earth's origin, fathers and sons have bred horses together, thirty generations of fathers, thirty generations of sons and grandsons" clearly associate a line of agnates with the procreative potential of brood mares. The warden taxed the fertility of horses just as the Guomindang taxed the fertility of fathers and sons with forced conscription.

The warden's price was governed by the same principle of reciprocity that organized the *ts'iɛi's* duties as host. To associate the "price of horse feed" with the warden's job of smoothing the way for the hated "dog's legs" was to acknowledge that higher powers would always demand tribute. In the case of forced conscription, this price was the sons on which the future procreative potential of any family was supposed to depend. While the burden of forced conscription could not be distributed equitably, the warden's chanted insistence on taking only from the prosperous—those who had mares—was an assertion that the analogous tax on the fertility of horses, at least, should be distributed among those who could bear it best.

THE SPEAKER'S PRICE

The idiom of procreative potential also informed the rules for compensating the speaker and the bearer. The title to about ten *mu* of Zhizuo's most fertile river-bottom paddy land circulated with the title of *ts'ici*. These twelve contiguous fields, said to have been granted to the *ts'ici* by the original ancestors, were farmed communally, and their entire product went to the *ts'ici* household. A few hundred yards upstream of these fields, where a bend in the river on one side and terraces on the other made a warm, protected corner, was another plot of land, of about one *mu*. This was the seedbed in which rice that was to be transplanted into the larger fields grew for its first fifty days. Custodianship of this land, too, rotated with the *ts'ici*, and it too was farmed communally, by workers organized by the *ts'ici* household. It was called the *lòrɔmi*—the "speaker's field." A tenth of the rice seedlings grown in this field were transplanted back into it, and the speaker received their harvest.

In many contexts, Zhizuo residents compared growing rice to raising children. Sowing rice was likened to insemination, uprooting and transplanting seedlings to giving birth, hoeing, weeding, and fertilizing the growing plants to feeding and clothing children, harvesting rice plants to the labor of helping people die, and storing rice seeds to keeping ancestral souls in preparation for their rebirth. Men of the *ts'ici's* and his siblings' households lavished attention on the womblike speaker's field, fertilizing it with ashes from nitrogen-fixing tree species and several applications of manure, and soaking, plowing, and harrowing it repeatedly until the earth blended into a thick, nutritious, uniform mud. After smoothing the bed with a wooden dressing bar, the *ts'ici* himself chose a time when no women were nearby to hang a bag of seed on his belt and scatter it over this warm, even, sheltered earth. Fifty days later, female kin and friends of the *ts'icimo* pulled up the seedlings to transplant into the larger fields on a festive occasion in which this work was explicitly associated with giving birth (see Mueggler 1996).

One afternoon Luo Baolin, one of the most loquacious of my sources on the *ts'ici's* "rules and procedures," suddenly switched topics from the speaker's right of conversation to the people of nearby Zhenamo. In that group of villages, he said, people do not replant rice seedlings in their seedbeds after the seedlings have been pulled up. Instead, they spend the entire year intermittently plowing and fertilizing their seedbeds to prepare them for the next year's seeds. "Every time a Mátɕʻip'ò [a derogatory term for Zhenamo residents] has spare time, he is out plowing his seedbed," he laughed. "They are very stubborn people. That's what Mátc'ìp'ò means: stupid, stubborn people. They never learn anything new; they always sow the same fields their ancestors sowed. Even now the Party can't convince some to transplant back into their seedbeds. They say the seedbed is the mother and the seedling the son, and to replant the seedling in the seedbed would be like the son fucking the mother."

Those listening laughed, as though at an off-color joke. People in Zhizuo *do* transplant seedlings back into their seedbeds. Not to do so in a place where every inch of irrigable land is precious, one would have to be as stupid as a Mátc'ìp'ò. I never heard anyone explicitly deny that "the seedbed is the mother, the seedling the son," but to say it out loud disrupted the neat homology Zhizuo residents habitually make between procreation and rice production. As he told how Zhenamo residents extend the logic of procreative metaphor one step further than Lòlop'ò usually care to do, Luo Baolin's implication was clear: by accepting the harvest from seedlings transplanted back into the seedbed as his due, the speaker consumed the issue of a son's sexual relations with his mother.

THE "PRICE OF GRASS"

If someone had to eat this scandalous by-product, the speaker was an appropriate choice. I came to understand this as people who had been members of *ts'ici* households repeatedly contrasted the offices of speaker and bearer. The speaker had a famous time eating, drinking, and chatting, while the bearer's job was a heavy burden. The speaker should be a sophisticate, while the bearer was best an idiot. The speaker wore stylish "Han" clothing that buttoned down the front, while the bearer dressed in old-style hempen clothes that buttoned down the side. And the speaker accepted every opportunity for social intercourse, while the bearer rarely spoke and ideally was celibate.

In these recollections, speaker's and bearer's opposite orientations toward eating, speaking, sexual activity, and signs of Lòlop'ò ancestry were of a piece with their opposite relations to the boundaries of the Zhizuo *ts'ici*. In collecting his compensation, the bearer was a boundary maker. His recompense for his year of service was called "the price of grass" *(ci p'ù ṣo)*. At the end of the year, he undertook a tour of the small high-mountain settlements on the *ts'ici* borders, collecting money or grain from those living outside who grazed their goats and cattle on land within. There was no common understanding of how much this fee should be, and what the bearer collected depended on his own industry and the thickness of his skin. In negotiating which hamlets should pay for the right to graze their animals on what land, the bearer established the *ts'ici*'s territorial boundaries. As he hauled visitors' baggage out of the valley and carried letters through it, he worked to preserve these boundaries by facilitating the movement of outsiders through and away. His hempen clothing, monolingual speech, and presumed celibacy reproduced in his person this boundary-making status. His clothing signaled his intimate connection with the original Lòlop'ò ancestors, his laconic speech and celibacy that he eschewed an excess of social relations with people other than close kin.

The ideal speaker, on the other hand, specialized in boundary traversals. His job of cultivating and enlivening relations with powerful outsiders was centrifugally oriented. His "Han" clothing, multilingual facility, conversational skills, and indulgence in food and alcohol all directed his person toward promiscuous and facile sociability, especially with outsiders. His task was to take on the qualities of those who most directly threatened the community in order to deflect part of that threat. Indiscriminate in his social relations, the speaker may have been supposed to be indiscriminate sexually as well: his personal qualities fit to a tee the stereotype of a successful adulterer in Zhizuo. And, in Zhizuo as in many places, the forbidden indiscrimination par excellence was incest between mother and son. The speaker too reproduced his boundary-traversing status in his person. To pay him with the issue of an unavoidable sexual relation between mother and son was to recognize the social promiscuity with which he helped preserve Zhizuo's boundaries by continuously transgressing them.

Recollections of the speaker's transgressive character help illuminate the proscriptions Zhizuo residents remembered being applied to the *ts'iɛi* couple. At the household's center, in their inner room, the *ts'iɛi* couple combined all the most powerful signs of Lòlop'ò ancestry with restricted speech, sociability, sexuality, and abstention from food and drink associated with "Han" outsiders. At its margins (in the courtyard, porch, and outer rooms) the speaker stoked the fires of hospitality with everything the *ts'iɛi* and *ts'iɛimo* were enjoined to avoid—a specialist in scandalous unrestraint managing the unrestrained speech, sociability, and sexuality that transgressed the house's walls from outside. As designated hosts for the entire territory of Zhizuo, the *ts'iɛi* couple made it possible to imagine this territory similarly as a household, sheltering both a powerful productive union and potentially troublesome guests, who must be fed, flattered, and hurried on their way.

Zhizuo residents' insistence on the bearer's contrasting character participated in this imaginative constitution of a houselike territory in a different way. The proscriptions applied to the bearer's diet, speech, clothing, and sexuality were identical to (if not as strict as) those applied to the *ts'iɛi* and *ts'iɛimo* because of his association with the reliquary box they served. In their relation to this reliquary, the *ts'iɛi* couple acted as a conduit through which the procreative power of the ancestral union it represented descended on the entire valley-house of Zhizuo. In *his* relation to the reliquary, the bearer made this union move, passing it like a bride from one village and one household to the next, making it into the sister, wife, and mother that bound each Zhizuo household to many others. In this way, Zhizuo residents could imagine the *ts'iɐi* couple and the bearer to combine in their persons the principles of descent and affinity on which all relations of kinship were built, extending these principles to saturate the house of Zhizuo to its outer boundaries. As they recollected the "rules and procedures" of the *ts'iɐi* system, Zhizuo residents used ideas about the fluidity and fixity of speech, sexuality, and sociability to imagine Zhizuo as, at once, a household descended from a single set of ancestors and a circle of households connected through marriage alliances.

CONCLUSION

The ethnographers who in 1953 bravely set out to classify the inhabitants of thousands of mountain villages like Yijichang and Zhizuo learned to be extremely flexible in applying the four criteria of common territory, language, economic base, and psychological makeup that Stalin had declared defined a nationality (Stalin 1956, 294–95). They tempered this definition with the older associations with racial origin and inheritance that the term *minzu* (nationality) had gathered since its adoption into Chinese around 1900 (Dikötter 1992; Lin 1963). To these ethnographers, Zhizuo residents clearly shared a territory, language, economy, and historical origin with the speakers of the Central dialect of Yi who surrounded them (if only more problematically with the far-flung groups also labeled Yi in other parts of the southwest). Even in the 1980s and early 1990s, county and prefectural officials frequently employed these criteria to pass off Zhizuo residents' claims to a separate *minzu* status as ignorant or delusional.

People in Zhizuo, however, took advantage of associations of *minzu* with origin, inheritance, and descent to link the problem of "nationality" to a large and systematic body of expert knowledge about the past. Their accounts of the *ts'iɐi* system used moral ideas about speech, sociability, and sexuality to create an imagined unity for all those who claimed to be Lòlop'ò. Creating terms of comparison between agricultural cycles and lifetimes, and the spatial arrangements of households and those of the territory of Zhizuo, these recollections compounded mutually contradictory ideas about descent and affinity into a single institutional container (Lévi-Strauss 1983, 185). Zhizuo was a single productive unity, a household descended from a single set of ancestors, or a series of households bound together through marriage exchanges and mutually involved in the intimate processes of household reproduction. From within this imagined unity, Zhizuo residents could deal with powerful outsiders as a household would, flattering them with the honors and privileges of guests while excluding them from internal household affairs.

Ethnographers and administrators could easily pass off this self-consciously formal and reflexive talk about the past as innocuous nostalgia for a defunct "nationality custom." But under the cover of its formality, it created a forceful strategy of self-representation, in which spatial descent and symbolic affinity took the place of the racial and historical genealogies that preoccupied the ethnographers and officials who defended *minzu* classifications. Claims that the *ts'ici* is "the heart of our nationality" and "our nationality's most important custom" employed the troubled political potency of the term *minzu* to give this self-representational strategy force in the present. Much has been written about how colonizing regimes create ethnicities for their subjects. Studies of ethnicity and "nationality" in China especially have repeatedly shown how local identities are forcefully produced or molded by state policies (cf. Harrell 1990, 1995a; Mackerras 1994; Gladney 1991, 1994; David Wu 1990). Zhizuo residents' accounts of the "rules and procedures" of a long dead but fondly remembered institution point to another side to this dialectic, in which older local self-representations engage or absorb state discourses about ethnicity to create new possibilities for struggle or self-definition.

CHAPTER 11

Native Place and Ethnic Relations in Lunan Yi Autonomous County, Yunnan

Margaret Byrne Swain

Belonging to a native place is an important piece of a person's identity in China. The intersections of this identity with other ways of categorizing people, specifically ethnicity, family, class, and gender, create hierarchies of resource claims and behavioral expectations within regional systems. Native-place identity and associations in Chinese urban environments are well-documented sojourners' phenomena (Skinner 1976, 1977; Honig 1992; Goodman 1995), but native place is also a factor within rural areas. This essay looks to the less-studied periphery, exploring issues of rural native-place identity *(bendiren, bencun, laojia, guxiang)* and ethnicity or nationality *(minzu)* between Han Chinese and Sani Yi now settled in Lunan Yi Autonomous County in eastern Yunnan (see Map 11.1).[1]

My goal is to show how native-place and ethnic identities interact in local rural resource competition through time. Throughout China there exist ethnically distinct populations with claims to the same rural place. In rural China, migration over time is a significant factor in identity formation. Two types of population movements can be distinguished: those undertaken by migrants (for resources, in the wake of devastation or for colonization), who perhaps re-create their native-place identity, and those by emigrants, sojourners to urban centers (individuals expected to return to their abode) who maintain their native-place identity (Skinner 1976, 335–36).[2] Throughout China, histories of antagonistic relations between immigrant and native

1. Han Chinese and Sani Yi are respectively the two largest groups, approximately 67 percent and 30 percent, of a total 201,215 population in 1990. I gratefully acknowledge the support of the Committee on Scholarly Communication with China for field and archive research in Yunnan during 1993.

2. With reference to Lunan, in the past migration and sojourning were present in the rural local system, which used to be in the periphery of Kunming (Shih 1944). In the 1990s Lunan

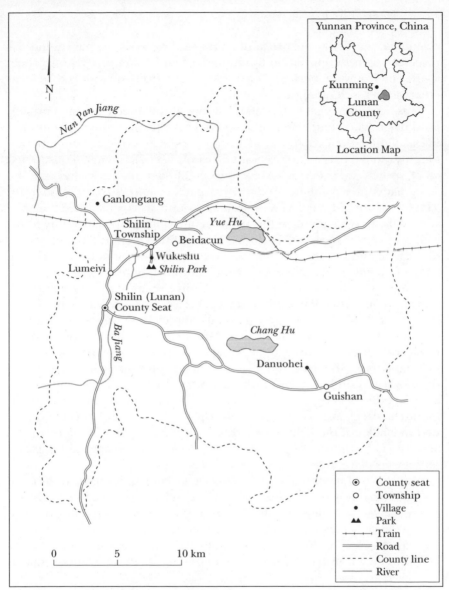

Map 11.1. Lunan Yi Autonomous County

populations underlay the use of the term *bendiren* to signify natives in their place of origin in opposition to immigrants and colonizers (Honig 1992, 5–6). The "common heritage" of an immigrant group may indeed be ideas created as a result of migration (ibid., 8).

This essay interrogates the need to distinguish between ancestral origins, local native place, and birthplace, as people in China do among themselves in establishing their composite identities.[3] The state's role in contemporary identity issues is particularly relevant to people who carry a state-constructed label, such as the pan-Yi *minzu* category codified in the early Mao era. The state may confer or limit, conflate or negate, resources based on identity. The formation of Lunan Yi Autonomous County in 1956 marked the occasion of the state mapping of this region as an Yi minority nationality place, while the census recorded a growing Han Chinese majority. Today, contradictory commodification of identities can be seen in the political museumizing of origins by the Lunan government tourism bureau. It promotes Lunan County as the unique Sani heroine Ashima's native place or hometown *(guxiang)*. On the other hand, bureau plans for the "Ashima Cultural Center" negate local group claims of cultural uniqueness by importing many external Yi ethnic groups to participate. Museumizing of local ancient origins ties in with map and census projects that have distinct agendas to define who belongs where (Anderson 1991, 183). Lunan people's practices manipulate their own and others' ideas of who and what they are as local natives, *bencunde* (of the local or native village) or *bendiren* (local or native person), in hierarchies of claims to their local "native place." The idea of "local" is closely tied to images of the land reflected both in the standard Chinese *(difang)* and Sani *(mitw)* gloss, using the word "land" (*di* and *mi* mean land or earth; *fang* means place or location).

My study of Lunan looks at native-place identity as it forms in the local community and is used in the distribution and control of resources. I ask where native-place identity comes from and how is it used locally over time in an ethnically mixed region.[4]

Harrell's (1995a) three civilizing projects are all present in Lunan County and provide a framework for understanding local ethnic relations. Lunan

---

is officially located in the Kunming urban metropolitan district, and its resources are incorporated directly into the regional center. The location has been redefined due to transportation, communication, and population shifts.

3. For example in the 1990s, a person may have a Lunan native-place identity (Lunanren), despite being born in Kunming and having a Sani ancestral origin "to the west" of Yunnan. The occurrence of ethnically mixed people who may have the same (Lunan) or distinct (Lunan and Nanjing) parental native places also occurs, and it depends on circumstances whether the father or mother's native place is given precedence.

4. So, how is local native-place identity distinct from village community identity? There can be people without a native place—those who are immigrants and who do not fit in the local

Han, culturally identified with the Confucian and Communist projects of the majority society, are also subjected to the ruling center and influenced by their "uncivilized," ethnically distinct neighbors. In contrast to their Han neighbors, Lunan Sani became identified with the Christian project, represented by French Catholic missions initiated by the indefatigable Paul Vial. Sani also have their own highly localized identification with the Communist project. Each group has distinct claims to native-place identification and resources in Lunan through ancestors, colonial histories, cultural hegemony, and the state.

ETHNIC ORIGIN AND MIGRATION STORIES

In the distant past, ethnic origins for both Han and Sani Yi were claimed to have occurred in places far from Lunan. These two peoples' histories mark both as immigrants to the region. In their own stories the idea of being a Lunan native is not based on some autochthonous origin, but rather on having generations of family claims to places in Lunan. Ancestral native place as a site of group origin is part of the distinction made between ethnic groups who are now co-positioned in local space.

Much of Sani early history has been transferred over the generations by *bimo*, Sani male religious leaders, through their writing system and oral records. By the mid-twentieth century, warfare and some Western missionaries endangered the written records of many Yi groups. One effort to save various Yi texts was made by the renowned linguist Ma Xueliang,[5] who shipped documents off to Beijing for safekeeping. Ma subsequently wrote a detailed study of Sani Yi language (1951) and encouraged publication of Sani folklore, such as the flood epic *Nimishi* that he translated from Sani texts with the Sani scholar Ang Zhiling (Ma 1985). The poem recounts the creation of Sani ancestors, and their relationship to other nationalities, in a story of how three generations of protohuman beings survived various disasters including ice, drought, and floods. Ultimately only a brother and sister, Aher and Ahshe, were left, and they reproduced. The final lines of the

---

community or have a specific ancestral native place. These are the test cases—the ones who clarify the distinctness of this identity. Niangjia (mother's household) can be seen as the intersection of gender hierarchy and native place.

5. Ma's essay "How Imperialism Destroys Our Brother Nationality's Culture" (1951, 381–85) recounts his efforts in the 1940s to preserve Yi books in the Jinsha area, acting before missionaries destroyed the books. Ma argued that the missionaries had destroyed local culture by creating foreign language alphabets so the natives would learn quickly and convert their souls. Missionary bible myths also took away their history. "Some people even say they are not Chinese now, because of the story of Adam and Eve taught to them by the missionaries. This story which told people that they are all descendants of one family or all the same people is typical of the kind of poison missionaries spread," wrote Ma.

poem, based on an English translation by the Sani scholar Zeng Guopin, relate the following:[6]

> The sister gave birth to a large flesh ball that the siblings then chopped into pieces and cast into many directions. The flesh of the ball ran down to a flat plain *[pingba]* where they *[sic]* became the Han nationality who live there; the blood flowed into a big river and became the Dai nationality who live by the riverside; and the bone of the ball went into the forest where they *[sic]* became the Yi nationality who live in the forest:

> There are six places in the forest.
> Six places became six villages.
> One village is for Black Yi, who speak Black Yi language.
> One village is for White Yi, who speak White Yi language.
> One place is for Red Yi, who speak Red Yi language.
> One village is for Gan Yi, who speak Gan Yi language.
> One village is for Sani, who speak Sani language [as in 1985 Chinese version, no Yi attached to Sani or Axi].
> One village is for Axi, who speak Axi language.
> Year after year, generation [follows] generation.
> The population has flourished, the world has been lively, and all things on earth have come back to life.[7]

The *Nimishi* can be understood as a metaphor for the beginning of each new family, and in the past it was chanted at Sani weddings (Vial 1898,

---

6. The use of the term "Yi," a PRC state-constructed ethnic-linguistic group, unhooks and elides local manifestations, developments, and expressions often masking political suppression of local names. The choices of Chinese and English translations of Sani writing made by the Sani scholars cited here reflect current state policy rather than the Sani original, written from a Sani (not "Yi") point of view. If we look at the Sani writing system originals and compare Chinese and English translations, we can see that the character pronounced *ni*, meaning the self-name of Sani people, is also translated as "Yi." The Sani character pronounced *vi*, meaning family (*jia* in Chinese), is translated as *zu* (nationality) and "Yi," while *nivi* is translated as "Yi Zu" and "Sani" in various English stanzas. There is a parallel of colonial essentializing in nineteenth-century Euro-American reports, including Vial's, that use the gloss "Lolo" to mean both the larger language group in general and specific groups like the Sani (as in "my Lolo"). Vial was aware of derogatory meanings attached to the term but felt its general use, much as "Yi" is used today, was necessary because there was none in the language system itself to indicate linguistic and cultural ties between groups. In this essay, instead of "Lolo" I use the term "Yi" when referring to Vial's and others' writings about the classificatory macro group, and "Sani" when referring to the local "Ni" people in Lunan, whom Vial called "Lolo" or "Gni."

7. In his introduction, Ma (1985, 1) remarks, "So, this poem highlights that all people today come from the same source. Even though there is no theoretical evidence, it is a good wish for humanity's childhood. After all, it is what binds together a union of nationalities." This sounds like the reverse of his critique of the missionaries. The long narrative "Ashima" has been interpreted by Ma to be a continuation of Sani history since Nimishi times, making them "sister poems" (Ma 1985). In most popular retellings, Sani life is portrayed through this story of a young woman of renown called Ashima, who is stolen away by the evil landlord Rebubala. Her

19–20). It also reflects internal colonialization, mapping regional hierarchies of space in which Han live on the desirable plains, while culturally distinct groups of Yi settled up in the forested mountains. Sani genealogies, epic poems of creation and heroes, and geography chants *(mifeke)* of past homelands also relate how the Sani were pushed out from various settlements by competing groups, including Han Chinese. Accounts from the turn of the twentieth century (Vial 1893–94, 1902, 1905, 1908; Lietard 1904) and contemporary observations (Li et al. 1993) confirm the persistence of a spatial configuration by ethnic groups in Lunan.

Various Sani histories relate how their ancestors descended from three brothers and amalgamated into two groups. Later some descendants of one group migrated over three distinct routes into the Lunan region (Vial 1898, 1–2). In a version collected by Vial in the 1890s, the details are as follows: ancestors of all Yi peoples formed into two major tribes, with the families of the youngest brother mixed into both groups. The second brother's family became the conquerors (the Black, "Na") of the eldest brother's family (the White, "Tou"), who became their serfs. The Black married only among themselves, controlled all the territory, and as local lords *(midzemou)* demanded rent from the White, who worked the land. There were many civil wars, as the White Yi peoples' (Vial 1905, 335–36) population grew and they expanded their need for territory. Over time the White subdivided into many groups, becoming the Sani *(gni)*, Axi *(ashi)*, and so on.

In Vial's analysis, little by little each White group has formed a tribe with its ethnographically distinct costume, customs, and dialect, and with territorial claims. Some groups emigrated under the conduct of a "minor chief" to look for new lands. Thus, some Sani recollected to Vial places where they stopped en route from the Dali region to where they are now settled. They migrated to Lunan under the leadership of three powerful men, whose house sites were still memorialized in Vial's day.[8] As we can see, Vial perceived the Sani as an indigenous people who were in the Lunan region first and had claims to the soil that perhaps neither their own Black Yi overlords nor the Chinese rulers could abrogate.

Another understanding of Sani history is provided in the late twentieth century by Sani scholars (Ang Ziming 1996, 10) studying local variations in

---

companion Ahei, who is identified as either her brother or her lover, rides to her rescue. After surmounting many trials, tricks, and tigers, they are trapped in a raging flood that sweeps Ashima way from Ahei. She returns as an echo heard in the karst stone forest of Lunan.

8. "Mais il est vraisemblable qu'ils étaient conduits par les chefs de familles ou tribus; peut-être méme n'étaient-ils que deux, l'un appelé Blanc (tou), l'autre appelé Noir (na); c'est, pour moi, le seul moyen d'expliquer cette tradition qui divise les Lolos en deux especes, les blancs et les noirs. D'apres une version indigène, ceux-ci seraient descendus de trois frères; mais les descendants du plus jeune se seraient confoundus avec les deux autres frères. Ce qui est constant, c'est que le blanc était l'ainé et le noir le cadet; mais par une inversion inexpliquée, les

the "Mizhi," an earth-centered annual ritual cycle. The scholars trace three sources of this variation, reflected in distinct histories without reference to possible Han Chinese influences. According to their research, one group of proto-Sani intermixed with local aborigines *(tuzhu);* another branch migrated as a group from the west (Dali) during the time of the Nanzhao Kingdom, and the third branch migrated as a group from Guizhou and northeast Yunnan. From their perspective, Sani people have evolved a shared appearance, society, economy, and beliefs, with local characteristics based in unique histories.

Who might have been the aboriginal people of Lunan and what happened to them are questions taken up in contemporary government histories. Recent discoveries of Paleolithic artifacts and art in several Lunan sites indicate early human habitation (Lunan Yizu Zizhixian 1986, 27–29). Cave paintings have been interpreted by He Yaohua (1994, 41) to be the cultural heritage of "primitive Lunan indigenous people" who then mixed with in-migrating non-Han peoples from the northwest and Chinese from central China, creating ancestors of the Sani people. A Lunan County gazetteer (Lunan Yizu Zizhixian 1996, 120) states that most Sani are descendants of the "Luomengbu," a tribe who had settled in Lunan (and actively fought and negotiated with the Chinese), but there has also been a blending with immigrant people settling from the outside. Chinese language patronyms used by Sani clans can be linked to specific locations outside of Lunan (including Nanjing, Guizhou, and Kunming) and the routes that their ancestors followed to Lunan before merging into the Sani people.

As early as 109 B.C.E. there are historical records of Han dynasty dam- and canal-building projects in the region now called Lunan County, according to an official state history (ibid.). By A.D. 225, the famous Han leader from the north, Zhuge Liang, used wealthy local officials to control the area. As war waged in the middle of China, a Luomengbu family named Cuan became very powerful in central Yunnan, including Lunan. During the Dali

---

descendants du noir ont formé la tribu patricienne appelée napou, et les descendants de l'ainé sont devenus les serfs de l'autre, tout en se subdivisant en un grand nombre de tribus (naseu, ko, hotou, gnisou, gni, ashi, adje, etc.). . . . Les Lolos éraient soumis a dix-huit seigneurs ou midzemou à qui le peuple payait une redevance annuelle; quant au bien foncier il appartenait à celiu qui le cultivait. C'est encore actuellement le régime de la propriété chez cette race; en sorte qu'un seigneur peut aliéner la redevance qui lui est due, mais il ne puet pas aliéner le fond qui ne lui appartient pas. . . . Les Chinois, en s'emparant plus tard de ce pays, n'ont fait que mettre des mandarins où habitaient les signeurs; et dans les parties conquises, mais non soumises, ils ont donné le titre de mandarin aux seigneurs indigènes, c'est ce que on applle de les 'tusiguan.' . . . Les Lolos en se multipliant débordent de leurs anciennes limites et forment de nouveaux noyaux indépendants des seigneurs, mais encore il se trove au milieu d'eux des hommes audacieux qui les dominent. Ansi, la tribu gni, que j'évangélise, se souvient des étapes qu'elle a du faire pour arriver de Tali jusqu'ici; elle garde la memoire de trois hommes puissants qui se sont fait un nom: Adle, Joke, Dzeshi."

Kingdom era (A.D. 902–1252), Chinese sources called the Lunan area "Ludian." In a Yuan dynasty geography record of the region, a fortified Luomengbu city called Salu is noted.

Various attempts by government historians to link ancestors of Lunan Yi people to the Luomengbu build on language clues. The *Yunnan Sheng Lunan Yizu zizhixian dimingzhi* (Lunan Yizu Zizhixian 1989) relates that in Sani language, a word that sounds like *luo* means tiger and a word like *meng* means very great, powerful. In A.D. 1270 three tribes including the Luomengbu, totaling about thirty thousand households, united in the middle region. One leader of the Luomengbu became the prefecture administrator, and the Yuan government appointed another one the military leader of Lunan. When the three tribes merged, the name "Lunan" came into use. In Sani language this name was pronounced *lu*, meaning stone, and *nai*, meaning black. Throughout all of these histories, written down by Sani intellectuals, government officials, and a French missionary, there is a repeated emphasis on the number three to explain local Sani variation: three brothers, three leaders, three routes, three tribes, and three sources of Sani ancestors from other places.

Sani ancestors became incorporated into the state under the Ming, in 1383, when a hereditary land administrator *(tusi)* was appointed in Lunan (Lunan Yizu Zizhixian 1989). Meanwhile in 1382, some 2,627 Han soldiers were sent into Lunan with their families to guard the city and cultivate agricultural land. Prisoners from central China were also sent down for agricultural work (He Yaohua 1994, 41). In the Lunan plain, Han people continued to settle, but in Guishan and other remote areas, the *tusi* system dominated non-Han people, in some cases until liberation in 1949.

Groups called Black Yi and White Yi by the Han were once different strata in one society in various mountain regions (ibid., 30). The *County Annals* reported that in some places Lunan people called White (Bai) Yi were dominant and owned a lot of land and forest, while Black (Hei) Yi depended on working for landlords.[9] Feudalism dominated Lunan, where whole forests, water systems, plants, mountains, and hamlets were owned by landlords. The landlords were *tianzhu*, masters of the fields, while peasants were *dianhu*, or tenants. Tenants had freedom and permanent rights to *fen*, or units of land— for planting, forestry, and housing—that they could sell or rent out. According to government research, before Land Reform some 7 percent of the population were landlords, who rented out 59 percent of the land (ibid., 31). In some areas landlords experimented with improvements in agricultural and working conditions, and elsewhere coal mining developed. The Lunan area has been administered in various districts since Han dynasty times into the present. In 1956 the Lunan Yi Autonomous County was founded,

9. Of course it could also be argued, as Vial (1908, 22) did, that even if these groups were once one society, they have become separate ethnic groups over time.

and in 1983, by national government action, the county became part of the Kunming Municipality.

Han and Yi groups in Lunan have moved for water, conquered, rented or purchased lands in areas controlled by another ethnic group, and migrated for cash employment out of their home communities.[10] The oldest Sani communities in Lunan are believed to be in the eastern remote areas of Guishan district, where the Sani subvernacular (one of four) spoken there is the standard for Southeastern Yi (Bradley n.d.). Locally, Lunan Han and bilingual Sani speak a regional variation of Southwestern Mandarin Kunming vernacular called "Hanhua." Lunan communities have distinct histories that detail when the ancestors arrived and how families became rooted there. As we have seen, in general ethnic enclaves migrated for new resources and/or in response to dominant groups.

Ethnic distinctions between Han and Sani societies beyond language and material culture differences were well marked in Lunan. In their relationship to the landscape, Sani ancestors established sacred groves and rocks in each community, venerated immediate family ancestors for two generations, and kept long genealogical chants. While Han have portable ancestor worship and lineage systems, they also have *tudigong*, local minor deities invested into the local landscape, and practice geomancy (*fengshui*) to understand the influence of regional natural forces. Sani society is kin based, with rotating community leadership, multicommunity clan affiliations, cross-cousin marriage, and relative gender equality in contrast to hierarchical Han society directly incorporated into the state, as well as regional patrilineage systems and exogamous marriage practices. Sani like Han however were also inserted into the Chinese state political economy with their tenant status, taxation, and cash employment.

What seems critical to note in this discussion of native-place and ethnic identities is that Sani ancestors stopped migrating into the Lunan area and settled there about five hundred years ago. Meanwhile Han people have continued to move from various places into Lunan through time, and the region has been controlled to some degree by a Chinese state system since the Han dynasty. The presence of Han in Lunan County over the centuries was a direct result of the Confucian civilizing project, while French missionaries brought in a competing Christian civilizing project.

10. Vial interpreted ethnic relations between the Sani and other local groups as being shaped by their sociocultural "character" differences, as well as by the dynamics of political inequalities and their physical proximity to each other. The relationship between Sani and Chinese was his primary emphasis. He rarely noted Sani relations with neighboring indigenous groups such as the Noeso (Nuosu) Lolo, Ashi (Axi) Lolo, or Miao. Muslims allied with various indigenous groups, including the Sani, during their grueling twenty-year revolt, but they often became enemies, according to Vial. He cites Muslim treachery as the reason why there was so much postrevolt enmity between them, despite their common Chinese oppressor (1898, 4).

THE FRENCH COLONIAL ERA

During Yunnan's mid-nineteenth-century Muslim Revolt, peasants and miners began a local, multiethnic (primarily Han and Yi) rebellion against their oppressors in Lunan County (He Yaohua 1994, 42–43). With the help of Hui Muslim rebels, the locals took control of Lunan in 1859, but were then defeated by Qing government troops. Containment of the province-wide revolt by the 1870s did little to resolve underlying inequalities and competing resource claims.

In the immediate postrevolt era, European imperialists strengthened their presence in southwest China. French Catholic missionaries with ties to colonial holdings in Indochina established themselves in Yunnan. Père Paul Vial began the first Lunan-region mission in 1888. He learned spoken and written Sani language and immediately began publishing observations of Sani Yi society, filtered through his religious civilizing project. It was useful to him that the Sani were very different from the Han, as Vial targeted the Sani for conversion into a modern, global Catholic identity.

Foreign influence became a new part of China's regional landscape in the late nineteenth century, affecting class structure, the economy, and concepts of modernity. Sometimes foreigners, such as Vial, were active agents in the construction of these changes (Honig 1992, 15). His writings form a valuable record of thirty years of life in Lunan and provide insights into the motivations and perspective of a European colonizer who purposively inserted himself between Han Chinese and the "indigenous" Yi, specifically in Sani communities.

Vial moved into Lunan as a secondary colonial force, and found that he had to deal with a layered social system crosscut by ethnicity and a cash economy. The Yi hereditary landlord class *(midzemou)* extracting from communal village tenants had been co-opted by the state-designated *tusi* system. A Han landlord and "mandarin" government system also controlled various resources. This situation was further complicated by the fact that all landlords could sell their various rights. Some Lunan districts long ago were established as primarily Sani Yi (in Guishan) or Han (in Beidacun) holdings, but control of Lunan land has been fluid over time, shifting between local Yi, Han, and nation-state control.

Almost a hundred years ago, Vial described this region as follows: "The Lunan plain (1650m altitude) is not a plain, but a suite of little and fertile valleys, running in a north-south direction. . . . The [highland] limestone belongs to the Yi and the [lowland] sandstone belongs to the Chinese[,] . . . who spread out where life is easy, and the earth is fertile and well irrigated. The Yi are spread out among the rocky peaks where no river flows, but there are numerous pools and abundant pastures" (1908, 22).

Western Lunan villages were tied to regional market systems near the main road running from Yunnan's capital to Guangxi Province. The population was about half Han, half Sani Yi, living in segregated villages (Vial 1902, 160; 1917, 537). The eastern Lunan population was mainly Sani. Every year Sani women, men, and children migrated from compact communities in the east, while their crops were still green, for temporary wage labor harvesting ripe rice on Chinese lands in the Lunan plain. Han preferred to hire indigenous laborers "who speak less and work better," rather than other Han (Vial 1893, 201). This migration was shaped by a Sani gender system of shared work and equitable cash property rights, and perhaps population pressure on the land (Vial 1908, 22). The Yi (Sani and others) were increasing faster than the local Chinese, and generally lived in less productive areas, where their ancestors had been pushed by incoming Han.

In the 1880s, the Yi began to migrate back west into the lowlands, forming new villages along the eastern border of the plain "that are half Yi and half Chinese and will become all Yi" (Vial 1908). Vial's fellow missionary Alfred Lietard (1904, 105), who worked with neighboring Axi Yi, maintained that indigenous Yi were buying up Lunan land from Han forced to sell due to opium addiction.[11]

Chinese property, Vial noted (1908, 23), "was in very small pieces and the landlords were infinite" due to real estate, financing, and inheritance practices. Furthermore, many Yunnanese tenants were displaced from one region into another by poor and hungry Han Chinese immigrants from Sichuan and Guizhou, who were very bad tenant farmers and soon abandoned the land. According to Vial, the ideal agriculturists in the region were the Yi, who "loved only the land and obeyed only the land," responsibly paying rent to the landlord (ibid., 17).

The landlord had a great deal of authority in Yi society, but not within village affairs, which were autonomous and closed. Sani villages had two types of nonhereditary leaders, called permanent chiefs and annual chiefs by Vial (1905, 338–39; 1908, 79). Permanent chiefs (*boudze* in Vial's Sani orthography, translated to *guansi* in Chinese) became leaders by circumstance and acclaim rather than election. They formed a council that resolved problems by drawing from oral traditions handed down by the elders. Many disputes were about the land: separation of property, limits of fields, or the conservation of woods and prairies. The Sani village council had ultimate authority over its community. When a judgment was made the guilty party had no recourse to Chinese authorities or to other villages, and had to submit to the community will.

Annual chiefs (*okotso,* meaning headman; *jiatou* in Chinese) were in charge

---

11. In one comparison of Sani and Chinese family life, Vial (1893, 258) portrayed the Chinese as opium sots incapable of productive life, while the Sani were seen as hardworking saints.

of a subsection of the village composed of five to ten families. Vial reported that "they are the ones who received strangers, managed the communal house, gave hospitality to the landlords or their envoys, brought together the Council when there was a need, and executed the Council's decisions. In a word, theirs was a true corvée, as everyone had a turn" (1905, 339). The *okotso's* responsibilities also included caring for the group's musical and dancing instruments and their communal feasting pots.

There are strong parallels between the duties of the *okotso* and the rotating *huotou (ts'ici)* headman among the Lòlop'ò, discussed by Eric Mueggler in chapter 10 of this volume. Among the Sani, in 1939 Fang Ho reported that there was still a monthly rotating village leadership, by clan and household, although this was changing to a system of state-organized leaders. At that time, in a significant distinction between Sani and Han gender roles in village life, if there was no male available a Sani woman would serve the family's turn as headman.

Lunan Landlords, Commoditization, and the French

In Vial's time, control of Lunan land resources and local folk claims to native place were situated in terms of who belonged to which landlord system in what place, as landlords or as tenants.[12] Vial (1893, 237) recounted a popular story of upward mobility and state control that continued to be told in the late twentieth century: During the Yuan dynasty, Chinese armies advanced to the Luliang plain. A mighty indigenous lord ruled the region from

12. Sorting out the linguistic distinctions between types of indigenous and Han landlords in Lunan during the last century is not easy. There is a veritable forest of terms. For example, Lietard wrote: "It is improper to give the name *tuzhu* to those landlords [propriétaires] of the revenue among the indigenous people, as these words in Chinese translate as 'landlord, master of the ground.' Here, the Chinese are masters of revenue or rent, not masters of the ground or soil. When they sell to others, they can only sell the rights to revenue" (1904, 105).

Vial asked, "Who is the one called 'seigneur'? The one Chinese call *tusi* and the Lolos *midzemou?* It is only the landlord [propriétaire]. But this title confers on him the right of high and base justice over all his tenants" (1905, 335). In Vial's Sani-French dictionary (1908–09) there are clues to the puzzle confounded by French-Sani-Chinese-English glosses for words: *mi* in Sani language means earth and is in many related concepts. In summary, the Sani word, over the past hundred years of French, Chinese, and Sani scholarship, has been defined as landowner *(propriétaire)* and translated into Chinese as *tusi, dizhu,* or *tianzhu. Dzmo* has been used to mean Lolo lord, *tusi,* and later, mandarin, while *sep'a* means master but was also used for mandarin and lord. I have not found a consistent pattern in Vial's usage of terms *propriétaire* and *maître* in reference to the landlord role, using one term for relationship with tenants, the other for relationship with earth, or an ethnic distinction between Han and Yi landlords. Neither is there agreement in other sources as to consistent translations of Sani terms into Chinese. Perhaps the structural position as extractor from the peasants, whether Yi or Han, agent of the state or private businessman, made the landlord's relationship to, if not the effect on, the peasants much the same.

a river island village that was unreachable until an indigenous shepherd offered to show the army a river ford. The Chinese subsequently seized the countryside, and their political leader rewarded the shepherd with all the land that his horse could cover in one day's riding. The place where the young man stopped on his horse was in Vial's time still the site of a huge house owned by an old Yi lord *(tusi)* who governed some forty-eight rent-paying villages.

Lietard wrote with passion about the actual conditions of landlords and tenants in Lunan in the early 1900s: "The indigenous people are treated as slaves. . . . When the Chinese conquered Yunnan . . . the mandarins, in order to collect taxes, sent into the interior clever, sly men who conferred with the indigenous people [who] . . . believed they had found protection in their intermediaries with the mandarins. . . . Alas, these men without hearts abused their [the villagers'] confidence and greedily charge them 400 percent interest on loans. . . . The Chinese leaders, who are always insatiable, demanded more. This is the situation now in most non-Christian villages" (1904, 105).

The system is typical of a "tribute-paying mode of production" found in many pre-capitalist state societies (Gailey 1987, 32) where the state claimed the land, forcing peasants to pay tax-rents for use of hereditary indigenous lands. Native-place claims in Lunan at that time can be seen to have been based in sentiments about who belonged where, overlaid with external controls and commodification of land resources. According to Vial (1905, 336), the landlord was lord of all his tenants, who owed him rent regardless of their ethnicity (various Yi or Han). Landlords were all-powerful, but when they sold their property rights, they lost this power based on collecting rent. The land itself was inalienable from the tenants. Besides rent, landlords also passed on taxes and demanded forced labor or corvée. The Chinese government registered landlord rights and imposed the taxes that were extracted from the tenants.

Yi "indigenous" lords, or *tusi,* held hereditary positions and passed on their rights to their heirs. However, the heirs might sell their titles if they were low on resources. Vial lamented (1905, 337) that Yi lords often preferred to sell to Chinese who were looking for a good business deal. The Chinese perceived Yi communities as ideal tenants who paid on time and would host the landlord, and as places where, Vial wrote, they would "have the pleasure of eating their chickens and beating the folk, without fearing the mandarin!"

In Vial's perspective, the Chinese landlords, who demanded more grain and cash payment for taxes and often demanded corvée labor, were much more corrupt than Yi *tusi.* Furthermore, Chinese landlords ignored community attempts to defend the Yi tradition of communal sacred groves *(mizhi)* belonging to each village, often cutting down the groves and selling the wood. Given the ritual, symbolic importance of the *mizhi* to Sani communities, embodying their ties to that place, this type of control was a frontal assault on ethnic group–native-place ties.

Vial saw himself as the Sani's valiant protector against the Chinese (Swain 1995), even going to prison at one point for interfering with local landlords. He ultimately set about to become a landlord himself, highly aware of the irony. His goal was to create a model village with modern hygiene, kitchen gardens, a safe drinking-water supply, advanced agricultural methods, and educational opportunities. Vial purchased almost three hundred *mu* of land over a nine-year period, in the borderlands between the "Chinese plain" and the Sani settlements to the east. Despite elaborate plans, Vial had problems persuading many of his converts to join in his experimental community of Qingshankou. In his own analysis, the problem had to do with the Sanis' ties to native place, their communities, and sacred groves and rocks. He noted that young Sani girls, in contrast to Chinese virilocal ideas of gender and native place, often refused to marry if expected to move too far away (twenty or twenty-five km) from home. If a community became overcrowded, then some people would migrate as a group to establish a new permanent village. Thus Vial decided that the Sani would take his new village seriously only if he assumed the duties of landlord and assured them that this was a village whose title would pass on to his successor, as should happen (Vial 1908, 23, 26–30).

Within many Sani villages, Vial established schools and long-term links with the Catholic Church. Vial's colleague Père Lietard reported (1904, 106) that many schools for both girls and boys were in place by the 1890s, financed with contributions from France and Sani village "requisitions" (Vial 1917, 547). Students were taught using Catholic religious materials translated into Sani script, as well as materials in Chinese and French. Local mission schools had primarily indigenous students, but the seminaries for advanced religious training recruited both Han and Yi students. In 1939, Fang reported that the Yi students from Lunan worked hard in the seminary. Often, though, there was some tension between Han and Yi in the school over what Han perceived as Yi privileges.

Vial's legacy in shaping Lunan ethnic relations and native-place identities in Lunan was virtually obliterated from local public memory by the 1960s in the revolutionary zeal to blot out old imperialist, foreign ways. In some official histories (Lunan Yizu Zizhixian 1986, 29) he is vilified as a bad landlord, and in others (He Yaohua 1994) the French presence in Lunan is simply not mentioned. The Sani, French-trained priest Laurent Zhang has responded (1987, 33–34) to criticisms of Vial by noting that he was far from perfect but also did many good deeds. Zhang relates that Vial's relations with Han were often strained because he much preferred working with and for Sani Yi people.

Vial's use of "les indignes" when writing about the Sani codified his position as an actor shaping perceptions by Sani and non-Sani alike of their claims to Lunan as native place. Now at the close of the twentieth century, Lunan history, and Vial's role in it, is being reassessed by Sani, Han, and foreign scholars, and the interplay of ethnic and native-place identities in Lunan resource allocations is evident at the local and county levels.

CONTEMPORARY NATIVE PLACE, ETHNICITY, AND RESOURCES

Resource allocations in Lunan continue to be based on the interlocking categories of ethnicity and native place, affected by local practice and external state and global policies. Variation in migration patterns, settlement, and local history in Lunan can be well illustrated by comparing the rural communities of Danuohei in Guishanxiang, Wukeshu in Shilinzhen, and Ganlongtang in Lumeiyixiang. In these locations some aspects of a Communist civilizing project since 1949 can be seen in the implementation of numerous policies regulating economic and social development, including land use, residence, birth control, education, and registration of ethnic identity.

Danuohei

Danuohei is located in the southeastern quarter of the county at an altitude of 1,985 meters above sea level, in the Guishan district. This is the region thought to have the most ancient Sani settlements, where people speak a distinct subvernacular and are believed by local scholars to be the most authentic. The village name is a Chinese transliteration of a Sani name meaning a pond *(hei)* where monkeys *(nuo)* drink. Sani settlement of the area started more than five hundred years ago with waves of migration from the west. In 1754 the Sani peasants of Danuohei were granted a free charter by the imperial court, allocating village lands to peasants in exchange for direct payment to the court rather than to a landlord as in the past. This charter still exists in the keeping of the community.

French Catholic missions opened in the Guishan area during the early twentieth century in a number of neighboring communities, including Haiyi and adjacent Xiaonouhei, but not in Danuohei. Meanwhile by the 1930s Danuohei had become a center of Communist resistance against the Guomindang. A valorized history of Danuohei, combined with its identification as Ashima's real hometown during the state myth-writing project in the 1950s, promises a hyperreal touristic image for the community in the future. Changes in this previously isolated community as a result of tourism development will provide great contrast. Meanwhile in Danuohei, commodification of tobacco production and the introduction of the household responsibility system by the state have accelerated family income growth since 1983. Completion in mid-1993 of an all-weather road linking the village to the main highway and the villagers' improvements in their local elementary school are also contributing to this community's transformation.

In Danuohei, land area in cultivation is approximately 2,600 *mu*, planted in primary food crops of corn and potatoes and, increasingly, in tobacco. Virtually every Danuohei household in 1993 grew tobacco with introduced seed and fertilizer supplies provided by the county tobacco extension service (He Yaohua 1994, 47). He Yaohua believes that under a market economy local differences between Yi and Han in terms of both economy and culture are diminishing. To substantiate this argument, He describes a Sani family situated at midlevel in the village economy. The household head is a forty-year-old man with a first-year middle-school education. His spouse graduated from sixth grade. They have a fifteen-year-old daughter in the first grade of middle school and a twelve-year-old son in primary school. In 1992 this family farmed fourteen *mu* of land that is allocated by the village in equal shares to all family members and can be leased. Keeping back some crops for seeds and food for domestic animals, they sold 450 kilograms of corn in the market for 360 yuan, 2,700 kilograms of potatoes for 600 yuan, and 650 kilograms of tobacco for 2,500 yuan, for a gross income of 3,460 yuan. They had a total of 883 yuan in agricultural expenses, leaving a net annual income from various crops of 2,577 yuan, or 644.3 yuan per person.

In areas like Danuohei with limited paddy, rice is procured through a two-to-one exchange of corn for rice. He records (ibid.) that in 1992 this family exchanged some 2,000 kilograms of corn for rice. Buckwheat, the old Sani staple, is now consumed only on special occasions, and the preferred staple is rice (that might be cooked with ground corn). While this does indicate an economic change linked with a change in cultural practice, my own observations and interpretive lens would keep me from making any pronouncements of cultural homogenizing. According to He (ibid.) this family earned a typical midlevel, mountain Yi (Sani) rural agricultural income. They were still not rich, because they could not yet replace their old home with a new one or buy an Eastwind or Liberation truck (there were five in Danuohei in 1993), but they had much more income than in the past. The family owned a sewing machine (very useful in handicraft production), a radio, and two watches, and were preparing to buy a color television. Their three-room house was a mixture of old mud construction and new brickwork, with glass windows. Many families in Danuohei had started construction on new houses.

Village population in 1993 was officially 937 people in 203 households, according to village leaders. Four of those households were designated Han, the rest were Sani, although some of the 13 Han residents listed in the household registry lived in Sani households. It is interesting to note that in the county atlas (Lunan Yizu Zizhixian 1989, 67), population figures for the late 1980s recorded 39 Han residents in Danuohei's population of 884 people living in 67 households. Redivision accounts for a tripling of the number of households, with a 6 percent increase in population, but not for the drop in Han residents. Why there may have been a shift in ethnic identification is a fascinating question we will return to.

Wukeshu

How many Han were living in a Sani village became a deep concern in Wukeshu, where residents during 1993 would often assert, "We are all Sani here!" Located west of Danuohei, Wukeshu (which means "five trees") Village sits at 1,763 meters altitude in the karst topography of central Lunan, in the Shilin Township. Wukeshu has clan ties with Sani communities to the east but represents a later wave of Sani migration speaking a distinct subvernacular. The village was founded about five hundred years ago in a region controlled by *tusi*. Until the recent explosion of tourism development at Shilin (stone forest), this was an agricultural village removed from main transportation routes. In late 1993 the status of this community, next to the entrance of Shilin national park, was changed from peasant village to the "Stone Forest Peasant Industry and Commerce General Corporation" (Shilin nong gongshang maoyi zonggongsi) for tourism. All 760 indigenous villagers—women, men, and children, including several Han women married into Sani families and their offspring—became corporation members. This process had started in 1987 when the village's administrative classification changed from township unit to one under direct control by the Shilin Tourism Bureau. At that moment all the village lanes were unpaved, all livestock roamed freely, and most houses were rammed-earth and thatch. The village population at that time—708 people in 144 households—was all Sani except for 2 Han family members (Lunan Yizu Zizhixian 1989, 18), and virtually all adults farmed their adjacent lands, which used to include the park itself. Wukeshu was also the site of a regional elementary school (kindergarten through sixth grade). While villagers had enough to eat, they were not considered a rich village by neighboring Sani. Before Liberation, French Catholics from the west visited, but this village has never been missionized.

By 1993, as the surrounding tourism business grew, Wukeshu was regionally known to be "well-off" *(you qiande)*. The village lanes were all paved to benefit the locals and wandering tourists, and an edict from the Shilin Tourism Bureau enforced with fines the confinement of all livestock, even the pigs (sometimes). Almost all houses had tile roofs, and a new house-building boom was going on at the village periphery as non-Sani workers rented old buildings in the center. The official village population of 760 people is still almost all Sani, but households have divided into 193 smaller units. The status of 229 people has been reclassified from peasant *(nongmin)* to Kunming resident, and the village land base has shrunken from 434 *mu* in 1988 to 191 *mu* in late 1993 as the Tourism Bureau has bought up rights for further park development.

The Tourism Bureau has constructed a modern shopping plaza for tourists just outside the park gates, renting out little shops to Wukeshu residents and outsiders (Sani and non-Sani alike) running restaurants and souvenir shops. Economic competition and cooperation across ethnic boundaries have become a factor in the production and sale of Shilin tourism. Han tailors (mostly men) from as far away as Sichuan have moved into Wukeshu during the past few years to craft "Sani" goods to sell themselves or to wholesale to Sani traders. Fourteen emigrant Han families lived in the village in fall 1993, producing vast quantities of piecework bags and children's Ashima costumes for Sani and Han retailers.

In Wukeshu, there is also a plan being promoted by the Shilin Tourism Bureau and local officials to museumify the village, moving all the residents away and setting up a Sani-tized tourism village with beautiful young people in quaint costumes acting as guides to the past. The transformation of the village into a corporation has been seen as a first step, but Wukeshu folk in interviews during late 1993 tended to dismiss the name change of their community as yet another government scheme and were skeptical about rumors that they would have to move out into other communities because their homes would be transformed into an idealized tourist attraction. Talking to the two elected Sani village leaders *(cunzhang)* also gave me disparate impressions about the village's future. The old farmer–village leader acknowledged the flow of money and the need to change, but saw this as a very gradual process. The younger village leader, a bureaucrat who has been sent all over Southeast Asia by the Tourism Bureau, literally said, "You won't recognize this place in 1995." As none of these plans has been publicized and the Shilin Tourism Bureau maintained that the future of the village was now strictly Village Corporation business, it was hard to say what the village would be in a few years. Today, economic class distinctions are growing; young men and women are finding that their futures, so different from those of their farmer parents, are no easier to negotiate; and the sense of Wukeshu as a community is endangered. In 1995, the village was still very recognizable, with some new houses being built on the periphery and more stores opening up on the village side of the lake. By late 1997, the young village leader had been replaced by another man with close ties to the Tourism Bureau, and the older village leader had consolidated his power base.

With the advent of cultural commodification, local ethnic tourism, and mass tourism in minority-cultural-village theme parks in Kunming, Beijing, Shenzhen, and even Orlando, Florida, there is even a new kind of "Sani sojourners" whose native place in the Stone Forest of Lunan is an important part of their work qualifications and provides a network of ties back home. On the road between Kunming and Shilin Park, outside of Wukeshu, construction was started, then halted in 1993, for a local cultural village, the Ashima Culture and Art Company, Ltd. *(Ashima wenhua yishu youxiangongsi),* a very ambitious joint venture, with a hotel, performance hall, observatory, museum, and artisan handicraft production, exhibition, and sales hall. The chief of the Lunan County Culture Bureau was enthusiastic about the project both as economic development and a means to promote ethnic arts and culture. What would be the actual impact of this project—which is named for the Sani heroine but is intended to have representatives of some twenty distinct Yi peoples from three provinces—remains to be seen. Local Sani have commented that the company should either drop the name Ashima if the project is to include all Yi groups or have only Sani culture as its focus.[13]

Ganlongtang

Among the many sources of employees for Stone Forest tourism development are the surrounding villages, including old and new Ganlongtang (meaning "dry dragon pool"). In a landscape of caves and springs in the eastern part of the county, Lumeiyi district, the paired villages of Ganlong-tangxinzhai (new dry dragon pool) and Ganlongtang lie at 1,775 meters. The older village is made up of Yi people: primarily Bai Yi who migrated down from the northern Qujing region in search of water more than eighty years ago and settled in with Sani. The newer village is mainly Han. In this area, Han and indigenous villages have developed side by side, often sharing resources and markets that have ties both to the eastern mountains and the western plain.

This area's ties to the Lunan plain are reflected in the mixed ethnic composition of villages. In the late 1980s old Ganlongtang had a population of 88 people, 28 or 31 percent of whom were listed as Han, the rest as Yi (Lunan Yizu Zizhixian 1989, 30–31). Field study in 1993 recorded a population of 117, only 5 (4 percent) of whom were identified as Han, 46 as Sani, and 66 as Bai Yi, distributed in 25 households. No household was designated as Han, but 3 were Han-Yi mixed. This dramatic drop in the Han population does not signify migration of people, but rather a realignment of ethnic identity from a majority status to a minority status with specific rights to resources. In New Ganlongtang, the 1980s population was 215 total, 61 of whom were Yi; the rest, 154 or 74 percent, were Han. The 1993 field study recorded a population of 206, with 158 Han (76 percent), 44 Sani, and 4 Bai Yi listed in the household registry *(hukou).* Officials designated 4 households out of 44 as Bai Yi (with Sani members), while the registry showed 10 Yi (Sani) households, 2 of mixed Han and Yi composition, and 28 Han

13. Lack of international funding slowed down construction, and the facility had not yet opened in late 1995.

households. Although the Han population in this village has held steady in numbers, all may not be what it seems.

Fluidity in this ethnic classification system is well illustrated by the elected leader *(cunzhang)* of the new village. He is listed on his state identification card as Han but has said that he thinks of himself as *minzu*. His relatives are Bai Yi, Hei Yi, and Sani, so it is not too clear which branch *(Bu tai qingchu shemma zhi)* of the Yi he should be assigned to. When he was younger it was easier to be listed as Han, even though he has the unusual family name of Ba.

The land base of Ganlongtang villages included some 212 *mu* in the new village and 87 *mu* in the old, worked in a small valley adjacent to the village sites, which are separated by a small ravine. A small shared elementary school (grades one through four) is located in the new village, which first developed as a settlement about a hundred years ago. As a community, Ganlongtang is oriented toward Lumeiyi due to marriage ties and the settlement of several Lumeiyi Sani Catholics in the new village. Past commune ties from the 1950s through 1970s and future tourism employment pull Ganlongtang people toward Shilin. Improved roads between limestone quarries and the main highway have made it easier for people to find work in the cash economy.

CONCLUSION

Non-Han minorities, targeted over the millennia for colonization and assimilation into the Chinese nation-state, respond to current situations in constructing their local identities. At times such as the Cultural Revolution, ethnic differences strategically had to be suppressed for survival, while at the end of the twentieth century, cultural commodification reinvents ethnic cultural differences within and between ethnic groups. As we have seen in Lunan County, multiethnic regional identities respond to changing political economies that situate relations between groups in hierarchies of influence, value, and cultural forms. Just as origin stories, myths, and historical records are reinterpreted to serve current uses, so are the roles of past actors, such as Paul Vial, in shaping local identities. In the 1990s, one hundred years after he built his mission in Lunan County, Vial is no longer vilified by revolutionary rhetoric, but instead influences various groups within Lunan. For Sani intellectuals he provides tantalizing clues to what the language and culture was like, as well their long-term legitimacy as a distinct group. For the state Tourism Bureau, Vial's history of European activity and his photographs are very useful in marketing Lunan as a unique international destination. For local Catholics, who are no longer "underground" but are building churches in several communities, Vial is revered and remembered for bringing a new heritage to Lunan. Alliances within and across native-place and ethnic identities through marriage, work, and politics are shaping the character and future of Lunan County as a place where Han and Sani must cooperate. As we have seen in the past, strong ties to native place for the Sani—expressed in Sani origin songs, government histories and policies, and French colonial descriptions of "indigenous" people in contrast to the Han—closely identify local Sani with Lunan County. At the same time, Han have settled in Lunan for many generations and Han emigrants continue to move in. Han now comprise more than twice the population of Sani in Lunan Yi Autonomous County.

Returning to the ethnic composition of the three study villages, the decrease of Han in old Ganlongtang and Danuohei could represent migration. However, the village household registers indicate another, more likely solution: the reidentification of *minzu* status during the 1990 census and subsequent registration. In these villages, virtually all children of ethnically mixed Han and Yi marriages listed in 1993 household registries were identified as Yi. According to various informants, from at least Vial's time in Lunan until the Cultural Revolution in the mid-1960s, there was virtually no Han-Yi marriage, although marriage across Yi groups such as Sani and Bai Yi did occur. Since the early 1980s a number of strategic advantages to minority status has evolved in Lunan as the state developed new policies, ranging from birth control policies allowing minorities to have at least one more child than Han (this was changed again in 1991 with rules limiting all rural couples to two children), to educational benefits, to economic development projects specifically targeting minority population, including the enormous tourism development surrounding Wukeshu.

While in the past to be a "native" in Lunan often meant subjugation by landlords, native minority status now may confer special advantages due to China's affirmative action policies. Ethnic-class considerations have become factors in marriages in new ways. Some Sani cross-cousin and uxorilocal marriage practices continue, in direct contrast to Han practices; but crosscutting the question of marriage occurring within or across ethnic lines is the issue of economic class. Hypergamy is crossing ethnic boundaries in a new way. While Sani and Han may marry up within their own groups, and Sani women may marry up into a wealthy Han family, there are now cases, as seen in Wukeshu, of Han women marrying up into wealthy Sani families. In general, mixed-ethnic families are choosing to give their children the advantage of a minority, indigenous identity.

Since the founding of the People's Republic, the advantages and disadvantages of ethnic identity and the uses of native place as ethnic territory in Lunan have built on the earlier history described in this essay. Lunan County is now faced with the tensions between modernity promoted by a homogenizing state "Communist civilizing project" and the promotion of ethnic variation and status. A series of Yunnan newspaper stories on development in Lunan county (Li et al. 1993) illustrates this, when the stories both laud the county for its ethnic charms as an ancient Yi place—Ashima's hometown—with a thriving tourism business and also note that poverty is at its worst in the mountain areas where primarily Sani live. Lunan County is native place to the Han majority as well as the Yi minority. Having a Han Lunan local identity can also translate into local expertise and networks of information, kin, and work. In 1993 when I would engage local people for the first time in conversation, Han or Yi, the response to my attempts to ask Where are you from? *(Nide laojia zai nar? Guxiang shi shemma?)* would invariably be answered "Lunan." Both groups are well aware of Lunan's special local characteristics *(tese)* that build from Sani-Yi myth and material culture, but the two are also tied to the landscape that both Han and Yi claim as their native place. Their multiple histories underlie claims to native-place resources in commodities and identities.

The "Yi" in Lunan Yi Autonomous County are about 95 percent Sani (He Yaohua 1994, 40) and various small populations of Axi, Hei Yi, Bai Yi, and others. Since the county's founding in 1956, there have been at least three attempts by Sani to have their group declared a separate *minzu* rather than a branch or *zhi* of the Yi. Would it then be "Lunan Sani Autonomous County"? Such ideas may not occur to Lunan's tourism planners,[14] who both emphasize the "Yi-ness" and national patrimony of the region by promoting a Sani identity of the place with images of Sani folk as the native people of Lunan County, which is "Ashima's Home Town" *(guxiang)*, and ignoring the local Han majority. While it might appear to be more advantageous to have a "Yi" rather than a "Han" Lunan native-place identity at this time, the intersection of ethnic and native-place identities provides local actors with a range of options also shaped by gender, class, national, global, and perhaps just-emerging identity hierarchies in contemporary China.

In late 1997, claims to Lunan as name and native place took a new turn when the county name was officially changed by state mandate from Lunan to Shilin (Stone Forest). This bold move for tourism marketing was met with vocal disdain by local Han and Sani Lunan people.

14. Many of these planners are Han from the outside, who take a hierarchical "we know best" stance toward all locals. Local Han tourism administrators are more likely to advocate for all Lunan (Han and Yi). In local government work, Han employees sometimes complain of a "glass ceiling" that reserves all number-one positions for minority, usually Sani, workers.

PART IV

The Yi Today

CHAPTER 12

Language Policy for the Yi

David Bradley

MINORITY LANGUAGE POLICIES IN CHINA

Since 1950, official language and other policies concerning the group called Yi have been consistent with other practices of the Chinese state toward nearby minorities who did not pose a threat to Chinese rule and were for the most part willing to accept the Chinese civilizing project, as discussed in Harrell's 1995 edited volume. The overall political and economic goal for most of the time up to 1950 was to consolidate and expand central control. Of course this was less true in times of instability and during the early parts of rule by dynasties whose rulers were not ethnic Chinese, such as the Yuan (Mongol) and Qing (Manchu). When direct contact between Chinese and Yi existed, such as during the former and latter Han dynasties and again during the Tang dynasty, the two groups were at first accommodated into the system of indirect rule through local tributaries, which meant that the elite began to use the Chinese language. With large-scale Chinese migration into the plains and valleys of the Yi area over the last millennium, this contact became more pervasive. Thus the Chinese language began to influence Yi languages more and more, even to the extent that the Yi developed a cluster of writing systems based on the same principle as Chinese and using some Chinese characters (though mainly different ones).

The Chinese classification of minorities was rather procrustean, especially for smaller and more remote groups in the southwest like the Yi. Different groups tended to be lumped together under one term, and the terms used to refer to these groups changed fairly frequently. For example, the name Qiang (with a couple of variants) at various stages referred to a range of different groups in what is now Gansu and northern Sichuan. In general the policy concerning the languages of small groups or groups within the core political orbit of China was to assimilate them, initially by using Chinese as a lingua franca and medium of literacy, and ultimately by replacing the minority spoken languages with varieties of Chinese. There is evidence that substantial populations of Zhuang-Dong- (Thai-) language speakers were thus assimilated into the Yuè (Cantonese) over several millennia, and in the last millennium many members of minorities in the southwest, including quite a few Yi, have amalgamated themselves into the Chinese population who speak southwestern Mandarin.

When the ruling dynasty was not ethnic Chinese, as during the Yuan (Mongol) and Qing (Manchu), there was a much greater recognition and use, at least early in the dynasty, of the language of the rulers. Nominally Manchu remained the official language of the Qing court until 1911 and again in Manchukuo from 1932 to 1945; but by the nineteenth century this was very nominal indeed.[1]

During most Chinese dynasties, the main language workers were officials in charge of dealing with outside visitors, most of whom came with diplomatic and trading missions, which the Chinese court usually chose to regard as missions of submission and tribute. These officials were themselves often members of such missions or semihostages from the ruling families of adjacent territories who were kept, sometimes against their will, in the capital to work as translators and interpreters. This practice was reported as early as the Zhou dynasty.

In 1407, during the Ming dynasty, a separate translation office, the Siyiguan 四夷馆, was established. Staffed mainly by the descendants of previous translators, its work seems to have been rather ineffective. This office continued to exist under the Qing dynasty, under the slightly revised name Siyiguan (四译馆). Wild (1945) provides a description of this office and its activities. It produced a series of 740-word vocabularies of the languages it worked with, including those of a few large minorities like the Yi, thus starting the lexicographical tradition that has continued in the post-1950 linguistic surveys of minority languages. The Yi vocabulary is of an Eastern Yi variety then spoken in Yongning (modern Xuyong) County in south-central Sichuan, adjacent to Weining in Guizhou; it has been reproduced and analyzed in detail in Nishida (1979). This follows the usual arrangement of these vocabularies, with the Yi characters, the Chinese gloss, and Chinese characters to represent the phonetic value of the Yi characters. Another attempt at recording Yi is found in d'Ollone (1912), which includes two Northern Yi varieties from Xide and Zhaojue and an Eastern Yi variety from Weining in Guizhou.

During the Republican period, minority language policy continued to be one of assimilation and neglect. However, during the anti-Japanese war, many scholars moved to the southwest, and a few started serious linguistic research

---

1. For an excellent survey of the decline and current state of Manchu, see Kane 1997.

on minority languages including Yi. Among these scholars were Professor Fu Maoji, who worked in Sichuan on Northern Yi, among other languages, and Professor Ma Xueliang, who worked in Yunnan on Eastern Yi (Ma Xueliang 1948) and on Sani (Ma Xueliang 1951). These two scholars were the founders of modern linguistic study of the Yi, and continued to lead minority language work after 1949. On his return after earning his Cambridge Ph.D. on Northern Yi (Fu 1998), Fu Maoji became leader of minority language work at the Institute of Linguistics of the Chinese Academy of Sciences (later renamed the Institute of Nationality Studies of the Chinese Academy of Social Sciences; its work on varieties of Chinese remained in the residual Institute of Linguistics). Ma Xueliang became leader of the minority language department at the Central Institute (now University) of Nationalities, where he trained successive generations of people working on minority languages. At first this was mainly young ethnic Chinese, including many senior scholars still active in Yi language work. From the mid-1950s, but especially in the last twenty years, more and more of those trained have been members of the minority groups themselves.

After 1949, minority policy was revolutionized, and minority language policy along with it. In the 1954 and 1982 constitutions of the People's Republic of China, the right of each national minority to use and develop its own language is specifically recognized (1982, article 4); in practice, however, these rights have sometimes not been asserted or implemented, especially during periods of political change. The first stage in the development of the new minority language policy was to replace many of the old and often pejorative names for minorities formerly used in Chinese, and to start training, in 1951, groups of mainly majority-group Chinese language researchers to study minority languages at the Central Institute of Nationalities. At this time, much of the Yi territory, like much of Tibet, was left partially in the hands of its traditional rulers, though an increased Chinese administrative and military presence moved into areas such as Liangshan.

The major research effort to describe the existing minority languages and cultures and establish an official classification of national minorities took place from 1956 to 1958. This was a very large team effort, with the first generation of mainly ethnic Chinese language scholars training and leading teams of middle-school graduates. Different teams from the Institute of Linguistics of the Chinese Academy of Sciences surveyed minority languages and varieties of Chinese in every part of China; at the same time, ethnographic surveys were undertaken by other similar teams. Some of the best Yi and other minority workers from these surveys later became the first generation of minority scholars working on their own languages and cultures. The linguistic part of the survey collected a word list of over nine hundred items and a substantial number of sentences in thousands of locations; some of these manuscript materials, of variable quality, still exist and are occasionally used by scholars. A few Russian scholars also took part in the surveys.

At this stage the general language policy was to develop new romanized scripts for those languages that did not already have a suitable script. The Yi in Sichuan were among the first to have a romanized script, starting in 1951; this happened despite the existence of the traditional Yi script in this area. The romanization went through a number of revisions in the mid-1950s. One of these included a few Cyrillic letters, under the influence of Russian linguists working in the surveys; but with the break between China and the Soviet Union, these were removed from Yi and nearly all other romanized scripts in 1958. These Yi romanizations of the 1950s were never very widely used, and with political upheavals in the Yi areas from the late 1950s their use stopped.

The 1950s classification of national minorities followed the Soviet criteria: small groups were to be combined into larger national minorities that share a language, culture, territory, and economy. The ethnic Chinese majority is now known as Han; within this group the linguistic differences are very great, but literary and cultural unity has long been supported by the Chinese writing system. In parallel fashion, many related small groups have been combined into national minorities and in some cases renamed; this is the case for the Yi.

In general the degree of linguistic similarity within a national minority is similar to that within Chinese; that is, there are various related but often not mutually intelligible spoken varieties. This is true of the Yi and of many other groups in Yunnan and elsewhere, including the Lisu, Lahu, and Hani nationalities, whose languages are historically quite close to Yi. Non-Chinese linguists often say that the linguistic varieties within the Han Chinese majority and within some other groups are separate languages, not dialects as they are usually described within China; but this is actually a matter of non-congruity between levels of linguistic terminology. The Chinese term *yuyan* refers to a higher-level group than indicated by the English term *language;* and similarly the Chinese term *fangyan* refers to a higher-level group than indicated by the English term *dialect,* which corresponds better to the Chinese term *tuyu.*

When pinyin became the official phonetic representation of Chinese in 1956–58, a set of principles was adopted for minority languages and scripts, as follows:

1. There should be a standard variety, which should be that of a central area, with the largest number of speakers, intelligible to speakers of other varieties and preferably spoken in an economically, politically, and culturally advanced area.
2. New writing systems should be romanizations.

3. The values of letters should be according to Chinese pinyin.

4. Any reformed writing systems should also be romanized.

In practice, some existing scripts, such as the old Lisu script using roman capital letters and Arabic scripts for Turkic languages and Tajik in Xinjiang, were replaced by romanized scripts according to principle 4; but in most such cases the minorities have subsequently chosen to revert to the traditional script.[2] Principle 3 was intended to assist the minorities in learning standard Chinese (*putonghua*).

The most difficult and controversial aspect of language policy was often the choice of the standard variety. This was done in the late 1950s at meetings of leading figures of each nationality, with extensive participation by the Chinese scholars who were involved in the survey work. As in most such meetings in China, the outcome was largely determined in advance, but the consultative process was seen to be carried out in full. In the case of some nationalities with great internal linguistic diversity, several different standard varieties were chosen; these often followed political boundaries, and the relevant writing systems were used in different provinces or regions, prefectures, and counties. For Miao, for example, three different new romanizations are used in different parts of Guizhou and adjacent areas of Hunan, Sichuan, and Yunnan, while a modified version of a missionary script is used by Christian Miao in other parts of Guizhou and Yunnan; see Enwall (1994) for further details.

From 1958 the anti-Rightist campaign and its minority counterpart, the Nationalities Unity campaign, had a very severe political effect in many minority areas; the traditional rulers were deposed, often rather violently, as in Liangshan, and slaves were liberated. This set minority language work back greatly, as did the Great Leap Forward, which further disrupted economic activity. After the initial preparation and trials of romanized orthographies, some school and adult literacy textbooks were published, but it is not clear how extensively they were used. All language work, and indeed nearly all education, effectively stopped during the Cultural Revolution; sadly, many dictionaries and other manuscripts were destroyed, and others languished unpublished until the 1980s. What did get published in minority languages in the 1960s and early 1970s was mainly political: *Quotations from Chairman Mao Zedong* and similar treatises, using the romanized systems of the late 1950s; parallel editions of these were produced in various languages, using the same illustrations.

The original goal of the linguistic surveys of the mid-1950s was to produce a writing system, textbooks, grammar, and dictionary of each national minority

---

2. For details of the Uighur case, which is complicated by the use of Cyrillic scripts for this and other Turkic languages in the former Soviet Union, see Wei (1993); concerning Lisu, see Bradley and Kane (1981) and Bradley (1994).

language, based on a standard variety selected after the survey and discussions. The cultural surveys were to produce a history and descriptive ethnographic materials on each nationality. In most cases the initial textbooks containing the new writing systems first came out in the late 1950s. Two of the grammar volumes (Lisu and Jingpo) appeared in 1959, published by the Academy of Sciences; publishing of this series resumed in the early 1980s. Dictionaries mainly did not appear until after 1978, which is also when the histories and ethnographic volumes, mainly compiled in the late 1950s and early 1960s, also started to be published. Where the original classification into fifty-five national minorities proved too coarse, additional materials were also prepared: for example, for two varieties of Monba and several varieties of Luoba in Tibet, for additional varieties within the Nu and Jingpo nationalities in Yunnan, and for the Yi in the three provinces where most of them live.

After the end of the Cultural Revolution, from 1975 and especially after 1978, language work restarted in earnest; many pre-1965 materials that had not been destroyed were finally published, and a massive new effort started. This involved training large numbers of young members of national minorities to do linguistic and cultural research on their own groups, and assigning them to work in language-related units, such as translation bureaus, language bureaus, and cultural offices; research units of nationality affairs commissions; nationalities-publishing offices at various levels; or at all levels of education from primary to tertiary. Publishing in minority languages expanded exponentially, and the use of these languages in education, the media, and elsewhere became fully established during the 1980s. Some nationalities whose leaders had chosen not to implement a writing system in the 1950s, such as the Qiang, Bai, and Naxi, moved to do so; others whose writing systems had been in abeyance for over twenty years, such as the Hani, revised and reintroduced them; and some, such as the Lisu, reverted quietly to their previous writing systems in many localities.

The initial leadership of post-1950 language policy for national minority groups such as the Yi was largely Chinese; some of these people are still active, but most are approaching or beyond retirement. The younger generation—including nearly all practical language workers at the national, provincial, prefectural, and county levels in the Nationalities Commission, Education Commission, language offices, translation offices, and so on—is made up of members of the group whose language they work on. These people worked with great enthusiasm during the 1970s and 1980s and produced truly massive amounts of material in and about their own languages. They have now assumed full control of language work.

Since economic liberalization, some of the impetus has gone out of language work, and a backlog of very valuable unpublished materials has again developed: dictionaries, transcriptions of traditional manuscripts, and a great deal of other valuable linguistic and cultural work is languishing in drawers throughout China. What gets published usually has a more practical or popular orientation: health, agricultural and animal husbandry instructions, popular literature, and tourist-oriented picture books; such things are more likely to receive the publication subsidies from local government now required by most publishers in China, including the various nationalities publishing houses. Educational materials continue to be reprinted as needed, and a substantial linguistic literature in Chinese and in various minority languages, written by and for the new post-1978 generation of young minority scholars and their students, has started to develop.

THE YI AND THE YI LANGUAGES

Like many other groups, the Yi were called by a series of names through Chinese history. One early term was *Man,* which referred to a variety of non-Chinese groups in the southwest, including the Miao, Yao, Yi, and others. More specifically, the Yi were also sometimes referred to as *Wuman,* but this term included other groups of eastern Yunnan as well. Some more recent names for the Yi were derived from the names of dynasties, such as the Dian kingdom of the Kunming area, in close contact with the Chinese since the mid-fourth century B.C., and the Cuan kingdom (which later split into two) of the same area from the fourth to the twelfth century A.D. After this time, many Yi groups came to be known as Luoluo, written in various ways with characters containing the dog radical, *luo* 猡, or *luo* 猓, or the two together. Some Yi groups actually called themselves by these names, but most did not; naturally, these characters are pejorative. During the Ming dynasty, yet another collective term for southwestern non-Chinese groups, *Yi* 夷, became current. This was used for the Zhuang, Buyi, and other more or less Sinicized Thai groups, as well as for the more Sinicized subgroups of the Yi, but not for the more remote groups such as the Miao. With the establishment of the People's Republic of China, the old pejorative term *Luoluo* was eliminated, replaced by the new character *Yi* 彝, which is again homophonous with the Ming and Qing term; but it now refers only to the Yi, not to the various other groups previously included in those terms. When it is used as the former name of the Yi or in parts of names for certain subgroups within the Yi, the term *Luoluo* is now of course written with the human radical.

According to the traditional history, the Yi were divided into six clans, which migrated in various directions away from the Kunming area after the collapse of the Cuan kingdoms; modern linguists may have used this as one of the reasons for including six major *fangyan* groups within Yi. Several versions of these migration histories have been edited and published in Guo and Ding (1984). These relate to four subgroups of the Yi: the Southern Nisu, Southeastern Sani, Eastern Nasu, and Northern Nuosu.

The other two groups now included in the Yi nationality, the Central Yi and Western Yi, do not have a traditional writing system and are linguistically more similar to related groups further to the west and southwest, such as the Lisu and Lahu. The Central Yi call themselves Lipo in some areas and Luoluopo in others (see Erik Mueggler, chapter 10 in this volume); their language is so similar to Lisu that over fifty thousand Lipo in Luquan, Wuding, and Yuanmou Counties, northwest of Kunming, changed their nationality from Yi to Lisu between the 1982 and 1990 census. The Western Yi mostly call themselves Laluo; their speech is also rather closer to Lisu than to the rest of Yi.

The modern names of the subgroups of the Yi are based on geographical location. Of the four subgroups who trace their origins back to the Cuan kingdom and traditionally use the Yi script, the most numerous is the Northern Yi, or Nuosu, who live mainly in southern Sichuan but also in northwestern and northeastern Yunnan. Very close to this group linguistically is the Eastern Yi, or Nasu, with many subgroups dispersed across northeastern Yunnan, western Guizhou, and a small part of northwestern Guangxi. The group classified as Southern Yi, or Nisu, of south-central Yunnan includes some subgroups with quite different names, including the Pula whose speech is distinct and who are recognized as a separate nationality from the Lôlô (Yi) in Vietnam. Concentrated in the area to the southeast of Kunming are the Southeastern Yi, with four major named subgroups: Sani mainly in Shilin County, Axi farther south in Mile County and surrounding areas, Azhe further south again, and Azha to the southeast. The "Southern Yi" Pula extend eastward, south of these Southeastern Yi subgroups.

Map 12.1 shows the approximate locations of these groups; but note that in many areas there is overlap: for example, there are some Lipo and some Nuosu in rural areas of Panzhihua (formerly Dukou) City and Yuanmou County, with the Lipo mainly to the south of the Jinsha River and the Nuosu mainly to the north. Similarly, there are some Lipo and some Nasu in Wuding and Luquan counties, with the former mainly but not exclusively to the west; and some Lipo, some Nisu, and some Laluo in parts of southwestern Chuxiong Prefecture.

Northern Yi or Nuosu is divided by speakers into three subgroups. The northern subgroup is the "large trousers," or Yynuo (Chinese, Yinuo),[3] with a fairly distinct northwestern variety around Lindimu (or Tianba 田坝, the Chinese name of the same place); the latter is the variety described in Fu (1998). The central "middle trousers," or Shynra (Chinese, Shengza), are the majority of the Northern Yi, and the type of Shynra spoken at Xide County was

---

3. Yi names are given in the romanization introduced in the 1970s; these are usually represented in Chinese by the characters shown in the glossary corresponding to their Hanyu pinyin form.

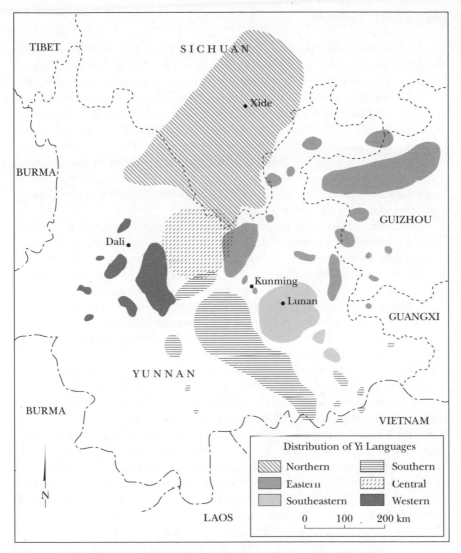

Map 12.1. Distribution of Yi dialects in Sichuan, Yunnan, and Guizhou

selected as the standard.[4] The southern are the "small trousers," or Suondi (Chinese, Suodi), with a subdivision into western Adur and eastern Suondi proper. Of these varieties, Yynuo and Shynra are easily mutually intelligible, but speakers of Suondi must make a considerable effort to learn Shynra. There are a few villages in western Zhaojue County that are linguistically transitional between Suondi and Shynra. The trousers referred to are the men's; women's clothing, especially the headdress, also differs greatly. There are several hundred thousand Shynra in Ninglang and adjacent counties in northwestern Yunnan and a smaller number in western parts of Zhaotong Prefecture in northeastern Yunnan; and there are a few Suondi in Yuanmou and Wuding Counties, but most Northern Yi live in Sichuan.

Eastern Yi, or Nasu, contains a very large number of diverse varieties spread over northeastern Yunnan, western Guizhou, Longlin County in Guangxi, and parts of southern Yibin Prefecture in Sichuan. These actually form a dialect chain with Northern Yi, but dialects at the extremes are not mutually intelligible even within Eastern Yi. In Yunnan the main subgroup is the Hei Yi, or Nasu, as described in Ma (1948) but referred to in the Christian missionary literature as Nosu. A Luquan County variety of Hei Yi was selected as the standard for Eastern Yi in Yunnan. Other subgroups in Yunnan include the Gan Yi, or Laka, in the north, Hong Yi in the west, and Gepo (also referred to in the Christian literature as Kopu) in the east. In Guizhou the Nasu are divided according to former Yi kingdoms, Shuixi, Wusa, Wumeng, and Mangbu in different areas of northwestern Guizhou; several of these kingdoms actually overlapped into what is now Zhaotong Prefecture in Yunnan and Yibin Prefecture in Sichuan, and the same subvarieties of Yi are also spoken there. In Guizhou, as discussed below, several alternative varieties are accepted in educational settings; but the Shuixi variety of Bijie and Dafang Counties is regarded as the most standard. Two other types of Yi are also included in Eastern Yi by linguists in China. One comprises the various moribund varieties of the Kunming region of central Yunnan, including Samei, or Sami, just southeast of Kunming, Sanyie just west of Kunming, and Samaduo in one village in the southern outskirts of Kunming. The other is the rather divergent variety spoken in southwestern Guizhou around Panxian County and in adjacent areas of eastern Yunnan.

Southern Yi or Nisu also includes a large range of varieties spoken in a range from central Yunnan to northernmost Vietnam; many of these are quite different, and only very limited linguistic data are available about them.

Southeastern Yi is concentrated in the area immediately southeast of Kunming. Each of the four subgroups, Sani, Axi, Azhe, and Azha, feels itself to

---

4. All examples are given here in the standard romanization of the standard Xide variety of Shynra.

be a distinct group; only the Sani and Azhe have a literary tradition, and their characters are often quite different from those of the other three Yi literary traditions. The Sani call themselves Ni, which is of course also the traditional name of the Yi of several other subgroups. In the western literature, they are sometimes referred to as Gni or Gni Lolo, terms used by the French missionary Paul Vial, who published a great deal of material on them.[5] Though it does not really make sense to speak of a standard variety for these four groups, a local variety of Sani from the southeastern Guishan area was selected in the late 1950s; this is slightly different from the varieties described in Vial (1908–09) and in Ma (1951), and has been fully documented in Jin Guoku and colleagues (1983).

In the 1990 census the Yi were enumerated at 6,572,173. Of these, 4,060,327 were in Yunnan, or nearly 62 percent; just under 1.8 million, or over 27 percent, were in Sichuan; 707,275, or over 10 percent, in Guizhou; 6,074 in Guangxi; and the remainder scattered in various areas. The following list shows the estimated numbers of speakers of each type of Yi in late 1999.

Northern Yi (Nuosu) total	2,500,000
Yynuo (N)	450,000
Shynra (C)	1,500,000 (as first dialect)
Suondi/Adur (S)	550,000
Eastern Yi (Nasu, etc.)	1,000,000
Southern Yi (Nisu, etc.)	500,000
Southeastern Yi total	500,000
Sani	120,000
Axi	100,000
Azhe	80,000
Azha	100,000
Central Yi (Lipo-Luoluopo)	700,000
Western Yi (Laluo)	500,000

The above list includes the 6,500 Pula and 3,200 "Lôlô" of Vietnam in the Southern Yi total. Many of the Yi in China are bilingual in Chinese, and an increasing proportion of the younger Yi speak Yi less well than Chinese. In addition to the above totals, about 1.5 million Yi now speak little or no Yi. These nonspeakers are concentrated in Yunnan and Guizhou, especially among the Western Yi and also among the Eastern Yi. Quite a few Central,

---

5. See, for example, Vial (1908–09); for an account of Vial, see Swain 1995. For Sani society, see Swain 1995 and Swain, chapter 11 in this volume.

Southern, and Southeastern Yi, primarily but not exclusively the young, do not speak Yi; but most of the Northern Yi do. As previously discussed, the Central Yi and Western Yi speak varieties closer to Lisu and Lahu than to the other types of Yi.[6]

RECENT LANGUAGE POLICY FOR THE YI

In a truly impressive effort, Yi and Chinese linguists have preserved a large corpus of Yi traditional written materials. They have also developed three different revised versions of the traditional script and taught these very widely and maintained a fourth. Each province with a substantial Yi population has taken a completely different approach to script reform.

In Sichuan, the Shynra speech of Xide County was selected as a standard; a new syllabary of 819 syllables and one diacritic (representing a tone that arises mainly from sandhi) was chosen from the traditional characters in their Xide pronunciation. This new syllabary was officially approved on October 1, 1980, and has been very widely used ever since; up to 100 percent literacy is claimed in some areas. There is extensive publishing of school textbooks up to university level (see Harrell and Bamo 1998), adult literacy materials, traditional literature, new literature in traditional and modern styles, translated Chinese literature, agricultural and political materials, and even a daily newspaper. Regular radio broadcasts and public notices in the Yi areas of Sichuan are bilingual, and much of public life can be conducted in Yi. One result is rapidly increasing knowledge of the standard variety by speakers of other varieties, derived from its use as a lingua franca and language of education and the media. There are type fonts, including various ornamental ones, typewriters, and a computer font, for this script. In addition, a standard romanized phonetic form for Shynra has been agreed upon, though it is mainly used for teaching Yi to Chinese and others or in citing linguistic examples in scholarly literature.

One curious feature of this script is that all syllabic characters have been rotated ninety degrees clockwise compared to other versions of the Yi script; this is perhaps because the Northern Yi read their books by holding them at a right angle to the way books are held by other Yi, and the unreformed Northern script is still read right to left rather than top to bottom as the others are. Since the mid-1970s, when drafts of the new syllabary came into use, writing has instead been from left to right starting at the top left, like other modern Yi and Chinese books; but still with the syllabic characters in the rotated position. Early stone and bronze inscriptions indicate that this rota-

6. For a detailed survey of the historical linguistic relationships among the Yi Group languages including Yi, Lahu, Lisu, Hani, Jinuo, and others, see Bradley (1979).

tion is a Northern Yi innovation; the materials in d'Ollone (1912) show that it has been in use for some time.

The Northern Yi or Nuosu syllabic script is now extremely widely known and used in Sichuan and parts of Yunnan. This is especially so in Liangshan Prefecture in Sichuan and in Ninglang County in Yunnan. This syllabary has been in use since 1978 and has had official approval since 1980. One problem with this script is that it is based on the phonetic form of the standard Shynra dialect. In the Shynra dialect there is a semiproductive tone sandhi process that changes a midlevel [33] tone and in some environments a low falling [21] tone into a lower-high [44] tone; see Bradley (1990b) for further details. Other varieties of Northern Yi do not use this tone sandhi process in the same way; in Suondi and Adur it is almost completely absent, and in Ynuo it is used less, and another process that creates a higher-low [22] sandhi tone is used instead. There are other sandhi processes as well; for example, the morpheme *nyi* (many) occurs in all four tones and with two different vowels; and the morpheme *mga* (buckwheat) shows two tones and two vowels, as shown in the list below.

Shynra nyi (many), *mge/mga* (buckwheat)

many	*axnyi*	[a^{44}ɲi^{33}]
very many	*cypnyixnyip*	[tshz^{21}ɲi^{44}ɲi^{21}]
many slaves (a name)	*jjinyot*	[dzɨ^{33}ɲo^{55}]
buckwheat	*mgabie, mge*	[ŋga^{33}pe^{33}], [ŋgɯ^{33}]
bitter buckwheat	*mgapnuo*	[ŋga^{21}nø^{33}]
buckwheat chaff	*mgepu*	[ŋgɯ^{33}phu^{33}]
buckwheat flour	*mgepmop*	[ŋgɯ^{21}mo^{21}]

A speaker of Ynuo, Suondi, or Adur (or even a speaker of a local variety of Shynra where the rules are slightly different) must learn standard Shynra as a second dialect to achieve literacy, and will have considerable trouble learning all these arbitrary extra forms and their correct phonetic spelling; this problem would not have arisen if the characters had remained semantic rather than syllabic.

In the northwest of Yunnan, where Northern Yi is spoken, the Sichuan Yi orthography was introduced in the early 1980s, and continues in use in Ninglang County, though apparently not in Lijiang Prefecture as seen in the Yi village depicted in the television series *South of the Clouds (Yun zhi nan).* At first lecturers were sent from the Southwest Institute of Nationalities to train teachers and other language workers at the Yunnan Institute of Nationalities, but now students are sent from Ninglang County to study in Sichuan.

In Guizhou, the decision was to retain and standardize the traditional characters, but not to impose a standard pronunciation. This solution is similar to the traditional Chinese situation prior to the introduction of the *putonghua* policy, in which characters were read with a local pronunciation not necessarily intelligible to speakers of other varieties of Chinese. After publishing a provisional version of six school textbooks (Guizhou Nationalities Commission 1982–83) giving eight alternative local pronunciations, as well as adult literacy materials, the Guizhou Nationalities Commission textbook (1984) came out in early 1985, giving ten alternative local pronunciations, of which the former Shuixi standards, Bijie County and Dafang County, are listed first as the default. Several groups of Yi have been trained in this script at the Guizhou Institute of Nationalities, with the first group graduating in 1988. A recent dictionary, by Long Zhiji and colleagues (1991), gives four local pronunciation alternatives: first listed is a Weining County variety, second is a Dafang County variety, third is the divergent Panxian County type, and fourth is another Weining County variety. The two Weining varieties are both Wusa, but are substantially different from each other. All published materials in this script have been reproduced from handwritten versions, using a traditional style of characters with curves.

In Yunnan the policy is somewhat unusual; a completely new compromise script called "standard Yi" *(guifan Yiwen)* was devised between 1982 and 1987 by a committee of Yi working at the Yunnan Nationalities Commission, and approved for use from 1987 in most areas of Yunnan.[7] This is based on a character-by-character compromise between Eastern, Southern, Southeastern, and Northern Yi characters; some seventeen hundred characters were agreed on in the first stage by 1987, and a further five hundred by 1990 for a current total of over twenty-two thousand. The choice was by majority rule: the version of the character used in the majority of the four literary varieties of Yi was chosen. The original orientation as still used in Southern, Eastern, and Sani/Azhe—but not Northern Yi—is kept, but written from left to right starting at the top left. Since the Sani and Azhe characters are often somewhat different, few were chosen; on the whole, characters tend to come from Eastern and Southern Yi varieties. Compared to traditional handwritten Yi, these characters are usually written in a more squared-off form. Up to 1996, published materials in this script were produced from handwritten originals, but since 1997 there is a computer font.

Curiously, the first book to appear in this script was a collection of proverbs (Yang et al. 1989), followed by a word list (Yunnan Nationalities Language Commission 1989), and an adult literacy book (Yunnan Nationalities Language Commission 1990b), reprinted six months later (1990a) with identical Yi title and text, the same International Standard Book Number (ISBN), but a different Chinese title. More recently, the same commission prepared a children's textbook (1991), which has been put into use in

---

7. This is not to be confused with the Nuosu script based on the Xide Shynra variety, which is also referred to by the same name *guifan Yiwen*, or *Nuosu bburma* in Yi.

some Yi villages, including some near Kunming where the children speak no Yi at all. This textbook was reprinted in mid-1997 using the computer font, with a few errors corrected. This script has also begun to be used for public signs and banners and alongside Chinese on the covers of publications from the various Yi autonomous prefectures and counties in Yunnan other than Ninglang, which uses the Sichuan syllabary, and Lunan, which uses Sani. In the language policy debate, the government of the Chuxiong Yi Autonomous Prefecture, the only autonomous prefecture in Yunnan solely designated as Yi, weighed in with a dictionary in the traditional Nasu (Hei Yi) characters (Wang et al. 1995), which gives the pronunciation in two Eastern Yi varieties including Nasu, as well as two Central Yi varieties, Lipo and Luoluopo.

As in Guizhou, speakers may use their local pronunciation for the Yunnan standard Yi characters; but the only indication of pronunciation in any printed materials on this script is in a 1989 word list that uses Nasu (Hei Yi) of Luquan County, just north of Kunming. This had been the standard variety for Eastern Yi in Yunnan prior to the promulgation of the new standard, and several of the most active promoters of the Yunnan standard Yi are in fact Nasu from this area just to the east of Chuxiong.[8] There are serious problems with the new script, since it is a newly constructed compromise with no defined standard pronunciation and is derived from four distinct written traditions used by subgroups within the Yi whose speech is not mutually intelligible. For this reason it is very difficult for any Yi already literate in any existing variety of Yi to use. It is mainly being taught to young people, and many of them have limited speaking knowledge of their own variety of Yi. One must wonder how they will pronounce it!

In mid-1994 a two-year joint training class was started as a combined effort by the Yunnan Institute of Nationalities, the Yunnan Nationalities Language Commission, and the Southwest Institute of Nationalities; the students were forty Yi already working in language-related areas at the local level from all parts of Yunnan (and one participant each from Sichuan, Guizhou, and Guangxi). They were trained in the new Yunnan standard Yi, Sichuan Yi, and in Yi traditional scripts. These graduates have now returned to their work units. Since 1988 new classes of Yi-language students at the Yunnan Institute of Nationalities have all studied Yunnan "standard Yi" in addition to their own varieties. The Yunnan Nationalities Language Commission decided in 1996 that Yunnan "standard Yi" should be taught in all Yi areas and gave subsidies to places that started immediately. By 1997 this decision was reversed, and at present it is still very difficult for anyone, even the people who

---

8. The most active of these is Zhang Chunde of the Yunnan Institute of Nationalities, who has been involved in most efforts to train language workers and students in this script.

devised it and those who have taught it or studied it for several years, to read this script aloud.

In cooperation with the Institute of Nationality Literature of the Yunnan Academy of Social Sciences, I have been conducting a survey of varieties of Yi in Yunnan and producing textbook materials using a romanization parallel to pinyin to help speakers of some varieties of Yi when they wish to learn this script.[9]

The fourth variety of Yi currently in use is the traditional Sani script of Lunan County southeast of Kunming. A comparison of the versions of this script given in Vial (1908–9), the Sani migration story in Guo and Ding (1984), and a Sani dictionary (Jin et al. 1983) shows the degree of difference often seen within traditional Yi scripts: each religious practitioner had a slightly different version of many characters, which he transmitted to his chosen successor, usually a son or nephew. The recent Sani dictionary indicates that for nearly 90 percent of syllables there is only one character, and thus Sani appears to use considerably more characters phonetically with different meanings than other traditional kinds of Yi. On the other hand, the dictionary also gives a large number of alternative forms used for many characters by different religious practitioners. Various traditional stories, including that of Ashima, have been published in this script with Sani phonetic form and Chinese translation, as well as in Chinese and English translation only. The county government at various levels makes some limited use of this script in signs, banners, and letterheads, but it appears not to be taught in schools and is thus learned only by the successors of traditional religious practitioners, by scholars, and by Sani students who study their language at the Yunnan Institute of Nationalities or the Central University of Nationalities in Beijing.

In cooperation with several Sani scholars, we are collecting several versions of the traditional Sani death ritual text; this is particularly interesting because it traces the migrations of the Sani around northeastern Yunnan over many centuries.[10]

The list below exemplifies the degree of difference between the four currently used Yi scripts. The rotation of the Northern Yi variety can be noted, also the differences in rounding and shape between the Guizhou and Yunnan scripts and the greater divergence of the Sani script from the other three. The examples are the characters for the numbers one and two (whose ori-

9. I am very glad to acknowledge the financial support of the UNESCO Endangered Languages project and the very able assistance of Li Yongxiang, Maya Bradley, Deng Qiyao, and many local officials and speakers of Yi in various parts of Yunnan.

10. Again, I am very pleased to acknowledge the financial support of the UNESCO Endangered Languages project and the participation of Tseng Kuo-pin, Ang Zhiling, Maya Bradley, and a number of Sani religious practitioners.

gins from Chinese are clear), and the traditional name the Yi use for themselves. Also given are the different phonetic forms of this autonym.[11]

	Sichuan (Shynra)	Guizhou	Yunnan ("Standard Yi")	Sani
1, 2	⌐ ⌐	⌐ ⌐	⌐ ⌐	N ⌐
Yi autonym	♂	⌐	⌐	⌐
	[ni²¹]	[nɯ²¹][ɲi⁵⁵][no⁵⁵]	[ni²¹], etc.	[nɪ²¹]

In addition to the efforts to promote literacy in Yi among the Yi and to translate practical materials into Yi and Yi literature into Chinese, there are extensive efforts being made at the national, provincial, prefectural, and county levels to preserve traditional Yi literature and culture. County, prefectural, and provincial language offices, mainly within the Nationalities Commission, collect, transcribe, and translate manuscripts into Chinese (and in Sichuan into the new standard Shynra variety as well). Some of this material is published, mainly by the Sichuan Nationalities Publishing House but also by the Yunnan Nationalities Publishing House, the Guizhou Nationalities Publishing House, the Central University of Nationalities in Beijing, and by some prefecture and county governments as well as various scholarly journals.

In most cases, the traditional Yi religious practitioner (in Nuosu, the *bimo*) who wrote a text, or one of his trained descendants, is needed to read it with any certainty, so many of the manuscripts in official hands cannot be fully read. Also, as these texts have been transmitted for many centuries, there are many archaic and obscure passages. The texts also refer to historical and semihistorical places, events, and people for which there is no other source or that are known by other names in Chinese sources, and rituals that in some cases are not now fully understood. Furthermore, the manuscripts are traditionally regarded as secret, and payment for performing rituals was one of the main sources of income, so many religious practitioners are unwilling to help in transcribing them. The worst thing is that when the religious practitioner dies, his manuscripts are usually burned with him. As the traditionally trained religious practitioners are now mainly rather old men, recording and translation work is extremely urgent; but some of their sons and nephews have studied with them, and many of the religious practitioners of this generation, now aged in their twenties to forties, have been or are being trained in Yi linguistics at the Central University of Nationalities; at the Yunnan, Guizhou, and Southwest Institutes of Nationalities with various other Yi scholars; or at some of the leading research and translation bureaus, such as the Liangshan Translation Bureau in Xichang, Sichuan, the Yi Lit-

11. For a discussion of the historical connection of this autonym with those of the Hani, Lisu, Lahu, and other Yi Group languages, see Bradley, Bradley, and Li (1997).

erature and History Institute of the Yunnan Academy of Social Sciences at Chuxiong in Yunnan, the Yi Translation Bureau at Bijie in Guizhou, and elsewhere in numerous other language offices and other units.

The Lipo-Luoluopo and the Laluo have no tradition of using a script; rather, they share the widespread traditional story of the loss of writing: that it was given by god to every group, but that their group lost it through carelessness. Either the script fell out through a loosely woven basket, or it was written on some edible medium such as buffalo hide and eaten on the way home by the person carrying it or by some animal that stole it.

CONCLUSION: SUCCESSES AND PROBLEMS

In summary, very extensive efforts were made from the mid-1950s to the mid-1960s and again since the mid-1970s to standardize, teach, and use various versions of the traditional Yi script. There are now four varieties, one each for Sichuan, Guizhou, and Yunnan, and one used in Lunan County in Yunnan.

In Sichuan there are hundreds of Yi who do language work: in the Provincial and Liangshan Prefectural Translation Bureaus; in the Sichuan Nationalities Language Commission; in the Southwest Institute of Nationalities, which has a large Yi and Tibetan language department that teaches Yi to Yi, to Chinese speakers, and to a few foreigners; in teachers' colleges in Xichang and Zhaojue; in language offices in every county of Liangshan; in the Sichuan Nationalities Language Commission; and in the Liangshan Nationalities Commission, among other places. The Shynra syllabic script is very widely seen and used throughout Liangshan Prefecture and to a lesser extent in Ninglang County in northwestern Yunnan.

In Guizhou the new script is being introduced slowly as teachers become available; since the only Yi autonomous county in Guizhou is Weining, the other local governments are not promoting it as extensively as in Sichuan. Also, a rather high proportion of the Yi in Guizhou no longer speak any Yi. The Yi language workers in Guizhou are not as many as in Sichuan or Yunnan; they are concentrated in the Guizhou Nationalities Commission, both in the Research Institute of Nationalities and the Guizhou Nationalities Publishing House; in the Guizhou Institute of Nationalities at Huaxi; at Bijie in the Yi Translation Bureau; and scattered elsewhere in various government offices at the prefecture and county levels.

In Yunnan, the province with the largest number and greatest diversity of Yi, the Northern Yi script is used in Ninglang County, the Sani script is used for some official purposes in Lunan County, and the new Yunnan standard Yi script is starting to be introduced through the education system. The Yunnan Nationalities Publishing House has Yi staff who prepare and edit books in all three of these scripts, as well as in publishing old traditional texts. The Yunnan Nationalities Language Commission also has Yi staff from various backgrounds; those formerly involved in devising the new "standard Yi" have retired or moved elsewhere, but young colleagues continue the work. The Yunnan Institute of Nationalities has a substantial Yi-language section in its Department of Nationalities Languages and Literatures, and there are some scholars in the Yunnan Academy of Social Science in various institutes at Kunming and Chuxiong and scattered in various levels of local government.

It remains to be seen whether the very diverse Yi of Yunnan will accept the new Yunnan standard Yi script, and if so whether it will be possible to teach it successfully. The task is difficult, especially as there is no one who can comfortably read or write this script and no agreed-upon pronunciation. Indeed, many of the literate Yi in Yunnan are opposed to it, including most of the people who now work in language-related areas.

There is some cross-province coordination in Yi-language work. For example, the three main publishing houses printing Yi materials, those of Sichuan, Guizhou, and Yunnan, have regular meetings; and the Yunnan, Guizhou, and Southwest Institutes of Nationalities have exchanged staff over more than ten years and regularly meet at conferences. Yi-language scholars also meet at the more general Yi-studies conferences held every few years and at Nationalities Linguistics conferences. The most recent example of such cooperation is the sending of a Guizhou, a Sichuan, and a Guangxi participant in mid-1994 to attend the two-year Yunnan Yi traditional and Yunnan standard Yi script course. Of course, many Yi-language scholars also participate in general conferences on minority language and other issues and know each other well.

The commitment to Yi and other minority languages in China is much more than superficial. It has become an important part of the developing Yi identity. In many cases the children of cadres who have grown up in towns and cities do not speak Yi, but now some of this young elite wants to learn to speak it. Special classes for such students have been started in some of the institutes of nationalities. Furthermore, it is now expected that good Han Chinese cadres should learn some of the minority language of the area where they work, and teaching materials have been developed to help them do so, especially for Sichuan Shynra, but also for many other minority languages. I have also met many hardworking Yi cadres who speak not just their own variety of Yi but also one or more other varieties used where they work.

In general, the Sichuan syllabic script is a great success, the Guizhou revived traditional script is only starting to spread, and there may be problems ahead for the Yunnan standard Yi script.

CHAPTER 13

Nationalities Conflict and Ethnicity in the People's Republic of China, with Special Reference to the Yi in the Liangshan Yi Autonomous Prefecture

Thomas Heberer

Most of the earth's surface consists of states inhabited by several nationalities. Usually, minorities are openly or latently discriminated against or oppressed. The clashes that result constitute one of the main sources of domestic conflicts and instability. The French sociologist Raymond Aron predicted in the 1960s that, from a global perspective, ethnic conflict would take the place of class conflict (1962). If we look at contemporary developments in the world, this prognosis has already become fact.

From such conflict arises the critical need to provide ethnic minorities and folk peoples those rights that will allow them to survive and develop. Only in this way can the chronic potential for conflict be neutralized. This also involves the incorporation of minorities into the state with equal rights, as well as the protection of autonomous culture. This latter includes the protection of language and education; the right to identity, practice of religion, and protection from persecution; the right not to be discriminated against, and equality of rights and opportunities, from which follows the right to constitute one's own cultural organizations and interest groups.

The first part of this essay adopts a political science perspective to deal with basic problems that exist not only in Yi inhabited areas but as well in all areas inhabited by "ethnic minorities" in China (which will also be called non-Han peoples to differentiate them from the ethnic majority, the Han). After this, I briefly come to the crux of nationalities politics—regional autonomy. The second part focuses on a series of examples to discuss the problems of autonomy and the potential for conflict in Liangshan Yi Autonomous Prefecture. A third section summarizes patterns of conflict, perspectives, and possible preventive measures.

To begin with, it should be emphasized that genocide and forced assimilation are not aspects of today's nationality politics in China. Characteristics such as languages, writing systems, and customs are to a certain extent tolerated or even promoted. There are special quotas for non-Han peoples in birth planning and advancement to higher education. The state's opposition to strivings for autonomy comes clear through cultural insight. Equally important, a "Confucian path to assimilation," Sinification, casts its shadow over nationality politics: mass settlement of Han Chinese without recourse for affected minorities, penetration by Han Chinese education and culture, incorporation into the Han-dominated structures of Party and state, prohibition of "unhealthy" customs and habits that do not correspond to Han morality, interference with religion, forced "modernization" according to the conceptions of higher authorities, and the attempt at "assimilation" that is determined by it. The traditional Confucian way of assimilation was never aimed at elimination of non-Chinese people, but rather demanded their submission to the center (formerly, the emperor), as well as their incorporation into the general structure of the Chinese empire: the goal remained their "cultivation" by means of Confucian values, that is, cultural, nonviolent Sinification. And little of this foundation has changed up to today. This does not mean, as we will see below, that there has been no change in recent decades. The developments of the reform era also demonstrate that economic liberalization has not led to the disappearance of ethnic differences, but, as in other parts of the world, to an "ethnic revival."

TRENDS IN CHINESE NATIONALITIES POLICY AND THE YI

The Yi in the Liangshan Mountains, who call themselves Nuosu, had managed to maintain their social, cultural, and political identity virtually intact up to the mid-1950s, when Beijing attempted to integrate them into the socialist polity and society. Initial, gradualist attempts were quite successful, but radicalization of the process after 1956 provoked massive resistance in the form of a several-year guerrilla war against the Communist mission of eliminating the "reactionary slaveholding society."

Beginning with the so-called Great Leap Forward (1958–60), an attempt to achieve economic development and even "the final goal of the communist society of plenty" through "mass campaigns," a deliberate policy of forced assimilation was pursued. The illusion that communism was right around the corner was accompanied by the assumption that the knell of individual nationalities had rung. The "melting together of nationalities" led to coercive restrictions and even to prohibitions on the use of the language, script, customs, and religion of the Nuosu, as well as to forced elimination of social structures. Nuosu religious practitioners and members of the former ruling strata were sentenced to "forced physical labor." After a short interlude the Cultural Revolution brought the most extreme form of forced assimilation— physical elimination and cultural destruction.

For most Yi people political campaigns and movements were phenomena that did not concern their immediate sphere of living. As one Yi cadre put it in the 1980s, "In the 1950s the Party told us Gao Gang and Rao Shushi were bad guys and should be criticized; in the 1960s Liu Shaoqi had to be criticized. Lin Biao, the deputy of Mao, was at first magnificent, then an evildoer *[huaidan]*. We had even to criticize Confucius. All those people were Han, and we [didn't] know if they were good or bad. We [had] nothing to do with them."

At the beginning of the 1980s the Chinese leadership saw itself driven to a moderate policy because of dissatisfaction in minorities areas and in the interest of economic opening and modernization of these regions. The results of the Cultural Revolution had made it clear that the integration of non-Han people was to be achieved not through force, but through measures based on a broad consensus. The constitution of 1982 revalorized the minorities correspondingly, and a 1984 "Autonomy Law" formally extended to them the widest-reaching freedoms since the founding of the People's Republic. Accordingly, decisions and directives of higher organs that did not correspond to the concrete conditions of an autonomous region no longer had to be carried out (but only if the higher organs agreed!); the leading cadres were supposed to come from the nationalities that were carrying out the autonomy; the autonomous units received broader rights for regional planning and economic development, in protection and exploitation of their resources, in foreign trade, education, finance, public health, and other sectors (Heberer 1984a, 601–9). At any rate, most of the clauses are so vaguely worded that they would be unimplementable in the absence of accompanying laws. The Autonomy Law is thus a "soft law," that is, a process of setting goals that should be followed as far as possible by state policies. One misses reference to an effective system for protection of autonomy. In addition, there are no legal measures for implementation of this law. There are correspondingly many complaints that local authorities do not hold to it.

This law did not in any way quiet the calls of many minority leaders for wider-ranging, actual autonomy (up to the maximum degree: Beijing should, following the emperor's example, manage only the international relations and military interests of large regions like Tibet or Xinjiang and leave local politics to the peoples living there). Particularly among the larger nationalities, disappointment spread widely, and younger forces radicalized because they no longer expected Beijing to solve any of their problems.

To a great degree, the existing rights themselves occur only on paper. Because they are not actionable (in the end, there is no law independent of the Party and no constitutional or administrative court), the degree to which rights can be realized depends on the current Party line and is therefore quite arbitrary.

Thus, a basic conflict of Chinese society consists of the contradiction between the pretension to be an ideologically single-ethnic party and the fact of the existence of a polyethnic society. The Party, which, corresponding to the majority of the population, is dominated by Han Chinese, is the court of last resort. It is dedicated in its organizational structure to the leveling of all ethnic differences and is not subordinated either to the legal system or to autonomy. Therefore all forms of self-rule find their limits here. And this inhibits actual, implementable laws of autonomy.

PROBLEMS OF SELF-ADMINISTRATION AND POTENTIALS FOR CONFLICT IN THE LIANGSHAN YI AUTONOMOUS PREFECTURE

The problems of autonomy in Liangshan Yi Autonomous Prefecture are not fundamentally different from those in other regions. It should be emphasized again here that the central problem of autonomy does not lie in legal regulation, that is, in the lack of legal ordinances. Liangshan Prefecture, like other autonomous regions, enacts many local legal regulations. The weakness is rather that (a) there lacks a mechanism for implementation, and (b) the Party's authority is prior and superior to autonomy in every case.[1] In particular, the establishment of autonomy in the prefecture is oriented to the national autonomy law, with the corresponding restrictions. Even according to this law, decisions and policies of superior state organs do not need to be carried out when they do not correspond to the conditions of the locality. In any case it gives the local authorities the right to make a proposal and have it decided upon by the corresponding higher organs (usually the provincial authorities). The decision thereby remains with those who had the original power to decide. If they stand with their original decision, then their determination is decisive and must in every case be carried out according to "democratic centralism" (Liangshan Yizu Zizhizhou 1991, 39).

In the following paragraphs, I will use a few examples to problematize the rights of self-administration and the potential for conflict in Liangshan Prefecture. This is not intended to provide a comprehensive and systematic overview of autonomy, but rather to provide a selection that, on the one hand, deals with basic problems that have not yet been publicly problematized, such as ethnic names and the drawing of territorial boundaries, and on the other

---

1. The "Autonomy Regulation of the Liangshan Autonomous Prefecture" of 1987 confirms explicitly the Party's leading role. See Liangshan Yizu Zizhizhou (1991, 39).

hand, addresses the economic situation and social aspects connected to it and the policies dealing with customs and habits, concentrating on the *bimo* as well as on the politics of birth planning and language. These points should enrich the discussion of autonomy and its problems.

The Question of Names

In the 1950s, Beijing arbitrarily created nationalities and—in some cases— nationalities names. The criteria for these were set by the Party leadership. Stevan Harrell spoke in this context of a triple pattern of ethnic classification: ethnohistory, a scholarly discourse of the history of a nationality or an area; state discourse of ethnic classification, the official classification by Chinese authorities; and ethnic identity, the perception of one's own and others' ethnic identity (Harrell 1996b, 98). The official name *Yi* represents the state discourse of ethnic classification. In this respect it is necessary to problematize this official name: in the first place, the fact of putting together different groups, some of whom do not see themselves as part of the same ethnic unit, all under a unitary designation is problematic in itself (Harrell 1990, 521). In addition is the choice of the name itself, which differs from the name representing ethnic identity: The Yi in Liangshan call themselves either Nuosu or Nasu, which means nothing but "people."[2] Names that they were earlier known by, such as Lolo or Yiren (the first is derived from a pejorative name, the second means barbarian), were perceived as discriminatory. The current name, Yi, is said to have been the result of a majority opinion in a survey of representatives of this nationality in the 1950s. But Yi informants indicate that the only thing actually debated was a new character for *Yi*. The sound was still a historical product forced on them by earlier emperors. According to many Yi, among themselves they prefer the traditional name for themselves, Nuosu (Harrell 1996b, 104 ff; Luohong 1996, 88–91).

Territorial Boundaries

The Yi, the sixth-largest non-Han nationality in the census of 1990, with 6.58 million people, are distributed across the provinces of Yunnan (4.06 million), Sichuan (1.79 million), Guizhou (0.71 million), and Guangxi (7,200). In contrast to two smaller nationalities, the Yi have no provincial-level autonomous region of their own, but only five autonomous prefectures (four in Yunnan, one in Sichuan), and ten autonomous counties (seven in Yunnan, two in Sichuan, and one in Guizhou). Proposals for creation of a province-level autonomous region uniting the Yi areas in Yunnan, Sichuan,

2. This is a custom practiced by many nations, as evidenced, for instance, by the terms "Inuit," "Bantu," "Magyar," and "Alemannen."

and Guizhou were put forth primarily in the early 1980s. Many Yi in Liang-shan would have liked to see themselves united with the more than six mil-lion Yi in a unitary region. Although the proportion of Yi in the Yi regions is less than 50 percent (42 percent in Liangshan, as against 55 percent Han), it is higher than in most of the other autonomous regions. In addition, such a move would mean that the many Yi who live in mixed areas would be bet-ter protected against assimilation. Writing and a standard language could be better propagated among all Yi, and their culture could be better de-fended and protected. At the same time, an autonomous region could get stronger benefits from the center because it would be subordinate not to a province but directly to Beijing. As we will see (Table 3), Liangshan Yi Au-tonomous Prefecture gets many fewer benefits from the center in compari-son with provincial-level autonomous regions. At the same time, however, it is questionable whether the group that comprises "Yi" is interested in a provincial-level autonomous region.

Social Hierarchization

The classification as a cruel and brutal slave-owner society is another issue challenged more and more by Yi scholars. It assigns to the Yi a relatively low status in the hierarchy of nationalities. The Yi are seen as the only slave-owner society that existed in China as late as the 1950s. This assessment not only seems to verify the Stalinist historical concept of social hierarchy (develop-ment from primitive society to slave-owning, feudal, capitalist, and socialist society) that perceived China to be a nation consisting of nationalities rep-resenting different stages of development, with the Han at the top of eco-nomical, societal, cultural, and political development. Thus the Han had a concept that allowed continuation of their traditional function of raising the societies of the ethnic minorities to the level of the Han, and thus of equal-izing the various ethnic groups in the name of a modern theory (socialism). The Communist Party in its role as vanguard of all people living within the Chinese borders took over this traditional role of civilizing the national mi-norities. Henceforth, the Party decided which customs were useful, pro-gressive, and in the interest of a people and which were not and thus were to be abolished. This classification made equality between the Han and the minorities impossible. They could not be equal because the Han stood at the top of the hierarchy, and the minorities belonged to different stages of development below and had to strive to catch up with the Han. The policy and mode of catching up was set by the Han.

This concept of hierarchization perpetuates and approves inequality and tutelage. The philosopher Michael Walzer has pointed out that the idea of a cultural hierarchy always poses a threat to the people, whose culture is de-valuated. Hierarchies, said Walzer, are never "innocent," because they tend to a policy of discrimination (1996, 186). The classification as inferior is thus an obstacle for a true autonomy or self-administration, because those nationalities are seen as incapable of handling things and administering themselves.

Economic and Social Aspects

China's recent development demonstrates that the practice of actual rights of self-administration requires an economic foundation. The bigger the economy of a region, the greater is its maneuvering room vis-à-vis the center. And on the contrary, the more a region depends on the center or, correspondingly, a province, the less room it has for maneuvering. Autonomy is related not only to political decisions but also to economic strength.

Because the minority regions are among the poorest and least developed areas in China, their conditions for self-administration are not very good. Their economic and technological disadvantage when compared with other parts of China has, on the one hand, historical grounds. A large portion of the non-Han peoples has been, over the course of history, chased into poor regions. These peoples sealed themselves off from the outside in order not to be overwhelmed by the steadily increasing, land-gobbling Han population. On the other hand, the flawed, nationwide development policy of the 1960s and 1970s brought no progress for these areas.

In comparison with China as a whole and with the minority regions, Liangshan Prefecture ranks among the least developed regions, particularly when the economic potential of the Han-dominated prefectural capital of Xichang is not considered. The data in Table 13.1 demonstrate this quite clearly.

If we compare peasant per-capita income in the autonomous regions of Sichuan with the corresponding income in provincial-level autonomous regions, or with provinces that have a large portion of minority populations, the autonomous regions in Sichuan lie at the bottom end of the scale (Table 13.2).

Not only in comparison with other autonomous regions but also within Sichuan, Liangshan Prefecture is an especially poor region. Among the thirty autonomous prefectures in China, it was, in 1996, in terms of peasants' net income per capita, one of the poorest areas (793 yuan) (*Zhongguo minzu tongji nianjian* 1996, 283).

Twelve of the seventeen counties in Liangshan Prefecture in the mid-1990s were officially counted and registered as "poor counties" *(pinkun xian);* that is to say, they had a per capita income of less than 200 yuan per year (average: 129 yuan, less than the average per capita income of peasants for all of China at the end of the Cultural Revolution). In 1992, 860,000 of the 1.54 million Yi in Liangshan (55.8 percent) were counted as "very poor"; that is, their income was below the poverty line and they had a yearly income of less than 200 yuan, or US$25 (Qubi and Yang 1992, 33). With a 1992 peasant

TABLE 13.1 Comparative Economic Data (1990,* per Capita, in Yuan)

	China	Sichuan	Autonomous Regions in China	Autonomous Regions in Sichuan	Liangshan Yi Autonomous Prefecture 1989*
Gross output value	1,547	1,066	1,176	813	no data
Income	1,260	896	874	696	no data
Gross output value of industry and agriculture	2,393	1,729	1,731	984	542
Agriculture	670	589	724	547	314
Industry	1,723	1,131	1,007.5	437	228
Financial revenue	283	111	n.a.	86	77
Peasant per-capita income	683	505	312	357	317

SOURCES: Li Yihui (1993, 112); Qubi and Yang (1992, 32).
* Newer data not available.

TABLE 13.2   Comparison of Peasant Per-Capita Income (in Yuan)

	1990	1994
All China	693	1,221
Xinjiang Autonomous Region	623	947
Inner Mongolia Autonomous Region	607	970
Ningxia Autonomous Region	534	867
Qinghai Province	514	869
Guangxi Autonomous Region	500	1,107
Yunnan Province	490	803
Guizhou Province	435	786
Tibet Autonomous Region	437	976
Sichuan	505	946
Liangshan Yi Autonomous Prefecture	336	500

SOURCES: Li Yihui (1993, 118); *Zhongguo tongji nianjian* (1995, 280); *Zhongguo minzu tongji nianjian* (1995, 188).

income of 420 yuan (nationwide: 784 yuan), Liangshan Prefecture stood among the poor regions of China. This is particularly true if one disregards, as mentioned above, the city of Xichang, the industrial and cultural center with a predominantly Han population. In 1997 half of the population had no access to electricity and 95 percent of the villages were not integrated into the road network. The twelve poor counties had a financial average income of 13 million yuan and needed 300 million yuan in state subsidies. In the 1990s they had difficulty paying wages and providing social welfare and infrastructure (Sun 1997, 61–62).

Certainly, Liangshan Prefecture has profited from the general economic prosperity of the last fifteen years. Still, the gap between minority areas and other parts of China is growing. And this despite the increased state subsidies.

The reform policies have visibly diminished the state tutelage of the peasantry and moved toward a kind of economic regime more suited to local conditions, but this has not in any way brought advantages to the autonomous prefecture. This is related to the following points: Even according to official reports, the prefecture has not been given anywhere near sufficient consideration with regard to the provision of credit, subsidies, foreign exchange, and materials by the center or the province (*Zhongguo minzu jingji* 1993, 26). The financial subsidies to the autonomous regions of Sichuan at the end of the 1980s were far less than those for other autonomous regions or provinces with a high proportion of minorities (see Table 13.3).

The dismantling of subventions has in addition led to a great strain on prefectural endurance. Many offices and industrial enterprises find themselves in no condition to pay wages or accounts on time.

TABLE 13.3   Financial Subsidies from the Center
Per-Capita Minority Population (1988,* in Yuan)

All China	262
Inner Mongolia	762
Qinghai	610
Ningxia	572
Tibet	505
Xinjiang	272
Guizhou	199
Yunnan	183
Guangxi	123
Autonomous Regions in Sichuan	128

SOURCE: Li Yihui (1993, 115).
NOTE: The figures for financial subsidies for autonomous regions of Sichuan also include provincial subsidies, so the subsidies from
the center must be even less.
* Newer data not available.

In industrial colonization and the exploitation of raw materials, local interests are, as previously, not taken into consideration. The autonomous prefecture gets no fiscal advantage from them; the industrial colonization is directed mostly from outside and serves the extraction of cheap raw materials
in the interest of enterprises outside the prefecture. Laborers are recruited
outside the prefecture because of the low standard of local population: oc-
cupational training of the local population, which at most is undertaken only
for simple activities, is widely left undone.

Han Chinese skilled personnel (technicians and skilled laborers), brought
to the autonomous prefecture in the era before the reforms, moved back to
their native regions or out to coastal regions because living conditions and
living standards were better there. Thus the county of Zhaojue, one of the
counties that was supposed to constitute a key point in the fight against
poverty and which has a population that is 95 percent Yi, lost 995 skilled
personnel between 1979 and 1992, of whom 235 were college graduates and
760 higher vocational-school graduates. Most of these were young people
(Yang Jingchu 1994, 2).

Until the 1980s, trade in necessities for ethnic minorities was promoted
and subsidized by the state. The dismantling of this practice of subsidies led
to the collapse or weakening of the trade network.

Despoliation through deforestation, overgrazing, environmental pollution,
and ecological destruction through industrial colonization have led to cli-
matic change and lowering of the water table. Forested area in the three autonomous prefectures of Sichuan diminished from 29.4 percent at the be-

ginning of the 1950s to 12.5 percent at the beginning of the 1990s. About 5 percent of the native plant and animal species have become extinct, and 10–20 percent of the species must be counted as endangered. The rate of overgrazing—that is, the oversupply of domestic animals in proportion to the available pasture area—was already more than 12 percent in Liangshan at the beginning of the 1990s (Li Yihui 1993, 362–63).

The consequences of the transition to a "socialist" market economy also go beyond the economic sphere in Liangshan. For example, the removal of subsidies in the health and cultural sectors (free medical care and prevention of epidemics, free films and cultural activities) and the transfer of responsibility for these sectors to local authorities have led to the collapse of the health-care system and the discontinuance of cultural activities. Because of the local financial situation, clinics and health stations have been closed or made smaller. Epidemic diseases, which were thought to have been eliminated long ago, have broken out anew. In the three autonomous prefectures of Sichuan the number of local clinics diminished from 1,766 to 1,042 from 1978 to 1989, a reduction of 41 percent. Already in 1990, 53 percent of villages and 5 percent of towns and townships were without connections to the health-care-delivery network (Li Yihui 1993, 123–24, 436).

Similarly, in the educational and training sector considerable deterioration has taken place. In 1996, only 40 percent of Yi children in Liangshan attended school (in comparison to over 96 percent in Sichuan and 97 percent in the People's Republic of China, according to official reports). Only about 20 percent of girls attended school. In poor areas the school attendance rate was just 10 percent. Sixty percent of Yi over twelve years of age, according to official figures, were illiterate or semi-illiterate.[3] In spite of all the touted anti-illiteracy campaigns, this situation is little changed since 1980 (58.05 percent) (Heberer 1984b, 281). The return to family farming, which made the entry of children into the family workforce profitable again, the growing costs of school attendance, and not least the weakening of the school network are the reasons for this development. Related to this is the fact that the number of primary and secondary schools in the autonomous regions of Sichuan diminished by 3,135, or 35.5 percent, from 1980 to 1989, and their number of graduates by 33.2 percent (Li Yihui 1993, 122). In 1992–94 in Zhaojue County alone, only 3 of 80 applicants secured a place in a university, none of them Yi (Jiang , Lu, and Dan 1994, 193). Correspondingly low is the number of Yi with a university degree (the Yi are last among the nationalities with more than 500,000 people). According to the 1990 cen-

---

3. The population census of 1982 shows a much higher rate for the Yi in Liangshan area: 76.1 percent, of which are 62.0 percent male and 90.2 percent female illiterates. The illiteracy rate for Sichuan overall was 32.0 percent, and for the autonomous regions in Sichuan 62.3 percent (cf. Liu Hongkang, 1988, 342).

sus this proportion was .79 percent among Han, .28 percent among minorities in Sichuan, and .22 percent among the Yi (Renkou Pucha 1993, 700, 722).

It is interesting to look at a list of problems given by the magazine *Minzu* as most irritating to the peasants in Liangshan Prefecture. These problems do not appear much different from those in Han Chinese districts, but they are understood by many Yi as results of "Han policies":

> The prices for goods that are urgently needed in agriculture (such as means of production, diesel oil, chemical fertilizers, and insecticides) are rising faster than the prices for farm products, with the result that farm incomes are diminishing.
>
> State support monies for the agricultural sector in poverty areas (for the purchase of means of production, chemical fertilizers, insecticides, diesel oil, and so on) come significantly late. They are often paid only after the agricultural season for which they were needed is already over.
>
> There are practically no agricultural experts in the rural areas of Liangshan Prefecture.
>
> The prestige of cadres is at a nadir, because they often occupy themselves only as collectors of taxes and fees, and otherwise do not bother with the demands and needs of the peasantry.
>
> The rising number of false products (less valuable or worthless imitations) in the areas of seeds, diesel oil, fertilizers, and pesticides has developed into a considerable problem that has negative effects on agriculture.
>
> The medical network in the villages is practically shattered: there are hardly any doctors or medications, to the point where the death rate has begun to rise.
>
> Drug taking, dealing, and addiction are rising drastically, without any intervention by the authorities. (Wang Linlu 1994, 11)

In other parts of China, including, importantly, the province of Sichuan, peasants have defended themselves by force. For this reason, local authorities rightly fear that the potential for dissatisfaction in Liangshan could increase the potential for conflict in the province as a whole, particularly as the disturbances in Lhasa in 1993 over inflation have shown how quickly economic dissatisfaction can transform into politically and ethnically inspired demands.

"Unhealthy" Customs and Habits

Socially and economically caused dissatisfaction can mount when, simultaneously with economic liberalization, the often-intentional interference in Yi customs does not stop. As in the country as a whole, there is now a retraditionalization in Yi areas. The role of clans, shamans, and magicians, as well as that of religion, is growing.

Since the 1950s, "healthy" and "unhealthy" customs and practices have been differentiated. Unhealthy ones should be eliminated; healthy ones preserved. Because this definition has never been precisely clarified, it always has and continues to lead to local interference in the area of customs. Authorities usually judge customs and practices according to the scale of Han Chinese values. Rites or festivals which drive minorities to romance will continue to be forbidden because they violate the morality of Han functionaries.

The *Liangshan ribao,* the bilingual daily newspaper in Liangshan, reported in 1986 the prohibition of a predeath ceremony for an elderly couple. In this traditional ceremony all the friends and relatives assemble, bring gifts, and celebrate a communal feast for several days. The prohibition was announced by the prefectural government and was justified on grounds of "waste," even though the peasants used only their own money and consumed their own goods (*Liangshan ribao,* 5 June 1986). It is easy to imagine the feelings such a prohibition must have called forth among those affected. In 1996 a journal on nationalities affairs complained that, on the occasion of 383 funeral rituals in Meigu County, 5,202 head of cattle were slaughtered (Lü 1996, 104). In one township of this county alone 16.5 percent of the township revenues were said to have been used for "superstitious activities." In some areas half the income was reportedly spent on alcohol. According to the economic rationality of the Party, such behavior is wasteful. But, first, Yi may have a different rationality related to traditional social obligations ("moral economy"). Second, the state's interference is perceived as "Han" pressure on the Yi and their traditional customs. And last but not least, such "waste" could be interpreted as a kind of ethnic collective action that is more or less instinctive, and as a form of opposition against the perceived pressure of the Han.

Since the beginning of the 1980s, customs, practices, and festivals are again supposed to be officially respected. And in the constitution it says explicitly, "They [all nationalities] are free to preserve or reform unhealthy customs and habits of their own." At the same time, in the name of measures against "unhealthy customs" and "superstition," officials interfere in the system of customs. Because local authorities understand themselves to be representatives of local minorities, it is in practice not possible to resist such measures. This will be made clear in the following example of the *bimo.*

The Renaissance of the Bimo   Animism and animistic ideas shaped and shape the religious thinking of the Yi. Sickness, death, and misfortune all are ascribed to the influence of spirits. Because spirits can bring evil, there were many rituals to keep them under control. The *bimo* as priest and magician was an intermediary between spirits and people (see Bamo Ayi, chapter 8 in this volume). During the Democratic Reforms in the 1950s, in the course of which the traditional structure of power among the Yi was eliminated, the activities of *bimo* and *sunyi* (shamans that have a lower social position than the *bimo*) were classified as "superstitious activities" and prohibited and their practitioners persecuted. In times of political radicalization, the *bimo* and *sunyi* were designated as charlatans and class enemies and thus became the direct object of political persecution. Even at the beginning of the 1980s *bimo* who performed magical or healing activities and received payment, however small, were punished.[4]

In 1984 the State Council initiated a change with its decision that healers and magicians like *bimo* were to be dealt with like intellectuals. From then on, *bimo* could practice their activities for payment. Now there is again a training system in which young people from traditional *bimo* families are connected with the experience of their forebears. The *bimo* once again is part of the everyday life of the Yi, for officials as well as for ordinary members of that nationality. The crux of the reinstitution of the *bimo* was not a friendly disposition of the center. The above-mentioned collapse of the health-care network led already at the beginning of the 1980s to a resurgence of *bimo* and *sunyi* activities. These practitioners were the only ones in a position to fill the resulting gap, especially since the populace lacked the money to pay for increasingly expensive medical services.

The deterioration of health care, which was expressed, among other ways, by the fact that qualified doctors emigrated from poor areas and returned to their home districts, or changed to more remunerative occupations because of the low income in the health sector, stimulated the revival of *bimo* activities. In local clinics, severe diseases could in the main no longer be taken care of, and in the case of less severe diseases the local population often did not go to hospitals simply because of the cost. The roads to clinics are often long and difficult for rural inhabitants, and because of a lack of transport they often require a long walk on foot. Treatment was—and is—too expensive for peasants, who must pay the cost out of their own pockets, and anyone unable to pay would be quickly turned away from a clinic. In addition, the belief of the Yi population in the healing arts of *bimo* is as great as ever. News of healing results gets around quickly, and bad results, by contrast, can be attributed to supernatural powers. On top of that is the psychic function of the *bimo*, undervalued by the doctors of scientific medicine, as well as their knowledge of traditional healing procedures (Li Zhongfang 1994, 30–36). In the reinstitution of *bimo* activities the state thus was simply reacting to a change that was already in full course.

Still, it would be mistaken to attribute the *bimo* phenomenon solely to deficiencies in health care. And the prestige that the *bimo* have once again is not to be understood only in religious terms. Within Yi society the *bimo* assume the function of intellectuals, because of their knowledge and experience. We know from social anthropology that magicians function as guardians of knowledge in illiterate societies. In a rapidly changing world change will often be perceived as a threat, and nostalgia for the past will be

4. In 1996, for the first time an article in an academic journal spoke of a special "*bimo* religion" (*bijiao*) (Pu 1996, 66–72).

cultivated, in order to protect one's own identity. The flight to the *bimo* thus also effects mastery of the everyday world and its changes and preserves one's own ethnic identity. Under conditions in which the environment no longer seems predictable, in which identity is called into question, religion assumes a central value. As noted by Bassam Tibi, "The faster the social change, the more unpredictable the environment becomes for the individual, the stronger becomes the need for religion. Change is perceived simply as a threat, and as a result nostalgia for the past is cultivated" (1985, 166). The belief in soul worship, which is as strong as ever, and the role of intermediary between people and souls that the *bimo* derives from this are also part of this identity. Added to this are the aforementioned healing and exorcistic functions that reach beyond scientific medicine.

In case of illness, the *bimo* attempts to drive out evil spirits by magical means. Most Yi still believe that illnesses are caused by spirits and demons and can be healed only by exorcism. During the ceremonies, the *bimo* performs rituals according to the severity of the illness and the financial circumstances of the family.

Bimo keep in their houses many Yi documents, which they consult in cases of celebration, sickness, divination, marriage, and every kind of magical ceremony. These documents are composed in Yi script. The Yi script could survive over the centuries only because the *bimo* passed it on to their pupils and followers. Ordinary Yi had no chance to learn this script.

In the area of medicine, doctors from the Han nationality usually deny that the *bimo* have any medical abilities. But every Yi with whom I spoke, even local officials, expressed high regard for the *bimo* and their healing art. Peasants as well as officials agreed that the *bimo* possess many types of knowledge: knowledge of the Yi script, Yi history, meteorology, geology, and anthropology. On the negative side, Han Chinese officials most often mentioned the killing of animals for sacrifices, "interference in production," elements of exploitation, and superstition. But every Yi can give examples of miraculous healing from his or her own experience. A local official, for example, reported that his uncle had gotten only a diagnosis of end-stage liver cancer from the doctors in the county hospital. He had been advised to go home, since he would not live much longer. The uncle then placed himself in the care of a *bimo* and a year later went to the county hospital for an examination, where he was given a clean bill of health. A province-level Yi official likewise reported being healed by a *bimo*. As a child, he had been bitten by a rabid animal. The *bimo* had taken a young hen and first held it under the child's arm; then he held its beak in the child's mouth and had him blow two or three times into the hen's mouth. The *bimo* had next drowned the hen in cold water and plucked out the feathers; then he investigated the color of the skin and other things, and after that the innards. In the official's case, the skin and innards had shown changes from which the *bimo*, according to

Yi beliefs, could diagnose the illness and its cause. The *bimo* had then given the child a drug that had put him in a state like feverish delirium for two days, and on the third day he was healthy again. Many Yi thought that such methods were prescientific methods of medical investigation, because there had previously been no scientific methods of investigation, such as blood tests. In cases of infectious diseases, *bimo* boiled various medicinal herbs in the house of the patient and sprinkled the infusion in the room and on the patient, which had a disinfecting result. Yi ritual healing thus also acquired the force of science.

While many Han believe that *bimo* are consulted only by those who cannot raise money for treatment in a hospital, many Yi contradict this belief. The decision is based not only on the availability of money but also on trust and belief in the healing abilities of the shamans, as well as the continued existence of animistic and animatistic ideas.

But *bimo* are called for more than medical purposes, even today. In protracted bad weather, in the face of threatened bad harvests, in time of death, in questions of favorable and unfavorable outcomes, weddings, and so on—in all these situations the village *bimo* is present, and he performs the necessary ceremonies to placate or expel the spirits whose influence is still credited for most natural occurrences.

From the end of the 1950s the pursuits of the *bimo* were officially disapproved. A small portion of *bimo* went on to be educated as barefoot doctors (certainly the lesser *bimo*), but the overwhelming majority refused this offer. In knowledge, education, reputation, and social position, they felt themselves superior to doctors. *Bimo* were enrolled in "courses of study," with the object of "reeducation." Their activities, condemned as superstition, were forbidden, but in the villages *bimo* continued to practice. Even in the Cultural Revolution, when all *bimo* and *sunyi* without exception were defined as class enemies and "objects of class struggle," attempts to root out the shamans and their activities were unsuccessful. They and their store of beliefs were too closely attached to the worldview of the Yi, and they continued and still continue to count as an important component of Yi society, from which almost no Yi distance themselves.

Two still-practicing *bimo* in the county of Meigu—Nidi Ati and Qubi Vujisse—explained that there have been *bimo* for twenty-eight generations (counting one generation as twenty-five to twenty-eight years). One can distinguish three categories of *bimo:* (a) those who understand the sacred texts and have read many of them (little *bimo*); (b) those who, in addition to this, can also ask the gods for help and understand psychic healing methods (middling *bimo*); and (c) those who, in addition to having the abilities mentioned in the first two categories, also command the funeral ritual (great *bimo*). The training lasts, as it always has, fifteen years. *Bimo* are scientists who have discovered knowledge in the areas of history, medicine, meteorology, geology, and language. Because of this, local science could not develop without *bimo,* and the "four modernizations" in Liangshan would hardly be realizable. Peasants on their own would not be able to cultivate their fields well: they need the *bimo* to tell them when the weather will be optimal and which days are proper for sowing. The positive sides of the *bimo* must be promoted and preserved in the future.

According to these two bimo, *bimo* can save 90 percent of those afflicted with spirit illnesses before they die. But they understand that they cannot heal all illnesses. In the case of certain sicknesses, such as infectious diseases, it is better to go to one of the hospitals with modern equipment. *Bimo* strength is in psychological healing methods, supported by herbal remedies.

Even in the Cultural Revolution many young men demanded to be schooled as *bimo,* for several reasons. First, the deficiency in medical care made substitute care through the *bimo* network necessary; second, the schools were closed for a while and young people had few opportunities for education; third, the *bimo* and their professional standing enjoyed a high reputation among the Yi. *Bimo* are tolerated again today, but they remain a thorn in the side of Han cadres, who hope to convince the *bimo* "through educational measures" to give up their activities. But at most this succeeds only in very rare cases. The aforementioned Nidi Ati, among others, explained that the Chinese Academy of Social Sciences in Beijing had invited him to demonstrate his knowledge and skills there for scientific purposes. This he declined; he would transmit his knowledge only to his successors.

Though *bimo* today continue to possess great prestige in rural areas, it is declining in urban areas. There the opinion has spread that modern medicine is superior to archaic methods of the *bimo* in many respects and that modern hospitals "get better results with a lot of spirits" than do *bimo* (according to patients in the county hospitals at Meigu). With the increasing level of education and the popularization of modern medical and scientific knowledge, shamanism (including animism and animatism) is doomed to disappear from Yi society. However, for many young people *bimo* figure increasingly as scientific authorities who, at best, know the Yi, their history, their customs and usages, as well as their script (which certainly plays a role), and in rare cases work together with the Han.

Language Policy

At the beginning of the 1980s Yi script was released again in a reformed version. As early as the middle of the 1970s members of the Yi elite had intervened with provincial authorities and argued that, without their own script, the rate of illiteracy and school attendance could not be improved. The reintroduction was, at the same time, an expression of the failure of the policy to compel the Yi and many other people to use the Chinese language, along with Chinese script, as their only language. The Yi were clearly not ready to undertake the unlearning of their own language in favor of a foreign tongue.

Although the popularization of the Yi script has occurred at least in the Yi primary schools, and there is one newspaper, one magazine, and a limited selection of books in the Yi script, there are numerous problems. The language and writing are widely restricted to primary schools, at best; Chinese becomes the primary language beginning in middle school. Because of this, the level of Yi language remains restricted, and the language and writing remain insufficiently developed. Increasingly, Yi language is being degraded to a language of the rural population.

Yi-language speakers remain handicapped in comparison to Han speakers. It is a widespread conviction among Yi, particularly among cadres and skilled personnel, that bilingual education is "useless" because only knowledge of Chinese is required for learning trades or gaining access to wider educational opportunities. Because of this, the Yi script has only a limited area of usefulness and thus has no future. In any case students have enough to do just to learn Chinese. For this reason this circle of people is widely uninterested in bilingual education for further growth, but only in Chinese-language education (Zhang, Yu, and Ma 1992, 26). This particularly applies to people who speak only broken or no Yi, or who primarily speak Chinese. This circle includes a high percentage of people who live in cities or near cities, who have higher education (generally in a Han environment), or are active as officials.

Most of the children of officials or intellectuals, from whom the elite stem, generally know no Yi. In this way, the elite becomes linguistically Sinified. Whoever has enjoyed an education in a Han Chinese environment and speaks Chinese instead of his or her native language counts as more loyal and more integrable—in other words, less inclined to ethnonationalistic tendencies. But Chinese is not only, as is often maintained, a lingua franca. It is a means of transport for Han Chinese value concepts and norms of behavior, a not unimportant contributor to a process of cultural assimilation.

Where smaller speech communities count as "backward," where such an image is adopted by the elite of an ethnic group, where language is thus understood as a symbol for being dominated, the first step toward the extinction of the language has already been taken.

Birth Planning Policy

Birth planning policy can also lead to conflict. According to the population law of the province of Sichuan and the corresponding regulations of Liangshan Yi Autonomous Prefecture, members of ethnic minorities can have two, or in special circumstances, three children. Bearing more than three children is not allowed (Liangshan Yizu Zizhizhou 1991, 122–30). For this and other reasons, it is not surprising that the rate of natural increase is higher in Yi than in Han regions, where couples are allowed only one or two children. Indeed, Liangshan Prefecture shows the highest rate of increase in the province, with 10.6 per thousand, even when somewhat sensational figures are included. Thus it is reported that in an area in Leibo County, appropriate effort has brought the birthrate down from 23.43 per thousand in 1981 to 9.5 per thousand in 1993, thereby placing it below the provincial average of 9.6 (a paragon for all China) (Chen Xiangsen 1994, 44). Other reports show, however, that such "successes" are not by any means always reached through persuasion, and that attempts to carry through birth planning by force have now and then given rise to local revolts (Yang Ji 1982, 33).

CONCLUSION

Among the Yi in Liangshan since the founding of the People's Republic, we may observe the following seven trends.

No Separatist Tendencies, No Demands for Independence

In contrast to the minority areas on the borders, where minorities live together compactly in large areas (Xinjiang, Inner Mongolia, Tibet), there have never been separatist tendencies in Liangshan Prefecture in the sense of separating from China and establishing an independent state. The region does not lie in the vicinity of national borders and has never demanded or been able to expect political independence from China. But there was a strong sense of independence in the sense of a cultural and societal independence from China. And this spirit still exists among the Yi and manifests itself in their separation from Han influence. That 20 percent of the towns and 95 percent of the villages are not yet connected to the network of roads (Sun 1997, 62) may be interpreted not only as a sign of underdevelopment but also as an expression of the desire to live a way of life not much influenced by the Han. There still exists a strong tendency among the Yi to retreat into the mountains in order to avoid control by the Han.

Revolts in the 1950s Strengthened Han Chinese Presence

Up to the beginning of the 1950s the Yi attempted to preserve their relative independence within the Chinese state. After this attempt failed, they had to adjust themselves to the new political situation. Revolts in consequence of the Democratic Reforms in the middle of the 1950s were suppressed relatively quickly and led to a strengthened Han Chinese presence. The social reforms may have been welcomed by the majority of former slaves; what the Yi desired after that was the possibility of autonomous development, without radical interference in existing traditions and without loss of their national identity.

Massive Dissatisfaction with Policies in the 1950s, 1960s, and 1970s

Since the end of the 1950s there had been attempts to destroy these traditions and to make the Yi fit the notions of the Han or of the Party authorities in Beijing. Every phase of political liberalization showed that such attempts not only remained fruitless but also were harmful to development in this region and to relations among nationalities. Massive dissatisfaction among Yi generally necessitated state concessions in all areas. Economically, the Yi no longer want to be cheap providers of raw materials: they demand economic development and an economic policy that brings quick improvement of living standards. Politically, the wish for a larger measure of autonomy and for preservation of the identity of their nationality is getting stronger. But the current autonomy includes the problem that it is generally autonomy from above and does not contain the necessary democratic control mechanisms from below. Right now, demands for such control mechanisms are obscured by the improvements in individual income brought by the current economic policies. But surely not for long.

Social Change in the 1980s and 1990s

As well as in other minority areas, alcoholism, drug addiction, and collective action in the form of sporadic local unrest and criminality are on the rise (Lü 1996, 59–65). Drug addicts are such a tremendous social problem among the Yi that, for example, Yi teachers in Liangshan established "voluntary propaganda teams against drugs" in order to "save their own nationality" (cf. *Minzu* [November 1998]: 24).

The influence of traditional religion and of religious sects is growing tremendously, too. Chiliastic movements and sects organized by a charismatic leader *(mentuhui)* are spreading quickly in the Liangshan area, waiting for the end of the world and undermining Party organizations. More and more, these movements and sects control rural areas as well as access to Party and mass organizations and elections at village, township, and county levels (Shen 1997, 35). Such movements surface in times of erosion of traditional norms and relationships. A utopian, eschatological, and egalitarian idealism is created, a counterpoint to the symptom of decay and social disintegration and feelings of social and ethnic menace. These movements are a means to cope with the insecurity of life, particularly in a period of rapid social change.

And there is another new phenomenon: the emerging of jobless Yi in larger cities like in the provincial capitals of Chengdu and Kunming who organize themselves in informal groups (Lai and Mujie 1996, 66–72), not according to clan but nationality. This may be interpreted as a sign of growing ethnicity, since formerly Yi perceived themselves as members of clans rather than as members of a common nationality. And this ethnicity is promoted by strong feelings of discrimination and prejudice by the Han in Chengdu, who regard those organizations as just "criminal gangs." Poverty, unemployment, and the lack of educational opportunities drive young Yi into the large cities. Quite a few of them are drug addicts. Having no personal perspective at all, some of them commit criminal acts. In Chengdu, meanwhile, persons belonging to the Yi nationality are denied access to hotels due to an informal regulation of the city's Public Security Bureau. But criminal behavior must also be considered a kind of ethnic protest that results from perspectivelessness in the Liangshan area and the perception by many Yi that they are second-class citizens.[5]

Leaders of Clans and Educated Local Functionaries Emerge as a New Leading Stratum

It is true that the percentage of Yi cadres among all functionaries in Liangshan Prefecture is still quite low. Though 46 percent of the population in Liangshan are Yi, the minority cadres make up only 28.6 percent. Among the enterprise cadres they constitute only 9.6 percent (He Mingwei 1996, 16–18), and only one of sixty directors of enterprises in Liangshan is Yi (Yang Hui 1995, 50–52).

But there is a growing number of qualified Yi people taking over responsible functions and endeavoring to act in the interest of their nationality. The stratum driving the growth of ethnicity is the educated stratum among the non-Han peoples; that upper stratum is generally the primary supporter of ethnicity. Establishment of a school system in and for the minority areas, in order to educate skilled people needed locally, has significantly increased the number of people belonging to this stratum. Of course, higher education is in many ways designed to integrate members of non-Han peoples into the community of Chinese-language speakers and Chinese culture (through the use of the Chinese languages and through having institutions of higher education in Han Chinese areas); but in recent years, this

---

5. It is quite interesting that Yi who informed me about this development argued that those Yi only would steal from Han, not from Yi people. As soon as they found out that their victim was a Yi they would voluntarily return the stolen goods and apologize. Those statements were made by different Yi informants. There are two possibilities in this argument: First, that Yi are Robin-Hood-like thieves that take things away from the Han but not from members of their own nationality. This would imply a strong sense of ethnic feeling and therefore ethnicity. Second, that such stories are created by noncriminal Yi to defend their own nationality. This would also imply a strong sense of ethnic feeling and ethnicity, as the informants claim that those Yi are not simply criminals but have developed a strong sense of ethnicity and that their acts are only directed toward non-Yi, primarily Han. And the latter could even be regarded as a kind of ethnic opposition.

educated stratum increasingly has come to identify itself again with the culture, values, and traditions of their own peoples. The liberalization process since 1979 has led to the articulation of ethnonational interests among this stratum. Among the Yi, this "ethnic revival" manifested itself at the outset in cultural demands, but political issues have begun to be discussed as well.

Erosion of Party Organizations

Especially in the townships and villages in Liangshan Prefecture, Party organizations are eroding. Party organizations and Yi cadres are criticized as having weak "Party spirit" (He Mingwei 1996, 13; Yang Hui 1995, 50–52). The number of Yi cadres is decreasing, not because the Han want to dominate that area but rather because fewer and fewer Yi want to join the Party and its mass organizations. The institutional gap is filled by the clans and members of religious sects.

Reinterpretation of Yi History and Traditional Society by Yi Scholars

More and more Yi scholars question the Chinese interpretation of the Yi as a cruel, backward, reactionary, and brutal slave-owner society. On the contrary, the traditional society is interpreted by many Yi scholars as having been harmonious and well organized until the penetration of the Han in the 1950s.

At present we concurrently find retraditionalization as well as social uprooting among the Yi in Liangshan. On the one hand, the dominating influence of the Han in the process of opening Liangshan, and in economic development, has generated an erosion of traditional Yi culture and values, especially among Yi with weak clan bonds. Looking for better income and jobs, those Yi are migrating into urban centers. But just because they are Yi, poorly educated, and not accustomed to job conditions in urban areas where they are discriminated against, they don't find jobs; as a result they are frustrated that they do not participate in social prosperity. Thus they organize themselves in criminal gangs, making a living mainly through criminal offenses. On the other hand, we find a revitalizing of clan bonds, customs, and religious activities in remote areas and, particularly among educated Yi, a growing nationality consciousness.

The old leading stratum of the Yi is obliterated or sits superannuated in the People's Consultative Conferences. A new one is just beginning to form. One can hardly speak yet of a stratum of intellectuals, and all leading positions today are held by Party members. Education is thus a decisive means for the development of forces who will have at their disposal the necessary intellectual skills, who will possess a relatively great amount of knowledge of their position. It will depend on the future nationalities policies whether the Yi as a nationality will remain a loyal component of China, or whether they will develop a potential for dissatisfaction that will someday station itself in a nationalistic way against the prevailing relationships.[6]

Without doubt, the liberal policies of the reform era have given great latitude to Yi ethnicity (A. Smith 1996, 445–48). Social change following upon economic change, political liberalization, and the erosion of socialist ideology led to a new search for identity among all ethnic minorities in China and also among the Yi, particularly because the process of modernization is in many ways felt by many Yi to be a menace to ethnic identity, ethnic cohesion, and mode of life. Amid rapid social change many Yi therefore turn back to their ethnic culture, seeking protection and security, and this becomes a substantial motive for ethnonationalism and growing ethnicity (Rösel 1995, 117–30). Rising ethnicity has, on the one hand, a "protective function" for an ethnic group; on the other hand, it is a symptom of a crisis (Reiter 1991, 69). As Nash puts it: "The identity dimension of ethnicity . . . rests on the fact that fellow members of the ethnic group are thought to be 'human' and trustworthy in ways that outsiders are not. The ethnic group provides a refuge against a hostile, uncaring world. Like a family, it has a continuing claim on loyalty and sacrifice. . . . The idea of refuge, the place where one is fully human, whatever failure or success happens in the larger world, is the cement and power of ethnic membership and continuity" (Nash 1989, 128).

This psychological force of ethnicity thus reaches beyond the idea of national consciousness and attempts to explain psychologically why people cling to their identity. And this explains to us why all attempts at force or covert assimilation of the Yi are unavailing and why political liberalization has led to a stronger self-consciousness among the Yi.

The growing influence of *bimo* religion and traditional culture must be understood as another indication of rising ethnicity (Haynes 1994, 150–53). In this context, religion and traditions are not only reminders of one's own culture and cultural identity: embracing them is a reaction to the process of social change directed from above by the Han. The process of modernization and change threatens the cohesion of the Yi and thus often provokes mobilization for preserving the group identity.

The case of the Yi shows that it is difficult to address Chinese nationalities as a uniform group of ethnics. Moreover there are groups with a strong desire for independence, especially where a non-Chinese religion plays a major role (Uighurs, Tibetans, Mongolians): people with a broken identity who find themselves being assimilated and people in an ambiguous position be-

6. It is worth discussing here whether the so-called tremendous increase of criminality (like highway and train robbery, drug planting and dealing, murder, and clan wars) in the Liangshan area, which was especially mentioned in the *People's Daily,* is a reaction to social change and a sign of ethnic retraditionalization (see *Renmin ribao* [People's daily], 29 May 1996).

tween growing ethnicity and ethnic erosion. As there exist no interest associations representing the various nationalities, engaging in social violence and deviance is the only way of acting collectively. Despite all differences, the various nationalities have no choice but to act in a common way in order to enforce legal mechanisms to protect their rights in the face of the majority and the Chinese state, and thus create an institutional framework for carrying out the right of autonomy. In the last consequence, such a framework requires independent courts and the erecting of legal barriers against the majority. Also the Party should not remain superordinate to autonomy, but should be subordinate to the law. Further, care would have to be taken to ensure that not only individuals but also ethnic groups collectively are able to file lawsuits.

To guarantee the latter would require an organized representation of interests, because the right to autonomy can be represented or carried out only by organized communities. To counter the growing discrimination against members of ethnic minorities in urban areas requires intensified measures. While open discrimination is forbidden by law, it exists hidden and in daily life, and it increases in an alarming manner (reports about killing, injury, and insulting of minority peoples in urban daily life are increasing). The existence of such a phenomenon should be acknowledged, and special programs for reducing discrimination and prejudices established.

CHAPTER 14

Education and Ethnicity among the Liangshan Yi

Martin Schoenhals

Whether to assimilate or to separate is one of the most fundamental conflicts faced by members of ethnic groups, especially by members of small minority ethnic groups, upon whom the possibility of gaining access to wealth and power through assimilation asserts a strong pull in the assimilationist direction. Assimilation seems to offer not only access to wealth and power but also the pride that comes from being associated with, and becoming more like, the dominant segment of society. To attempt to assimilate, minority groups employ a variety of strategies, ranging from changes in dress, language, and custom to residing among and even intermarrying with the dominant group, participating in their social institutions, and attaining educational credentials that facilitate access to elite positions of power.

Yet while assimilation might buy power and prestige for those minority individuals who assimilate, it also, of course, comes at a cost. As the literature has documented, rejecting one's own cultural and social institutions in favor of those of the dominant group threatens the solidarity of those minority individuals who remain behind, sometimes leading them to feel a sense of betrayal by their upwardly mobile counterparts. Gradual loss of cultural heritage by the minority group because of those who leave it, and loss of those who reject its cultural ways, can give rise to increased feelings of alienation and inadequacy among minority group members.

One reaction to this process, and a means to challenge the dynamics of assimilation, is the affirmation by minority group members of their own culture, often through the conscious display and celebration of the icons of their

The Yi of Liangshan are called Nuosu in their own language and have a distinctive culture and social structure; this essay pertains to these people, and not to other Yi, such as those in Yunnan Province.

heritage. Socially too the group may reject participation in the society of the dominant group, seeking its own separate society.

Thus the minority group within a majority culture faces tension over competing alternatives—assimilation versus separatism—both of which may be perceived as beneficial by some and detrimental by others. For many minority individuals, the tension between cultural allegiances—to the dominant group or to the minority one—and the tension over the conscious affirmation of these allegiances through assimilation or separatism can be pronounced and sometimes painful, the source of a cultural and personal identity crisis (Fordham 1996).

Schools, of course, are prime loci for the enactment of all of these dynamics. Since education is often a primary route into the society and status of the dominant group, and since schools are usually run, for the most part, by members of that group, participation in, and success at, school can symbolically represent assimilation. Failure to succeed at school, rebellion against teachers, and refusal to participate in school at whatever level can come to symbolize separatism, or at least allegiance with the minority person's home community and home culture. It becomes a form of resistance by minority students to the wider oppression they face in society (Fordham 1996; Erickson 1987). Thus the literature on schooling and minorities is filled with examples of how minority students—African Americans, for example—manipulate their identity in school to "act white" or "act black," sometimes seeing success at school as part of the former process, and rebellion against school, and failure to learn, as part of the latter one (see Fordham 1996, especially chap. 7).

When I went to China to study the Yi people at a multiethnic school in Xichang, the capital city of the Liangshan Yi Autonomous Prefecture, I had expected to find ethnic dynamics similar to those described by scholars writing about Western ethnic contexts. Since the Yi are a numerical minority and live in a poor and remote region of China, I thought that those few Yi able to go to junior and senior middle school (basically, the equivalent of grades seven through twelve in the United States) would feel a cultural and personal tension over going to school. I also thought I would find Yi students commonly discussing this tension and the feeling that, in some way, they were betraying their parents, who are mainly uneducated peasants, and their language and culture, by entering a Han institution to prepare themselves for entry into largely Han-dominated society. I thought Yi students might feel an identity crisis, a conflict between the desire to assert a Yi identity and the desire to manipulate their personas (through dress, speech, behavior changes, and so on) so that they could more closely resemble the dominant Han.

Finally, I thought I would find what researchers working in multiethnic Western contexts have found—that discipline problems and achievement problems would be used by minority students to symbolize their opposition to the school and the dominant culture it represents. Perhaps Yi students might deliberately provoke their teachers and/or not do well in school, as a form of ethnic opposition. Or perhaps, while encountering Han society and Han teachers who sometimes secretly look down on the Yi as dirty, backward, and ignorant, they might come to perceive themselves as inferior, leading to feelings of depression and resignation.

But I found very little of what I expected, and when such phenomena did occur—such as Yi students not working as hard as Han students—it did not occur for expected reasons; it carried no symbolic weight as ethnic opposition. I found instead that caste and notions of Yi-ness make the Yi feel permanently Yi, so that the threat of Hanification becomes negligible. Assimilation versus segregation is not a genuine choice—one is always Yi by birth—so that ethnic identity, even in the multiethnic school context, does not become salient and politicized. Questions such as "Who am I?" and "Am I, and is my culture, worthy?" thus do not arise or are of minimal importance.

THE RESEARCH SITE

Liangshan Nationalities Middle School in Xichang *(Liangshan Minzu Zhong-xue)*, the site of my nine months of ethnographic research in 1994–95, is the most prestigious nationalities middle school in Liangshan Yi Autonomous Prefecture. MZ, as I will henceforth refer to the school, was established in 1990 when a vice-prefect of Liangshan at the time persuaded high-level government officials to help fund a school for nationalities to draw students from the entire Liangshan region.[1] The Sichuan provincial government contributed money for construction; currently money for operating expenses comes from the Liangshan government.[2]

MZ is one of the many "nationalities" *(minzu)* schools established throughout China at the primary, secondary, and even college levels in regions such as Liangshan, where there are high concentrations of ethnic minorities.[3] These schools exist alongside regular schools in the same regions. While the

1. The story I heard from students, though I could not confirm it, is that the vice-prefect, a Yi man who is highly respected among the Yi for his dedication to the Yi people and for his proud refusal to be intimidated by powers stronger than himself, put on his Yi cape and went to Beijing and demanded money for a prefecture-wide nationalities school, telling the higher authorities he would not leave until they granted his demand.

2. Shortly before I began my research in fall 1994, a Japanese company had searched throughout China for a needy school to which it could give a very large donation and, for some reason that no administrators of Liangshan Nationalities Middle School really knew or understood, had selected this school as the object of its largesse. During my stay in China, the final contract specifying the terms of the donation was still being negotiated.

3. I translate *minzu* as nationalities, following the Chinese approach, but the word really means something closer to ethnicities—that is, a school for students from different ethnic groups.

presence of nationalities schools within Liangshan is related to its status as a minority area, the distribution of such schools within Liangshan bears no strong relationship to the degree of minority group concentration. In Liangshan some counties have a predominantly Yi population while others have mixed populations of Yi and Han (and other nationalities), but all counties, even those that are predominantly Yi, have regular schools and nationalities schools, and even in predominantly Yi counties there are more regular than nationalities schools. Butuo County, for example, a county with a heavy concentration of Yi, has three nationalities primary schools and eighteen regular primary schools.[4]

Minzu in the titles of these schools means, in effect, minority. Thus, the nationalities schools' target populations are the ethnic minorities. In Liangshan, Yi and other minority students have the option of attending either regular schools or nationalities schools (provided that, in both cases, they meet the school's admission requirements). When asked the reason for establishing separate schools for minorities alongside regular schools that serve both the majority and minority populations, Liangshan educators normally explain that minority students have special needs that are best served in separate schools. In fact, regular schools in Liangshan sometimes maintain segregated classes within the school by putting minority students in their own classroom, ostensibly to better serve their special needs. When I asked the principal of MZ, a Yi man who normally gave me honest, straightforward answers to my questions, why there was a need for a separate nationalities school such as MZ, he answered rather incoherently and did not give any of the reasons one could have expected—such as the need to instill greater pride in minority students by teaching about their heritage in schools geared to them, or the use of special curricula or teaching methods.

Thus the nationalities schools do not in actuality differ fundamentally from regular schools, nor do they really seem to be administered with any conscious purpose of catering to special minority needs, other than the perception (often valid) that minority students need remedial help upon entering secondary school due to inadequate preparation at the remote, rural primary schools they often attend. During the nine months I spent living at MZ, I also visited other secondary and primary schools throughout Liangshan. I found the nationalities schools' curricula to be identical to those used in regular schools throughout all of China, a situation occasionally making for awkward ethnic moments, as when a Han primary school teacher of an all-Yi class (specifically designated as such) within a regular primary school taught a lesson from a national textbook about the ancient accomplishments of "we" the Han people.

4. The source for this is an unpublished Butuo County government chart on education, 1995.

The one way in which the curriculum differs from that of regular schools is that many nationalities schools offer Yi language courses that teach native Yi-speaking students to write their own language. This class is of course taught in the Yi language, but in all other classes the language of instruction—for speaking, reading, and writing—is Han Chinese. (In the early years of primary school, Yi teachers sometimes use Yi intermixed with Han Chinese for Yi students who have trouble understanding.) There are a few schools, considered experimental, where students are taught in the Yi language, including one entire middle school in Xide where all courses are taught in Yi. Educational administrators I met, however, told me that the general feeling is that such schools do not significantly raise Yi students' achievement level in school, and that the experiment may soon come to an end. As for the teaching staff, the nationalities schools have both Han and Yi teachers, but Han are usually in the majority.

MZ, like all nationalities schools in Liangshan, uses the same curriculum, in Han Chinese, used in regular secondary schools throughout China. The goal of this curriculum is the same as it is for secondary students throughout China: to prepare students to take and pass the college entrance exam (gao kao), the primary way to gain admission to college. Without a college degree, it is very difficult to get a good job in China, thus the college entrance exam exerts a very strong influence on teachers, students, and curricula. The one curricular difference when compared to regular schools is that MZ has two Yi teachers who teach the Yi writing system to Yi students. This is, however, an elective course (whereas all other courses at MZ are required), which students take because they can get added points on the college entrance exam if they can pass a Yi writing section. Six years of Yi language are taught, and in the upper years students read literature—both Yi literature and Han classics that have been translated into Yi. Since MZ students can already read and write Han characters well when they start to learn Yi, and Han writing is the predominant mode of communication between literate Yi as well as literate Han, the learning of the Yi written language does not seem to have a genuine pragmatic purpose as far as educational advancement is concerned. It is more useful for adult literacy—some adults write in Yi frequently, and the Yi language is being used to run voluntary adult literacy classes. Thus, while learning to write Yi does not have a clear pragmatic or cultural resonance for MZ students, the potential nonetheless exists for a growing use of the written Yi language and for a growing cultural pride in its use. Certainly, MZ Yi classes will facilitate this process, even if that is not their explicit motive.

MZ boasts that it has twenty-two Yi teachers, out of a total of eighty, but many of these are not culturally Yi—they have one Yi parent (usually their father) and one Han parent, and grew up in an urban Han area, speaking Han Chinese, and they have little or no comprehension of the Yi language.

According to a knowledgeable informant, only six teachers—three of whom are the Yi-language teachers—and the principal of the school are unambiguously Yi: those whose parents were both Yi, and who grew up in a Yi area speaking Yi at home. The teachers' teaching styles, their general attitudes, and the overall tenor of school life at MZ are similar to those at Third Affiliated, the Han Chinese key school located in a very different part of China, which I described in an earlier work (Schoenhals 1993). MZ, like the school I studied previously, is a well-respected school and, as the one nationalities middle school designated to draw students from all over Liangshan, is considered to be the best nationalities middle school in Liangshan and one of the best middle schools in general in Liangshan. It is not yet an official key school, although it has applied to be considered such.

As is the case with any well-respected middle school in China, MZ has earned its reputation by placing a very high percentage of its graduates into college through the college entrance exam, resulting in pressure to preserve the school's reputation by keeping its rate of students accepted into college *(shengxuelü)* high. Teachers push students to study, and students themselves seemed to study quite hard—probably harder, I would guess, than those at Third Affiliated. One difference I noted, however, was that teachers at Third Affiliated spoke glowingly of the students' abilities, while teachers at MZ frequently commented that their students lacked a "foundation" because most of them had attended inadequate rural primary schools. In addition some Han teachers told me, in a confiding but not malicious manner, that the majority of MZ non-Han students did not study very hard because some colleges (in particular the nationalities colleges) give preference in recruitment to non-Han students, and thus they can get into college with less effort.

The student body at MZ is 74 percent Yi, 16 percent Han, and 10 percent other minorities, such as Hui and Zang. The school is mandated by its charter to recruit students from all over Liangshan and to affirmatively recruit students from peasant families. Slightly lower admissions standards for students from especially poor regions of Liangshan help MZ attempt to realize its mandate, although the principal admits the school has difficulty achieving full geographic diversity since Yi families from counties with a very high percentage of Yi traditionally do not encourage their children to go to school, so the school has relatively few students from such counties as Zhaojue, Meigu, and Butuo, but many from Yuexi, Xichang, Huili, Ningnan, and so on. The overwhelming majority of MZ students are, however, from peasant backgrounds, and many are from poor families and/or from poor, remote mountain villages, and their education poses a heavy economic burden on their families. Among the forty-seven Yi students in a survey I conducted, twenty-three said they had considered dropping out of school for financial reasons.

MZ does not have statistics on the percentage of Yi males versus females at the school. However, I found in my survey of two senior middle school classrooms *(ban),* one in the humanities and the other in the sciences, that sixteen out of forty-seven Yi students—about one-third—were female. In contrast, among Han students in the same two classrooms, eighteen of thirty-one, or 58 percent, were female.

Given that MZ is a nationalities school, I was surprised to discover a fairly significant percentage of Han students—about 18 percent of the senior middle school student body and 15 percent of the junior middle school student body is Han, a majority of them from peasant backgrounds. When I asked the principal why there were Han students at the school, he explained (as did many teachers and students whom I asked this same question) that the school recruited Han students who are exceptionally qualified in order to spur the school's Yi students to study harder—by providing a model of good behavior and by arousing Yi ethnic pride and hence the desire to study in order to compete with the Han. The motive for Han students to come to MZ is simply that it has a good general reputation and is less expensive than, for example, the most prestigious regular Liangshan middle school. I never found any Han student who said he or she came to MZ specifically to learn more about the Yi and make contacts with Yi. It is perhaps not to be expected that Han students would have idealistic motives for going to school with the Yi, but it is, in fact, surprising that no one articulated the practical benefits of making contact with the future Yi leaders of Liangshan.[5]

WHY MORE YI ARE NOT IN SCHOOL: THE NATURE OF THE RHETORIC

According to educational documents from the Liangshan Committee on Education, only 63.4 percent of minority children seven to twelve years old are actually in school (Liangshan Prefecture Education Commission 1994a, 2). Percentages for junior middle school and senior middle school are not given, but based upon available statistics it is easy to calculate that about 15 percent of minorities attend junior middle school and only 2 percent attend senior middle school.

Why don't more Yi go to school? I questioned many informants, but almost none of their answers reflected ethnic identity conflict issues. Instead the most common reasons given were, first, lack of money: middle schools charge tuition. In addition, since most Yi students live a great distance from the nearest middle school, they must live at the school if it provides housing

5. I am not sure why this is so but have a strong feeling that the Han parents in Liangshan cannot conceive of encouraging their children to make connections with the Yi, a group the Han consider clearly inferior culturally despite their local power.

for students, or with a relative or friend who lives near the school. In either case the student's parents must give money for room and board. The cost of tuition, room, board, and miscellaneous expenses is substantial. In the case of MZ, for example, the total of these items is two thousand to twenty-five hundred yuan, an amount equal to, or greater than, the annual income of many Yi MZ students' families.

In most cases families simply spend almost all of their cash income to send one child to school. For a fair number of students, relatives provide a portion of the money for education. It is not surprising, then, that so many Yi students reported having considered dropping out of school for financial reasons. One, for example, wrote, "My home is poor. I often can't afford both food and school and so often go without food. Therefore, I want to quit school." Another Yi student wrote, "My father is old and my mother is often sick." This is a typical answer—the student's awareness that his or her education is putting a large burden on his older parents, and that the sickness of one or both of them makes continuing in school difficult.

A second common reason given for not going to school is the need for children's labor at home. Yi children start helping their parents—for example, herding sheep or goats—early, around seven years of age in the case of several male informants. Many students said that Yi parents oppose sending their children to school, or send only one to school, because of the need for children to help with farmwork.

A third reason given was the distance of schools from home. The Yi often live in the mountains. In fact, there are Yi living almost at the tops of mountain peaks, at around 3,500 meters. Just to get to an elementary school can sometimes require a child to walk one or two hours each way, on an often dangerous mountain path. Because of this, many Yi parents are reluctant to send their children to school. At the very least, they delay sending them to school for several years, until they are around ten years old, because parents believe that by this age children can handle the long walk to school more safely.

A fourth reason, for females, is that they will just "move away." Because Yi marriage is patrilocal, young women move away from their natal families after they get married. Therefore the Yi are reluctant to educate their daughters, because the investment spent educating them is considered lost to the family when a daughter moves away to her husband's family. Also, some traditional Yi believe that educated women make less obedient wives.

According to statistics from the Liangshan Prefecture Education Commission, the percentage of children ages seven to twelve in school is about 80 percent as a whole for Liangshan but only 37 percent for Yi females (Liangshan Prefecture Education Commission 1994c, 1). While the Yi rationale for not educating women is similar to the Han, its effect is much stronger. Han peasant females at least start school, and many of them in Liangshan enter secondary school. For the Yi, however, most girls who start school go only for a year or two. Out of the scores of students at the several countryside primary schools that I visited in Butuo County, for example, only a handful were female. The inequities of the lack of schooling for females are recognized by Yi intellectuals, both females and males. Many male Yi students whom I interviewed were quite vocal in criticizing the Yi reluctance to educate girls. The principal of MZ (who is Yi) made it a priority to try to recruit larger numbers of Yi females to MZ, and the school has been moderately successful in its efforts (although the majority of Yi students at the school are still male).

What thoroughly surprised me in interviewing students is that, with the exceptions described below, no one mentioned ethnic identity issues as a reason for not attending school. No one said that Yi students are reluctant to attend school because the schools are usually run by Han, conducted in the Han language, attended mostly by Han students, and located in Han areas. The possible loss of one's own cultural values and beliefs, as well as one's mother tongue, as one spends one's prime years away from that culture and its socializing agents—parents and other relatives—was never mentioned as a concern. This is all the more surprising considering that the Yi do not like the Han and see them as culturally quite different; the observation made universally throughout Liangshan by the Yi is that the Yi are honest whereas the Han are dishonest and sneaky. The traditional Yi antagonism toward the Han (who were often seen as slaves and captured by the Yi) remains, and is perhaps most evident in the fact that one of the worst insults a Yi can give another Yi is to call him *Hxiemga* (Han), since it means that person's ancestors were slaves.

The lack of ethnic identity issues affecting school participation is also all the more surprising given the very strong presence of such issues in Western educational contexts. Of course, one might suppose that my informants were reluctant to talk about ethnic identity issues because of the sensitivity of such issues. But in fact, the Yi pride themselves on their frankness and honesty, and I found that informants never hesitated to tell me things about interethnic relations, which were much more sensitive than the issue of whether they felt ambivalent about leaving home to attend school in a Han area. Whenever I felt that an informant was opening up and being very honest, I would use the occasion to ask about ethnic identity issues and schooling. Many times I would explain that some people have commented that in America some African American students see school, and success in school, as representative of acquiescence to the majority white culture that usually controls the educational system. Thus these students respond by dropping out of school or at least withholding their full effort from school.

But even my closest informants were quick to deny any parallels between my description of the American system and the Yi response to school, even though in other respects the Yi identify with African Americans, recognizing that they are a disenfranchised, poor minority group whose social situation resembles that of the Yi. The Yi never spoke to me of going to school as a betrayal of their own Yi culture and society. School was simply a means to get ahead, in order to help oneself and one's family and hometown.

The one exception arose when discussing the very clear asymmetry between school participation of Yi from mixed-ethnic counties versus those from pure-Yi counties. The latter were much less likely to send their children to school. One informant, whose ancestors had been proud practitioners of the occupation of *bimo* (see Bamo Ayi, chapter 8 in this volume), told me that many of his Zhaojue County (a county with a high concentration of Yi and few Han) relatives scolded him for receiving a Han education. He said that his relatives who are *bimo* are reluctant to send their children to school, which I would suggest is because *bimo*, the traditional teachers of the Yi, feel that the ascendant Han education is in conflict with, and a threat to, the traditional teachings of *bimo*. Many *bimo* know that the Han, as well as many Yi who have been educated in Han schools, look down on *bimo* as unscientific, superstitious frauds. *Bimo* may resent this attitude toward their profession and refuse to send their own children to schools run by, essentially, the competition. (To get a sense of the potential magnitude of this phenomenon it may be useful to know that, according to recent figures, *bimo* and *bimo* students comprise 8 percent of the male population in Meigu County, one of the counties with an overwhelmingly Yi population and low school attendance [Gaha 1996, 21–22].)

The hostility of *bimo* to modern schools may explain why my informant's relatives, many of whom are descendants of *bimo*, chided him for attending "Han schools." But why are even non-*bimo* Yi from Zhaojue, Butuo, and other counties with high Yi populations unlikely to send their children to school? The principal of MZ said that he believed it was because such areas lacked a long tradition of schools, whereas areas where Han and Yi lived together had schools. In mixed areas wealthy Yi occasionally hired Han tutors and this, the principal said, led those Yi to develop a tradition of education and a recognition of its value. A principal at a country elementary school from Butuo agreed. He believed that in his native Yuexi County Yi parents felt that it was valuable to send their children to school. In fact they competed to do so—if X's neighbor sent his children to school, X felt obligated to do the same in order to keep up with his neighbor. No such dynamic exists, however, in Butuo, this principal told me, and hence school participation rates there are very low.

What all of the above suggests is that for the Yi, with the possible exception of *bimo*, schools do not symbolize majority Han culture, so that going to school never becomes a polarized and politicized act of capitulation to the majority. Instead, Yi from areas where there is a tradition of schooling view schools as a pragmatic means to get ahead.

This meaning of education really became clear to me during conversations with a *quho* (White Yi) MZ student from Yanyuan County, a county with a mixture of Han and Yi. This student, whom I will call by his Han name Li Xiaoping, told me how he had ended up going to school rather than working on the family farm. He had two older brothers, both of whom were educated, and so Li's father had decided that Li did not need to attend school because his brothers could obtain for Li's relatives the perks of an educated person— a paying job with a steady cash income and the possibility of influence with local government officials. In addition, Li's father, although fairly well off financially, believed he could save tuition money by not sending Li to school, and he would have Li at home to help with the family's farmwork.

But on one memorable day seven-year-old Li was tending the family sheep when he passed by the open door of a local elementary school. Li stood in the back of a classroom listening, and felt overwhelmed with excitement at what he heard. Soon after this incident he told his brothers that he wanted to go to school, and they helped persuade their father that Li should go. After graduation from junior middle school, Li was preparing to leave Yanyuan for senior middle school in Xichang, a fair distance away. A large group of males from Li's clan gathered together to send him off. They gave him a large sum of money and told him to study diligently. They said their clan had not raised a well-educated person in a long time, and they promised to help him whenever he needed help.

If Li and his relatives saw school as a way to get ahead, this is also how the Han living near Li's home viewed education. And many of them did not like the idea of their Yi neighbors going to school. The elementary school Li attended was located in the valley, about an hour-and-a-half walk from Li's home. Han teenagers would linger near the school and try to prevent Yi kids from getting to school. Groups of them would often beat up the Yi students, and Li himself was beaten up by them. This, and other experiences, left Li feeling that the Han were mean and bullying, while the Yi were polite and kind—an observation he often shared with me.

During MZ's winter vacation I went to visit Li's family. While sitting outside in the courtyard of the Li home on a cool but sunny February day, a neighbor rushed in with some bad news. He told Li's father, a man to whom the local Yi turned to for leadership when there were problems, that a group of Han—several dozen men, with one or two of them representing each family— had come earlier that day to the construction site of a primary school the local Yi were building. They had come to protest the building of the school, claiming that the school interfered with the grazing of their livestock. (Even to me, it was very clear upon seeing it that the school, only the foundation of which had been built, was far too small to interfere with anyone's grazing, especially since it sat high up in the foothills, a forty-five-minute walk from the Han areas in the valley.) The Han had argued with the few Yi at the school construction site, a fight had ensued, and the Han men had trampled on the school's mud-wall foundation, destroying it. This was all very bad news, and Li told me he did not know what would happen but predicted a large fight between the Yi and Han later that night. My visit was cut short in the later afternoon, and as Li walked me to the town where I would get a ride back to Yanyuan County Town he explained that the Han do not want to see the Yi progress in any way, and often interfere with any Yi attempts to improve their community. The primary school would have been a big help for the Yi because then they could have sent their children to a nearby school, rather than to the school that was over an hour's walk away, down in the valley.

ARE ETHNICITY IDENTITY ISSUES SALIENT
FOR THOSE YI WHO DO GO TO SCHOOL?

In Western contexts one of the explanations for discipline problems and the lack of effort among disenfranchised groups in schools is that misbehavior and the withholding of effort are means by which ethnic minority students symbolize their refutation of their teachers and the dominant culture they represent, and their allegiance to their peers and more generally their minority identities (Fordham 1996; Erickson 1987).

In order to see if this occurred among students at MZ, I interviewed dozens of Yi students and asked the following questions: Who does better academically in school—Han or Yi students—and why? What students are popular in your class and why? Yi student informants, the principal, and Han and Yi teachers almost unanimously agreed that Han students at MZ do better than Yi students. As noted earlier, one reason often given for why Yi do not do as well as Han is that Yi, having gone to inadequate rural primary schools, lack a good educational foundation (*jichu*). Many Yi also explained that they have difficulty in school because instruction is given in the Han language, which is not their mother tongue. (Surprisingly, even students who had been living in Han areas as students and attended years of school claimed that the Han language was a major barrier preventing them from doing well in school.)

The most commonly given explanation for a difference in academic achievement was that the Han study harder than the Yi, and that the Yi like to "play" (*war*).[6] When I was told that Yi do not study as hard, I always pushed for further explanation. One Yi student explained that the Yi do not study

---

6. It was true that the top-ranked students at MZ were mostly Han, and it is my impression that those students worked very hard. However, both Han and Yi students may have been somewhat misled about the nature of Han students due to the fact that the school intentionally recruited a certain percentage of academically outstanding Han students in order to spur on the Yi students to study more diligently. The Han students at MZ were thus quite probably not representative of Han students in general. My impression is that they studied harder, for example, than students at the prestigious urban school where I conducted my previous research.

that hard because they know they can always rely on their very strong and supportive clans (*cyvi*, or *jiazhi* in Chinese) if they encounter financial distress. The Yi have a dependent nature (*yikaoxing*), which this student criticized. A Han teacher said that she believed the lower threshold that Yi must meet to be accepted to college means Yi students do not study as hard. But many informants could not give any explanation for why the Han study harder than the Yi.

But what is especially important is the explanations I did not get. First, no one—Yi or Han—claimed that the Yi were intellectually inferior to the Han. In fact quite a number of Yi informants (but no Han informants) said they believed that the Yi are intellectually superior to the Han. Second and even more significant, no one said that the Yi withheld effort in order to "act Yi." While working hard was clearly identified as Han behavior, no one said that the Yi choose not to work hard so that they do not seem like Han. Just as Yi students denied that Yi avoided or dropped out of school as a statement of ethnic protest, they also denied that they misbehaved or did less work in order not to be like Han. In fact when I asked students what they had learned, if anything, by going to school with Han students, a common answer was that they had learned to study more diligently. This was seen as a Han virtue, and one that the Yi should adopt. Many students told me that the Yi should have a sense of pride in their ethnic group (*minzu zizunxing*), and when I asked what this meant, they usually explained that one should strive to earn honor for one's own ethnic group (*wei women minzu zheng guang*) through diligent study. (Han students often use a similar phrase, except that they say they want to earn honor for their *country*, something I never heard the Yi say.) Perhaps especially indicative of the absence of the ethnic politicization of effort is the fact that MZ's principal has specifically tried to increase the percentage of Han students at the school so that the Yi will emulate Han assiduousness. This strategy would not work if Yi were prone to do the opposite of what the Han do.

What is especially interesting about the issue of effort is that while whether one works hard or not is not ethnically symbolic for the Yi, effort is politicized (in the sense of symbolizing a contest of allegiances) for the Han, at least among urban Han. When interviewing students at Third Affiliated, I was often told that students who are too diligent are disliked. They are viewed as too much the teacher's pet and, because of their diligence, not friendly enough to peers. It is the student who is intelligent (*congming*) whom students respect. *Congming* generally indicates a person who can learn things without really trying too hard. It also connotes someone who is naughty (*tiaopi*) and rebellious—the opposite of the obedient and simple, honest (*laoshi*) person. Third Affiliated students often liked and respected social, smart, somewhat rebellious and naughty classmates.

I asked Yi students who they most liked and who was most popular. In con-

trast to the Third Affiliated urban Han, Yi students looked up to hard-work-
ing, obedient *(ting hua)*, straightforwardly honest *(laoshi)*, polite classmates.[7]

Nor did the Yi politicize disobedience to the teacher. Whereas urban Han
students, caught in a complex social structure that rewards those who can
display their morality and competence, thrilled at the prospect of disobey-
ing an incompetent or immoral teacher and viewed the consistently obedient student as dull in both a social and a mental sense, the Yi looked up to
students who were consistently obedient and polite toward their teachers.
Hence I did not see Yi students trying to challenge or disobey teachers in
order to score points with their Yi (or Han) peers.

I must add however that, ironically, both Yi students and Yi and Han
teachers viewed the actual behavior of MZ Yi students as less polite than
that of Han MZ students. This is one aspect of MZ that I never fully understood, since the Yi seemed to me to be as polite, if not a bit more polite, than
the Han students. Perhaps the explanation for this lies in different cultural
definitions of politeness. For me, and for many American teachers, Han
students are too talkative out of turn during class; the Yi, on the other hand,
are quiet and are good listeners and thus seemed polite according to my
own, admittedly American, standards of politeness. For Han teachers at MZ,
however, a student who is in the wrong should be apologetic and contrite
(just as anyone whose immorality is exposed should be—see Schoenhals
1993). Han students at MZ were this way, at least to their teachers' faces,
whereas Yi students were less sycophantic and hence were viewed as im-
polite by their teachers. But when not in a confrontation with the teacher,
Yi students were less gratuitously naughty, and disobedient, than the Han
I studied at Third Affiliated; and therefore disobedience, like effort, does
not symbolize the ethnic or generational opposition of the Yi toward their
teachers.

ANALYSIS: THE NATURE OF YI ETHNIC IDENTITY AS AN EXPLANATION FOR THE YI RESPONSE TO SCHOOLING

Why, then, do the Yi not view school as a site for the contestation of ethnicity? I maintain that this is because Yi identity does not conform to the traditional dynamics of ethnicity as described by anthropologists who have
worked in other ethnic contexts.

My basic premise is simple: The Yi do not see school as a setting for ethnic
identity contestation because, among the Yi, identity—ethnic and social—
is fixed at birth and therefore not contestable. Yi society is divided into two

7. My focus at MZ was Yi students and so I did not formally study Han students' attitudes.
It may be that MZ Han students, who were mainly from peasant backgrounds, shared many of
the Yi students' views about honesty and hard work.

ascribed, ranked, endogamous castes, the *nuoho* (Black Yi) and the *quho* (White Yi). No amount of money earned or education acquired can ever make a *quho* person into a *nuoho,* nor can a *nuoho* fall to *quho.* Nor, for that matter, will a *nuoho* ever want to marry a *quho,* even if the latter is rich and well educated. In the past, customary law dictated that *quho* and *nuoho* who tried to marry would be forced to commit suicide. Today this penalty can no longer be enforced, but the threats are nearly as severe. Many of my informants said their families, even their clans, would ostracize them if they married cross-caste. Several informants' parents told their children they would commit suicide if they tried to marry cross-caste or married someone who was not Yi. Thus who a Yi person is in terms of social status and marriageability is set at birth. Going to school does not change the way a Yi person sees himself or how others see him, in contrast to the situation in societies where status is achieved, and accessible through education.

Yet why is ethnicity politicized in schools in other caste societies? Surely race in America is one of the purest ascriptive ideologies in the world, and yet blacks and whites in America still struggle over their identities, and the manipulation of them in and out of school. In America, however, ascribed ideologies of race coexist with the ideology that status is achieved depending upon one's merit. The achieved and ascribed aspects of the ideologies interact and counteract each other, so that race becomes seen as manipulable to a certain extent. One's actual race may not be changeable, but in the arena where status becomes contested—in schools—racial allegiances and racial statuses can be contested: Doing well in school is viewed by, for example, some blacks as allegiance to white society and a betrayal of their own black communities (Fordham 1996). For other blacks, doing well in school becomes a means to challenge the low status of blacks by challenging the dominant majority's stereotyping of blacks as academically less capable (ibid., especially chap. 6).

But for the Yi, social status and ethnic status are both incontestable. And in fact they are really the same thing! The *nuoho* think of themselves as higher status precisely because they are pure Yi, whereas they believe the *quho* have some Han and other non-Yi blood mixed in. Those at the very bottom of Yi society are Han and other non-Yi who were captured as slaves shortly before the end of slavery in 1958. Thus Yi social hierarchy is based on an ethnic hierarchy. This link in hierarchies is manifested in marriage too, since the reason *nuoho* do not marry *quho* is because the latter are not pure Yi, and no Yi will marry a non-Yi, who is by definition lower in status. Even the Queen of England would be rejected by Yi men as a spouse, one *nuoho* informant jokingly told me (although the point he was making was a serious one). The social-ethnic link ensures that no fundamental aspect of Yi identity is contestable, hence the noncontested nature of education for the Yi.

The ethnic-social status link, curiously enough, means that ethnicity is defined in both an absolute dichotomized fashion (Yi versus non-Yi) and in a graded, relativistic fashion as well: those who are more versus those who are less Yi. (This relativism is most clearly seen among the *quho*. All of them are below *nuoho* because of their impurity, but some of them are higher than others because they are less impure, hence more Yi.) Thus, there is a sense in which Yi feel their ethnic identity to be essential, given at birth and from one's ancestors, and not merely constructed in opposition to the ethnic "other," a dynamic anthropologists have described so often as central to ethnicity (Barth 1969, especially 14–15). Nor is one's ethnicity constructed based upon one's culture. As one informant insisted to me, a Yi-ancestry person who cannot speak Yi and knows nothing of Yi culture is more clearly Yi, and more clearly worthy of marriage to a Yi, than a Han-ancestry person who has become Yi culturally and linguistically (a not uncommon occurrence in some parts of Liangshan). Thus a young person can go to a Han school, speak Han, and yet not have the sense of giving up Yi identity. His or her Han teachers could just as well be absorbed into Yi society, but only as inferiors.

Thus the Yi, though poor and numerically insignificant in China, see themselves as superior to the Han. Therefore they do not act, with regard to school, like a minority group. This superiority is, again, not a construction based upon an opposing Ethnic Other. The Yi do not feel good about themselves by looking down on other ethnicities, as one informant explained to me. They simply know and feel that their essence makes them better. Thus there is no Yi feeling of inferiority at being a minority, nor is their sense of self-worth insecure and always in need of assertion, in contrast to the Han, who always look down on others in order to bolster their own insecure self-esteem. What all this means is that doing well or not doing well in school is not tied up with ethnic esteem issues. The Yi neither feel doomed to educational insignificance because they are minorities—in fact, as noted, many Yi believe they are smarter than the Han—nor, however, do the Yi feel they must prove their superiority educationally. How one does in school and in work is, in large part, due to fate, one informant explained, thus taking school attendance and performance out of the realm of personal, cultural, and ethnic identity. The one exception to this is the Yi recognition that the Han work harder at school, but again this observation causes no Yi any real sense of cultural inferiority or angst (as it might the Han). It is simply a fact—benign tradition, which can be easily changed without an identity conflict about becoming too Han if one works too hard.

OTHER ISSUES BEARING ON SCHOOL

There are a few other issues that help to explain the Yi response to school. First, while technically school attendance is required through grade nine by law, this law is not enforced, so school is optional. Rarely does any official make the rounds of Yi homes to make sure their children are in school. Since there is no feeling that the state or adults or the Han are enforcing school attendance, the individuals who go, go there voluntarily. In fact, since parents often oppose sending their children to school because of the distance, the expense, and their need for their children's labor, it is often the child who desires to go (as for example with Li), not the parent forcing the child to go. Thus students in school do not display opposition to school and teachers as they would if forced to be there.

Second, very rarely do Yi females get to go to school. Thus education is seen as a privilege—male privilege. There is, therefore, no sense that going to school, or doing well in school, is emasculating for males. Good male Yi students are not teased or socially ostracized, as sometimes occurs among the Han. (It is important to add, however, that several Yi and Han females who did especially well at science were teased repeatedly by a group of Yi males from a humanities classroom. This seems, unfortunately, to be consistent with the Yi view of education as male privilege—a privilege these females were violating, and doing so at the expense of Yi male egos, since both Yi and Han more greatly esteem those who do well in science than in the humanities.)

Third, there is no perception, or reality, of widespread job discrimination against the Yi in Liangshan and consequently no sense among the Yi that they might do well in school yet fail to secure a good job because of discrimination. The Yi make up over half the prefectural officials in Liangshan, and these jobs are won by going to college and then being appointed to such a position. Thus the Yi feel confident that if they do well in school, and get into college, they will be rewarded with a good job. This is in clear contrast to, for example, the American situation, where the legacy of open discrimination is only a generation back, and the perception of its persistence deters some minority students from really working hard in school (Ogbu 1974).

Fourth, the Yi communities are still quite autonomous in Liangshan, culturally, socially, and linguistically. There is thus no real reasonable fear that education will lead to the Yi assimilating Han ways of doing things, and thus lead to the destruction of Yi culture. The position of Yi communities high in the mountains and Yi pride in their culture ensure that the Yi language, culture, and communities will persevere into the indeterminable future.

CONCLUSION

The Yi present an interesting case study for the study of ethnic identity and its relationship, or lack thereof, to academic achievement and behavior in school. The ascribed nature of Yi status and ethnicity means that the assimilation/separation dilemmas faced by minority ethnic groups in a multiethnic society are not confronted by the Yi, even those who go to largely

Han schools. One is born into a set status, and one's ethnicity is fixed by birth and the identity of one's ancestors. Therefore, going to school poses no real threat to the maintenance of a Yi ethnic identity or to one's inborn Yi social status, and so going to school does not symbolize rejection of Yi culture or affirmation by Yi students of Han culture and institutions. Studying hard and obeying the teacher, likewise, carry little meaning as symbolic opposition to one's own ethnicity.

Not only does the ascribed nature of ethnicity preclude assimilation dilemmas and the politicization of ethnicity, but the relativized nature of ethnicity—in which every Yi person is slightly more or less Yi, rather than Yi or not-Yi—leads Yi identity to not depend on a dichotomized Ethnic Other for its own definition. It is hard to convey what I nevertheless felt very strongly about the Yi: The Yi do not think of themselves or their own worth as deriving from a contrast with an inferior Ethnic Other. They do not need to constantly look down on, for example, the Han, to make themselves, as Yi, feel superior. They simply feel they are Yi at birth, and by birth, are good. Thus, whereas in most multiethnic settings one group often derives its identity and value through repeated performances of opposition to an Ethnic Other, the Yi show no such dynamic. Consequently, the Yi do not need to do the opposite of a dichotomized Ethnic Other such as the Han in order to define and defend their own identity. They can do well in school, or fail at school, with little effect on their sense of who they are as Yi.

CHAPTER 15

Nuosu Women's Economic Role
in Ninglang, Yunnan, under the Reforms

Wu Ga (Luovu Vugashynyumo)

ECONOMIC DEVELOPMENT AND RURAL WOMEN'S STATUS

Scholars writing about women and economic development are divided on the question of whether the penetration of capitalist markets into communities previously practicing subsistence agriculture is helpful or detrimental to women's position in family and community. Boserup (1970), for example, suggested that in many colonial situations, development, along with Eurocentric ideas about the proper role of women, led to erosion of women's traditional social rights and economic autonomy. Dauber and Cain (1981) and Ahmed (1985) pointed out that the development of commercial agriculture and wage labor had deleterious effects on rural women. Other literature has stressed the "feminization of subsistence agriculture" in situations where men have switched to cash crops or migrant labor and left women with the burden of providing for the family's subsistence needs (Staudt and Jacquette 1982; Tinker 1990).

Afonja (1980), however, disagreed with these blanket statements, pointing out that it may be wrong to imagine that the predevelopment world was one where women always had a significant degree of independence. She also noted that the feminization of agriculture has not occurred everywhere, that there are places where women's agricultural contribution remains small and others where commercialization has increased both women's and men's agricultural labor inputs. Boserup's general formulations are thus applicable only under certain conditions.

Since the late 1970s, China's economic reforms have greatly changed the structure of agricultural economy and rural society. The introduction of the household responsibility system and the creation of related economic incentives have significantly stimulated agricultural productivity. As a result, surplus labor in the agricultural sector has become a serious problem. In the early 1980s scholars such as Elizabeth Croll suggested that under the reforms there would not be many nonagricultural opportunities for women, because "where there is employment other than in agriculture[,] . . . then in all probability women will remain as agricultural labourers and the men will increasingly move into other, non-agricultural occupations" (1983, 29). In this same study, Croll also suggested that under the new system, once women were forced to remain as agricultural laborers, their labor would become invisible.

My field study of Nuosu women in Ninglang County, Yunnan, presents a more complicated picture. In some villages, there are new forms of stratification and inequality, while in others the reforms have brought new economic opportunities for women. Because of the nature of Nuosu society, including the patrilineal clan ideology, women's social roles are different from those found in Han villages. Detailed examination of these case studies will show that it is impossible to generalize about the effects of economic reform on women's status even for people of a single ethnic group in a single county, let alone for China as a whole.

NUOSU WOMEN'S ROLES BEFORE THE REFORM PERIOD

When economic reforms were first implemented in the 1980s, the rural economy of places like Ninglang, and the role of women in that economy, had already been through considerable changes under the collective agricultural regime of the 1950s through the 1970s. Before the 1950s, what evidence we have from Han-language sources indicates that Nuosu women played a variety of roles in the traditional agricultural economy. In general, it seems that in traditional society in the Ninglang area, women's economic role was determined by class. Among wealthy families, who also tended to belong to the high-status *nuoho* stratum, women's work consisted primarily of herding sheep and other domestic animals; the women rarely plowed fields or grew crops. Among commoners, women's economic roles seem to have been more varied. I have recorded the following roles: planting fruit trees; herding sheep; carrying wood; planting and harvesting buckwheat, corn, and potatoes; gathering mushrooms; and gathering medicinal plants from the mountains for sale in the market. In addition, both high- and low-caste women engaged in crafts such as weaving wool, dyeing cloth, making hats, and spinning and weaving silk linings for skirts. Even before 1956, there was also local variation in women's agricultural work: in buckwheat-growing areas women tended to have a greater role in agriculture than in oat-growing areas, where fields were fallowed in alternate years and labor requirements were less intensive.

In 1956, socialism came to Ninglang with the implementation of the Democratic Reforms. Despite the geographic remoteness and ethnic minority status of the Ninglang population, nationwide policies of collectivization, com-

munization, and agricultural intensification were implemented here as elsewhere. During the Great Leap Forward, over forty thousand laborers were
enlisted in the "war against bad weather," while twenty thousand were mobilized to make iron and steel and another forty-five hundred to build roads.
Agriculture was organized in communes with thousands of members, and
Ninglang joined in the nationwide effort to increase the scale and yield of
grain production.

After 1960, the large communes, here as elsewhere, were broken down
into smaller collective units, which resulted in a recovery from the famine
of 1960–62; but soon the reradicalization of policy during the Cultural Revolution caused further troubles for local farmers. The emphasis on "grain
as the key link" brought particularly deleterious results to a mountainous
area like Ninglang, where the traditional economy had emphasized—in addition to grain—forestry, livestock raising, and fruit growing. In order to raise
more grain, large areas of forests were cut down. In addition, local peasants
had no experience with high-yielding varieties of rice and wheat and could
not obtain enough fertilizer to grow these new varieties efficiently. As a result, there was an overall decline in agricultural productivity.

How did Nuosu women fare during the period of collective agriculture?
My interviews with several local women concerning this period indicate that
they had been dissatisfied and had displayed a fair amount of resistance to
what they considered unsuitable policies. Some had used their private land
for sideline enterprises and crop diversification. Others had engaged in the
illegal practice of reclaiming wasteland without official permission in order
to be able to plant freely. Jare Anyumo recalls this time: "There are Yi
proverbs that say, 'In the high mountains, animal husbandry is fit; in the lowlands, honeybee production is proper,' and 'Lower land does not need plowing; the land itself is fertile.' Here we live in high mountain conditions, which
have low productivity due to weather conditions. The project of scientific
agricultural experiments to double-crop rice and wheat, disregarding local
conditions, brought disaster here." She also pointed out the deleterious effects of collective incentive and compensation systems: "Before the economic
reforms of the 1980s, for a long time there was no private land. Peasants always talked during working hours. They never cared about fertilizer or seeds.
There were no training classes on how to plant corn covered with plastic during the winter. There was no migration policy, and no plan for planting fruit
trees. During the commune period, I got 14 points a day,[1] and at the end of
the year this worked out to a cash income of 60 yuan. If you add work-point

1. During the period of collective agriculture from 1956 to the early 1980s, production
team members were paid in "work points" (gong fen), and the proceeds of the collective harvest
were shared among the team's households according to the points earned by the households'
members.

grain, it might add up to 100 yuan. In Ninglang we had many villages with less than 250 yuan household cash income."

Jare Gagativumo could earn 300 yuan per year doing miscellaneous work in the township grain station, but the jobs were arduous: washing bedclothes for the township hotel, gathering wood for sale to cadres, mending and washing grain bags, digging ditches, and building roads.

Women also faced difficulties and inequities related to childbirth. Alur Zhoshy's wife, Lypimo, recalled, "After my first birth I only got eighteen days' rest, and my husband's mother was not at home. I had to garden food for my family. According to the rules, women who had given birth only received basic grain *[jiben gongliang]*, but no work-point grain *[gongfen liang]*. I had to go back to the fields after giving birth. It was difficult for the whole family. Qumo Guoguo was right when she told you that during the 1950s, male peasants could earn 10 work points per day, but women could only earn 8. When a woman was resting after birth, in addition to her basic grain she received only 2 work points."

Not all women had similar experiences. According to Qumo Lydimo,

During the 1950s and 1960s, I was part of the "hardworking youth team," which was building the road into Yongningping. Each day I earned 10 work points. After this, I started working in Zhanhe, loading goods at the grain station. I received 10 yuan per day, and sometimes also could make 3 yuan per day making clothing; in addition I sold a pig for about 200 yuan and soybeans for another 200 yuan each year. I did almost anything to get money for my family: plowing and planting, loading goods, and working in a sewing shop. Women usually got only 7 or 8 points; the best received up to 20, while children got 2 points for herding the animals. There were many taboos against women climbing to the loft for grain, pruning apple trees, or plowing the land like men. Because my husband was working in a cloth factory, however, I did everything. He was not at home, so I had to do these male things. After six months, I had to bring children to the field and set them down there while I worked.

In general, then, Nuosu women's economic role was expanded in some ways during the collective period—they worked on road construction projects during the winter slack season, for example—and curtailed in others: forestry, animal husbandry, and craft production were all limited by the grain-first policy. When the economic reforms came in the 1980s, however, Nuosu women gained opportunities to both resume traditional economic activities and develop new ways of making money in the market economy.

WOMEN'S ROLE SINCE THE ECONOMIC REFORMS

The economic reforms came to Ninglang, as they did to the rest of the country, beginning in the early 1980s. The former emphasis on subsistence production and self-sufficiency has been replaced, here as everywhere, with a market economy in which the state has given up control over agricultural production, distributed land among peasant households, and allowed households to control their own production and marketing as long as they pay certain agricultural taxes and sell some products to the state at below-market prices (Oi 1986; Skinner 1985; Nee 1988). Socially and politically, the commune system was dismantled and replaced with a system of township and village governments.

The relaxation of control over agriculture and the incentives of the market have had a profound impact on the Ninglang economy. In particular, traditional economic activities such as sheep raising and forestry have been revived on a large scale. Sheep are once again raised for wool and meat, and women play a large role in this industry. As Bbuyo Anyumo from Yongningping explained, "Shearing sheep wool is a woman's job. Nowadays the price of wool is 2 yuan per *jin*. We shear three times a year, in March, July, and October. The wool from July is the best. Generally 1 sheep produces about half a *jin* per shearing, for a total of 1.5 *jin* per animal per year. My family has 10 sheep, so we have 15 *jin* of wool per year. Women use the wool to make *shapa*, a special skirt and dress for winter time. We also make bedcovers. Sheep are also very important for parents, as gifts especially before they die. According to Nuosu custom, there should be a sheep killed for each person when they die. This is called 'following-parents sheep.'"

Forestry has also become available to peasants again. In 1981, the county government distinguished state from collective forests, and in 1984 it further divided collective forests into collective and private forests and began using the contract system to divide up collective and private mountains. The government also instituted incentives for reforestation, paying families a certain amount for every *mu* of mountains reforested after cutting.

Forestry has thus become a significant source of peasant income in some areas. But unlike animal husbandry, forestry offers few opportunities for women. According to Jjisse Anyumo, "Tree cutting is only for men; women are not allowed to participate. Cutting trees is the most lucrative economic activity in the Xilaping area, but gender bias and discrimination exclude women from this job. For example, the 1992 lumber quota assigned to Yongningping Township is 10,000 cubic meters, and 5,000 for Xilaping. A wage of 24–30 yuan is paid for each cubic meter of wood cut. Women have no right to earn these wages, since they are not permitted to cut trees like men. Brothers and fathers are very proud of their special contribution to the family economy. Women can be road builders, but they are not permitted to cut trees. Why?"

Another new source of income is planting "covered corn," an activity in which both men and women can participate. Sete Guojiamo explained,

To plant covered corn, you must spend money on the plastic cover. In Wanhe Village, we have five households who planted this corn. Special seeds cost

7 yuan per *jin*, with the government paying 5 and the household 2. This kind of corn is a high-yield crop, with up to 1,000 *jin* per *mu*, where 500 is generally considered a high yield here. To plant the corn we also need water, and some lazy households did not plant this corn since it requires too much water, and bringing water up to these mountain areas is very difficult. Other families are very industrious and weed three times.

The first year I helped other people to plant, and the second year I started to plant myself. In Yongsheng County they started to plant this corn in 1985, but here we did not start until 1992. There were five households here who planted. We started on April 10–17, after the [Han Chinese] Qingming holiday, the Nuosu time of preparing the land, watering, fertilizing, planting, and covering it to try to maintain the temperature. Actually, we learned many new scientific methods, especially in pig feeding, from Mr. Sun [Han Chinese], a twenty-seven-year-old technician who has a nice attitude toward Nuosu women, and also from the station head, Hielie Lybusse, a Yi man who taught us how to use fertilizer.

It is thus evident that Nuosu women are once again playing a wider role in the local economy of Ninglang. But precisely because the reform policies had recognized the error of imposing a uniform, grain-growing regime on all areas, I found that the reform economy was taking very different directions in the three townships in which I worked, and that women's roles varied greatly from one part of Ninglang to another.

Yongningping

Yongningping is the most isolated and remote of the villages that served as my field sites. Of the forty villages in the township, twenty-eight lack water. Many parts of the township are not accessible to transport systems and thus not suitable for growing cash crops for export. In this area, women's work consists mainly of collecting water and firewood, preparing food, and engaging in the many tasks of preparing fields for and planting, fertilizing, and harvesting corn, the main subsistence crop in most of the township. In lower-lying areas, women also cultivate sweet potatoes, and they grow buckwheat in the higher regions. There is some fruit orchard development in Yongningping, and women plant, tend, and harvest fruit. Training classes have been held for Yongningping women to teach them proper spacing between crop rows, which crops can be interplanted with which trees, and how to tend trees for maximum yield.

Domestic livestock production is also very important in Yongningping. Taking care of livestock is the first job for younger girls, one that often prevents them from attending school. Women also build fences to protect crops from the incursions of domestic animals.

Xingyunpan

Household productivity in Xingyunpan is higher than in Yongningping, with corn yielding 800–1,000 *jin* per *mu* (in contrast to about 500 in Yongningping), and potatoes as much as 3,000 *jin* (contrasted to 2,500 in Yongning-ping). There is also more double-cropping in this area, which increases the amount of labor women perform. According to the women's director of the township government, "Nowadays, people favor brides from Xingyunpan, because they are more skilled at planting new crops than women from other regions."

Xingyunpan is also Ninglang's model township for growing apple trees. According to the government plan, the 50,000 *mu* of land in the township was to be divided, with 24 percent planted in apple trees, 4 percent in *hua-jiao* (Sichuan peppercorn trees), 4 percent in plums, and 12 percent in forest species. Women are heavily involved in apple and other cash-crop production in Xingyunpan, as explained to me by the township head, Jiesha Wani:

> The women of Xingyunpan benefited from the basic infrastructural construction of the 1950s: electricity from the reservoir built at that time has benefited seventeen villages. Since 1986, this water has helped women with apple tree planting, and there are now 12,000 *mu* producing apples. For example, the Alur Aguo family harvested 1,200 *jin* of apples in 1991; the Jiesha Guoguo family in Maoguping had only two apple trees, but their income was 500 yuan, and the Liu Yipu family planted 300 apple trees, and harvested 10,000 *jin* of apples, for a cash income of 5,000 yuan. Bbuyo Fuha's family won the first prize in the 1991 provincial apple competition in Kunming. The county policy is that both apples and green-manure crops can be exchanged for rice at the county grain station, and that the families developing these crops will pay no new taxes for six years. In the Xingyunpan area, these policies have resulted in 12,000 *mu* of apple orchards, with about 45 percent of the trees now producing fruit.

All this prosperous commercial agriculture has meant an increase in women's workloads. Green manure crops are planted in October and harvested in June. In June, sweet buckwheat is planted, and it is harvested in December. The busiest times for women are the harvest in September and planting season in March and April.

Wanhe

Of the areas in which I conducted research, Wanhe Village in Zhanhe Township is the most favored economically. Economic reform here brought privatization of land for villagers, but an unfair land policy has increased the inequality among village households. According to Aku Shama Gaga,

> Wanhe Village divided its land in 1982, and at first there were three big groups contracting land from the village. My husband was head of the third group. Even at the beginning, the three groups were not given land of equal quality. Jjiggu Ajie's group had the best land, and Jjiesse Yoqie's and my husband's groups had so-so land, so that when the land was further contracted to individual house-

holds, the quality of the land you got depended on which group you had originally belonged to. Some families with insufficient land have opened up new land illegally, and been fined by the village, whereas other families have had too much, and have tried to sell to other people. Other people have plowed up land that was supposed to belong to public animal rights-of-way. So some people get more land than others, and some must open up new land illegally. I don't know whether the government will readjust this policy or not.

In Wanhe No. 1 Village, many better-off households owe their success to the nonagricultural employment of husbands or daughters, rather than to hard work in agriculture. Poor households, on the other hand, are vulnerable to the effects of late planting, poor weeding, lack of cash for seed, transport problems, labor shortages, lack of agricultural knowledge, poor soil, and the inability to hire machinery.

Migration has also played a part in the agricultural division of labor in Wanhe. On the one hand, many male laborers have left the village in search of off-farm employment. This has left women from these households to participate in every aspect of agricultural production. They also purchase seed, fertilizers, and chemicals; hire extra labor; and market the surplus produce. On the other hand, because of the village's favorable location, thirteen families moved to it during the reform era. These people typically do not have land of their own, so they lease from families with a land surplus, and the latter now count rent as a major source of income.

Ward (1986) pointed out the paradox that increasing women's work often simply meant longer workdays with no improvement in status, but it is clear that women's work in Ninglang differs greatly according to social status. Rich households in Wanhe are more likely to hire labor, while poorer people in Xingyunpan are more likely to rely on themselves, meaning that the workloads of women in Xingyunpan increased more than those of Wanhe women. Wanhe women from wealthy households are also more likely to set up shops to earn money, and this, along with their involvement in nonagricultural craft enterprises, has raised the value of their work for their families. At the same time, Wanhe women are more likely to engage in wage labor during the agricultural slack season. In other words, Wanhe women have achieved considerable economic independence in the reform era.

Women in Xingyunpan, by contrast, take a much more active role in agricultural work and take on multiple roles in the agricultural sector, aided by government extension services. In Yongningping, the most remote area, kinship-based social organization still survives, and women's work is mainly concerned with the care of animals belonging to their husbands.

Women and the Market

In Zhanhe, the commercialization of agriculture and the commoditization of the household economy, along with the increased control exercised by women in households where husbands have emigrated in search of wage labor, have resulted in women's playing an unprecedented role in local markets. Women of all social classes have entered the market to sell household-produced goods.

Much feminist research has concentrated on analyzing the social and economic background of women's move to the marketplace. Factors listed by Gugler and Flanagan (1978) and Vandsemb (1995) include divorce, widowhood, premarital pregnancy, barrenness, and escape from social pressures or disagreements between kin. Other scholars have in contrast stressed changes in the gender division of labor, as well as simply the expansion of the market itself. In the Zhanhe market there were many kinds of women active in trade. For example, divorced women moved from farming to marketing, and their market activity sometimes provided the sole support of their households. They were able to work in the market because their work did not depend on rigid separation of the home from the workplace. Women whose husbands had low incomes moved to the market as part of a strategy for coping with economic change. Some younger women entered the market to escape unhappy marriages. And others simply wanted to take advantage of newly diversified economic opportunities or, in the case of wealthy families, to further supplement their income. Some market women in Zhanhe were known to be very rich—Molie Agamo, for example, who told me,

> I was married in 1972 and this year I am 41 years old. My sons are 19, 16, and 13, and are very helpful to me. We used to live in Dahosan Village, Sibuhe Township, but in 1981 we moved to Wanhe because the location of this village is very good for commercial production. My husband returned from army service in 1989, took out loans to buy a tractor, and we made money from transport work. Last year, we sold pigs for 800 yuan, and I have used 10,000 yuan of family money to set up my first shop, and have now earned almost 30,000. I have also helped some women sell their mushrooms, medicinal plants, animal skins, wool, garlic, and vegetables. I pay a tax of 40 yuan to the government each year, along with an administrative fee of 15 to the village. I am a very lucky person, and I think I have also made some contributions. In our village, the Jjiesse brothers are the wealthiest—they have opened the first hotel. Zhanhe is a very complicated place; people even call it "Little Shanghai." But the market of Zhanhe has helped many women, both rich and poor.

Alur Vugashoviemo is another woman who works in the market. She is a model laborer in animal rearing, with twelve pigs and fourteen chickens at her home when I visited her in 1993:

> At first I only sold them to the county, but later on I learned that if I kill the pigs first and then sell them in the market, I will make more money. For example, if you sell live pigs to the county, you might get 100 yuan, but in the market you might make as much as 700, since the price is about 2.9 yuan per *jin* for live pigs, but good meat in the market might sell for as much as 5.8 or

even 6 yuan. My husband is so proud of me for this job—I can sometimes make more than he does.

I started to learn to rear animals three years ago. I first talked with my friend, then I bought feed and high-quality pigs. I could not read the instructions on the feed bag, so I always had to bother Yang Qingning to read them for me. When my pigs got worms, I could not read the instructions, and put too much medicine in their food, so five of them died, and my husband was very angry. I cried also. This job can be difficult, too, but the market here has indeed helped me a lot. Compared with before 1982, when the government did not allow markets here, I really like the new situation.

With the rise of the market, women have stepped into the marketplace to make their careers and seek independence, but they also face new problems such as sexist violence. For example, Jiho Nyunyumo's fiancé accused her of being a prostitute and beat her so severely that she had to be hospitalized. Many men still see women, even those who work in the market, as property, and when incidents of sexual violence have happened in the Zhanhe market the police have played a rather passive role, either arriving late or not interfering, in deference to the power of male kin over women.

Since the Zhanhe market was formally established in 1986, there have been 116 women registered as traders. The majority of these come from the nearby counties of Huaping and Yongsheng. There are 11 women who belong to the special category of women with bad fate—divorced or widowed. Jjiesse Vuji Aqiemo reported,

> After my husband went to military service, I came back to my own village. They [her husband's family] asked me back but I decided to divorce, and a friend helped me come here to work. After the death of her second husband, with a daughter and a son in school, Shama Lyviemo, at age forty-three, had to find some way to support them. Shama Viemo of Wanhe received her dowry of 3,000 yuan back after her divorce. She used 1,000 to rent a room and buy a sewing machine and some cloth to open a shop. Jjiesse Alymo, forty years old with no education, is from Wanhe No. 2 Village. Her first marriage ended in divorce, and she then married her former husband's brother, but this also ended in divorce. After the second divorce, she came here to open a shop in the market. She wants to help her two sons to go school.

CONCLUSION

The experiences of Nuosu women in Ninglang County demonstrate that there is no single trend that affects the status of female rural subsistence producers when they move into a market economy. The women of remote Yongningping have returned to something resembling their role in the traditional economy—animal husbandry, housework, and supplementary agricultural work, all within an economy mostly controlled by the men of their households. In Xingyunpan, where cash crops have taken over, women's agricultural participation has increased because they have learned many new techniques for cultivating fruit and other cash crops. At the same time, the burden of agricultural labor has increased for these women: they have added the new agricultural activities to their traditional roles. And in wealthy, accessible Wanhe, women have taken on different roles according to their social class position, with wealthy women almost liberated from agricultural labor, but women of all social classes active in the newly bustling market in that area.

CHAPTER 16

The Yi Health Care System
in Liangshan and Chuxiong

Liu Xiaoxing

There are, as yet, very few scholarly studies of the health care system of any Yi people, despite the presence of both a flourishing traditional sector and a biomedical sector advocated by the Chinese state. This chapter explores what causes changes and what remains the core of continuity in the health care system of two Yi peoples: the Nuosu in Liangshan Yi Autonomous Prefecture in Sichuan (see chapters 2–9, 14, and 15), and the Lolopo in Chuxiong Yi Autonomous Prefecture in Yunnan (see Erik Mueggler, chapter 10).

The field of health care was a major frontier where the Chinese state promoted scientific knowledge and techniques along with communist ideology, expecting ethnic minorities to give up their "backwardness" and identify themselves with the progressive nation-state. Under pressure by the state and the dominant Han ethnic group, the Yi neither gave up their ethnic identity and medical culture nor resisted loudly. Instead, people took their ritual performance underground during the years when it was officially forbidden. They pragmatically made use of the official health care, adopted some scientific knowledge, and eclectically modified their own medical practices, so as to survive and develop in the circumstances in which they were situated.

CULTURAL BACKGROUND OF THE YI HEALTH CARE SYSTEM

Ethnic Identity

Study of Yi health care is complicated by the fact that the different local groups classified in the 1950s as belonging to the Yi *minzu* (nationality, ethnic group) have different histories of interaction with the surrounding Chinese national culture and with Han people. According to recent research on ethnicity, particularly that of the Yi in China, we have to be aware that "Yi" is a politically defined ethnic category, and the ethnic identities of various subgroups of the Yi people are quite different from each other. Therefore, when studying the ethnic identity of a group of Yi, certain factors need to be considered; that is, how they have been labeled by the state, how they are addressed by their neighbors, and how they represent themselves.

There are similarities and differences between the Lolopo and Nuosu. *Lolo* is the reiterative of *lo*, which means tiger in Lolopo dialect (Liu Yaohan 1985, 40). Men call themselves Lolopo while women call themselves Lolomo among this group of the Yi. Nuosu also called themselves Lolo less than a century ago (Liu Yaohan 1980, 122). In Nuosu language, *la* means tiger, as do its variants *lo, le,* and *lao,* recorded in the literature (ibid., 120). People from both groups are proud of themselves for their special connection with the tiger (Liu Yaohan 1985, 41, 42). Before the Communist takeover, both state officials and their Han neighbors called them Lolo, which in Chinese, though similar in pronunciation to what they called themselves, carried the derogatory meaning "savages" or "barbarians." Now, the state refers to the whole group as the Yi; what the people call themselves depends on which language they are speaking. They call themselves Yi when speaking Chinese; they call themselves Lolopo, Lipo, Nuosu, and so forth when speaking their own languages. Their Han neighbors simply call them *minzu* or sometimes *lao Yi bao* (old Yi brothers), which connotes incomprehensibility, dirt, and laziness, as Harrell has observed (1990).

Economic Life

Most Yi in China live a rural life that depends on agricultural production. Long Jianmin, in his article on the historical restriction of production in the Yi area, points out that there are neither broad lowland plains nor large grasslands in the mountains where the Yi reside, since valleys and rivers cut them into small pieces. The Yi engage in both swidden and sedentary agriculture and animal husbandry. They grow buckwheat, potatoes, and oats in high mountain areas and maize, wheat, peas, and beans in the lower uplands, planting corn and rice where conditions permit. They farm extensively using simple tools and techniques. Slash-and-burn as a form of cultivation was practiced at least until the late 1980s and may be practiced still (Long Jianmin 1987, 196–210; Yu Hongmo 1988, 21). The Yi also raise domestic animals, including sheep, goats, pigs, cattle, and horses. To a great extent, this industry provides resources for maintaining and promoting relations based on lineage or family systems, such as gifts and sacrifices. The characteristics of Yi trading activities well portrayed the influence of clan principles.

Until a few decades ago, Lolopo were not good at commercial activities in their homeland. Many of them were ashamed to sell their products at local markets. On the other hand, the same group of the Yi have long enjoyed the reputation of being good at long-distance caravan trading. Long suggests that these seemingly contradictory attitudes toward internal and external group exchanges indicate that clan principles are valid among many Yi at present (Long Jianmin 1987, 201); that is, they can trade with people who have no close relationship with them. To clan members and relatives, they are obligated to give, rather than sell, their products.

Traditionally, these peoples' food supply and cash income have depended predominantly on local agricultural production. All things related to agriculture are meaningful, and some are especially significant to them, such as mountains, streams, rains, fire, crops, and animals. Myths and legends describe the close relationships between human beings and these natural phenomena and entities in the physical world. Each subgroup of the Yi has festivals and ceremonies celebrating and reinforcing such cosmic relations. Nowadays, many Yi people live in cities and have entered production sectors other than agriculture, such as factories, mines, businesses, governmental institutions and services. The education they receive and the health care services they use have led them to know more about the germ theory and biomedicine than their fellow villagers know. Yet, the majority of the Yi are peasants, and most of them maintain traditional notions of health and illness.

Social Organization

Social organization among the various Yi groups is not all the same, because the Yi are so diverse. Generally speaking, however, there are two models. Most Yi in Yunnan and Guizhou were strongly influenced by Han Chinese hundreds of years ago. Their political systems fit into the systems of Chinese dynasties. The most important social unit is the family, a term that conveys both political connection to the regional community and blood ties to the broader family system. Most Yi families are nuclear families. Normally a household consists of a husband, wife, and their unmarried children. When the children grow up and get married, they form a new family and live in a separate house. Usually a woman marries into her husband's family. However, it is not uncommon for a man to marry into his wife's family and carry on her family name if her parents do not have a son.

Unlike these subgroups in Yunnan and Guizhou, Nuosu in Liangshan maintained the administrative function of their patrilineage system (see Anne Maxwell Hill and Eric Diehl, chapter 3 in this volume) until 1956, when the Chinese Communist Party carried out the Democratic Reforms, replacing lineage systems with all levels of political institutions. Nuosu mainly live in and work as nuclear families, but the lineage remains significant to most of them and still affects their lives. Before 1956, the Yi society in Liangshan was divided into four social strata: *nuo* or *nuoho* (elites), *qunuo* or *quho* (commoners), *mgajie* (settled dependent farmers), and *gaxy* (household slaves). According to the Nuosu tradition of stratum endogamy, a *nuo* will not marry a *qunuo* and a Yi will not marry a Han or a person of other ethnic origin. The Yi never established a unitary regime in Liangshan, but organized the society by blood ties and administered public affairs through the lineage systems.

In sum, among the Yi, the nuclear family is the basic unit of production and living, while the patrilineage is the institution for keeping social order and security among Nuosu in Liangshan. Ancestors, who brought people into the world and held them together in families and lineages, are highly respected, and their blessing is desired by their descendants. As a result, a great number of healing rituals involve the ancestors (see Bamo Ayi, chapter 8 in this volume).

THE HEALTH CARE SYSTEM

The health care system of the Yi community is what Charles Good called an ethnomedical system that includes the total medical resources available to and utilized by this community (1987, 22). It is concerned not only with how to manage bodily suffering but also with the economic lives, ideologies, and sociopolitical relationships among the Yi people and their interactions with the outside world. The Yi, like any other people, have, over time, developed their own ways to cure and prevent illnesses by integrating other people's ideas and techniques into their healing practices. Yi healing practices are thus a mixture of indigenous beliefs and outside influences.

Theory of Illness

Yi consider etiology in terms of both natural and supernatural aspects. According to Azi Ayue, a Yi physician trained in traditional Chinese medicine, the Yi consider "wind" to be the most important cause of illness. Normally, wind is the dynamic of life and production, but it also causes sicknesses under certain circumstances. Poisons and worms also lead to illnesses (1993, 98–99).

Supernatural causes are many. For example, an illness may result from the fact that an ancestor blames the living descendants for not providing sacrifices on time. Or perhaps one's ancestors are too weak to protect their descendants because they have not received enough offerings. Or an illness may be a message that an ancestor injured by wild spirits sends to living descendants in order to ask for their assistance. Spirits avenge themselves on people who offended them, and this may take the form of an illness. People lose their souls by being frightened or seduced. People see strange phenomena, such as snakes copulating or a cow's tail tangled with a tree, phenomena considered to be signs of evil spirits. Someone breaks a taboo and is punished by the ancestors. Some people can deploy sorcery or witchcraft to make others ill.

Although many Yi do not reject biomedical causes of sicknesses, most interpretations of illnesses are still based on the traditional theory of supernatural causes. These beliefs are constructed by the Yi people from their cosmology and other aspects of ideology, and constitute one of the major factors that determine patterns of illness behavior and health-care decision-making. Some of these beliefs are less important, so people are not very serious about them. Others, such as evil caused by various spirits, and ancestors' roles in health problems, have been deeply rooted in most people's minds at both conscious and unconscious levels over time. Therefore, it is very difficult to change or eliminate them.

Spirits as the Cause of Illness

Yi divide spirits into good and evil. Some spirits attack people aggressively, some punish people who offended them, while still others help ritual practitioners heal patients. Spirits are usually named after the illness they cause, such as the spirit of leprosy, of headache, of red eyes, of the drowned, of the people who jumped off cliffs, and so on. Regarding the latter two, a person seduced by one of these evil spirits would lose control of his or her mind and jump into deep water or off a cliff; thus these are considered the result of illness. The Yi call on ritual healers to invoke a certain kind of spirit to release the relevant sickness from the patient when possible. There are so many spirits in the world of the Yi that the interactions between human beings and spirits take place at least as frequently as those among people themselves. Spirits resemble human beings in that both need food and both have feelings, so, like people, spirits can be pleased or offended. Although people carefully maintain good relations with their ancestors and good spirits, and endeavor to stay away from bad spirits, they cannot avoid offending or running into the latter because the spirits are invisible. Dissatisfaction, anger, punishment, and invasion by the spirits are common causes of sickness (Lin 1961; Qin et al. 1988; Ma Xueliang 1943). Punishment can be the result of the spirits' dissatisfaction and anger, but invasion can be initiated by ancestors and other spirits for other reasons, such as by request of the victim's human rivals. Of all supernatural beings, ancestors are particularly significant to the Yi.

The Role of Ancestors in Health Care

In contrast to Han Chinese, who see ancestors primarily as benign beings, the immediate concern of the Yi with their ancestors tends to be etiologic, though they do trace their origin and respect their ancestors. The Yi attitude toward their ancestors is ambivalent because of the dual character of the latter, who can do both good and harm to them. Analyzing the dual character of Yi ancestors, Bamo Ayi observes that whether they bless or harm their descendants depends both on the ancestors themselves and on outside influences. Ancestors' spirits can cause sicknesses in their descendants either directly or indirectly. Direct causation is an expression of ancestors' dissatisfaction with and anger toward—that is, punishment of—their descendants; indirect causation is the result of ancestors not being strong enough—or being unwilling—to protect their descendants. Some ancestors have the evil tendency to harm their descendants; they are called "the ancestors who eat people." Some suffer from illness and injury in the other world, and some are bothered by animals or worms at their resting place. Whatever the problem, the descendants can take action to deal with it, such as providing offerings to please and support ancestors, holding rituals to heal their illness, using magic to control or change their evil intentions, and so forth. That is why the Yi developed very elaborate rituals for worshiping their ancestors and making sure they receive an adequate supply of energy and entertainment over time (1994, 28–31).

Cosmology

Yi have a strong interest in, and keep searching for, the origin of the universe and of human beings. This is manifested in Yi traditional culture in the form of myth, both in oral epics and classic literature written in the old Yi scripts. Expressions of the cosmology of Yi people vary from one subgroup to another. Some describe water as the origin of the universe. They say that "the first thing evolved from Chaos was water," then all things on the earth were developed from it (SFAS 1960). Some suggest that the air or fog formed the sky, the earth, and all kinds of beings and items in the world (Luo and Chen 1984; GINS 1982; Guo and Tao 1981). In an Axi epic the original form of the universe and everything in the world was a cloud (HIFY 1978). A well-known Yi myth in Yaoan entitled *Meiguo* describes how a tiger's body became the universe and all planets and things on the earth were gradually generated from it (CIFY 1959).

No matter how diverse the ideas about the origin of the universe are, all emphasize movement and change. The word *universe* is written in old Yi as two symbols, O ⊙. Although Yi characters are primarily phonetic, some of them, such as these two, are hieroglyphic. O indicates the space in which all things exist; ⊙ is an egg, which implies life and relentless movement (Bai 1995, 67, 93; Zhu Juyuan, personal communication, 1995). As far as the origin of human beings is concerned, myths and legends express awareness of the close relationship between the Yi and neighboring groups. There is a myth about human origin among Yi groups living in Yao and Dayao counties in Yunnan tells that ancestors of the Han, Yi, Lisu, Hmong, and some other groups came from the same parents (CIFY 1959, 1–46). Many *minzu* in China, including the Yi, Hani (Akha), Lahu, Lisu, Miao (Hmong), and Yao, have similar legends about human beings coming from a gourd or squash, and usually the ancestors of several groups came out together (Liu Xiaoxing 1990). The myth of the Axi Yi group asserts that the existence and development of the world and all things in it depend on their pairing as female and male (Xia 1990, 124). Quite a few peoples categorize things into male and female, the Moso and Lahu being the groups most similar to the Yi in this regard.

Male and Female   In the Yi myth of creation, uplands, trees, grass, stones, and people are all divided into male and female. Things exist and develop only as pairs, such as the sun paired with the moon, the sky paired with the earth, big stars paired with small stars, and black clouds paired with white clouds (CIFY 1959; HIFY 1978). One can still see the trace of dual cosmology in Yi daily life. For example, the Lipo subgroup of the Yi in Tanhuanshan, Yunnan, divides natural objects and household utensils into female and male according to their size: the larger objects are female and the smaller ones, male. The Yi in Ninglang had used a solar calendar composed of ten months in a year and thirty-six days in a month. The Yi named the months after five pairs of elements—wood, fire, earth, copper, and water—so they had five female months and five male months each year (Liu Yaohan 1985, 59). Yi astrology, according to the associations of sun-female-bright and moon-male-dark, divides a day and night into female day and male night (ibid., 96). Some Lolopo families in Yunnan enshrine their ancestors in calabashes. Each calabash contains a couple's spirits: parents, grandparents, and great-grandparents. The calabash inhabited by the souls of male and female ancestors is called *nielomo*. Portraits of ancestors (male and female together) are worshiped in some Yi households. The descendants call this portrait *nielomo* as well. *Nie* means ancestral spirit, *lo* means tiger, and *mo* means female. That is, they use the female ancestor to represent the ancestors of both sexes. Interestingly, the way the Yi categorize the features of male and female is very similar to that of the Moso and the Lahu, among whom women are highly respected (Du Shanshan 1992; Yan and Song 1983).

Seven and Nine   The Yi use the number seven to signify female and nine to indicate male. In a Nuosu cremation, for example, they make a coarse wooden chair with two long boards on either side and a wooden plank across the middle—altogether, nine pieces of wood for a man and seven pieces for a woman. When a *bimo* (healer and ritual practitioner) makes the spirit abode of the dead, he uses cotton thread to bind together a slip of bamboo shoot (which represents the spirit of the dead) and a little wool—nine rounds for a man and seven for a woman. Then he puts them into the spirit house, which is a piece of wood split and hollowed inside for the purpose, then binds the upper outside with hemp twine—again seven rounds for a woman and nine for a man. In Yi divination, "an odd number betokens good luck, an even number, bad luck" (Lin 1961, 129, 134).

Left and Right   According to Liu Yaohan, the Yi, unlike many groups in the world, see the left as positive, the right as negative, and they associate female with the left and male with the right (1985). *Meiguo,* a Yi myth about the universe being developed from the body of a tiger, says the tiger's "left eye became the sun and right eye the moon" (CIFY 1959). The Yi highly value the left. When a *bimo* holds a ceremony, he calls the souls of the ancestors with his left hand while he drives away evil spirits with his right hand. Some Yi literature recorded the ancient custom of handing things to ancestors, respected ones, seniors, and parents with the left hand, and to wild ghosts and belittled ones with the right hand. The Lolopo in Yunnan make ancestral tablets with the female on the left and the male on the right. All these data indicate that the left is considered better, stronger, and more positive than the right in Yi cosmology, and that the Yi relate the female to the left, the sun, and ancestors (Liu Yaohan 1985, 48–49).

The above discussion of cosmology may seem a digression from the subject of the Yi health care system, but it signifies the ideological and historical aspects of Yi culture. It is on this cultural ground that Yi developed their health beliefs, forged their interpretations of illnesses, and evaluated health care providers in each sector. These peoples' understanding and evaluation of different health care sectors affects what kind of health care they choose— how they make their decisions and act on them. Having examined these basic cosmological beliefs, we can now consider where the Yi seek medical help.

Sectors of the Health Care System

As far as health care is concerned, both Arthur Kleinman (1980) and Charles Good (1987) suggest that people choose methods from three different sectors. The popular sector, Kleinman states, can be seen as a matrix containing several levels: individual, family, social network, and community beliefs and activities. The traditional (folk) sector refers to medicine and is frequently classified into sacred and secular parts, but the division is often blurred in practice and the two usually overlap. The professional sector comprises the organized healing professions (Kleinman 1980, 50–59). In most societies, the later is simply biomedicine, as Good mentions in his definition, but in China this also includes mainstream traditional Chinese medicine.

The Popular Sector   Among most peoples in the world, the family is the first place to seek healing for illness and injury, an estimate of the seriousness of one's health problems, and help in making decisions for further treatment. Many people in Yi communities know at least some methods of curing an ailment or minor injury and are able to hold simple rituals for the purpose of healing illness. Commonly, the Yi people ask for medical help from neighbors or kin. Most ailments are actually handled within households. For example, to stop bleeding Yi apply a kind of efflorescent stone powder, a glue made from spider webs, or chicken feathers to the wound. To treat different kinds of pains, they use massage, steam, and/or single or combined herbal remedies. The Nuosu patrilineage plays an important role in preventing and curing illness in Liangshan. Some healing rituals involve a whole lineage: when a ritual is held to imprecate evil spirits or divine the agent who cast a spell on the patient, each family has a representative attending the ritual to join the chanting or shouting, because a collectivity will make this kind of ritual powerful. Hu Qingjun (1985) describes a sort of children's gathering called *axyi momge* in the Liangshan area. To halt a disease that was quickly spreading from village to village, all children of the village attended the meeting under the guardianship of their parents. This meeting, held by one of the headmen of the lineage, was actually an exorcism of the evil spirit that causes this disease. In this way, the lineage serves to manage children's health problems, both by decision making and ritual performance.

The Traditional Sector   The traditional sector of a health care system is classified by Kleinman (1980) as having both secular and sacred components. In Yi areas, the secular part includes herbalists, massagers, bonesetters, and midwives. Most of these healers inherit prescriptions from their older generations, as well as collect valid therapies through their own experiences. Some of them were recruited by the local government into the state-run township clinics after 1956.

The sacred components of the traditional sector of the Yi include mainly two kinds of healers: *bimo* and *sunyi*. *Bimo* are also called *baima, beima, abeima, bumo, xipo, xibo, duoxi*, and so on, depending on the dialect and translation. *Bimo* work as diviners, ritual practitioners, and healers who communicate with both natural and supernatural worlds. In the Yi language, *bimo* means "teacher" and "the one who knows." It is an office achieved rather than inherited, though it is important for a person to have *bimo* family or lineage background in order to become a powerful *bimo* (see Bamo Ayi, chapter 8 in this volume).

Of all kinds of knowledge preserved by *bimo*, medical theory and techniques have been sought most frequently. During a healing ritual, a *bimo* reads or recites ritual scriptures for hours, sometimes for a few days. He also makes sacrifices or sticks twigs into the ground symbolizing the way for the return of the patient's soul. As healers, some *bimo* also use herbal medicine or other healing techniques, such as massage. A *bimo* named Nurtiha was so good at massage that people called on him mainly for this, rather than for prayer, though he was also a very good ritual practitioner (Li Shikang 1995, 108).

Another kind of sacred healer is the *sunyi*. Unlike *bimo*, *sunyi* can be either male or female and need not be literate in Yi writing. *Sunyi* do not inherit the position and skills from their family or lineage members, nor is their education systematic like that of the *bimo*. However, they too must learn from experienced *sunyi* (Azi 1993, 11). Usually, those who become *sunyi* are people who have had the experience of suffering from mental illness. After recovering, they have a *bimo* divine for them and hand them a drum made of sheepskin, which is their major ritual implement. *Sunyi* drive evil spirits away from patients by beating the drum and by whirling and dancing with the whole body shivering while muttering chants of exorcism (Lin 1961, 127; Hu 1985). Although *bimo* and *sunyi* are different in many ways, their distinctions are blurred in practice. Usually *bimo* rituals are language-oriented, while *sunyi* rituals are performance-oriented; most practitioners conduct their kind only. However, some practitioners can perform both kinds of rituals. *Bimo* and *sunyi*, together with herbalists, have traditionally taken responsibility for protecting the health of Yi people.

The Professional Sector   Western missionaries introduced biomedicine to the Yi. The earliest hospitals in both Liangshan and Chuxiong were built by missionaries, who brought biomedical techniques into the areas where they were preaching, in the early twentieth century. Later, the Guomindang government established some biomedical facilities in cities and towns. By 1949, in the fourteen counties of Chuxiong prefecture there were 10 clinics, with a total of 20 beds and 47 medical personnel. Some people in the cities could reach the facilities if they wished, but before the establishment of the People's Republic of China in 1949 the Yi living in the uplands had much less access to the clinics (WLYG 1985; WCYG 1986), so biomedicine was of little importance to them as a means of resolving health problems.

It was the Chinese Communist Party state that made it possible for peasants in remote rural areas to use biomedical health care. After the Communist revolution, the state set up a medical network in the early 1950s reaching from the capital city to the villages. The People's Hospital of Chuxiong was established in 1951, and dispensaries in surrounding counties were gradually built. By 1984, there were 28 hospitals, 422 institutions of curing, protection, and immunization, 4,926 beds, and 6,466 health care personnel in Chuxiong Prefecture. In the rural areas, there were 151 dispensaries at the district level, with 1,785 health workers and 1,982 beds. At the village level, there were 1,044 medical stations and 1,949 village health workers. The rural area's lack of doctors and medicine has been changing over time.

The morbidity and mortality rates for infectious diseases diminished notably. For example, the morbidity rate of leprosy was .2 percent in 1962, but it was reduced to .046 percent by 1984, and the relevant medical institutions expect to reach the goal of eradicating leprosy by the end of this century. In the 1950s some vaccines began to be used, including smallpox vaccine, T.A.B. vaccine,[1] cholera vaccine, and bacillus Calmette-Guerin for tuberculosis. Since the 1960s, vaccines for polio, measles, and epidemic encephalitis have been used. The morbidity rate and breadth of epidemics of these diseases have been greatly reduced; special attention has also been paid to malaria, dysentery, and hepatitis. Health care for women and children has improved since 1953. The prefecture started to train midwives in new methods of delivery, and had retrained more than a hundred traditional midwives by 1954. By 1984, in Chuxiong Prefecture there were 749 rural midwives in addition to village health workers (WCYG 1986).

The biomedical sector is now organized in the following way: At the lowest level, the village, there is usually one health worker (known during the 1970s and 1980s as a barefoot doctor) who serves more than a thousand people. The most important responsibilities of this position are family planning, immunization, and sanitation. The village health workers treat ailments, perform first aid, and refer patients to higher-level medical facilities as well. At a higher level, there is the township clinic with several physicians, who are usually trained in a middle-level medical school. The physicians supervise the work of village health workers, perform family planning surgery, and treat patients with both biomedicine and Chinese medicine. Physicians at this level usually do not go to the villages; rather, patients come to see them. These physicians avoid, at least publicly, communicating with religious healers because clinics are seen as official, scientific institutions, while healers are private and seen by the state as "superstitious." Township physicians treat most diseases, but if the patient's situation is severe or requires surgery or mental health care, they refer the patient to a higher-level (county or prefecture) hospital, which has better equipment and doctors with medical degrees. In fact, very few patients are sent to provincial hospitals, because hospitals at the prefecture level are able to heal most diseases, and patients from rural areas usually cannot afford to pay for care far from home, even if it is necessary.

1. The vaccine for typhoid and paratyphoid A and B.

THE ROLE OF THE STATE AND
THE IMPLICATIONS OF THE RESEARCH

The Role of the State

Charles Keyes and his colleagues suggest that in Asia there is a general tendency to view ethnic, local, and religious identities as an obstacle during the process of nation-state building. They state, "The perpetuation of primordial identities was, indeed, seen by political leaders and social scientists alike as a fundamental problem in the development of modern nation-states" (Keyes, Hardacre, and Kendall 1994, 4). However, the basic differentiation of communist and capitalist ideologies, and the historical backgrounds of the nations, had different impacts on the medical practice of the people. Robert Thorp comments that, particularly in the case of the Chinese, creating a sense of national cultural identity requires persuading all of the non-Han peoples that they have a stake in the fate of the Han majority. If ethnic groups always place their "Chinese" citizenship behind their own ethnicity, the state will fragment (1992, 18–19).

The state knew this well and made great efforts to avoid letting it happen. The political leaders, just like the scientists, policy makers, and religious fundamentalists that Byron Good (1994) observed, see "a similar benefit from correct belief"; they have adopted the attitude that they will "get people to believe the right thing and our public health problems will be solved." The difference is that, compared with other nations trying to promote modernization and eliminate local religion, China has been particularly successful in forcing its policies all the way down to the village level; until the implementation of the economic and administrative reforms in the 1980s and 1990s, the government was able to officially stop local practices. This was mainly because the Chinese Communist Party was well organized and the Central Committee had greater control of the nation, from the top to the bottom, than many other parties and states in Asia. Policies were the tool by which the state directed the thoughts and actions of the nation, and the local officials disciplined the activities of people. Although freedom of religious belief has been guaranteed by the Constitution in China, the religious practices of the Yi, like those of many other ethnic groups, are not recognized as a religion *(zongjiao)*, but as superstition *(mixin)*. It therefore legitimated the action against Yi sacred healers and forced them to stop their practices for about thirty years (Qumo 1993, 148; Wang Linlu 1994, 150; Li Shikang 1995, 109). Their experiences with state-run health care services, the education program, and the campaign against "superstition" have together caused the Yi people and their religious specialists to make changes in their ideology and health care practices.

As a result, many Yi people now recognize and accept the efficacy of bio-medicine in curing infectious and many other diseases, as well as the importance of immunization and public hygiene. These changes, along with the elements of the Yi medical tradition that have remained in use during the process of new China's nation-building, reinforce the Yi idea of "double solution by divinity and medicine"—that is, the urge to use both healing rituals and medicines in their health care practices.

The content of ritual healing has also changed. In addition to the traditional concern of relationships with lineage members and relatives, there are new rites for helping local officials adjust their relationships with higher-level government and helping private car owners drive safely. Some ritual healers, especially those of the younger generation, are becoming interested in biomedicine and are even trying to learn biomedical methods of diagnosis and prescription to better control illness (Tang Chuchen, personal communication, 1994). Others, however, have hardly been able to shake off the nightmare of the campaign against them. Jike Zehuo, one of the most powerful *bimo* of the Jike lineage, published his autobiography before his death. In the book, perhaps fearfully, he continued to criticize himself for practicing harmful superstitious rituals and praised the Party for bringing liberation to him and the Yi as a whole (Jike 1990, 17, 31). Another *bimo* kept saying "praise the Communist Party and praise Mao Zedong" during an interview about his ritual activities (Quomo Yuozhi and Li Shikang, personal communication, 1994).

Ironically, after nearly two decades of economic reform, which the official news media claims is a great achievement of socialist modernization, the state is no longer able to control the country's widespread religious activities. I personally can attest to this. When I investigated economic reform in a Yi township ten years ago, the Yi were very hesitant to talk about the topic of ritual practice. Yet in 1995 and 1996, I ran into various ritual events in almost every village I visited during my pilot research and observed many rituals during my fieldwork. More dramatically, starting early in the 1980s, *bimo* began to be called "ethnic intellectuals" (*minzu zhishifenzi*) rather than "superstitious activists" (*mixin huodongzhe*) in Chuxiong and later in Liangshan. The number of *bimo* grew quickly after this. A special institute was established for studying *bimo* culture in Liangshan in 1996. One cannot help but ask why these changes happened.

Implications of the Research

The change in the Yi medical system we have been examining here is not a spontaneous process occurring in some isolated community. The Yi, though peripheral and remote, are part of Communist China and the global movement of modernization. The causes of change range widely from the development of the group itself to the influence of neighboring groups to the state and the state's intervention, which is the dominant cause. Its efforts in establishing health care networks in rural areas; training health care personnel of different levels; carrying on immunization, prevention, and family planning programs, together with the campaign against "superstition," have had a strong impact on health conceptualization and medical practices of the Yi. Their health-seeking behaviors have changed to some extent and their physical condition has improved.

People such as the Yi who live in remote areas, although constrained by their natural circumstances and the available means of communication with the broader outside world, are not as "stubborn" and "backward" as some political leaders and policy makers have perceived. In contrast to the presumed backwardness and ignorance, such people have developed methods of seeking knowledge about the world and resolving problems in their daily lives. These methods include divination and healing rituals, which are not ancient artifacts but a dynamic knowledge system. Many anecdotes demonstrate that these people are not narrow-minded at all. For example, almost all ethnographers in Africa, China, and other places have had the experience of villagers requesting biomedicine from them. These people accept new medicine and therapy as long as they see them to be helpful. When the immunization program in Chuxiong started in the early 1980s, it was difficult for health workers to locate the children who should have had the vaccines, because the scared mothers tried their best to avoid having their babies injected. Nowadays, a notice bearing the vaccine information and date is enough to attract enthusiastic parents who may walk many miles to bring their children to the health station to get the shots. Some ritual practitioners also accept new medicines and therapy. A young *bimo* in Dayao County, for instance, learned to use biomedicine while simultaneously performing healing rituals. Such examples show that these people are open to new information, knowledge, and techniques and accordingly adjust their behaviors to the changed environment.

Ironically, many well-educated people, including political leaders and policy makers in China, are not able to treat local healing rituals as openly as the Yi treat biomedicine and science. These officials are actually restrained by their ethnocentrism and desire for political power over Yi people. Byron Good argues that it is difficult to avoid the strong opinion that one's own system of knowledge is a progressive one (1994, 7). Similarly, when the state in China labels local ritual practices as superstition, this implies that the people are ignorant, backward, and uncivilized and therefore in need of education and direction. According to officials, the state had to replace these people's primordial tradition with scientific knowledge, to replace their "false beliefs" with "correct beliefs." Chinese political leaders have claimed that the scientific will defeat the superstitious, the advanced will defeat the backward, and the correct will defeat the wrong. That is why they have been confident that the Yi and other *minzu* would finally give up the "primordial" traditions and identify with the progressive nation-state. Now, facing the revival of Yi healing rituals and other religious activities, these officials are confronting the question, "What on earth is wrong: the argument about the final victory, or the judgment on the nature of local ritual practice, or both?" Anthropologists such as Good have realized the profoundly negative influence of the deeply felt assumption that claims superiority of the researcher over the researched, and they are trying to change this situation. However, quite a number of political leaders, policy makers, and scientists in China still cling to the ideas they had about this subject decades ago: they still call *minzu* healing rituals "crazy superstitious activities" and blame these rituals for disturbing the officially provided health care service.

Although the Chinese state is penetrative in terms of its power over Chinese people, and was especially so during the 1960s and 1970s, there has still been space for ritual practitioners to survive under its rule. This basically results from the Party's own nature. The policies of the state are not always consistent. In Yi areas, the campaign against "superstition" started officially in the early 1950s, and, as I noted, *bimo* were not allowed to practice openly for about thirty years. However, they were not always persecuted in the same way. In fact, most never stopped holding rituals, such as "guiding the way for the deceased" and healing rituals, at the request of villagers in the rural areas, though the rituals were of smaller size—less complex and with fewer attendees—and shorter than those held before the prohibition.

Discussing the situation in rural China, Ann Anagnost suggests that the "campaign against superstition" has not been a ceaseless but rather a fitful impulse. The consequence of this practice has been an intermittent policing that "must be read . . . within its wider political context" (1994, 227). One cannot discuss government policy in China without considering the internal situation of the Chinese Communist Party. The policies reflect the outcomes of factional struggles within the Party. How local governments interpret and carry on the policies also makes a difference. In recent years, local governments have seen the advantages that cultural tradition may bring: economic benefits such as making local strengths visible, appealing to tourists, and the possibility of attracting investments from developed areas of both China and overseas. As a result, Yi *bimo* were transformed from "superstitious specialists" to "ethnic intellectuals," and some were even recruited into local social-science research institutions. Their status and treatment were changed by what Anagnost called "the power of naming" (ibid., 228), not for their good but for the political needs of the state.

CONCLUSION

In an attempt to obtain a better understanding of change and continuity in the Yi health care system in contemporary China, I have examined Yi medical experiences and relevant issues in light of medical anthropology literature generally. The existence and development of Yi medical tradition is indeed "the triumph of practicality," as Stella Quah has called the prosperity of traditional healing in Asia (1989). As far as the Yi health care system is concerned, the government-sponsored biomedical service compensated for the lack of this element in local health care systems. The modifications that the Yi made in their traditional practice updated their ability to deal with current problems. Therefore, Yi medical practice is doing well, rather than dying out. The Yi might not have intentionally done anything counter-hegemonic, but the rituals' importance lies, as Anagnost puts it, in "their ability to disrupt the totalizing claims of power," so that "the little resistances of everyday life are not readily visible, yet they do subvert the values and symbolic order of a totalizing structure of power" (1994, 247).

REFERENCES

Afonja, Simi

1980   "Current Explanations of Sex Inequality: A Reconsideration." *Nigerian Journal of Economic and Social Studies* 21 (2): 198–209.

Ahmed, Iftikhar, ed.

1985   *Technology and Rural Women: Conceptual and Empirical Issues.* London: Allen and Unwin.

Alting Von Geusau, Leo

1983   "Dialectics of Akhazang: The Interiorizations of a Perennial Minority Group." In *Highlanders of Thailand,* ed. John McKinnon and Wanat Bhruksasri, 241–78. Kuala Lumpur: Oxford University Press.

Anagnost, Ann S.

1994   "The Politics of Ritual Displacement." In *Asian Visions of Authority: Religion and the Modern States of East and Southeast Asia,* ed. Charles F. Keyes, Laurel Kendall, and Helen Hardacre, 221–54. Honolulu: University of Hawaii Press.

Anderson, Benedict

1991   *Imagined Communities: Reflections on the Origin and Spread of Nationalism.* 2nd ed. New York: Verso Press.

Ang Zhiling

1986   "Sani yu gaikuang" (A survey of Sani language). *Lunan wenshi ziliao xuanji* 2:1–9.

Ang Ziming, ed.

1996   *Lunan Yizu Mizhi jie yishi geyishu* (Translations of the Lunan Yi nationality "Mizhi" Festival ritual songs). Kunming: Yunnan minzu chubanshe.

Appadurai, Arjun

1992   "Putting Hierarchy in Its Place." In *Reading Cultural Anthropology,* ed. George Marcus, 34–47. Durham: Duke University Press.

Aron, Raymond
1962   *Paix et guerre entre les nations.* Paris: Calmann-Levy.
Azi Ayue
1993   *Yizu yiyao* (Yi medicine). Beijing: Zhongguo yiliao kexue jizhu chubanshe.
Bai Xianyun, ed.
1995   *Yi Han zi dian* (A Yi-Chinese dictionary). Kunming: Yunnan minzu chubanshe.
Bamo Ayi
1994   *Yizu zuling xinyang yanjiu* (Research on ancestral spirit beliefs of the Yi). Chengdu: Sichuan minzu chubanshe.
1996   "Ryoosan bimo kaisoo no tokuchoo no shiron" (A preliminary discussion of the characteristics of the *bimo* social stratum of Liangshan). *Hikaku minzoku kenkyu* (Tsukuba) 3:193–217.
Barth, Fredrik
1969   Introduction to *Ethnic Groups and Boundaries: The Social Organization of Culture Difference,* ed. Fredrik Barth, 9–38. Boston: Little, Brown.
Bboshy Zhyxti et al.
1990   *Gamop atnyop.* Chengdu: Sichuan minzu chubanshe.
Bentley, G. Carter
1987   "Ethnicity and Practice." *Comparative Studies in Society and History* 29 (1): 24–55.
Bi Zhiguan
1989   "Saniren de yuanyuan chutan" (An initial examination of Sani people's origins). *Lunan wenshi ziliao xuanji* 4:32–44.
Bloch, Maurice
1986   *From Blessing to Violence: History and Ideology in the Circumcision Ritual of the Merina of Madagascar.* Cambridge: Cambridge University Press.
Boserup, Ester
1970   *Women's Role in Economic Development.* New York: St. Martin's Press.
Bourdieu, Pierre
1977   *Outline of a Theory of Practice,* trans. R. Nice. Switzerland: Librairie Droz, S.A., 1972. Reprint, Cambridge: Cambridge University Press.
Bradley, David
1979   *Proto-Loloish.* Scandinavian Institute of Asian Studies Monograph Series 39. London: Curzon Press.
1990a   "Language Planning for China's Minorities: The Yi Branch." In *A World of Language: Presented to Professor S. A. Wurm on His 65th Birthday,* ed. D. Laycock and W. Winter, 81–89. Canberra: Department of Linguistics, Australian National University.
1990b   "The Status of the 44 Tone in Nosu." *La Trobe Working Papers in Linguistics* 3:125–37; also (in Chinese) in Proceedings of the International Yi Linguistics Conference, Xichang, 1991.
1994a   "Building Identity and the Modernisation of Language: Minority Language Policy in Thailand and China." In *Modernity and Identity: Asian illustrations,* ed. A. Gomes, 192–205. Bundoora: La Trobe University Press.

1994b   *A Dictionary of the Northern Dialect of Lisu: China and Southeast Asia.* Pacific Linguistics C-126. Canberra: Australian National University.
1997   "Onomastic, Orthographic, Dialectal, and Dialectical Borders: The Lisu and the Lahu." *Asia Pacific Viewpoints* 38 (2): 107–17.
n.d.   "The Yi Nationality of Southwestern China: A Linguistic Overview." Bundoora: La Trobe University Press.

Bradley, David, Maya Bradley, and Li Yongxiang
1997   "The Sanyie of Kunming: A Case of Yi Language Death." Paper presented to the 30th International Sino-Tibetan Languages and Linguistics Conference, Beijing.

Bradley, David, and Daniel Kane
1981   "Lisu Orthographies." *Working Papers in Linguistics, University of Melbourne* 7:23–38.

Butuo County
n.d.   *Minjian wenxue san tao jicheng: Butuo xian juan* (Three sets of collected folk literature: Butuo chapter). Butuo: Butuo County.

Cancian, Frank
1965   *Economics and Prestige in a Maya Community: The Religious Cargo System in Zinacantan.* Stanford: Stanford University Press.
1992   *The Decline of Community in Zinacantan: Economy, Public Life, and Social Stratification, 1960–1987.* Stanford: Stanford University Press.

Carsten, Janet, and Stephen Hugh-Jones, eds.
1995   *About the House: Lévi-Strauss and Beyond.* Cambridge: Cambridge University Press.

Chen Shilin, Bian Shiming, and Li Xiuqing, eds.
1985   *Yiyu jianzhi* (A brief ethnography of Yi language). Beijing: Minzu chubanshe.

Chen Tianjun
1987   "Lun Yizu gushi fenqi" (Discussion of the periodization of ancient Yi history). In *Xinan minzu yanjiu, Yizu zhuanji* (Research on southwestern *minzu,* Yi special collection), ed. Zhongguo xinan minzu yanjiu hui, 107–19. Kunming: Yunnan renmin chubanshe.

Chen Xiangsen
1994   "Mohong Yiqu wu chaosheng" (No over-quota births in the Yi area of Mohong). *Minzu* 10:44.

CIFY (Chuxiong Investigative Team for Folk Literature in Yunnan Province)
1959   *Meiguo* (A Yi myth). Kunming: Yunnan renmin chubanshe.

Cohen, Myron L.
1990   "Lineage Organization in North China." *Journal of Asian Studies* 49 (3):509–34.

Comaroff, John, and Jean Comaroff
1992   *Ethnography and the Historical Imagination.* Boulder, Colo.: Westview Press.

Combs-Schilling, M. E.
1989   *Sacred Performances: Islam, Sexuality, and Sacrifice.* New York: Columbia University Press.

Constitution of the People's Republic of China
1986   Beijing: Falü chubanshe.

Croll, Elizabeth
    1983   *Chinese Women since Mao.* London: Zed Books; Armonk, N.Y.: M. E. Sharpe.
CYZZ (*Chuxiong Yizu Zizhizhou zhi* Writing Group)
    1993   *Chuxiong Yizu Zizhizhou zhi* (Chuxiong Yi Autonomous Prefecture gazetteer). Vol. 1. Beijing: Renmin chubanshe.
    1994   *Chuxiong Yizu Zizhizhou zhi* (Chuxiong Yi Autonomous Prefecture gazetteer). Vol. 2. Beijing: Renmin chubanshe.
Dauber, Roslyn, and Melinda L. Cain, eds.
    1981   *Women and Technological Change in Developing Countries.* Boulder, Colo.: Westview Press.
Diamond, Norma
    1988   "The Miao and Poison: Interactions on China's Southwest Frontier." *Ethnology* 27:1–25.
Dikötter, Frank
    1992   *The Discourse of Race in Modern China.* London: Hurst and Company.
d'Ollone, H. M. G.
    1912   *Ecritures des peuples non chinois de la chine: Quatre dictionnaires Lolo et Miao Tseu.* Paris: Leroux.
Dreyer, June Teufel
    1976   *China's Forty Millions.* Cambridge: Harvard University Press.
Du Shanshan
    1992   "Western Biases in the Gender Dichotomy in Feminist Anthropology: The Case of the Lahu of Southwest China." Paper presented at the 91st American Anthropological Association Annual Meeting, San Francisco.
Du Yuting
    1984   "Yunnan Xiao Liangshan Yizu de nuli zhidu" (The Yi slave system in Xiao Liangshan, Yunnan). In *Yunnan Xiao Liangshan Yizu shehui lishi diaocha* (Investigations into the history of Yi society in Yunnan's Xiao Liangshan), 1–24. Kunming: Yunnan renmin chubanshe.
Durrenberger, Edward Paul
    1971   "The Ethnography of Lisu Curing." Ph.D. diss., Department of Anthropology, University of Illinois at Urbana-Champaign.
    1983   "Lisu: Political Form, Ideology, and Economic Action." In *Highlanders of Thailand,* ed. John McKinnon and Wanat Bhruksasri, 215–26. Kuala Lumpur: Oxford University Press.
EGSP (Editing Group of Sichuan Province)
    1985   *Sichuansheng Liangshan Yizu shehui lishi diaocha* (Sociohistorical investigation on the Yi in Liangshan of Sichuan Province). Chengdu: Sichuan shehui kexue yuan.
Enwall, Joakim
    1994   *A Myth Become Reality: History and Development of the Miao Written Language.* Stockholm East Asian Monographs, no. 5. Stockholm: Institute of Oriental Languages, Stockholm University.
Erickson, Frederick
    1987   "Transformation and School Success: The Politics and Culture of

Educational Achievement." *Anthropology and Education Quarterly* 18:335–56.

Fang Guoyu
1984   *Yizushi gao* (Draft history of the Yi). Chengdu: Sichuan minzu chubanshe.

Fang Ho
1939   "Lunan Sani Axi er zu xianji" (Communities in two groups: Lunan Sani and Axi). *Yi shi bao* (Nanjing), 24 July.

Fei, Xiaotong
1981   *Toward a People's Anthropology.* Beijing: Renmin chubanshe.

Feng Yuanwei, ed.
1986   *Le'e teyi* (*Hnewo teyy,* The book of creation). Chengdu: Sichuan minzu chubanshe.

Fordham, Signithia
1996   *Blacked Out: Dilemmas of Race, Identity, and Success at Capital High.* Chicago: University of Chicago Press.

Fortes, Meyer
1953   "The Structure of Unilineal Descent Groups." *American Anthropologist* 55 (1): 17–41.

Foucault, Michel
1984   "Truth and Power." In *The Foucault Reader,* ed. Paul Rabinow, 51–75. 1977. Reprint, New York: Pantheon.

Freedman, Maurice
1958   *Lineage Organization in Southeastern China.* New York: Humanities Press.

1966   *Chinese Lineage and Society.* New York: Humanities Press.

Fried, Morton H.
1967   *The Evolution of Political Society.* New York: Random House.

Fu Maoji
1998   "A Descriptive Grammar of Lolo." *Linguistics of the Tibeto-Burman Area,* no. 20:1–242.

Gaha Shizhe
1996   "Meigu Yizu bimo de jianjie" (A brief introduction to the *bimo* of Meigu). In *Meigu Yizu bimo diaocha yanjiu* (Investigation and research into the *bimo* of Meigu), ed. Shama Guri, Gaha Shizhe, and Moxi Zihuo. Meigu: Meigu Yizu bimo wenhua yanjiu zhongxin.

Gailey, Christine Ward
1987   *Kinship to Kingship: Gender Hierarchy and State Formation in the Tongan Islands.* Austin: University of Texas Press.

Ggelu Asa
1986   *Hoyi Ddiggur.* Chengdu: Sichuan minzu chubanshe.

GINS (Guizhou Institute of Nationality Studies)
1982   *Xinan Yi zhi xuan* (Selections from the *Record of Southwestern Yi*). Guiyang: Guizhou People's Press.

Gladney, Dru
1991   *Muslim Chinese: Ethnic Nationalism in the People's Republic.* Cambridge: Council on East Asian Studies, Harvard University.

1994   "Representing Nationality in China: Refiguring Majority/Minority Identities." *Journal of Asian Studies* 53 (1): 92–123.

Good, Byron J.
1994   *Medicine, Rationality, and Experience: An Anthropological Perspective.* Cambridge: Cambridge University Press.

Good, Charles M.
1987   *Ethnomedical Systems in Africa: Patterns of Traditional Medicine in Rural and Urban Kenya.* New York: Guilford Press.

Goodman, Bryna
1995   *Native Place, City, and Nation: Regional Networks and Identities in Shanghai, 1953–1937.* Berkeley and Los Angeles: University of California Press.

Gu Yanwu
1831   *Tianxia junguo libing shu* (The book of strengths and weaknesses of (Late 17th c.) regions around the empire), ed. Long Wanyu. Chengdu: Xie tang.

Gugler, Josef, and William Flanagan
1978   *Urbanisation and Social Change in West Africa.* Cambridge: Cambridge University Press.

Guidieri, Remo, Francesco Pellizzi, and Stanley Tambiah, eds.
1988   *Ethnicities and Nations: Process and Inter-Ethnic Relations in Latin America, South Asia, and the Pacific.* Austin: University of Texas Press.

Guizhou Nationalities Commission
1982–83   *Guizhou Trial Yi Textbooks* (in Guizhou Yi [eight varieties] and Chinese). 6 vols. Guiyang: Guizhou Nationalities Commission.
1984   *Yi Literacy Textbook* (in Guizhou Yi [ten varieties] and Chinese). Guiyang: Guizhou Nationalities Commission.

Guldin, Gregory
1994   *The Saga of Anthropology in China: From Malinowski to Moscow to Mao.* Armonk: M. E. Sharpe.

Guo Ji and Ding Ha
1984   *Selected Ancient Records of Migrations of the Six Clans of Yi* (in Chinese and Yi [4 varieties]). 6 vols. Beijing: Central Institute of Nationalities.

Guo Sijiu and Tao Xueliang
1981   *Chamu* (A Yi myth). Kunming: Yunnan renmin chubanshe.

Guo Xie and Xi Zuanxiu, eds.
1924   *Yanfeng Xian zhi* (Yanfeng County gazetteer). Kunming: Yunnan kaizhi gongsi.

Harrell, Stevan
1982   *Ploughshare Village: Culture and Context in Taiwan.* Seattle: University of Washington Press.
1989   "Ethnicity and Kin Terms among Two Kinds of Yi." In *Ethnicity and Ethnic Groups in China,* ed. Chien Chiao and Nicholas Tapp, 179–97. Hong Kong: New Asia College.
1990   "Ethnicity, Local Interests, and the State: Yi Communities in Southwest China." *Comparative Studies in Society and History* 32:515–48.
1993   "Linguistics and Hegemony in China." *International Journal of the Sociology of Language* 103:97–114.

1995a   "Introduction: Civilizing Projects and the Reaction to Them." In *Cultural Encounters on China's Ethnic Frontiers,* ed. Stevan Harrell, 3–36. Seattle: University of Washington Press.

1995b   "The History of the History of the Yi." In *Cultural Encounters on China's Ethnic Frontiers,* ed. Stevan Harrell, 63–91. Seattle: University of Washington Press.

1996a   "Languages Defining Ethnicity in Southwest China." In *Ethnic Identity,* ed. Lola Romanucci-Ross and George DeVos, 97–114. 3rd ed. Walnut Creek, Calif.: Alta Mira Press.

1996b   "The Nationalities Question and the Prmi Prblem [sic]." In *Negotiating Ethnicities in China and Taiwan,* ed. Melissa J. Brown, 2–23. Berkeley: Institute for East Asian Studies, University of California.

1997   *Human Families.* Boulder, Colo.: Westview Press.

In Press   *Ways of Being Ethnic in Southwest China.* Seattle: University of Washington Press. (Forthcoming 2001.)

Harrell, Stevan, ed.

1995   *Cultural Encounters on China's Ethnic Frontiers.* Seattle: University of Washington Press.

1996   *Chinese Historical Micro-Demography.* Berkeley and Los Angeles: University of California Press.

Harrell, Stevan, and Bamo Ayi

1998   "Combining Ethnic Heritage and National Unity: A Paradox of Nuosu (Yi) Language Textbooks in China." *Bulletin of the Concerned Asian Scholars* 30 (2): 62–71.

Haviland, John

1977   *Gossip, Reputation, and Knowledge in Zinacantan.* Chicago: University of Chicago Press.

Haynes, Jeff

1994   *Religion in Third World Politics.* Boulder, Colo.: Lynne Rienner.

He Mingwei

1996   "Liangshan zhou minzu ganbu xianzhuang he xuqiu yuce yanjiu" (Research into the present situation and the demands of minority cadres in Liangshan Prefecture). *Minzu yuanjiu* 3:10–18.

He Yaohua

1994   "Lunan minzu guanxi de lishi he xianzhuang" (The history and status quo of national relations in Lunan). *Yunnan shehui kexue* 6:40–56.

Heberer, Thomas

1984a   "Gesetz über die Gebietsautonomie der Nationalitäten der VR China" (The PRC law on local autonomy of nationalities). *China Aktuell* (October): 609.

1984b   *Nationalitätenpolitik und Entwicklungspolitik in den Gebieten nationaler Minderheiten in China* (Nationality policy and development policy in national minority areas of China). Bremen: Universität Bremen, Beiträge zur Geographie und Raumplanung.

1989   *China and Its National Minorities: Autonomy or Assimilation?* Armonk: M. E. Sharpe.

Herman, John
1997 "Empire in the Southwest: Early Qing Reforms to the Native Chieftain System." *Journal of Asian Studies* 56 (1): 47–74.

HIFY (Honghe Investigative Team for Folk Literature in Yunnan Province)
1978 *Axi de xianji* (The ancestors of the Axi). Kunming: Yunnan minzu chubanshe.

Honig, Emily
1992 *Creating Chinese Ethnicity: Subei People in Shanghai, 1850–1980.* New Haven: Yale University Press.

Honig, Emily, and Gail Hershatter
1988 *Personal Voices: Chinese Women in the 1980's.* Stanford: Stanford University Press.

Hsu, Francis L. K.
1967 *Under the Ancestors' Shadow: Kinship, Personality, and Social Mobility in China.* Stanford: Stanford University Press.

Hu Qingjun
1955 "Da Liangshan Yizu shehui gaikuang" (The social situation of the Yi in Greater Liangshan). In *Zhongguo minzu yanjiu jikan.* Vol. 2. Beijing: Zhongyang minzu xueyuan yanjiu bu.

1981 *Ming-Qing Yizu shehuishi luncong* (Essay on the social history of the Yi in the Ming and Qing). Shanghai: Shanghai renmin chubanshe.

1985 *Liangshan Yizu nulizhi shehui xingtai* (The social structure of the Liangshan Yi slave system). Beijing: Zhongguo shehui kexue chubanshe.

Huang Kaihua
1968 "Mingdai tusi zhidu sheshi yu xinan kaifa" (The opening of the southwest and the establishment of the native chieftain system during the Ming Dynasty). In *Mingdai tusi zhidu* (The native chieftain system during the Ming dynasty), ed. Y. She. Taipei: Taiwan xuesheng shuju.

Jiang Liu, Lu Xueyi, and Dan Tianchen, eds.
1994 *1993–94 Nian Zhongguo: Shehui xingshi fenxi yu yuce* (China in 1993–94: The situation and prognosis for society). Beijing: Zhongguo tongji chubanshe.

Jiang Yongxing
1985 "Cong Guizhou minzu shibie gongzuo tanqi" (Discussion on the basis of Guizhou's ethnic identification work). *Minzu yanjiu jikan* (Guangxi) 2:303–16.

Jiemei Yi xue yanjiu xiao zu (The Three Sisters' Yi Studies Research Group)
1992 *Yizu fengsu shi* (Records of Yi customs). Beijing: Central Institute of Nationalities Press.

Jike Erda Zehuo
1990 *Wo zai shengui zhijian: Yige Yizu jisi de zishu* (I among the spirits: An autobiography of an Yi priest). Kunming: Yunnan renmin chubanshe.

Jin Guoku et al., eds.
1983 *Concise Yi-Han Dictionary* (in Chinese and Sani). Kunming: Yunnan minzu chubanshe.

Jjissyt Dalyt
1980   *Hnewo teyy* (The book of creation). Chengdu: Sichuan minzu
             chubanshe.

Kane, Daniel
1997   "Language Death and Language Revivalism: The Case of Manchu."
             Central Asiatic Journal 41 (2): 231–49.

Keane, Webb
1995   "The Spoken House: Text, Act, and Object in Eastern Indonesia."
             American Ethnologist 22 (1): 102–24.

Keesing, Roger M.
1975   *Kin Groups and Social Structure.* New York: Holt, Rinehart, and Winston.

Keyes, Charles F.
1976   "Toward a New Formulation of the Concept of Ethnic Group." *Eth-
             nicity* 3:203–13.

Keyes, Charles F., Helen Hardacre, and Laurel Kendall
1994   "Introduction: Contested Visions of Community in East and South-
             east Asia." In *Asian Visions of Authority: Religion and the Modern States
             of East and Southeast Asia,* ed. Charles F. Keyes, Laurel Kendall, and
             Helen Hardacre. Honolulu: University of Hawaii Press.

Kleinman, Arthur
1980   *Patients and Healers in the Context of Culture: An Exploration of the Border-
             land between Anthropology, Medicine, and Psychiatry.* Berkeley and Los
             Angeles: University of California Press.

Kligman, Gail
1988   *The Wedding of the Dead: Ritual, Poetics, and Popular Culture in Tran-
             sylvania.* Berkeley and Los Angeles: University of California Press.

Lai Yi and Mujie Keha
1996   "Xianshi de minzu xin wenti" (Real new ethnic problems). *Xinan
             Minzu Xueyuan xuebao* 5:66–72.

Lary, Diana
1996   "The Tomb of the King of Nanyue: The Contemporary Agenda of
             History." *Modern China* 22 (1): 3–27.

Leach, Edmund
1954   *Political Systems of Highland Burma.* London: Athlone Press.

Lehman, F. K.
1967   "Ethnic Categories in Burma and the Theory of Social Systems." In
             Southeast Asian Tribes, Minorities, and Nations, ed. Peter Kunstadter,
             93–124. Princeton: Princeton University Press.

Lei Chin-liu
1944   "Yunnan Chengjiang Luoluo de zuxian chongbai" (Ancestor worship
             of the Lolo in Chengjiang, Yunnan). *Bianzheng gonglun* 3 (9): 31–36.

Leibo
1796–1820 *Leibo Ting Zhi* (Gazetteer of Leibuo Subprefecture) (Jiaqing Period).
             N.p.

Leng Guangdian
1983   *Vonre* (The snow clan). Chengdu: Sichuan minzu yanjiu suo.

1988   *Yi wangxi Yige Yizu tusi de zixu* (Retrospection of the past: Autobi-
            ography of a Yi *tusi*). Kunming: Yunnan renmin chubanshe.

Lévi-Strauss, Claude
1983   *The Way of the Masks,* trans. S. Modelski. London: Jonathan Cape.
1984   *Paroles données.* Paris: Plon.

Lewis, Paul, and Elaine Lewis
1984   *Peoples of the Golden Triangle: Six Tribes in Thailand.* London: Thames
            and Hudson.

Li Guantian, ed.
1960   *Ashima.* Kunming: Yunnan renmin chubanshe.

Li Li, et al.
1993   "Maitou kugan zhong shixiao, shanggu kanhao 'Ashima'" (Paying
            attention to efficiency, merchants think they will benefit from
            "Ashima"). *Yunnan ribao,* 6 March.

Li Min and Ma Ming
1983   *Liangshan Yiyu yuyin gailun* (Introduction to the Yi phonetics of Liang-
            shan). Chengdu: Sichuan renmin chubanshe.

Li Shaoming
1986   "Lun Chuan-Dian bianjiang Nari ren de zushu" (Discussion of the
            ethnic categorization of the Nari people of the Sichuan-Yunnan bor-
            der area). *New Asia Academic Bulletin* 6:279–90.

1992   "Lun min gai qian Liangshan Yizu shehui de dengji jiegou" (On the
            structure of ranking in Liangshan Yi society before democratic re-
            forms). *Liangshan minzu yanjiu* 1:65–72.

Li Shikang
1995   *Yiwu liezhuan* (Biographies of Yi priests). Kunming: Yunnan renmin
            chubanshe.

Li Shiyu
1990   "Luelun tusi zhidu yu gaitu guiliu" (A brief discussion of the native
            chieftain system and bureaucratic consolidation). In *Zhongguo gudai
            bianjiang zhengce yanjiu,* ed. Ma Dazheng. Beijing: Zhongguo shehui
            kexue chubanshe.

Li Xingxing
1994   "Chuan-Dian bian 'Nari' ren zucheng wenti de youlai yu xianzhuang"
            (The history and current status of the question of the ethnonym of
            the "Nari" people of the Sichuan-Yunnan border). *Minzu yanjiu dong-
            tai,* no. 1:7–11.

Li Yihui, ed.
1993   *Sichuan Sheng minzu zizhi difang fazhan yanjiu* (Research into devel-
            opment in minority autonomous areas of Sichuan). Chengdu: Si-
            chuan minzu chubanshe.

Li Zhongfang
1994   "Shehuizhuyi shiqi Liangshan Yizu bimo jianxi" (A simplified analy-
            sis of the *bimo* of Liangshan in the socialist period). *Xinan minzu
            xueyuan xuebao* 4:30–36.

Liang Zhaotao, Chen Qixin, and Yang Heshu, eds.
1985   *Zhongguo minzuxue gailun* (Introduction to Chinese ethnology). Kun-
          ming: Yunnan renmin chubanshe.
Liangshan Prefecture Education Commission
1994a   "Gongzuo zong jie" (Work summary). Unpublished educational doc-
          ument. 12 pages.
1994b   "Liangshan Zhou jiaoyu zai fazhan qianjin" (Liangshan Prefecture
          educational advances). Unpublished educational document. 5 pages.
1994c   "Mama de nüer yao du shu" (Mama's daughter wants to go to school).
          Unpublished educational document. 8 pages.
Liangshan Yizu Zizhizhou (Liangshan Yi Autonomous Prefecture)
1991   "Liangshan Yizu Zizhizhou zizhi tiaolie" (Autonomy articles of the
          Liangshan Yi Autonomous Prefecture). In *Sichuan minzu fagui huibian,*
          comp. *Sichuan minzu,* 38–56. Chengdu: Sichuan minzu chubanshe.
"Liangshan Yizu Zizhizhou jihua shengyu banfa" (Methods of birth planning in Liang
shan Yi Autonomous Prefecture).
1991   In *Sichuan minzu fagui huibian,* comp. Sichuan minzu, 122–30. Cheng-
          du: Sichuan minzu chubanshe.
Lietard, Alfred
1904   "Le District des Lolos A-chi." *Les Missions Catholiques* 36:93–96;
          105–108; 117–120.
Lin Yaohua (Lin Yueh-hwa)
1961   *Lolo of Liang Shan* (Translation of *Liangshan Yijia*). New Haven: HRAF
          Press.
1963   "'Guanyu minzu yici de shiyong he yiming de wenti'" (On the prob-
          lem of the uses and synonyms of the term *minzu*). *Lishi yanjiu* 2:175.
1987   "Zhongguo xinan diqu de minzu shibie" (Ethnic identification in the
          southwest Chinese area). In *Yunnan shaoshu minzu shehui lishi diaocha
          ziliao huibian* (Collection of materials from historical and sociologi-
          cal investigations of minority nationalities in Yunnan). Kunming:
          Yunnan renmin chubanshe.
1990   New China's Ethnology: Research and Prospects. In *Anthropology in
          China: Defining the Discipline,* ed. Gregory Eliyu Guldin. Armonk, N.Y.:
          M. E. Sharpe.
Lin Yaohua and Jin Tianming
1980   "Cong lishi fazhan kan dangqian woguo minzuxue de duixiang he
          renwu" (The tasks and goals of our country's ethnology from the per-
          spective of historical development). *Minzu yanjiu* 2:50–57.
Lipman, Jonathan N.
1998   *Familiar Strangers: A History of Muslims in Northwest China.* Seattle: Uni-
          versity of Washington Press.
Litzinger, Ralph A.
1995   "Making Histories: Contending Conceptions of the Yao Past." In *Cul-
          tural Encounters on China's Ethnic Frontiers,* ed. Stevan Harrell, 117–39.
          Seattle: University of Washington Press.

Liu Hongkang, ed.
1988   *Zhongguo renkou, Sichuan fence* (China's population, Sichuan volume).
          Beijing: Zhongguo caizheng jing ji chubanshe.
Liu Jiahe
1963   *Spartan.* Series Books of Foreign History. Beijing: Commercial Press
          (in Chinese).
Liu, Lydia
1993   "Translingual Practice: The Discourse of Individualism between
          China and the West." *positions* 1 (1): 160–93.
Liu Xiaoxing
1990   *Muti chongbai: Yizu zulinghulu suyuan* (The worship of mother's body:
          Seeking the source for using the calabash as Yi people's memorial
          tablet of ancestors). Kunming: Yunnan renmin chubanshe.
Liu Yaohan
1980   *Yizu shehui lishi diaochayanjiu wenji* (A collection of papers on histor-
          ical investigation of Yi society). Beijing: Minzu chubanshe.
1984   *Yizu tianwenxue shi* (A history of Yi astrology). Kunming: Yunnan ren-
          min chubanshe.
1985   *Zhongguo wenming yuantou xintan* (A new approach to the origin of
          Chinese civilization). Kunming: Yunnan renmin chubanshe.
Liu Yaohan and Lu Yang
1986   *Wenming Zhongguo de Yizu shiyue li* (Civilized China's ten-month Yi cal-
          endar). Kunming: Yunnan renmin chubanshe.
Long Jianmin
1987   "Lishi de yueshu" (Restriction of history). In *Yizu wenhua* (Yi culture),
          195–209. Chuxiong: Yizu wenhua yanjiu suo.
Long Xianjun
1993   *Zhongguo Yizu tongshi gangyao* (An outline of the comprehensive his-
          tory of the Yi nationality in China). Kunming: Yunnan minzu
          chubanshe.
Long Zhiji et al.
1991   *Concise Yi-Chinese Dictionary* (in Guizhou Yi [four varieties] and Chi-
          nese). Guiyang: Guizhou minzu chubanshe.
Lowie, Robert H.
1929   *Are We Civilized?* New York: Harcourt, Brace, and Company.
Lü Qing
1996   "Shilun minzu shehuixue de yanjiu keti" (An attempted discussion
          of the research project of ethnosociology). *Xibei minzu xueyuan xue-
          bao* 1:59–65.
Lunan Yizu Zizhixian (Lunan Yi Autonomous County)
1986   *Lunan Yizu Zizhixian gaikuang* (General description of Lunan Yi Auto-
          nomous County). Kunming: Yunnan minzu chubanshe.
1989   *Yunnan Sheng Lunan Yizu Zizhixian dimingzhi* (Gazetteer of Lunan
          Yi Autonomous County). Lunan: Lunan Yizu Zizhixian renmin
          chubanshe.
1996   *Lunan Yizu Zizhixian zhi.* Kunming: Yunnan minzu chubanshe.

Luo Guoyi, and Ying Chen
1984   *Yuzhou renwen lun* (On the universe and humanity). Beijing: Minzu chubanshe.

Luohong Rongzhi
1996   "Lun Yizu de zicheng he tuteng jiqi guanxi" (On the Yi's names for themselves and their relation to totemism). *Xinan minzu xueyuan xuebao* 1:88–91.

Ma Erzi
1992   "Qiantan Liangshan Yizu Degu" (A superficial discussion of the *Ndeggu* of the Liangshan Yi). *Liangshan minzu yanjiu* 1:99–107.

1993   "Dui jiu Liangshan Yizu shehui jiegoude zai renshi ji 'Heiyi' 'Baiyi' de bianxi" (On a reexamination of the social structure of old Liangshan, and of the distinction between "Black Yi" and "White Yi"). *Liangshan minzu yanjiu* 2:38–48.

Ma Erzi and Qubi Shimci
1996   "Chuugoku Kyuu Ryoosan Yizoku ni okeru kashi inseki no satsujin to sono jirei ni kansuru kosatsu." *Hikaku minzoku kenkyu* 3:177–92.

Ma Xueliang
1943   "Exorcism, a Custom of the Black Lolo." *Bianzheng gonglun* (Frontier affairs) 3 (9): 27–30.

1948   "Explanation and Annotation of the Luoluo Text for Performing Ritual" (in Nasu and Chinese), 14:341–55 ff. Beijing: Chinese Academy of Science.

1951   *Sani Yiyu yanjiu* (Research on the Sani Yi language). Yuyanxue zhuankan, no. 2. Beijing: Chinese Academy of Sciences.

1992   *Minzu yanjiu wenji* (Collected works on nationalities research). Beijing: Minzu chubanshe.

Ma Xueliang, with Ang Zhiling, Li Hongwen, and Mei Yu
1985   *Nimishi.* Kunming: Yunnan minzu chubanshe.

Ma Yin
1984   *Zhongguo shaoshu minzu* (China's minority nationalities). Beijing: Renmin chubanshe.

1989   *China's Minority Nationalities.* Beijing: Foreign Languages Press.

Mackerras, Colin
1994   *China's Minorities: Integration and Modernization in the Twentieth Century.* Hong Kong: Oxford University Press.

Malinowski, Bronislaw
1942   *A Scientific Theory of Culture and Other Essays.* New York: Van Rees Press.

Matisoff, James A.
1991   "Sino-Tibetan Linguistics: Present State and Future Prospects." *Annual Review of Anthropology* 20:469–504.

Mueggler, Erik
1996   *Specters of Power: Ritual and Politics in a Yi Community.* Ph.D. diss., Department of Anthropology, Johns Hopkins University.

Nash, Manning
1964   "Capital, Saving, and Credit in a Guatemalan and a Mexican Indian

Peasant Society." In *Capital, Saving, and Credit in Peasant Societies,* ed. Raymond Firth and B. S. Yamey. Chicago: Adeline.

1989   *The Cauldron of Ethnicity in the Modern World.* Chicago: University of Chicago Press.

Nee, Victor

n.d.   "From Redistribution to Interactive Market: Who Gets Rich First in a Socialist Market Economy?" Paper presented at the Conference on Social Consequences of Economic Reform in China, 1988.

Nishida Tatsuo

1979   *A Study of the Lolo-Chinese Vocabulary Lolo I-yu. The Structure and Lineage of Shui-Liao Lolo* (in Japanese). Kyoto: Shokado.

NYZXGBZ (*Ninglang Yizu Zizhi Xian gaikuang* bianxie zu) (The Editorial Group for *A General Survey of Ninglang Yi Autonomous County*)

1985   *Ninglang Yizu Zizhi Xian gaikuang* (A general survey of Ninglang Yi Autonomous County). Kunming: Yunnan renmin chubanshe.

Ogbu, John U.

1974   *The Next Generation: An Ethnography of Education in an Urban Neighborhood.* New York: Academic Press.

Oi, Jean C.

1986   "Peasant Grain Marketing and State Procurement: China's Grain Contracting System." *China Quarterly* 106:272–90.

1989   *State and Peasant in Contemporary China.* Berkeley and Los Angeles: University of California Press.

Pan Jiao

1998   "Theories of Ethnic Identity and the Making of Yi Identity." Paper presented at the Second International Yi Studies Conference, Trier, Germany.

Pan Wenchao

1987   "Shilun Liangshan Yizu nuli shehui de deng ji huafen" (Preliminary discussion of the allocation of caste statuses in Liangshan Yi slave society). In *Xinan minzu yanjiu, Yizu zhuanji* (Research on southwestern *minzu,* Yi special collection), ed. Zhongguo xinan minzu yanjiu hui. Kunming: Yunnan renmin chubanshe.

Peek, Philip M., ed.

1991   *African Divination Systems: Ways of Knowing.* Bloomington: Indiana University Press.

Pu Tongjin

1996   "Yizu xinyang de bijiao" (The bi[mo] religion of the Yi). *Yunnan minzu xueyuan xuebao* 3:66–72.

Qian Mingzi

1982   "Yingxiong shidai jian lun" (A brief discussion of the heroic age). *Minjian wenyixue luncong* 3:91.

Qin Guangguang et al.

1988   *Zhongguo shaoshu minzu zongjiao gailuan* (A general survey on religion among minority nationalities in China). Beijing: Zhongyang minzu xueyuan chubanshe.

Quah, Stella R., ed.
1989   *The Triumph of Practicality: Tradition and Modernity in Health Care Utilization in Selected Asian Countries.* Singapore: Institute of Southeast Asian Studies.

Qubi Shimei, ed. and trans.
n.d.   *Hnewo teyy* (The book of origins). In *Liangshan Yiwen ziliao xuanyi* (Selected translations from Yi language materials from Liangshan), ed. and trans. Qubi Shimei. Xichang, n.p.

Qubi Shimei and Yang Liping
1992   "Liangshan Zhou pinkun wenti de duice yanjiu" (Research on the solutions to questions of poverty in Liangshan Prefecture). *Liangshan minzu yanjiu* 1:31–39.

Qumo Yuozhi
1993   *Liangshan Bai Yi Quomo shizu shijia* (The White Yi Qumo clan of Liangshan). Kunming: Yunnan renmin chubanshe.

Qumo Zangyao
1933   *Xinan Yi zhi* (Survey on the southeastern minorities). Nanjing: Bati Shudian.

Reiter, Albert F.
1991   "Theorie der Ethnizität—eine allgemeine Entwicklungstheorie?" (The theory of ethnicity—a theory of general development). *Österreichische Zeitschrift für Politikwissenschaft* 1:59–72.

Renkou Pucha (Census)
1993   *Zhongguo 1990 nian renkou pucha ziliao* (Data from the 1990 census). Vol. 1. Beijing: Zhongguo tongji chubanshe.

Rösel, Jakob
1995   "Ethnic Nationalism and Ethnic Conflict." *Politik und Gesellschaft* 2:117–30.

Schein, Louisa
1990   "Barbarians Beautified: The Ambivalences of Chinese Nationalism." Paper presented at the American Anthropological Association Annual Meeting, New Orleans.

Schoenhals, Martin
1993   *The Paradox of Power in a People's Republic of China Middle School.* Armonk, N.Y.: M. E. Sharpe.

SFAS (Society of Folk Literature and Art in Sichuan)
1960   *Le'eteyi* (*Hnewo teyy*, The book of origins). In *Daliangshan Yizu minjian changshi xuan* (Selective collection of Yi folk literature of Liangshan). Chengdu: Sichuan renmin chubanshe.

She Yizi
1947   *Zhongguo tusi zhidu* (China's native chieftain system). Shanghai: Zhongzheng shuju.

Shen Jun
1997   "Feifa zuzhi 'mentuhui' huodong weihai da" (Great harm is done by illegally organized "disciples" organizations). *Minzu* 8:35.

Shih, Kuo-Heng
1944   *China Enters the Machine Age.* Cambridge: Harvard University Press.

Shue, Vivienne
  1988   *The Reach of the State.* Stanford: Stanford University Press.
Sichuan Sheng bianji zu (Sichuan Province Editorial Group)
  1985   *Sichuan Sheng Liangshan Yizu shehui lishi diaocha zonghe baogao* (Sum-
              mary volume of historical and social investigations on the Yi of Liang-
              shan in Sichuan Province). Chengdu: Sichuan Sheng shehui kexue
              yuan chubanshe.
  1987   *Sichuan Yizu lishi diaocha ziliao, dangan ziliao xuanbian* (Collected and
              edited materials from oral history and archival sources on Yi history
              in Sichuan). Chengdu: Sichuan Sheng shehui kexue yuan chubanshe.
Skinner, G. William
  1976   "Mobility Strategies in Late Imperial China: A Regional Analysis." In
              Regional Analysis, ed. Carol A. Smith, 327–64. New York: Academic
              Press.
  1977   "Introduction: Urban Social Structure in Ch'ing China." In *The City
              in Late Imperial China,* ed. G. W. Skinner, 521–54. Stanford: Stanford
              University Press.
  1985   "Rural Marketing in China: Repression and Revival." *China Quarterly*
              103:394–413.
Smith, Anthony D.
  1996   "Culture, Community, and Territory: The Politics of Ethnicity and
              Nationalism." *International Affairs* 3:445–58.
Smith, Kent
  1970   "Ch'ing Policy and the Development of Southwest China: Aspects of
              Ortai's Governor-Generalship, 1726–1731." Ph.D. diss., Department
              of History, Yale University.
Spivak, Gayatri Chakravorty
  1988   "Can the Sub-Altern Speak?" In *Marxism and the Interpretation of Cul-
              ture,* ed. C. Nelson and L. Goldberg. Urbana: University of Illinois Press.
Stalin, Joseph
  1956   *Sidalin quanji* (The collected works of Stalin). Vol. 2. Beijing: Renmin
              chubanshe.
Staudt, Kathleen, and Jane Jaquette, eds.
  1983   *Women in Developing Countries: A Policy Focus.* New York: Haworth Press.
Su Ping
  1989   "Zhizuo Yizu huotou zhidu" (The Yi *huotou* system of Zhizuo). In *Yong-
              ren lishi ziliao xuanji* (Selected materials on Yongren's history),
              1:118–21. Wuding: Wuding xian yinshua chang.
Sun Qingyou
  1997   "Da Liangshan de xingxiang fupin" (Toward poverty alleviation in
              Greater Liangshan). *Minzu tuanjie* 2:61–62.
Swain, Margaret B.
  1990   "Commoditizing Ethnicity in Southwest China." *Cultural Survival
              Quarterly* 14 (1): 26–29.
  1995   "Père Vial and the Gni-P'a: Orientalist Scholarship and the Christian
              Project." In *Cultural Encounters on China's Ethnic Frontiers,* ed. Stevan
              Harrell, 140–85. Seattle: University of Washington Press.

Taipei Ricci Institute
.1998   *Liangshan Yizu Qu Gui Jing: Ritual for Expelling Ghosts.* Taipei: Taipei
Ricci Institute.
Thorp, Robert
1992   "Let the Past Serve the Present: The Ideological Claims of Cultural
Relics Work." *China Exchange News* 20 (2): 16–19.
Tibi, Bassam
1985   *Der Islam und das Problem der kulturellen Bewältigung des Sozialen Wan-
dels* (Islam and the problem of the cultural management of social
change). Frankfurt: M. Suhrkamp.
Tinker, Irene, ed.
1990   *Persistent Inequalities: Women and World Development.* Oxford: Oxford
University Press.
Toynbee, Arnold J.
1939   *A Study of History.* Vol. 3. London. Oxford University Press.
1957   *A Study of History.* Vols. 7–10. London: Oxford University Press.
Vandsemb, Berit
1995   "The Place of Narrative in the Study of Third-World Migration: The
Case of Sri Lanka." *Professional Geographer* 47:411–25.
Vial, Paul
1893–94   "Les Gni ou Gni-P'a: Tribu Lolotte du Yu-Nan." *Les Missions Catholiques* 25:160–61; 178–80; 189–90; 200–202; 208–9; 222–25; 236–
38; 244–46; 258–60; 268–70; 281–83; 293–94; 308–10.
1898   *Les Lolos: Histoire, Religion, Moeure, Langue, Ecriture.* Chang-hai (Shanghai): Imprimerie de la Mission Catholique.
1902   "Les Joies du Retour." *Les Missions Catholiques* 34 (1707): 85, 89–90;
(1708): 105–6; (1709): 111 15; (1710): 121; (1711): 139–42; (1712):
147–49; (1713): 159–61; (1714): 169, 173–77.
1905   "Nadokouseu, Chapitre III." *Annales de la Société des Missions-Étrangères*
48 (November-December): 334–59.
1908   "Miao-Tse et Autres." *Annales de la Société des Missions-Étrangères* 61
(January-February): 15–32.
1908–09   *Dictionnaire Français-Lolo, Dialect Gni.* Hong Kong: Imprimerie de la
Société des Missions-Étrangères.
1917   "A Travers la Chine Inconnue: Chez les Lolos." *Les Missions Catholiques*
49: 254–57; 537–38.
Walzer, Michael
1996   *Lokale Kritik—Globale Standards.* Hamburg: Rotbuch.
Wang Guangrong
1994   *Tong tianren zhiji de Yiwu "Lamo"* ("Lamo," the Yi priests who communicate between humans and spirits). Kunming: Yunnan renmin
chubanshe.
Wang Linlu
1994   "Liangshan nongmin you ba pan" (The peasants of Liangshan have
eight hopes). *Minzu:* 11.
Wang Quangen
1985   *Huaxia mingming mianmian guan* (An overview of personal names
among the Chinese). Nanning: Guangxi renmin chubanshe.

Wang Tianxi et al., eds.
1995   *Yi-Chinese Dictionary* (in Eastern Yi, Central Yi, and Chinese). Kun-
            ming: Yunnan minzu chubanshe.
Ward, Kathryn B.
1986   "Women and Transnational Cooperation Employment: A World-
            System and Feminist Analysis." Women and International Develop-
            ment Working Paper No. 120, Michigan State University.
Watson, James L.
1982   "Chinese Kinship Reconsidered: Anthropological Perspectives on His-
            torical Research." *China Quarterly* 92:589–627.
1986   Anthropological Overview: The Development of Chinese Descent
            Groups. In *Kinship Organization in Late Imperial China, 1000–1940*,
            ed. Patricia Ebrey and James L. Watson, 274–92. Berkeley and Los
            Angeles: University of California Press.
1988   "The Structure of Chinese Funerary Rites." In *Death Ritual in Late Im-
            perial and Modern China*, ed. James L. Watson and Evelyn S. Rawski,
            3–19. Berkeley and Los Angeles: University of California Press.
WCYG (Writing Group of *Chuxiong Yizu Zizhizhou gaikuang*)
1986   *Chuxiong Yizu Zizhizhou gaikuang* (A survey of Chuxiong Yi Auton-
            omous Prefecture). Kunming: Yunnan minzu chubanshe.
Wei Cuiyi
1993   "An Historical Survey of Modern Uighur Writing since the 1950s in
            Xinjiang, China." *Central Asian Journal* 37 (3): 249–322.
WGLJ (Writing Group of *Lisuzu jianshi*)
1983   *Lisuzu jianshi* (A short history of the Lisu). Kunming: Yunnan ren-
            min chubanshe.
WGYJ (Writing Group of *Yizu jianshi*)
1987   *Yizu jianshi* (A short history of the Yi). Kunming: Yunnan renmin
            chubanshe.
Wheatley, Julian K.
1985   "The Decline of Verb-Final Syntax in the Yi (Lolo) Languages of
            Southwestern China." In *Linguistics of the Sino-Tibetan Area: The State
            of the Art*, ed. G. Thurgood, J. Matisoff, and D. Bradley. Canberra: Aus-
            tralian National University.
Wild, Norman
1945   "Materials for the Study of the Ssu I Kuan." *Bulletin of the School of Ori-
            ental and African Studies* 11 (3): 617–40.
Winnington, Alan
1959   *The Slaves of the Cold Mountains*. London: Lawrence and Wishart.
WLYG (Writing Group of *Liangshan Yizu Zizhizhou gaikuang*)
1985   *Liangshan Yizu Zizhizhou gaikuang* (A survey of Liangshan Yi Auton-
            omous Prefecture). Chengdu: Sichuan renmin chubanshe.
Wolf, Eric R.
1955   "Types of Latin American Peasantry: A Preliminary Discussion."
            American Anthropologist 57:452–71.
1957   "Closed Corporate Peasant Communities in Mesoamerica and Cen-
            tral Java." *Southwestern Journal of Anthropology* 13:1–18.

1986   "The Vicissitudes of the Closed Corporate Peasant Community." *American Ethnologist* 13:325–29.

Wu, David Y. H.
1990   "Chinese Minority Policy and the Meaning of Minority Culture: The Example of the Bai in Yunnan, China." *Human Organization* 49:1–13.

Wu Xiongwu, ed.
1990   *Yizu zhexue sixiangshi lunji* (Collection on the history of Yi philosophical thoughts). Beijing: Nationalities Press.

Xia Guangfu
1990   "Yizu bimo ji qi jingdian de sixiangshi kaocha" (An intellectual-historical investigation of the Yi *bimo* and their texts). In *Yizu zhexue sixiangshi lunji* (Collection on the history of Yi philosophical thoughts), ed. Wu Xiongwu, 111–36. Beijing: Nationalities Press.

Yan Nukun and Liu Shaohan
1984   "Ninglang Yizu Zizhi Xian shaliping xiang Yizu shehui jingji dianxing diaocha" (Investigations into some typical economic cases among the Yi in Ninglang Autonomous County, Shaliping Township). In *Yunnan Xiao Liangshan Yizu shehui lishi diaocha* (Investigations into the history of Yi society in Yunnan's Xiao Liangshan), 65–112. Kunming: Yunnan renmin chubanshe.

Yan Ruxian and Song Zhaolin
1983   *Matrilineal System of the Naxi in Yongning*. Kunming: Yunnan People's Press.

Yang Hui
1995   "Lun Liangshan Yizu qiye guanli ganbu de peiyang" (On the training of enterprise management cadres among the Liangshan Yi). *Xinan minzu xueyuan xuebao* 3:50–53.

Yang Ji
1982   "Zhengque jiejue minzu diqu de renkou wenti" (Correctly solving the population problems of minority areas). *Zhongyang minzu xueyuan xuebao* 2:33–37.

Yang Jingchu
1994   "Shehuizhuyi shichang jingji yu minzu guanxi de jige wenti" (The socialist market economy and some questions of ethnic relations). *Minzu yanjiu* 5:1–9.

Yang Jizhong et al., eds.
1989   *Selected Yi Proverbs* (in Yunnan "Standard Yi" and Chinese). Kunming: Yunnan minzu chubanshe.

YSB (Yunnan Sheng bianjizu, Yunnan Province Editorial Group), ed.
1986   *Yunnan Yizu shehui lishi diaocha* (Investigations of Yunnan Yi society and history). Vol. 162. Kunming: Yunnan renmin chubanshe.

YSRTB (Yunnan Sheng renkou tongji bangongshi, Yunnan Province Demographic Statistical Office), ed.
1990   *Yunnan Sheng disici renkou tongji shougong huizong ziliao* (Manual tabulation of major figures from the fourth population census of Yunnan Province). Kunming: Yunnan renmin chubanshe.

Yu Hongmo
    1988   "Qian Xibei Wumengshan Qu de Yizu" (The Yi in the Wumeng
                Mountains of Northwestern Guizhou Province). In *Yizu wenhua* (Yi
                culture), 19–32. Chuxiong: Yizu wenhua yanjiu suo.
Yunnan Nationalities Language Commission
    1989   *Yi-Chinese Writing Textbook* (in Yunnan "Standard Yi" and Chinese).
                Kunming: Yunnan minzu chubanshe.
    1990a   *Yi Literacy Textbook* (in Yunnan "Standard Yi" and Chinese). Kunming:
                Yunnan minzu chubanshe.
    1990b   *Yi Trial Textbook* (in Yunnan "Standard Yi" and Chinese). Kunming:
                Yunnan minzu chubanshe.
    1991   *Children Look at Pictures and Memorize Characters* (in Yunnan "Standard
                Yi" and Chinese). Kunming: Yunnan minzu chubanshe.
Zhang Fu, ed.
    1999   *Yizu gudai wenhua shi* (History of ancient Yi culture). Kunming: Yun-
                nan jiaoyu chubanshe.
Zhang Wenchang (Père Laurent Zhang)
    1987   *Deng Mingde shenfu xiaozhuan* (A short biography of Father Deng
                Mingde [Paul Vial]). Kunming: Self-published.
Zhang Yurong, Yu Huina, and Ma Jinwei
    1992   "Sichuan Yizu diqu shuangyu jiaoyu xianzhuang ji qi fazhan qiantu"
                (The current situation and future development of bilingual educa-
                tion in Yi areas of Sichuan). *Xinan minzu xueyuan xuebao* 6:24–30.
Zhongguo minzu jingji (Economy of China's nationalities)
    1993   Beijing: Minzu chubanshe.
Zhongguo minzu tongji nianjian (Statistical yearbook of China's nationalities)
    1995   Beijing: Minzu chubanshe.
Zhongguo minzu tongji nianjian (Statistical yearbook of China's nationalities)
    1996   Beijing: Minzu chubanshe.
Zhongguo tongji nianjian (Statistical yearbook of China)
    1995   Beijing: Minzu chubanshe.
Zhou Qingsheng
    1992   "Aspects of Chinese Ethnosociolinguistic Studies: A Report on the
                Literature." *International Journal of the Sociology of Language* 97:59–73.
Zimei Yi xue yenjiu xiao zu (Sisters' Yi Studies Research Group: Bamo Ayi, Bamo
    Qubumo, and Bamo Vusamo)
    1992   *Yizu fengsu zhi* (Records of Yi customs). Beijing: Central Institute of
                Nationalities Press.
ZYSZY (Zhonggong Yunnan shengwei zhengce yanjiushi, Yunnan Province and Party
    Committee Office of Policy Research), ed.
    1988   *Yunnan di zhou shi xian gaikuang: Chuxiong Yizu Zizhizhou fence* (The
                local situation of Yunnan's prefectures, municipalities, and counties:
                Chuxiong Yi Autonomous Prefecture). Kunming: Yunnan renmin
                chubanshe.

CONTRIBUTORS

BAMO AYI is a Nuosu from Liangshan, born in Zhaojue. She received her B.A. in political science and her Ph.D. in minority languages and literatures, both from Central Nationalities Institute (now University). She is Associate Professor of Comparative Religion, as well as Director of the Division of International Exchanges at Central Nationalities University. She has done field research on the *bimo* and their role in Nuosu society, on women and development in Liangshan, and on Protestant Christianity and the social gospel in Seattle. She is author of *Yizu zuling xinyang yanjiu* (Researches into the Ancestral Spirit Beliefs of the Yi) and coauthor of *Yizu wenhua shi* (The History of Yi Culture).

DAVID BRADLEY is an Australian linguist who has been working on Yi Group languages for nearly thirty years. He is the author of *Proto-Loloish* (Curzon Press, 1979), which also appeared in Chinese, as *Yiyuzhi yuanliu* (Sichuan Nationalities Press, 1993), and of the *Lonely Planet Burmese Phrasebook* and *Lonely Planet Hill Tribes Phrasebook,* among numerous other works. Bradley is one of the editors for a variety of language atlas projects, including the *Language Atlas of China* (Chinese Academy of Social Sciences and Longmans, 1987). His main interest is sociohistorical linguistics of the Yi Group and related languages.

ERIC S. DIEHL is a graduate of the Department of East Asian Studies at Dickinson College. He is currently a Henry M. Jackson China Studies Fellow in the Department of Anthropology at the University of Washington. His research interests include medical anthropology, rural health care in China, and marginalized identities.

STEVAN HARRELL is Professor of Anthropology at the University of Washington, Seattle, and curator of Asian Ethnology at the Burke Museum of Natural History and Culture. He has conducted field research in Liangshan and Panzhihua intermittently since 1988. He is the author of *Ways of Being Ethnic in Southwest China* and cocurator (with Bamo Qubumo and Ma Erzi) of the exhibit *Mountain Patterns: The Survival of Nuosu Culture in China.* He is now working on a multimedia CD-ROM ethnography titled *Liangshan Journeys.*

THOMAS HEBERER is Professor of East Asian Politics and Director of the Institute of East Asian Studies at Gerhard-Mercator University at Duisburg, Germany. He studied social anthropology, political science, and sinology at the universities of Frankfurt, Goettingen, and Mainz, and at Heidelberg, where he received his Ph.D. in 1977. From 1977 to 1981 he worked as a lector and translator at the Foreign Language Press in Beijing. From 1981 to 1982 he carried out field research in Liangshan, publishing *Nationalities Policy and Development Policies in Minority Areas in China.* Since then he has conducted field research on various aspects of East Asian development and social change. He is the author of *China and Its National Minorities: Autonomy or Assimilation,* as well as coauthor or editor of books on corruption in China, Chinese rock music, Mao Zedong, political participation of women in East Asia, and most recently, the transformation of China's rural society.

ANN MAXWELL HILL is Associate Professor in the Departments of Anthropology and East Asian Studies at Dickinson College. She recently published *Merchants and Migrants: Ethnicity and Trade among Yunnanese Chinese in Southeast Asia* (Yale Southeast Asia Studies, 1998). Her current research centers on Nuosu social stratification in Ninglang County, Yunnan Province.

LI YONGXIANG is a Nisu Yi from Xinping County, Yunnan. He was educated at Yuxi Teachers' College and the Central Nationalities University. He is now Assistant Researcher at the Institute for Minority Literature in the Yunnan Academy of Social Sciences and a doctoral candidate in anthropology at the University of Washington. He is the author of two books, *Azhi and Azuo, Funeral Rites, and Documents of the Nisu,* and *The Lady Bimo and Her Family Stories,* along with numerous articles on Nisu ritual, bilingual education, and Yi linguistics. Most recently, he collaborated with David Bradley on a survey of Yi dialects in Yunnan.

LIU XIAOXING received her Ph.D. in social cultural anthropology from the University of Illinois at Urbana-Champaign in October 1998. She is currently teaching Chinese language at Northeastern Illinois University. Liu has been studying the Yi and other ethnic groups in China since 1985, and has published investigative reports, research papers, a book, and some translated works. Her research interests include medical systems and practices, rituals, interethnic relations, family and society, state and ethnicity, and the cognitive aspect of knowledge acquisition.

LIU YU comes from a Yi background in Yunnan. She was educated at People's University and Central Nationalities Institute, both in Beijing. From 1985 to 1996 she was a researcher in the Division of Antiquities of the National Museum of Chinese Ethnology in Beijing. She has published articles on a variety of ethnological themes and has recently completed a monograph on the heroic age of the Liangshan Yi.

LU HUI was born in 1962 in Kunming, China, and is Yi on her father's side and Han on her mother's. She graduated in 1982 from Yunnan University, with a B.A. in French language and literature. From 1982 to 1986 she worked at Yunnan Nationalities Institute, before leaving to study in France. She received an M.A. in 1989 and a Ph.D. in 1994 in social anthropology and ethnology from the Ecole des Hautes Etudes en Sciences Sociales, under the direction of Professor Georges Condominas. She was a postdoctoral research fellow in the French institutions ORSTOM and CNRS from 1994 to 1997, and is now a consultant in the Unit of Intangible Heritage at UNESCO, in Paris.

MA ERZI (MGEBBU LUNZY) was born in Yangjuan Village, Yanyuan County, Liangshan. He was an elementary and high school Yi-language and physical education teacher and a translator for the Language Bureau of Yanyuan County before he went to Beijing to study Yi documents at the Central Nationalities Institute. Ma was a curator at the Liangshan Museum of Slave Society before becoming a researcher at Liangshan Nationalities Research Institute, where he is now Associate Director. He is also the managing editor of *Liangshan minzu yanjiu* and cocurator of the exhibit *Mountain Patterns: The Survival of Nuosu Culture in China* at the Burke Museum, Seattle.

ERIK MUEGGLER is Assistant Professor of Anthropology at the University of Michigan. He conducted fieldwork in Yi communities in Yunnan in 1989, 1990, and 1991–93, when he lived in a Lolopo village in Yongren County for over a year. His work on memory, grieving, poetics, and politics has appeared in the *Journal of Asian Studies, Comparative Studies in Society and History, Journal of the Royal Anthropological Institute, Cultural Anthropology,* and *Modern China.* He is now completing a book on ritual and memory of violence in a Yi community, and plans to return for more fieldwork in 2000.

QUBI SHIMEI is a Nuosu from Mabian County, born in 1936. He comes from a *bimo* clan. He began studying Yi classical books in childhood. After 1950 he began studying Chinese and participated in field research organized by the Chinese Academy of Sciences, which resulted in publication of the book *Liangshan Yizu nuli shehui* (The Slave Society of the Liangshan Yi). Afterward, in cooperation with Feng Yuanwei, he compiled, translated, and published three Yi classics: *Hnewo Teyy* (The Book of Origins), *Hmamu Teyy* (The Book of Knowledge), and *Amo Nisse*. With Jjilu Tisse and Ma Erzi, he wrote *Nimu Teyy* (The Book of Ritual) and *Jiu Liangshan Yizu xiguan fa* (The Customary Law of the Liangshan Yi).

MARTIN SCHOENHALS is Chair of the Anthropology Department at Dowling College in Long Island, New York. He conducted field research on education in a large Chinese city in 1988–89, resulting in the book *The Paradox of Power in a Chinese Middle School*, which deals with the concept of face and the micropolitics of interaction. Based on his second extended period of fieldwork, in Xichang in 1994–95, he has just completed a book on ethnicity, caste, and race in an ethnic educational setting.

MARGARET BYRNE SWAIN, an anthropologist at the University of California at Davis, began her conversations with Sani women handicraft peddlers in Kunming during 1987. She subsequently studied the commodification of Lunan County for tourism, engaging her desire to understand what this state-mandated "development" meant to the local Han and Sani, the "Yi" in "Lunan Yi Autonomous County." The writings of French missionary Paul Vial became an important historical resource in her project, augmenting a year of fieldwork in 1993 and continued site visits. Her ethnography of tourism, globalization, and modernity, as they intersect local gender and ethnic hierarchies in Lunan, is forthcoming.

WU GA (Luovu Vugashynyumo) was born in Puge, Sichuan. She was a "sent-down youth" in Zhaojue in 1974, after which she worked as a reporter for *Sichuan Daily*, from 1975 to 1977. In 1982, she received her B.A. in philosophy at the Central Institution of Nationalities in Beijing. For the next two years she worked as a research scholar at the Sichuan Nationalities Research Institute and then spent about a year at the Yunnan Academy of Social Sciences, where she earned a master's degree in history. She received her Ph.D. in anthropology from the University of Michigan in 1998, conducting field research in Ninglang County, Yunnan. From 1994 to 1997, she was a visiting scholar at Tulsa University, Oklahoma. From 1998 to 1999, she was one of the principal advisors for the Chinese Society for Women Studies (CSWS) workshop, "Poverty, Ethnic Minority, and Development in Chengdu." Since 1993, she has worked as a researcher and a China adoption program director for the Family Resource Center in Chicago.

WU GU is a member of the Big Black Yi group from Luxi, Yunnan. He is Chair of the Yunnan Office for the Editing of Minority Classics, the editor-in-chief of the *Collected Works of Yunnan Minorities*, and Vice Secretary-General of the Chinese Association for the Study of Minority Literature. He has translated over ten Yi classics into Chinese, including *Annotated Ashima* and *Annotated Kejisi,* and is the author of *Minzu guji xue* (The Study of Minority Classics) and over a hundred thousand characters' worth of articles, including "Cong Yizu yingxiong shishi 'Zhygge alur' kan Yizu gudai shehui" (Looking at Ancient Yi Society from the Perspective of the Yi Heroic Poem "Zhygge Alur") and "Lue lun yinan Yizu dianji shouji he yanjiu" (A Preliminary Look at the Difficulties of Collecting and Researching Yi Classical Books).

WU JINGZHONG is a Nuosu from Mianning. He was educated at Beijing Normal University and is a former Director of the Sichuan Provincial Nationalities Research Institute. He is the author of *Liangshan Yizu fengsu* (Customs of the Yi of Liangshan) and many articles about society, culture, and development in Liangshan and other regions.

INDEX

Academy of Sciences, Chinese, 197, 230
Academy of Social Sciences, Chinese, 197
Academy of Social Sciences, Yunnan, 211
acculturation, 12–13, 16
adaptation, ecological, 32
administration: lack of territorial, in Liangshan, 107; in Nanzhao Kingdom, 31
Adur (Nuosu subgroup), 204; phonetics,
  207
Adur *tusi*, 70, 107
affinal relations, 55, 73–75. *See also* marriage, alliances
affirmative action. *See* preferential policies
Afonja, Simi, 256
African Americans, 239, 246–47, 252
afterworld. *See* Ngomi
Agàmisimo, earth vein spirit, 155; as
  ancestor for Lòlop'ò, 157; as bodily
  metaphor, 156–57
Agge clan, conflict with Ajy, 44–46
agriculture, 27, 29, 53, 268; collective
  period, 257–59; feminization of, 256,
  263; prices, 225; traditional period, 257;
  women's role in, 260–61
Ahe Aggo, *bi*, 43
Ahe Atu, 40–41
Ahe Ave, *mo*, 43
Aho clan, 108, 109
Ailao, Mount, 138
Ailao Yi (Nisu), 135–43

Aji and Ajuo (spirit brothers), 141
Ajy clan, conflict with Agge, 44–46
alcoholic beverages: "alcohol culture," 27;
  from Chengdu, 47; and councils, 45;
  expenditures on, 226; manufacture, 27;
  rituals and, 27
Alu clan (*nuoho*, Meigu), 101, 108
Alu clan (*qunuo*, Ninglang), 57–58, 62–63
An clan, 77
ancestors, 119; abode after death of, 135,
  136, 138; alcohol offered to, 27; cause
  of illness, 270–72; lack of receptivity to
  homicides, 95; nature of, 124; praise of,
  112; reliquary box for, 154, 155 fig 10.1,
  167–68; reserve lands, 154–55; shrines,
  154–56; spirit house for, 274; tablets, 23;
  trust lands, 154, 155, 165–66; worship,
  23, 40, 56, 59, 63, 121, 123, 124, 126,
  154–56, 178, 270, 272, 273
Ang Zhiling, 173
Ang Ziming, 175–76
Ango Ngole, *nzymo*, 43
animal husbandry, 47, 52
animals, twelve, 87
animism, 28–29
anti-Rightist campaign, 199
anti-Japanese war, and Yi research, 22
Apopo, *nzymo*, 4
apple cultivation, 262
apukuo shrine, 63